Killing by Remote Control

Killing by Remote Control

The Ethics of an Unmanned Military

EDITED BY
BRADLEY JAY STRAWSER

OXFORD
UNIVERSITY PRESS

OXFORD
UNIVERSITY PRESS

Oxford University Press is a department of the University of Oxford.
It furthers the University's objective of excellence in research, scholarship,
and education by publishing worldwide.

Oxford   New York
Auckland   Cape Town   Dar es Salaam   Hong Kong   Karachi
Kuala Lumpur   Madrid   Melbourne   Mexico City   Nairobi
New Delhi   Shanghai   Taipei   Toronto

With offices in
Argentina   Austria   Brazil   Chile   Czech Republic   France   Greece
Guatemala   Hungary   Italy   Japan   Poland   Portugal   Singapore
South Korea   Switzerland   Thailand   Turkey   Ukraine   Vietnam

Oxford is a registered trademark of Oxford University Press
in the UK and certain other countries.

Published in the United States of America by
Oxford University Press
198 Madison Avenue, New York, NY 10016

Library of Congress Cataloging-in-Publication Data

Killing by remote control : the ethics of an unmanned military / edited
by Bradley Jay Strawser.
pages cm
Includes bibliographical references and index.
ISBN 978-0-19-992612-1 (hbk.: alk. paper)   1. Military robots—Moral and ethical
aspects.   2. Drone aircraft—Moral and ethical aspects.   3. Robotics—Moral and ethical
aspects.   4. Robotics—Military applications.   5. Military ethics.   I. Strawser, Bradley Jay.
UG479.K55 2013
172'.42—dc23
2012043807

ISBN 978-0-19-992612-1

5 7 9 8 6 4
Printed in the United States of America
on acid-free paper

For Abbilynn

CONTENTS

FOREWORD

Jeff McMahan

There is increasing enthusiasm in government circles for remotely controlled weapons. Such weapons are especially attractive in democracies when political leaders want to fight a war or attack enemies in remote locations but are constrained politically by the aversion of citizens to being killed or having their children killed for the sake of aims they think may not be worth the cost. The Barack Obama administration is particularly enamored with these weapons, the use of which carries no risk of becoming encumbered with "detainees," which have become a political liability in the wake of the George W. Bush administration's rebarbative policies of detention and torture.

What differentiates the newer models of remotely controlled weapons from traditional long-range precision-guided munitions is that they allow their operators to monitor the target area for lengthy periods before deciding whether, when, and where to strike. These are capacities that better enable the weapons operators to make morally informed decisions about the use of their weapons.

But remotely controlled weapons are associated in the popular imagination with targeted killing, especially of terrorist suspects outside of traditionally delimited combat zones. Yet they can be, and are, used in combat as well and have the same advantages in each of these roles: that is, they function without risk to their operator, can be highly discriminating in the targets they destroy, and can be used in places that are inaccessible to soldiers or prohibitively dangerous for their deployment. The objections to targeted killing are not, therefore, necessarily objections to remotely controlled weapons—though if targeted killing is objectionable then it is one objection to remotely controlled weapons that they make targeted killing safer and politically more palatable than it would otherwise be.

The distinction between using remotely controlled weapons in war and using them for targeted killing is not always easy to draw. There seems to be little difference morally between using a drone to kill members of the Taliban in remote areas of Afghanistan or Pakistan when they are not engaged in violent or coercive activities and using the same weapons in the same areas to kill members of al Qaeda, who are not combatants in a war but criminals preparing to engage in terrorist action.[1] It can, indeed, be argued with considerable cogency that the use of remotely controlled weapons to kill Taliban fighters in their "safe havens" can be legally justified as the killing of enemy combatants in war, while their use to kill al Qaeda operatives in their havens can be legally justified as police action against dangerous criminals who cannot be arrested and tried at a reasonable cost so that the requirement of arrest must be suspended, as it sometimes must be even in domestic law enforcement. Critics of this suggestion will say that the difference between targeted killing and cases in which the requirement of arrest must be suspended in domestic law enforcement lies in the imminence of the threat. In domestic cases, the requirement of arrest is suspended only when a criminal is on a rampage and is resisting arrest, posing a danger to the police and perhaps to innocent bystanders as well. But targeted killing is necessarily preventive: it is done when there is no imminent threat from the terrorist. If a terrorist posed an imminent threat, killing him would not count as targeted killing but simply as third-party defense of others, about which there is no legal controversy. But to have any plausibility, the imminence requirement must be understood as a proxy for considerations of probability or necessity. Usually threats that are not imminent are either below some threshold of probability or can likely be dealt with in some other way. But in the case of committed terrorists who are protected by the political and legal authorities where they live, targeted killing may be necessary for defense of the innocent in the same way it is in the case of a rampaging murderer.

Killing by Remote Control is a book about remotely controlled and preprogrammed weapons, not about targeted killing, though the latter obviously receives some discussion. What should we think about the use of remotely controlled or preprogrammed weapons in war?

Some writers, including the editor and some of the other contributors to this book, argue that in war the fact that remotely controlled weapons can be used without risk to the operator makes them unambiguously good in the hands of just combatants—that is, those who fight in a just war. I think this is right. But of course their possession and use cannot be restricted to those who will use them only in the pursuit of a just cause and only against those who are liable to attack. So just as their availability may diminish inhibitions

---

[1] For a defense of the claim that al Qaeda terrorists are not combatants, see Jeff McMahan, "Targeted Killing: Murder, Combat, or Law Enforcement?" in Andrew Altman, Claire Finkelstein, and Jens David Ohlin, eds., *Targeted Killings: Law and Morality in an Asymmetrical World* (New York: Oxford University Press, 2012).

against fighting in justified wars, especially wars of humanitarian intervention, it may also weaken deterrence of wrongful aggression. As a practical matter, then, trade-offs must be made between ensuring the safety of just combatants and preventing war and targeted killing from becoming safer for unjust aggressors.

Perhaps surprisingly, there are some who argue that the elimination of risk even to just combatants is morally problematic. Michael Walzer, in an essay on the Kosovo intervention written in 1999, claims boldly, and in italics, "*You can't kill unless you are prepared to die.*"[2] He follows this declaration by saying that the leaders of the North Atlantic Treaty Organization (NATO) "cannot launch a campaign aimed to kill Serbian soldiers, and sure to kill others too, unless they are prepared to risk the lives of their own soldiers.... They cannot claim, [and] we cannot accept, that those lives are expendable, and these not."[3] I am uncertain how to interpret this passage, as it is uncharacteristically obscure. Whose are "those lives?" If the phrase includes the lives of Serbian soldiers, then Walzer's claim challenges the permissibility of using remotely controlled weapons on the ground that their use somehow implies the unacceptable judgment that the targets of such weapons are expendable while the operators are not. Yet something akin to that judgment is made by every combatant who tries to kill enemy combatants in war. Perhaps what Walzer means is only that it is not permissible for combatants to fight in a way that minimizes the risk to themselves by shifting the risks to civilians instead. If this is all he means, then he is largely right, though there are two qualifications. First, it is possible that some civilians are liable to suffer certain harms as a side effect of military action. It might, for example, have been permissible for NATO combatants knowingly to harm certain Serbian civilians as a side effect rather than expose themselves to certain risks if they had known that those civilians were collaborators with the Serbian soldiers in Kosovo. Second, it is also possible that the civilian beneficiaries of humanitarian intervention can permissibly be made to share some of the risks with the combatants who intervene on their behalf. Still, if all that Walzer is claiming is that combatants must take certain risks if that is necessary for them to avoid harming or killing civilian bystanders, then nothing he says impugns the permissibility of using remotely controlled weapons.

The case against remotely controlled weapons is clearer in the writings of Yale law professor Paul Kahn, who argues that "riskless warfare" threatens to undermine the moral justification for killing in war even in its application to just combatants. What Kahn takes to be the moral justification for killing in war is closely related, though not identical, to the one defended in Walzer's

---

[2] Michael Walzer, "Kosovo," in his Arguing about War (New Haven, CT: Yale University Press, 2004), p. 101, italics in original.

[3] Ibid., pp. 101–102.

Just and Unjust Wars, according to which the "right not to be attacked...is lost by those who bear arms...because they pose a danger to other people."[4] Kahn first claims, as Walzer does, that combatants have no control over which wars they are commanded to fight in or whether to fight when they are commanded to do so. They lack free choice in these matters and are thus morally innocent. But how, he asks, can it be permissible to kill them if they are morally innocent? His answer is that there is a "distinct morality of the battlefield" in which "the fundamental principle of the morality of warfare is a right to exercise self-defense within the conditions of mutual imposition of risk."[5] When all combatants are morally innocent, "the rule of reciprocal self-defense" permits combatants on each side to defend themselves from attack by combatants on the other. The goals for which they fight are irrelevant to the moral justification for the harming and killing they do in combat, and the contribution their action makes to the achievement of those goals is morally incidental: "Defending himself, the combatant advances the political objectives for which force is deployed."[6] Provided that it remains within the limits imposed by the principles of *jus in bello*, the harming and killing that a combatant does on the battlefield is morally justified on the ground that it is instrumental to his own defense or to the defense of his fellow combatants.

But if this is the justification for killing in war, a war fought entirely with remotely controlled weapons seems a moral impossibility, no matter how important its just cause might be, for the operators of the weapons would not be under threat and hence could not use the weapons in self-defense. But perhaps one can claim that if the operators of the remotely controlled weapons are citizens of a state that is the victim of armed aggression, they are necessarily under some sort of threat, so that if the threat they face as individuals is sufficiently serious to make killing a proportionate response, they can be justified in using their weapons against the aggressors. This response is, however, limited to wars of national self-defense. It does not apply to wars of collective defense or to humanitarian intervention, in which the intervening combatants are antecedently under no threat at all. It seems, therefore, that Kahn's morality of warfare rules out humanitarian intervention, not just with remotely controlled weapons but also with weapons of any type. For "the soldier's privilege of self-defense" cannot justify the initial harming and killing of soldiers in the state that is the target of the intervention when neither the soldier nor any of his comrades is threatened by them. Perhaps Kahn's view implies that intervening soldiers must wait until they come under attack before they may use

---

[4] Michael Walzer, *Just and Unjust Wars* (New York: Basic Books, 1977), p. 145.

[5] Paul W. Kahn, "The Paradox of Riskless Warfare," *Philosophy and Public Policy Quarterly* 22 (2002): 2–8, p. 3.

[6] Ibid.

force to stop the perpetration of atrocities. If so, those committing the atrocities could deprive the interveners of a justification for the use of force by simply ignoring them.

Kahn claims that intervention can be justifiable, provided that there is "*a prior and continuing symmetrical application of force*" by the parties in whose conflict the intervention occurs.[7] But this seems to rule out intervention to stop a campaign of genocide against an entirely defenseless and unresisting civilian population. It seems inescapable, then, that a view that rules out "riskless warfare" because it justifies killing in war only as the exercise of individual rights of self-defense by combatants on the battlefield, thereby making the aims of their war irrelevant to the justification of their action, cannot be the correct account of the morality of warfare. This critique of riskless warfare thus leaves the moral case for the use of remotely controlled weapons by just combatants unscathed.

Advocates of "unmanned" weapons claim that they are not just less risky but also more discriminating, in that they have, or can have, sensors that can detect such things as concealed weapons that ordinary combatants cannot and are not subject to the distorting effects on judgment of such passions as rage or the desire for vengeance.[8] But this claim does not apply to remotely controlled weapons because these weapons must be fired by a human operator. The weapon may have sophisticated sensors, but the judgment about the status of the target remains with the operator, who may misinterpret the data or act irrationally.

New generations of preprogrammed robotic weapons will, however, be equipped with features that, according to their proponents, will enable them to discriminate between combatants and noncombatants more reliably than ordinary combatants can in the stress and fog of combat. Yet there are reasons to doubt the proponents' claims. If the weapons were better able than soldiers to recognize certain markers of combatants, enemy soldiers could simply dispose of those markers. Doing that in the face of human combatants of course involves the risk that the combatants will simply give up trying to discriminate between combatants and noncombatants and begin to kill indiscriminately. But weapons that are preprogrammed not to fire on people whom they identify as noncombatants would simply not fire on anyone. To become useful again, they would have to be reprogrammed and would no longer be discriminating in the way their advocates claim. A naïve response to this problem would be that the weapons could be programmed to attack only those bearing arms. One is

[7] Italics in original.

[8] "Unmanned weapon" is an unfortunate term because it suggests that women do not operate weapons and perhaps because "unmanned" also calls to mind the alternative meaning, "emasculated." But it is useful because it covers remotely controlled, preprogrammed, and semiautonomous weapons.

invited to imagine the use of a weapon of that sort in a society such as the contemporary United States, where it seems that every other civilian now carries a concealed weapon.

The ability to distinguish between combatants and noncombatants will remain morally and legally important no matter what the correct view of *in bello* morality is. But it is less important if the traditional theory of the just war is mistaken in asserting that this distinction coincides with the distinction between legitimate and illegitimate targets. Some revisionist critics of the traditional theory have argued that the relevant moral distinction is not between combatants and noncombatants but between those who pose a just or justified threat and those who pose an unjustified threat, or a threat of wrongful harm. Even preprogrammed or semiautonomous weapons cannot distinguish between unjust and just wars or therefore between those who are responsible for a threat of wrongful harm and those who are not. If the revisionists are right, these weapons cannot distinguish between morally legitimate and illegitimate targets, for no sensors can detect moral liability to attack.

Among the most significant concerns about weapons that do not require continuous control by an operator is that if there were enough of them they could enable a relatively small number of people to initiate and conduct a war without the cooperation or consent of others. Much of the work the revisionist just war theorists have done has sought to discredit the traditional view that soldiers who fight for an unjust cause do no wrong provided that they obey certain neutral rules governing the conduct of war. It seems likely that this traditional view has been instrumental in persuading many soldiers to put their qualms of conscience aside when they have been commanded to fight in a war they believed to be unjust. Thus, the work of these revisionist theorists has a practical as well as a theoretical aim, which is to enlist the consciences of ordinary soldiers in the effort to prevent the initiation or continuation of unjust wars, which until recently could not be fought without the involvement of a great many people who needed to be convinced that what they were doing was not immoral. This situation changed with the advent of nuclear weapons and other weapons of mass destruction, but the use of such weapons is fraught with so much uncertainty and risk even for those who would use them that the temptation to fight a war with them has, since their first use by the United States, never been very great. Preprogrammed or semiautonomous robotic weapons, however, could enable a government to fight an unjust war while bypassing the problem of convincing soldiers that it was just. To the extent that such weapons make this possible, their development will subvert the practical project of the revisionist theorists of limiting unjust wars by appealing to the consciences of those who would fight them.

I have briefly reviewed only a few of the moral issues raised by both the advent of remotely controlled and preprogrammed weapons and the prospect of even more sophisticated semiautonomous weapons. Many other such issues are raised and discussed in this timely and important book, which I hope will serve as a catalyst for serious debates not only in moral philosophy but also, and more importantly, among philosophers, political and legal theorists, policy analysts, and the public at large.

PREFACE

BRADLEY JAY STRAWSER

I first began thinking seriously about the issues debated in this book when I was teaching philosophy at the United States Air Force Academy as a junior faculty member in 2006. My job was to teach these incredibly bright, eager, and talented students an introductory ethics course focused primarily on the ethics of war. These students were on their way to becoming officers in the United States Air Force. Indeed, many of them were seniors and would be leaving my classroom and, in but a few short months, be on active duty. Many wanted to become pilots, and some wanted to become fighter pilots, in particular. At the same time I began teaching these unique students, the lethal employment of unmanned drones by the US rose precipitously. This naturally posed an extremely relevant real-world case study to discuss in the classroom. In these discussions, two things became apparent.

First, the ethical issues surrounding killing by remote control are both more complicated and subtler than they first appear. I found this complexity and subtlety to be true of the ethics of drones in surprising ways. That is, the ethical problems I expected to find with drones were often, I would discover on close inspection, actually illusory. And, vice versa, things that I had originally thought would be rather fleeting or inconsequential worries, have turned out to be persistent, tenacious sources of ethical concern (what remote killing does to the pilots of drones and issues surrounding military virtues, for example). Indeed, even more surprising to me, in following the arguments where they led, I ultimately arrived at several conclusions rather far afield from my initial "gut instincts" that first got me interested in the topic.

The second thing I discovered in exploring these questions was that many of my students were not happy with the recent trend of ever greater military employment of these unmanned aerial vehicles (UAVs). For many of them their initial objections to UAVs were not ethical ones, although many did have genuine moral concerns over their use. Rather, many of them had dreamed of being a pilot for as long as they could remember. This sudden increase in drone employment made it clear that this dream of piloting an aircraft in military service would likely mean flying a drone remotely rather than operating a manned aircraft as they had always envisioned. Remotely flying a UAV from a desk— one contributor to this volume calls pilots in such a role "desk jockeys"—is not nearly as exciting or sexy as being, say, a traditional fighter pilot.

Of course, through these discussions, nearly all of my students with these kinds of initial complaints would eventually come to embrace a view of professional obligation for military officers that dissuaded them of such protests. On this view of professional military ethics, society entrusts them with a duty of military service requiring that they serve in their capacity as officers in the way that the military, and ultimately the society that fields it, determines is best. If that means flying unmanned rather than manned aircraft, then they would proudly take on that charge. However, we discovered along the way that their initial discomfort with the idea of flying drones was not grounded purely in an immature machismo and desire to be a "fighter jock." Indeed, as we worked through the question of what it meant to kill by remote control we uncovered a handful of deep-seated ethical concerns over this form of warfare at the root of their initial worries. Several of my students' earliest apprehensions are found within the scholarly debates undertaken in this book.

Many of my former students have gone on to become pilots of various stripes (as well as military engineers, doctors, judge advocates, support officers, and so on), and most of them eventually served in Iraq or Afghanistan (or both), often on multiple tours. Some of them are in those theaters as I write this preface and edit this volume. Many have become fighter pilots, as they had dreamed of doing from a young age, while others have gone on to become UAV pilots, something they never envisioned themselves doing when they first enrolled in the Air Force Academy.

I'll admit that once I first set my mind to the question of whether or not drones were ethically permissible, I thought the primary moral issues here were rather transparent. It seemed to me that what matters in this discussion is whether or not a given military action is itself justified in the first place. I simply didn't see what the significant *moral difference* could be in a missile being fired from a manned F-15 fighter or from a remotely controlled Predator drone. In either case, the central moral questions surround what or who that missile is going to hit and why—not the platform from which it was delivered. Other things being equal, whether the platform was controlled remotely or controlled with someone inside of it seemed irrelevant.

To a large extent, I still think this, as I argue for in this book's introductory chapter and elsewhere. But I remember discussing this point with Martin Cook (deputy head of the Air Force Academy's Philosophy Department at the time) and other colleagues and being surprised to find widespread disagreement over this, to me, seemingly transparent point. While Professor Cook himself agreed with me, he convinced me that many in both the military and scholarly communities would not and that this debate was worth pursuing. Now, several years later and with no end in sight for this debate (or for the use of UAVs), it is clear he was right in his assessment. As the essays in this volume will attest, widespread disagreement persists over the ethics of employing lethal unmanned weapons. Since killing by remote control is now occurring at an ever-increasing pace, the importance, timeliness, and pragmatic significance of the work proffered in this volume is evident.

I am indebted to many people for this book. Each of the contributors to this volume has my sincere gratitude and appreciation for moving the scholarly work on this crucial debate forward. My deepest thanks are owed to each of them: Asa Kasher, Uwe Steinhoff, David Whetham, Julian Savulescu, Zack Beauchamp, Rebecca Johnson, Rob Sparrow, and George Lucas. Three contributors in particular stand out for their extensive efforts put into this volume, both for their own chapters and for their help and advice on my work: Matthew Hallgarth, Avery Plaw, and Stephen Kershnar. Each has helped in countless ways, and I doubt that the volume would have come together were it not for their tireless work. I am also indebted to Pauline Kaurin, Andrew Ely, Deonna Neal, and Ken Himma for their work on this volume's behalf.

Special thanks are also due to Jeff McMahan both for writing the foreword to this volume and for the tremendous influence he has had on my thinking (and so many of the contributors' thinking) over these and other matters pertaining to the ethics of war. Thanks are also due to many others, including Steve Wall, Michael Lynch, David Rodin, Henry Shue, Martin Cook, Peter W. Singer, Seth Lazar, Jai Galliott, Patton Dodd, Ken Himma, Peter Asaro, Patrick Lin, Noel Sharkey, Randy Dipert, Ronald Arkin, Armin Krishnan, Daniel Brunstetter, Murtaza Hussain, James Cook, Donald Joy, John Sherman, Carlos Bertha, Bill Rhodes, Richard Schoonhoven, Luciano Floridi, James Moor, Peter Lloyd, Michael Dolbec, Paul Bloomfield, Rik Hine, Alexis Elder, Casey Johnson, Kathy Fazekas, Stephen Coleman, Ed Barrett, Michael Skerker, Mike Rak, Kalev "Gunner" Sepp, Michael Freeman, Doug Borer, John Arquilla, Gordon McCormick, George Lober, Larry Strawser, Todd Strawser, Abbilynn Strawser, and all of my former students at the United States Air Force Academy and the University of Connecticut. Thanks also to the participants at the 2010 International Society of Military Ethics Conference, the participants of the 7th Global Conference on War and Peace, the participants of the 2012 International Studies Association West Regional Conference, and the members of the UConn Ethics Summer Reading Group for valuable debates over some of the topics represented in this volume. Finally, thanks to Peter Ohlin and Lucy Randall at Oxford University Press for all of their extensive help. Even with such a list, I am sure I have forgotten many who have helped me think seriously about this difficult issue over the past several years. To all who have helped me along this road, thank you.

NOTES ON CONTRIBUTORS

Zack Beauchamp is a reporter and blogger for ThinkProgress at the Center for American Progress Action Fund. Previously, he was a research associate at the University of Oxford's Uehiro Centre for Practical Ethics and contributed to The Dish at Newsweek/Daily Beast. He has also worked at the Center for Strategic and International Studies and *Congressional Quarterly*. He holds an M.Sc. in international relations from the London School of Economics and Political Science and a BA in philosophy and political science from Brown University.

Matthew Hallgarth is assistant professor of philosophy and religious studies at Tarleton State University. A retired Air Force major, he served for many years at the United States Air Force Academy (USAFA), where he taught ethical theory, military ethics, medical ethics, history of philosophy, American philosophy, philosophy of religion, independent studies, and ethics for the USAFA scholars' program. Hallgarth served as the Chief of Honor Education at USAFA, where he wrote and edited the honor lessons for the cadet wing. He also managed the squadron professional ethics advisor program and the honor instruction for Basic Cadet Training program. Hallgarth was USAFA's Outstanding Academy Educator in Philosophy in 1996.

Rebecca J. Johnson is associate professor of National Security Affairs at the Command and Staff College at Marine Corps University, where she teaches courses in culture and military ethics. Previously, she taught international ethics at the Georgetown Public Policy Institute at Georgetown University and from 2004 to 2008 was assistant professor in the School of International Service at American University. Her current research explores how to prevent and respond to moral injury in complex operations. Johnson has published numerous chapters and articles related to military ethics and serves as the book review editor for the *Journal of Military Ethics*.

Asa Kasher is the Laura Schwarz-Kipp Professor of Professional Ethics and Philosophy of Practice and professor of philosophy at Tel Aviv University in Israel. His research covers a broad range of topics in philosophy and ethics, including especially military ethics, medical ethics, and philosophy of language, as well as issues of Jewish identity. During his service in the Israeli Defense Force, he attained the rank of major. In 1997, Professor Kasher was a recipient of the Itzhak Sade Prize for Military Literature (Military Ethics) and in 2000 was awarded the Prize of Israel (the most prestigious award made by the State of Israel) for his work in philosophy and ethics. He is the author of *The Israel Defense Force's Code of Ethics,* published by the Israel Ministry of Defense. He is the author of more than 150 articles, book chapters, and encyclopedia entries and twenty-three edited volumes and monographs. He is also editor of the Israeli philosophical journal *Philosophia, Philosophical Quarterly of Israel;* founding editor of *Hebrew Linguistics*; and founding member of the advisory board of the *Journal of Military Ethics.* He has served as president of the Israel Philosophical Association and head of the Military Ethics Committee IDF Personnel Division, has served as a member of the Executive Committee for the Israeli Society of Medical Ethics and the Israeli Press Council, was a member of the Ministry of Health Committee on Medical Administration of Drugs, and has been a representative for the Israel Delegation to UNESCO.

Stephen Kershnar is professor of philosophy at the State University of New York at Fredonia and also an attorney. He earned his B.A. from Cornell University, Ph.D. from the University of Nebraska–Lincoln, and J.D. from the University of Pennsylvania. His research focuses on applied ethics and political philosophy. He has written on such diverse topics as affirmative action, abortion, punishment, pornography, God, interrogational torture, the most valuable player in professional sports, hell, discrimination against women, and Batman. He has written five books: *Desert, Retribution, and Torture* (2001) (on the philosophy of punishment); *Justice for the Past* (2004) (on affirmative action and reparations for slavery); *Sex, Discrimination, and Violence: Surprising and Unpopular Results in Applied Ethics* (2009); *Desert and Virtue: A Theory of Intrinsic Value* (2010) (on the nature of goodness); and *For Torture: A Rights-Based Defense,* which is forthcoming.

George R. Lucas Jr. is Class of 1984 Distinguished Chair in Ethics in the Vice Admiral James B. Stockdale Center for Ethical Leadership at the United States Naval Academy (Annapolis) and professor of ethics and public policy at the Graduate School of Public Policy at the Naval Postgraduate School (Monterey, CA). He has taught at Georgetown University, Emory University, Randolph-Macon College, the French Military Academy (Saint-Cyr), and the Catholic University of Louvain, Belgium; has served as philosophy department chair at the University of Santa Clara in California; and has received research fellowships from the Fulbright Commission and the American Council of Learned Societies. Lucas is the author of five books and more than forty journal articles, translations, and book reviews and has also edited eight book-length collections of articles in philosophy and ethics. Among these titles are *Anthropologists in Arms: the Ethics of Military Anthropology*; *Perspectives on Humanitarian Military Intervention*; and a special issue of the *Journal of Military Ethics*, "New Warriors and New Weapons: Ethics and Emerging Military Technologies." Lucas is also coeditor (with Capt. Rick Rubel, US Navy, retired) of the textbook *Ethics and the Military Profession: the Moral Foundations of Leadership* and a companion volume, *Case Studies in Military Ethics*. These texts are used in core courses devoted to ethical leadership at the United States Naval Academy, the United States Air Force Academy, and Naval Reserve Officers Training Corps units at over fifty-seven colleges and universities throughout the nation.

Jeff McMahan is professor of philosophy at Rutgers University and honorary fellow of the Oxford Uehiro Centre for Practical Ethics. He studied at Oxford and Cambridge and works in normative and applied ethics, political philosophy, and legal theory. He has written countless articles and several books on such topics, including *The Ethics of Killing: Problems at the Margins of Life* (Oxford University Press, 2002). His more recent *Killing in War* (Oxford University Press, 2009) is based on the Uehiro lectures he delivered at Oxford in 2006.

Avery Plaw is associate professor of political science specializing in political theory and international relations with a particular focus on strategic studies and is director of the University Honors Program. Before arriving at the University of Massachusetts, he taught for three years at Concordia University's political science department, following which he received a two-year fellowship from the Social Science and Humanities Research Council of Canada to pursue research at New York University. He published a book in 2008 titled *Targeting Terrorists: A License to Kill?* in Ashgate Press's Ethics and Global Politics Series and just finished editing a collected volume titled *The Metamorphosis of War* (Rodopi Press, 2012). He has also edited a collected volume concerned with managing the challenges of philosophical and cultural pluralism titled *Frontiers of Diversity: Explorations in Contemporary Pluralism*. He has published fourteen peer-reviewed articles and chapters. In 2008 he won the American Political Science Association's Wilson Carey McWilliams prize. *Targeting Terrorists* was runner-up for the Canadian Political Science Association's Prize for Best Book of the Year in International Relations.

Julian Savulescu holds the Uehiro Chair in Practical Ethics at the University of Oxford. He is director of the Oxford Uehiro Centre for Practical Ethics within the faculty of philosophy. He is director of the Oxford Centre for Neuroethics, which is one of three strategic centers in biomedical ethics in the UK funded by the Wellcome Trust. He is also director of the Institute for Science and Ethics (formerly known as the Programme on the Ethics of the New Biosciences), which is one of the ten founding institutes in the Oxford Martin School at the University of Oxford. He is also principal investigator for a major Arts and Humanities Research Council grant on Science and Religious Conflict, co-investigator on a new Economic and Social Research Council award, and Louis Matheson Distinguished Visiting Professor at Monash University. In 2010 he was appointed as honorary professorial fellow at the Florey Neuroscience Institutes, one of the world's top ten neuroscience institutes, for a period of three years. He is a recognized world leader in the field of practical ethics. He is author of over 200 publications and has given over 120 invited international presentations and over 200 in total. Savulescu is editor of the *Journal of Medical Ethics*. His book, *Unfit for the Future: The Need for Moral Enhancement*, coauthored with Ingmar Persson, will appear in the Uehiro Series in Practical Ethics published by Oxford University Press in 2012.

Robert Sparrow is Australian Research Council Future Fellow at the School of Philosophical, Historical, and International Studies at Monash University, Australia, where he researches ethical issues raised by new technologies. He earned his Ph.D. from Australian National University and his B.A. from the University of Melbourne. He is one of the few professional philosophers with a significant research program on the ethics of robotics and has written a number of influential articles on the ethics of military robotics, including "Robotic Weapons and the Future of War" (forthcoming), "Predators or Plowshares? Arms Control of Robotic Weapons" (2009), "Building a Better WarBot: Ethical Issues in the Design of Unmanned Systems for Military Applications" (2007), and "Killer Robots" (2007). As well as some forty-four other refereed journal articles and papers in edited collections on topics in applied ethics, bioethics, and political philosophy. With colleagues at the University of Melbourne, Sparrow was awarded an Australian Commonwealth government–funded Australian Research Council "Discovery Grant" to study ethical issues raised by new military technologies over the period 2007–2009. He is also a founding member of the International Committee for Robot Arms Control.

Uwe Steinhoff is associate professor at the Department of Politics and Public Administration of the University of Hong Kong and senior research associate in the University of Oxford Programme on the Changing Character of War. He is the author of four books, including *On the Ethics of War and Terrorism* (Oxford University Press, 2007) and *On the Ethics of Torture* (SUNY Press, 2013), as well as of numerous articles on war, terrorism, and torture in such journals as the *Philosophical Quarterly*, *Journal of Political Philosophy*, *Journal of Applied Philosophy*, and *Journal of Military Ethics*.

Bradley Jay Strawser is assistant professor of philosophy in the Defense Analysis Department at the United States Naval Postgraduate School in Monterey, California, and research associate with Oxford University's Institute for Ethics, Law, and Armed Conflict. Prior to his current appointments, Strawser was resident research fellow at the Vice Admiral James B. Stockdale Center for Ethical Leadership in Annapolis, Maryland. Previously he taught philosophy and ethics at the United States Air Force Academy in Colorado and the University of Connecticut. Before his academic career, Strawser served as an active duty officer in the United States Air Force for nearly eight years. His research focus is primarily ethics and political philosophy, though he has also published on metaphysics, ancient philosophy, and human rights. His work has appeared in such journals as *Analysis, Philosophia, Journal of Military Ethics, Journal of Human Rights,* and *Epoché.*

David Whetham is senior lecturer in the Defence Studies Department of King's College London, based at the Joint Services Command and Staff College at the UK Defence Academy. Whetham initially took a degree in philosophy at the London School of Economics and went on to take a master's degree in war studies at King's College London, eventually followed by a Ph.D. in war studies. Before joining King's as a permanent member of staff in 2003, Whetham worked as a BBC researcher and with the OSCE in Kosovo, supporting the 2001 and 2002 elections. He now coordinates or delivers the military ethics component of courses for between 2,000 and 3,000 officers a year drawn from over fifty countries, that joins the British students at the UK Staff College. He is visiting lecturer in military ethics at the Baltic Defence College in Tartu, Estonia, and for the Royal Bruneian Armed Forces. His publications include *Ethics, Law and Military Operations* (Palgrave, 2010) and *Just Wars and Moral Victories: Surprise, Deception and the Normative Framework of European War in the Later Middle Ages* (Brill, 2009) as well as a wide range of journal articles and book chapters on subjects relating to ethics, norms, the laws of war, and professional military ethics education. He is a member of the editorial advisory board for the *Journal of Military Ethics* and co-convenes the European Chapter of the International Society for Military Ethics.

PART ONE

JUST WAR THEORY AND THE PERMISSIBILITY TO KILL BY REMOTE CONTROL

Introduction: The Moral Landscape of Unmanned Weapons

Bradley Jay Strawser

1. What This Book Is About

Human beings have come up with inventive and diverse ways to kill each other. These ways of killing vary widely in their range. Death can be wrought intimately, with our bare hands or a short melee weapon. With greater technology, we add greater physical distance. We can fire projectiles to create an intermediate distance from those killed, be it with a sling, a bow, or a rifle. With the modern machines of war, truly long-range means of killing are introduced via planes, cruise missiles, and the like. A new way to kill that's emerged in recent years is to use weapons fired from platforms, usually aerial in nature, which are controlled remotely from potentially anywhere on the globe. The essays in this book examine the ethical questions surrounding this latest inventive means of killing: *killing by remote control.*

If you are reading this, you probably know that killing by remote control has become a (relatively) common practice for a few Western states' military forces, particularly the United States. Although this kind of weaponry is not entirely new in military history, there has been a precipitous increase in their employment in recent years.[1] These weapon systems are called, among other names, unmanned (or uninhabited) aerial vehicles (UAVs), remotely piloted vehicles (RPVs), unmanned military systems (UMS, to capture the rising number of remotely controlled weapons that are not necessarily air-based), or simply

---

[1] That this weaponry is not entirely new will be discussed and debated in some of the chapters in this volume. See chapter 2, "Just War Theory and Remote Military Technology: A Primer," by Matthew Hallgarth and chapter 3, "Distinguishing Drones: An Exchange," by Asa Kasher and Avery Plaw. It's contentious just how "new" this kind of remote killing is in human history. For an argument that this way of killing has perhaps been around longer than most think, see "The Rise of Uninhabited Military Systems," in Galliott, Jai C. "Saving Soldiers and the Ethics of Uninhabited Military Systems," Doctoral Dissertation, Macquarie University, Forthcoming.

drones.[2] In this volume the terms drones and UAVs will be used most predominantly. Examples include the well-known General Dynamics MQ-1 Predator and the General Dynamics MQ-9 Reaper. Whatever we call them, these weapons are presently being used to kill people with remarkable efficiency and lethality. This book is premised on the simple idea that this lethal use of remote control weapons raises ethical questions requiring serious moral reflection and analysis.

2. The Infancy of a Long Conversation

One surprising feature of the discussion of the ethics of killing by remote control is how much of the conceptual terrain is yet to be fully explored by scholarly analysis. This collection contributes to filling gaps in this analysis, but it will not exhaust the issues raised by this technology. The literature on the ethics of lethal drones, and this discussion of remote control killing more broadly, is still in its infancy. This dearth of analysis parallels the fact that widespread actual employment of drones is itself, in some ways, still in its infancy. Yet the speed of technological change brought by these vehicles and the haste of their military deployment are quickly outpacing thorough ethical and policy analysis.

As a participant in this discussion over the past few years, I've noticed an emerging pattern—one common for any new area of analytic discourse and debate, and this issue has been no different. The pattern goes like this: First, a handful of popular articles and even some books (both scholarly and non-academic in nature) are published on the topic, which tend to simply describe some of the nascent and thorny ethical concerns, in laundry list fashion. While a useful conversation starter, this initial wave of work fails to substantively engage these concerns with positive arguments for or against the issues they raise. This journalistic approach usually provides a balanced presentation of the vexing problems but without providing any solutions to them. Later scholars slowly take positions on these issues and offer solutions that were missing in the first wave of journalistic attention getting. These scholars argue for or against various positions, better develop the grounds for the various concerns first broached, show why some are better or worse than originally thought for new and specific reasons, and so forth. This wave of work shapes debate over particular issues, usually polarizing into different camps. At this stage, areas of clearer discourse facilitate further debate, often producing a rough consensus on formerly disputed issues while discovering new ones.

---

[2] The shift to describing these weapons as "remotely piloted" in their moniker itself, rather than simply unmanned, has been on the rise of late, particularly within branches of the US military that operate them.

In my view, some of the debate over the ethics of drones is moving out of the first wave (or it *needs* to move out of it, at any rate), while other aspects of it are well into the second stage. Some positions have already received significant, albeit early, criticism and analysis. In any case, wherever exactly along this spectrum the current state of the conversation sits, those of us working on and thinking seriously about these questions need to move out of those early phases and push the scholarly conversation to a deeper analytic level. This is not for the purpose of creating yet another cottage industry of scholarly articles on a given subfield but rather to advance the debate toward productive and, one hopes, practical ends.

Killing by Remote Control: The Ethics of an Unmanned Military is part of that deeper analytic push. The contributors in this volume take definitive positions and defend them rather than simply rehearsing the common moral concerns floating around public discourse about drones. Some directly engage other scholars' views with critical scrutiny. Many in this book are highly skeptical of the moral justifiability of drone usage. Some argue for various reasons that the current and future employment of drones is morally unjustifiable. Others defend the opposite view: that drones are of course subject to moral scrutiny but are essentially no different from other weapons of war in that regard.

My goal in this volume is to move the conversation to a deeper level of critical analysis in concrete and specific ways. In what follows, I will describe some of the specific ways the contributors to this volume do precisely that. I'll refresh the reader with a survey that maps the current scholarly discourse on the ethics of remotely controlled killing technologies. I will also present some of my own views and arguments. Finally, I will then briefly describe the contributions to this volume and where they fall in the larger conversation.

3. Justifiable Killing

To understand the ethical landscape of killing by remote control, let's briefly discuss killing generally. Intentionally killing another human being, using any method or from any distance, is presumptively wrong. Yet most agree that *some* killing is morally justifiable. For most this is a first-order and rather simple moral truth that killing can, at times, be justified in some circumstances.[3] The reasons for justifying killing are more contentious. In my view, to justifiably kill a person, that person must have done something wrong, for which he is morally responsible, which makes it permissible to kill him to accomplish some specific end that is properly related to the wrong for which he is morally responsible.

---

[3] This view is not universal, of course. Some particular strains of pacifism hold that killing is never, under any circumstances, morally permissible.

That is, a person is for some specific reason liable to be killed. Usually this will be something like wrongful, unjustified violence toward another that can be prevented only by killing, that is, self-defense or third-party defense of others. But there are other cases of permissible killing, such as discriminate and proportionate killing in war. On the traditional just war theory account, the justification for killing in war is not necessarily based on individual moral liability like self-defense is but on the mutual threat that soldiers in a conflict pose toward one another. Recently, however, scholars have challenged this traditional view and argued that justified killing in war should mirror the moral rules guiding justifiable killing in ordinary life—that is, that soldiers can be justifiably killed when, and because, they fight and kill on behalf of an unjust cause and are thereby liable to be killed to avert that unjust cause.[4]

However, on either the traditional view or the new revisionist approach, there are moral boundaries to justifiable killing in war. There is, almost certainly, always some unjustified killing in war. And some killing in war (or, better, some killing in *some* wars) is justified as killing in other contexts (such as defense of self or others against unjust harm) is justified. Now, ceteris paribus, if killing is justified, then the method of killing may become morally relevant, but need not. Unjustified killing is wrong no matter how it is accomplished. But justified killing does not have a blanket justification attached that says the killing can be done in any possible way. Methods of killing that are merely more painful or cruel for no good reason are methods that can turn an *otherwise* justified killing into an unjustified one. For otherwise unjust killings, however, some methods simply make the moral crime *worse* than other methods, but any method would be unjust. That is, the bad method is simply a further way an already wrong act is wrong.

A quick example illustrates this simple point that there are cases of killing that we think would otherwise be justified if not for a particular method. Imagine a police officer who must kill a murderer to prevent him from killing some nearby children. Let's say the officer could shoot the murderer with a gun, or she could kill him with a potent nerve agent that would kill over the course of several hours of slow torturous agony. Presume that either method would be equally successful in defending the children from the murderer and that the police officer has both options available to her. Many would argue that the method used in this case *does* matter for our overall moral assessment of such a killing: justified if she uses the gun, but unjustified if she uses the nerve agent when she *could* have just as well used the gun. The reason we think the method is relevant to the moral permissibility of the killing is because she had a fast and more painless alternative with the gun; inflicting slow agony isn't necessary to

---

[4] In chapter 2, Matthew Hallgarth discusses the traditional just war theory framework in detail as well as this new revisionist strain of just war theory.

defend the children. Note that we likely think that the officer would be justified in killing the murderer with nerve agent if that were the only means available whatsoever to stop the murderer from killing the children. Of course, it would be better if she had a gun instead to defend the children, but, with no other alternatives available, saving the children justifies using the nerve agent.

This case applies well to killing by remote control. Is there anything wrong *in principle* with killing someone who should be killed with a drone? More specifically, is there any morally *relevant* difference between killing someone with a missile fired from a Predator drone or a missile fired from an F-15?[5] It may seem that the answer, prima facie, is no. If it is unjust to kill with one of these delivery methods then it will also be unjust with both. And if it is morally just to kill with the manned aircraft, then it is unclear why it would be morally unjustified to carry out the same killing via a remotely controlled aircraft. Those who would argue that drones are bad in a special way must cash out these morally relevant differences.

4. In Principle and in Practice

Answering the question of whether killing by remote control is distinct in any morally relevant way from killing by other methods constitutes a large portion of the current philosophical debate over the justifiability of the lethal employment of drones. I'll review what those various challenges to remote killing are in turn. First, however, I must explain a critical but often missed distinction right at the start. This is the distinction between the moral questions surrounding this form of killing in the abstract and the moral questions surrounding the actual, current, real-world lethal implementation of drones. While this distinction may sound prosaic, it is crucial to separate the moral questions surrounding drone warfare *in principle* from the moral questions over current implementation *in practice*. Not only is this distinction regularly missed in the public discourse over UAVs, but also the conflation of the two impedes clear debate of both issues. Indeed, I believe it is the failure to differentiate drone use in principle and drone use in practice that is the cause for so much of the current confusion in the present debate.

---

[5] Granted, the two platforms just named do (usually) fire different kinds of air-to-ground tactical missiles (AGMs). The Predator commonly fires an AGM-114 Hellfire, while the F-15E often fires an AGM-65 Maverick. The Maverick is essentially a larger, newer Hellfire and is primarily used by contemporary fighters such as the F-15, the F-16, and the F-18. The Hellfire, on the other hand, tends to be used by smaller platforms such as the Predator and Reaper drones and, of course, helicopters, for which it was originally designed. But this difference in armament is (almost always) not morally relevant. Moreover, in those rare cases where it is morally relevant (e.g., due to predicted impact damage), other armament choices are available for both platforms.

For example, a discussion over whether there is any moral reason, in principle, to put a combatant at greater risk by placing her in a given theater of combat rather than employ a remote weapon will often be hijacked by (perhaps entirely appropriate) complaints over the current US implementation of these remote weapons. Whether a given technology is being justly used in the real world is, of course, a critically important question for scholars to analyze and debate. But it is, to be sure, a separate question from moral issues intrinsic to technology that can be analyzed regardless of present context.

Some disagree that this distinction should be made as sharply as I argue for here. They contend that the only way to properly think about the moral principles surrounding drone use is to first and foremost look how they are actually being used. In chapter 9, Uwe Steinhoff will make this case in response to some of my views on drones. I disagree. In my view, there are good reasons to explore the abstract questions of whether remote control killing qua remote control killing holds any truly distinct morally relevant features, positive or negative. Steinhoff admits that there's nothing intrinsically wrong with UAVs, nor does he argue that their use is somehow intrinsically wrong. Given his criticisms of Western militaries' current employment of drones, this can be true only if we are able to separate the questions over killing by remote control in the abstract and the questions over its present incarnation (with which Steinhoff clearly takes issue).

Thus, in my view, the first question to engage in the ethical landscape surrounding drones is whether there is anything inherent in the nature of remote control killing that makes it wrong in some principled way rather than via an accidental or contingent feature of how drones are presently being used as the primary cause for moral apprehension. Consider, by way of comparison, the debate over the moral permissibility of torture. There are many who hold that torture is a practice that is intrinsically wrong: that it is wrong to torture people in principle, regardless of surrounding contextual factors. Others disagree and think that there is nothing intrinsically morally wrong about torture. Regardless of where one falls on this debate, we can agree that it would be odd to debate whether specific practices of torture are morally permissible if we have not first answered, or at least thoroughly engaged, the question of whether torture is intrinsically wrong. If one thinks that there is an absolute moral prohibition on torture, then it's moot to debate whether a specific instance of torture was morally permissible. Take the recent use of torture, specifically the use of the technique known as waterboarding, by the US in Guantanamo Bay against suspected terrorists. If one thinks that there is an intrinsic moral problem with waterboarding that makes it impermissible, regardless of the circumstances, then debating whether it was a morally acceptable practice in this case would be a fool's errand. Alternatively, if one thinks that a given instance of torture was morally impermissible yet holds that torture in principle could be permissible in some circumstances, then conflating the two questions between torture in principle and its specific use muddles our efforts for clear thinking in both inquiries.

We see this problem crop up frequently in the public discourse over drone use. Many believe that the present drone campaign carried out by the US in Afghanistan, Yemen, and the Federally Administered Tribal Areas (FATA) of Pakistan, among other areas, is morally dubious. But that view of this particular use of drones can prohibit a nuanced debate over the broader moral principles behind drone use itself. Perhaps surprisingly, this problem does not arise as often in the current scholarly conversation over the ethics of drones. This is probably because most academics working on the moral questions raised by drones do not think there are inherent moral problems with their employment that make their use intrinsically wrong. None of the contributors to this volume, for example, hold that there is an absolute moral prohibition against UAV use, in *all* cases real or imagined. However, many have principled issues with their use that could lead to larger problems in the abstract, still distinct from specific instances of their actual use. That is, some argue that there is something about this form of warfare that, although not absolutely prohibited in principle, leads to a judgment that they should not be used, all things considered. That is, some argue there is something about this form of remote warfare in general which should cause us to be morally dubious of it, even if it is not absolutely prohibited in principle. That view is far more common among scholars today, including some of the contributors to this volume.

One may still object to my emphasis on this distinction, however. One could argue that in the case of drones the matter at hand is different because nearly all present and likely drone use is carried out in this specific way, by the US, in these particular theaters of operation, against these kinds of targets. I think this is shortsighted. If history is any lesson, new military technologies only rarely go away. Indeed, far more likely is that the precipitous increase in drone use we have witnessed over the past few years represents just the beginning of the proliferation and widespread use of UAVs, across many contexts. Further, the actors who are currently killing by remote control (primarily the US and a few other nations) will likely do so in different ways, and for different reasons, in the future. Moreover, it is also likely that many more actors other than the US will eventually employ lethal drones for a multitude of different ends. Hence, the importance of exploring the abstract philosophical and moral questions over this manner of killing, apart from looking solely at their present use, should be clear.

I do not thereby mean to suggest, however, that the present and actual use of drones should not inform our thinking over the moral questions they raise. It would be foolish and naïve to explore the abstract without consideration of reality.[6] And the same is true with drones. My point is simply that it would also be shortsighted to look *only* at the current use of UAVs without considering the broader questions implied by remote killing more generally. So then let me return to the initial distinction that I said was so crucial yet so simple. We must distinguish the moral questions concerning lethal drone use in principle and lethal drone use in practice. Both inform what we think about the other, and both inform our conclusions regarding the overall moral permissibility of drones. But it is important to keep the difference in view to correctly identify the target of a given moral objection or moral commendation about drone employment. Some arguments deal directly with specific practices; others concern remote killing in theory. It is vital to keep this in mind while reading through the essays in this volume and in considering the debate over drones more broadly. There is an abiding tension here. Some, such as myself, find that drone employment is itself morally permissible in principle and even find some positive normative features that generate an obligation to use drones in some circumstances. Yet, as I will explain, those who hold this view may still often be uncertain as to the moral permissibility of actual drone employment in many cases of contemporary warfare.[7]

5. Mapping the Debate

I will now map the primary contours of the present debate over the morality of killing by remote control. To begin, I'll first briefly attempt to articulate the view just discussed that something is intrinsically wrong with this form of killing over other forms of killing, simply in virtue of being remotely controlled, across all possible circumstances. What do these positions tend to look like? They are surprisingly hard to articulate consistently and clearly. Like many claims about intrinsic qualities, efforts to defend this view often come down to assertions about how one *feels* about remote control killing and rely on appeals to moral sensation ("something about it just seems wrong") rather than specific moral reasons that withstand scrutiny for all cases.

Some attempts, however, have been made to express the feeling that there's something intrinsically wrong with remote control killing in more concrete terms. Take, for one example, the claim that killing by remote control crosses an asymmetry threshold between the relative combat abilities of differing

---

[6] I'm reminded here of a quote often attributed to Kant that "experience without theory is blind, but theory without experience is mere intellectual play." (It is disputed whether Kant ever directly claimed this, although he writes something similar in the first critique. See Immanuel Kant, *Critique of Pure Reason* (Penguin Classics, rev. ed., 2008), A51/B75.

[7] To say nothing of the moral status of autonomous weapons, which I will discuss and which chapters 10 and 11 address in depth.

sides in a conflict such that this kind of warfare becomes inherently ignoble and unjust in principle, regardless of surrounding context. This kind of objection is notoriously difficult to maintain because it is unclear why it could *never* be morally permissible to kill by remote control for at least two reasons. First, there's the problem with the primary premise: why think that asymmetry itself is even morally problematic for cases of otherwise justified killing? Certainly we do not want a military force fighting for an unjust cause to have an asymmetric advantage. But it seems to be a moral gain if a force fighting for a just cause has such an advantage. It is a good thing, for example, when the police have a significant advantage over criminals they are trying to apprehend; why should it be any different in war?[8] It seems whether asymmetry is a moral gain or loss is accidental to which side has the upper hand.

But let's presume for the moment that this could be shown to be false—that any radical asymmetry of the kind and degree brought about by drones really is morally problematic across all cases. Even then, the worry is still only a contingent one that would not prohibit all uses of UAVs. Notice that if both sides of a conflict had drones then the asymmetry itself would vanish. That is, in all cases, something in the equation could be modified to remove the (supposedly) troubling asymmetry while retaining the employment of lethal drones.

Some think that any warfare that is inherently "riskless" to warriors on either side of a fight is unjust according to the principles of the morality of war.[9] But it's unclear how trying to better protect one's soldiers, particularly those fighting for a just cause (or, in similar, morally analogous cases, protecting someone engaging in justified killing, such as the previously mentioned police officer), can be intrinsically wrong to do. Another related approach in this vein claims that we all have a right to not be killed remotely, by a "faceless" enemy who is not exposed to some risk. But it is unclear what moral principles this claim is grounded on, and, even if it is true, it is again unclear how it could hold for *all* cases. There are other attempts, of course, to articulate that killing by remote control is intrinsically wrong across all cases, but all appear to fail in similar ways. That is, again, most efforts to ground an intrinsic problem with remote control killing qua remote control killing rely on little more than intuition begging about how one feels about it instead of building a case on clear moral principles, which this form of killing necessarily violates. This is one reason that this approach is rarely seen in the majority of scholarly debate over drones. That's not to say that I think there is *nothing* to the unsettling

---

[8] Here I am relying on the revisionist strain of just war theory aforementioned and discussed briefly in the forward by Jeff McMahan. See chapter 2 in this volume for a more complete discussion. If one rejects the revisionist approach to just war theory, then this point still stands because the traditional just war convention does not have any moral prohibition against trying to give one's side as much of an advantage as possible.

[9] See McMahan's foreword to this volume for a brief discussion of this view.

intuitions many have over a remotely controlled robot killing human beings. Rather, such sentiments must be unpacked in a way that offers concrete moral reasons for why there is an intrinsic problem to this form of killing; an *argument* is needed, not mere assertion. At this point in the debate, we still await such an argument.

Since most of the current debate falls outside of this camp, an important point should be reiterated here, however obvious, before moving on: namely, even if one holds that the use of drones is permissible in principle, one may still hold that lethal drone employment is morally problematic for a wide variety of reasons. Setting aside worries over remote killing being intrinsically bad with that caveat, then, we see broad collections of views that hold contingent moral objections and concerns against the permissibility of lethal drone employment. As noted, this is where most of the action is in present scholarship. There are many such objections; here I will review only those that have been most influential in the present debate or in public discourse over UAVs, in either theory or practice. We also find a variety of arguments contending that drones have (at least the potential for) moral improvement and significant normative advantages over other forms of warfare. I will discuss some of those by way of introducing my own views in the next section.

The present employment of drones in service of the dubious practice known as targeted killing is cause for one of the most commonly heard objections to the moral permissibility of drones. Some contend that such a tactic should properly be called assassination and is little more than (or identical to) "extra-judicial execution." That drones are presently carrying out this practice has made the association of drones and targeted killing inseparable in the popular imagination. The moral and legal debate over targeted killing itself is long and surprisingly complex and has recently received renewed and intense scholarly attention.[10] But notice, of course, that targeted killing could be carried out by other kinds of weapon platforms or even soldiers on the ground with any weapon. That is, targeted killing need not be an objection against drones in principle. Still, however, their use to this end is widespread, and many think the capabilities of drones exacerbate or contribute to the moral questions surrounding the practice. Thus, whether targeted killing via drone strike can be morally permissible is a question of central importance in thinking through the morality of UAVs. A key chapter in this volume engages this difficult question head-on.

Another claim commonly heard against the moral permissibility of drones is that they are not discriminating enough in their strikes between properly liable targets and nonliable people. A similar objection is that they cause

---

[10] See Claire Finkelstein, Jens David Ohlin, and Andrew Altman, eds., *Targeted Killings: Law and Morality in an Asymmetrical World* (Oxford: Oxford University Press, 2012).

disproportionate "collateral harm" (that is, unintended death) to civilians, whatever their actual precision targeting capabilities may be, and thereby do not sufficiently adhere to the rules of *jus in bello*. Usually this objection is raised against drones compared with other weapon platforms (such as manned aircraft) or alternative means of carrying out a given mission (such as using troops on the ground to engage a particular target rather than from the air). That is, the objection is that drones are not as discriminate or proportionate, on par, with a given alternative means. Responses to this objection are varied and hinge heavily on the conflicting empirical evidence available for how much unintended death drone strikes actually do cause. Indeed, one of the most difficult problems with examining the present use of drones is that the facts of the matter regarding drone strikes are murky at best. The data that we would find most relevant for our deliberations over whether a particular strike or policy of strikes is morally justifiable (such as the specifics of who is killed and whether such people were morally liable to be killed) are exactly the kind of data that are most lacking, unreliable, unclear, or contradictory. This volume offers a chapter with new and, to my lights, some of the best analysis yet available of the evidence regarding proportionality and discrimination of drone strikes.

Others have argued that remote control killing results in a level of asymmetry between parties in a conflict that is new in kind or crosses some threshold that, while not ruling out the method's permissibility in principle, creates morally insurmountable problems in the real world. Similar to the previously given response to the claim that this asymmetry makes drones intrinsically bad, it is unclear why asymmetry is morally relevant to a given killing, if the killing is itself otherwise justified. Yet the concerns over asymmetry persist and are deeply ingrained in the discourse over drones. Many are troubled by the extreme difference in risk of harm between the killed and the killer brought about by the operators of drones themselves not being physically anywhere near the dangers of combat in which they engage.[11] Others fear that while the asymmetry itself may not be a problem in the particular instance of an otherwise justified killing, it creates long-term conditions for injustice and sets up an international power relationship that is inimical to peace. In response, several have pointed out that even if asymmetry is a real moral concern, then the asymmetry problem arose long ago in the history of ranged weapons. A pilot sitting in the cockpit of a modern bomber aircraft flying at high altitude and dropping munitions on targets far below is nearly as protected from harm as a drone operator is. Thus, if there really is a moral problem with asymmetry, it is

[11] Note, as Rebecca Johnson will discuss in chapter 8, that many of those who engage in insurgency warfare in some of the same places where drone operations occur also remove themselves from the locus of physical danger by using remotely detonated improvised explosive devices as their primary weapon. The point is simply that not only drones can create this sharp asymmetrical divide of physical risk in today's wars.

not relegated to UAVs. It does seem likely, however, that asymmetry in combat will continue to grow in direct relation to the increased use of remote control weapons and that drones will remain at the center of the broader debate over whether asymmetry is morally relevant for questions of permissible killing. Several chapters in this book discuss this problem, with one focused centrally on it.

Contemporary warfare, particularly that waged by the US, is presently dominated by what are known as "counterinsurgency" operations. In such military campaigns, the counterinsurgent forces must directly engage a given local populace and interact with them to create political stability and the conditions for peace. In such an environment, many object that air warfare broadly, and drone warfare in particular, is counterproductive to the aims of counterinsurgencies strategy. Related objections are raised by pointing to the views often held by civilians in areas where drone operations are taking place that UAVs represent a cowardly or ignoble form of warfare.[12] The worry for drones is that they will be incapable of succeeding in the mission for which they are deployed precisely because they are unmanned, and may even make matters worse, in either how they are perceived or their pragmatic abilities to deal with local populations. While these are difficult questions for how to best implement military strategy for a just cause, they are primarily empirical in nature. If drones cannot successfully implement a given military strategy, for whatever reason, then they should not be used, of course. But whether this is so and what the moral implication of some of these limitations is have thus far (until the contribution made in this volume) gone unexplored in the relevant literature and in the debate over drone warfare.

Here's another persistent and significant moral objection to remote control killing. It is that drones lower the threshold against lethal action (and war more generally) to a morally dangerous degree. They do this by being easier and cheaper to use (both monetarily and in lives lost for the side that employs them) and thereby less politically costly to national leaders than alternative means of war. That is, they make war too easy. (This has become known as the "threshold argument" or "threshold problem" for a variety of advanced military technologies.) This is usually proffered as a significant moral problem because

---

[12] A cluster of related concerns is occasionally heard regarding drones' inability to, for example, accept the surrender of an enemy combatant they are about to engage, since the war fighter is not physically present on the battlefield with the drone. Of course, this is already the case with any manned aircraft or ranged weapon of any kind where the operator is not physically present in the battlefield where his or her target is located. As such, it seems this whole range of objections to drones is misplaced insofar as they are meant to be specific to drones alone. Moreover, although drones (or, e.g., manned aircraft) do not allow for a combatant to accept the surrender of an enemy combatant, they can certainly choose (in the least) not to attack an enemy who has surrendered.

the presumption is that, as it is easier to go to war, more states will go to war when they should not, including when the cause is not just and the proper conditions for casus belli have not been met. Note, however, that this threshold problem could, in fact, be a moral benefit if it leads states to go to war when they *should* do so but do not because of being too risk averse. Clear moral analysis and well-articulated arguments on both sides of this threshold problem are badly needed in the debate over the morality of remote control killing. Two chapters in this volume do precisely that.

I'll note a related objection here that has been articulated of late in the increasingly elevated public discourse on drones. It takes the aforementioned premise—that drones make war too easy—and ties it to a kind of objection about broad proportionality considerations in war. The central premise is that, in weighing the predicted moral costs and gains in using drones, we must consider not only those potential costs (such as unintended damage or civilians deaths) of the immediate strike but also the medium-term and long-term potential costs that could come about through the use of this weapon. These include concerns over the proliferation and potential misuse of drones, perhaps by one's adversaries, and the long-term impacts on the population set living under drone strikes or the global attitude toward those states that employ UAVs. (This is a variant of the "it creates more terrorists than it kills" objection.) One problem with this concern is that it is, again, not drone specific. It is certainly true that any proportionality calculus should consider all relevant potential harms brought about by a given action, including long-term damage resulting from bad precedent and the like. But that is the case for *any* military action or war, not simply our thinking about drones. Moreover, because they are based on far-sighted predictions these long-term future costs cannot be known with any degree of certainty. Yet the future costs would have to be known with a high degree of confidence to have the significant effect this objection claims it should hold in our proportionality considerations. This is the most difficult problem to overcome for these kinds of objections and the threshold argument in general. Since we cannot have the required degree of confidence in such future estimates, the objection fails in the face of competing normative gains for which we can have greater epistemic confidence.

There are also a variety of concerns over how the use of remote control warfare (and particularly the risk-free aspect of it) impacts the warriors who engage in it, that is, the drone operators themselves. This nearly always includes worries over the drone pilots not engaging the operations with the proper sense of propriety or gravitas because they are too removed from the realities of combat. The fear is that the real-world killing the drones carry out and all of the resulting consequences will be treated more like a virtual video game by the operators and that *jus in bello* violations, among other moral problems, will surely result.[13] There are also concerns over the operators being harmed by a kind of cognitive dissonance that can arise from the radical displacement of their life and work from the battlefield itself. Indeed, there are some reports that UAV operators have experienced a higher degree of posttraumatic stress disorder (PTSD) than others carrying out similar missions, but in deployed locations in the theaters where the combat is taking place.

Another worry concerning those who fly drones is the impact remote control warfare might have on the martial virtues traditionally associated with warriors, such as bravery or courage. The concern is that, if soldiers can engage in combat with no physical risk to themselves (or very reduced or little risk, at any rate), then concepts central to the very notion of what it means to be a warrior will consequently be lost. Further, it is claimed that this is an overall moral net loss because of the morally restraining features of the "warrior ethos" and what these virtues can (in theory) bring to warfare and the profession of arms. This issue—how fighting a remote control war morally impacts the warriors who fly drones and, particularly, how it impacts our moral reasoning on issues such as the importance of bravery and other martial virtues—has been in the air for some time but, until this volume, has received virtually no scholarly analysis.

Finally, a variety of ethical concerns have been raised against the development and future use of what are known as "autonomous weapons." The term itself is highly contentious, but usually this refers to weapons that have an advanced artificial intelligence (AI) of some kind such that they can "choose" of their own accord certain mission actions and, in particular, can make lethal decisions "on their own." Although technically separate from concerns over remotely controlled killing (which is still controlled by human agents), such weapons, if they ever come to pass, will likely evolve out of present-day UAVs. Indeed, there are already

---

[13] In my view, much of this particular concern is vastly overplayed. In the public discourse over drones, a great deal of damage on this point seems to have been done by one solitary yet often cited quote by a drone pilot describing lethal UAV operations. The infamous quote is as follows: "It's like a video game. It can get a little bloodthirsty. But it's fucking cool." The comment received a lot of attention when it was published in Peter W. Singer, *Wired For War: The Robotics Revolution in the 21st Century* (New York: Penguin Press, 2009), pp. 308–309, n. 6. But the quote seems to have originated in Noah Shactman, "Drone School, a Ground's-Eye View," *Wired Magazine*, May 27, 2005, accessible at http://www.wired.com/science/discoveries/news/2005/05/67655. The quote was thereafter reiterated by countless other articles and sources, including Singer as mentioned, as well as by Robert Sparrow in his widely cited article, "Building a Better Warbot: Ethical Issues in the Design of Unmanned Systems for Military Applications," *Science and Engineering Ethics* 15 (2009): 169–187. The quote strongly suggests that drone pilots (or this drone pilot in particular, at any rate) displayed an attitude to their combat operations more befitting a teenage video gamer than a professional officer in the grave business of killing in war. In my own conversations with a large number of drone pilots, I have encountered precisely the opposite attitude: a deep-seated seriousness and professionalism regarding the business at hand and a high-level of conscientious critical questioning over every lethal drone strike decision they engage in. I have found this attitude prevalent across all levels of those involved in the drone community.

large research programs dedicated not only to developing AI capable of making such targeting decisions but also to enabling such autonomous weapons to behave ethically in such choices. Thus, the moral objections against the development and potential future employment of autonomous weapons are naturally linked to the debate over present-day UAVs and their continued research and development.

There are a wide variety of moral objections against autonomous weapons themselves. These include concerns over a lack of proper accountability if autonomous weapons were to violate the laws of war. Another issue is whether autonomous weapons, which would (arguably) not be proper moral agents themselves, should be in the business of making morally weighty decisions. Many find that such a thing would be a kind of "category mistake" in unleashing nonmoral agents into the world to make life-and-death decisions about actual, real moral agents (that is, about human beings). Some hold that the prospect of autonomous weapons is so morally dire, and that since they will likely be developed out of existing UAV platforms, this then constitutes a significant objection against even human-controlled UAVs. That is, the risk of autonomous weapons coming to fruition is so great, this argument runs, that we should block the use and development of current UAVs to prevent this greater moral problem. Because this issue is so important in thinking through the future of remote control killing, two chapters in this book address these moral quandaries.

6. A Moral Obligation to Kill by Remote Control

I mentioned already that most scholars working on the ethics of UAVs today do not think that there is anything intrinsic in the nature of such weapons that makes their use impermissible in principle. Let me take this line of reasoning a step further and argue that drone employment can be, in fact, morally *preferable* to using over alternative, manned systems (under certain conditions and granting some likely empirical assumptions). In fact, I think it's plausible that using UAVs rather than manned military aircraft can even be morally required in some cases.[14] If the same mission can be done with either, and the drone protects the pilot more effectively with no mission diminishment, then, *ceteris paribus*, we ought to use the drone. We are morally required to use drones over the manned aircraft to prevent exposing pilots to unnecessary risk. If adding risk to our troops is unnecessary and serves no defensible purpose, then subjecting troops to that risk is morally unjustified.

---

[14] I make this argument at length in "Moral Predators: The Duty to Employ Uninhabited Aerial Vehicles" *Journal of Military Ethics* 9:4 (December 2010): 342–368. I summarize much of that paper over the next few pages. My full formulation and defense of the PUR in that piece is critiqued by Uwe Steinhoff in chapter 9 of this volume, "Killing Them Safely: Extreme Asymmetry and Its Discontents."

This conclusion derives from what I have elsewhere called the *principle of unnecessary risk* (or PUR for short).[15] The basic idea is simple and intuitive. As I wrote, "It is wrong to command someone to take on *unnecessary* potentially lethal risks in an effort to carry out a just action for some good; any potentially lethal risk incurred must be justified by some strong countervailing reason."[16] Its technical formulation can get rather complicated, but its normative force is captured easily enough by some simple cases.

First, reconsider the previous story of the police officer killing the murderer to save children. Suppose instead that the police officer has a gun and a sword and is equally competent with either weapon and that each weapon has an equal chance of saving the children.[17] The only relevant difference here is that the gun significantly reduces her risk to being harmed by the murderer. A police commander would be foolish to insist that police officers used swords in these and similar cases. It seems that using the gun is not only preferable but also morally required. All the sword adds is risk to the police officer.

Here is another more elaborate example:

Two small towns, Prudentville and Recklessville, each have a local police force that includes a highly trained "bomb squad." Each bomb squad has been very successful in disarming and disposing malicious explosive ordinance throughout the years with few (but some) casualties. Recently, both towns acquired remotely controlled robots that can be used to disarm explosives while being operated from afar. Under the control of a trained explosive ordinance disposal (EOD) technician, these robots are just as capable at disarming bombs as the EOD techs are themselves working "hands-on." And with the robots, of course, the EOD technicians are not at any risk of injury or death. After some initial experimentation to ensure use of the robots did not cost them any bomb-disarming capability, Prudentville decides to have their bomb squad use the robots in any situation where it was possible to do so. They viewed the decision as a "no-brainer": saving the life of even one bomb technician would be well worth the cost of using the robot. Recklessville decides not to have its EOD techs use the robots, even though it has them available and are capable of doing so. Thus, it puts its bomb techs at risk for no reason (or no *good* reason, at any rate) and violates the principle of unnecessary risk.[18]

---

[15] Ibid., 344.

[16] Ibid.

[17] And assume that both weapons will kill the murderer if they are used to prevent him from killing the children—there is no nonlethal way for her to successfully stop him with either weapon.

[18] Ibid., 347.

It seems clear that "if it is possible for the bomb squad to use a robot to defuse the bomb remotely, with no significant or relevant loss of capability, then the bomb squad has a clear ethical obligation to use the robot in place of a human handling the bomb directly." These two examples are relevantly analogous to the current and future use of lethal military drones and killing by remote control more broadly. I argue that *if* a particular killing, which is otherwise justified, can be accomplished with a remote control weapon in place of a non–remote control weapon (presuming that the non–remote control weapon would put its operator at greater risk than the remote control weapon would) *and* if the remote control weapon is equal to or greater than the non–remote control weapon in all its relevant capabilities, *then*, ceteris paribus, there is a moral obligation to use the remote weapon to avoid putting the operator of that weapon at unnecessary risk. Call this conditional claim for a moral obligation to use remote weapons RW.[19]

This RW claim has attracted critical attention.[20] And rightly so, for there are many objections one can raise against such a moral obligation to use drones *actually* obtaining in the real world. But that is primarily because it is an entirely conditional claim reliant on certain real features of drone technology and how they can (or cannot), in fact, be used and what their actual usage entails. In this regard, the claim by itself is actually rather boring—the devil is in the details. But there is an advantage in approaching the conversation over the ethics of killing this way: the various objections raised against RW provide a useful way to chart the contours of the broader debate over the ethics of killing by remote control just mentioned. Working through the various conditions that would make RW either false or vacuous provides one with a fairly solid grasp of the entire larger debate.

RW is an entirely conditional claim that rests on the satisfaction of several caveats and a large ceteris paribus assumption. One can either object to any of these conditions or grant the conditions but reject the claim as false in principle. If one argues that one of the conditional caveats of RW fails to obtain in the *actual* world of drone usage, then the antecedent of RW is false and RW is only vacuously true. As I showed already, arguments over whether these conditional elements ever actually obtain constitute most of the debate on the ethics of killing with drones. This makes sense to me. For whether a given instance of killing by remote control *is* a justified

---

[19] This will be clear following, but note that "relevant capabilities" is actually incredibly broad and can include impacts that a weapon has (or does not have) on the operators (i.e., warriors) who use them, among many other considerations.

[20] See, for example, Jai Galliot, "Uninhabited Aerial Vehicles and the Asymmetry Objection: A Reply to Strawser," *Journal of Military Ethics* 11:1 (2012): 58–66, as well as several chapters in this book, which I will discuss here.

action to begin with or whether actual UAVs *are*, in fact, just as capable or accurate and so forth as manned aircraft (in a surprisingly wide number of questionable ways) are centrally important questions in our final judgment of the real and present lethal use of drones. Much of this, of course, rests on needed empirical work to assess whether the ceteris paribus assumption in RW ever holds up in practice. My previous summary of the many objections against the moral permissibility of drone employment are some of the kinds of issues that could make the antecedent of RW false, if they turn out to be true.

A second way to critique RW would be to reject it in principle. Even if the antecedent is true, the claim is false because the consequent is false. This objection claims that killing by remote control is wrong simply because it is killing *by remote control*. As we saw already, this view is less common in the present discourse and faces a large number of problems, but it has been argued and represents a watershed divide in the debate. Thus, the various ways RW could be shown to be false are precisely the various moral issues that are at the forefront of the debate over the ethics of drones.

Of course, it should be noted that none of the aforementioned approaches are mutually exclusive from the other. One could, for example, hold that there is nothing intrinsically wrong with lethal drone use and that their reduction of risk is a moral gain in the ways I have argued for via the PUR yet could also hold that some conditional problems (say, the way they impact the militaries who employ them) make their actual employment ultimately morally problematic and wrong to continue in practice. One could hold these views all while holding that there is something intrinsically wrong with autonomous drone killing and reject them as morally impermissible in their own right. Any number of combinations of overlap of the previous positions can be seen among the scholarly work assembled in this volume. That is an obvious point to make, perhaps, but the current public discourse over drones tends to be, in my view, utterly lacking of such nuance. Killing people by remote control raises complicated, morally vexing questions; we should expect, therefore, that the conclusions reached will often be equally, and rightly, intricate and multifaceted. This is highlighted by a question I am often asked by journalists and public figures: "Are you pro-drone or anti-drone?" I'm afraid the situation is not so simple as to allow for such a crude and blunt conclusion in either direction. In my view the question itself belies a naïve and oversimplistic view of both the moral principles behind remote control killing and the actual implementation of drones in the world today. Drones raise hard questions, both in principle and in practice. Those questions deserve correspondingly good, thorough, and thoughtful answers.

7. Outline of Chapters

The book is divided into three sections. The first section, "Just War Theory and the Permissibility to Kill by Remote Control," contains this introduction and two other chapters focused on background theoretic questions for this form of warfare and the principles of the just war tradition. In chapter 2, "Just War Theory and Remote Military Technology: A Primer," Matthew Hallgarth eloquently reviews the framework that has become dominant for most scholarly discussions over the ethics of war and the elements of it that are most relevant to questions surrounding killing by remote control. This provides a helpful foundation for the rest of the arguments in the book. Hallgarth argues that one of the just war tradition's great strengths is its adaptability to the changing realities of war. He thus concludes that it is able to handle the recent introduction of killing by remote control without need for wide revision.

Chapter 3, "Distinguishing Drones: An Exchange," presents an important and beguiling back-and-forth debate between Asa Kasher and Avery Plaw. The two scholars focus on several important questions such as whether drones present a particularly new form of warfare and whether we should look to revise the principles of the just war tradition in response to them. They also deliberate over the *jus in bello* principle of distinction and how it should apply to current operations being carried out by drones against terrorists, among other theoretic questions over the just war tradition's applicability (or not) to lethal drone employment

The second section of the book, "The Ethics of Drone Employment," directly addresses several of the pressing moral issues raised by the use of unmanned weaponry that I have reviewed already. In chapter 4, "Drones and Targeted Killing: Angels or Assassins?" David Whetham tackles the massive debate over the US active policy of killing specific persons via drone strikes. Whetham deftly works through the highly contentious questions surrounding this practice, such as whether targeted killing is really nothing more than a form of extrajudicial execution or if it can be morally defended. He argues that this kind of killing can be justified if our understanding and claims of it are restricted to a kind of defensive action against unjust threats. His conclusion carries with it sensible suggestions for safeguards that must be put in place to contain the dangerous potential abuses of such a practice.

I noted already the enduring worries many observers have over how fighting a war by remote control may impact the warriors themselves and the warrior ethos of the modern military. Rob Sparrow explores this issue in depth chapter 5, "War without Virtue?" After meticulous examination of the martial virtues and the potential impact of UAVs upon them, he arrives at a troubling conclusion regarding these changes to the nature of warfare. Sparrow's conclusions give ominous warning for what the development of remotely controlled warfare fore-tells for the conceptions of military virtues and their relevance (or lack thereof) to the future of war. Yet he concludes with a thoughtful consideration that it is still an open question whether such a change would be an overall moral gain or loss. As I noted earlier, Sparrow's chapter is the first serious scholarly treatment of this important issue in the debate over the morality of drones.

In chapter 6, "Robot Guardians: Teleoperated Combat Vehicles in Humanitarian Military Intervention," Julian Savulescu and Zack Beauchamp stake out a bold, new argument. They take the often-raised objection discussed already that drone use makes more war likely by making it too easy (that is, the threshold argument) and turn it on its head. Rather than see this as a necessar-ily morally problematic feature of drones, they argue persuasively that it can be a significant net gain by enabling states to engage in humanitarian military intervention when they should but otherwise would not due to improper risk aversion. Their argument will surely prove controversial, but also important, simply by providing a counterweight to the widely cited threshold objection against drone employment.

Chapter 7, "Counting the Dead: The Proportionality of Predation in Pakistan," by Avery Plaw, is a powerful and desperately needed analysis of the available data we have on the collateral damage wrought by drone kill-ings. I noted already that one of the persistent problems in the wider debate over the morality of drones is the scant and often contradictory empirical evi-dence to be had for the actual results wrought by drone warfare. This leads to the related objection that drone operations are disproportionate because they create large numbers of unintended civilian casualties. Plaw's analysis is careful, nuanced, and balanced in presenting evidence showing, in fact, that military operations carried out by drone tend to be far better in their ability to distinguish between combatants and civilians and that they ultimately result in lower rates of civilian causalities than other forms of warfare. He studies what these data can tell us about the common objection against drone war-fare: that it fails to meet the critical but contentious just war theory principle of proportionality.

Rebecca Johnson explores the role remote control weapons can and should play in counterinsurgency operations in chapter 8, "The Wizard of Oz Goes to War: Unmanned Systems in Counterinsurgency." As discussed, this new, population-centric approach to warfare has become dominant in the past few years in theaters such as Iraq and Afghanistan. Doubt over whether drones can play any kind of beneficial role in such environments has long been the source of many objections against drones. Johnson argues that drones can effectively aid in the efforts of counterinsurgency campaigns to better protect civilians from harm. To the extent to which they can meet a few important caveats, she finds their employment compatible with such operations.

To conclude section 2, Uwe Steinhoff argues that there is a general moral problem with the vast asymmetry between combatants in war that is generated by UAV-type weapons in chapter 9, "Killing Them Safely: Extreme Asymmetry and Its Discontents." Steinhoff presents his argument by taking aim at three seminal papers on the ethics of remote control killing and offering energetic critical attention to each. In particular, he first challenges Robert Sparrow's work on the moral permissibility of autonomous unmanned weapons. Next, Steinhoff critiques Suzy Killmister's argument that drone employment in war can force those being attacked by them to violate the traditional strictures of just war theory. Finally, he critiques my argument for the moral obligation to use drones based on the normative demand to avoid unnecessary risk. Steinhoff concludes that while neither remotely controlled unmanned systems nor even autonomous weapons present a special moral problem in principle, he thinks that the extreme military superiority resulting from their current use creates a more general problem that should make us very wary of such modern weapons. In so doing, Steinhoff offers perhaps the strongest and most passionate arguments against the moral permissibility of drones in the volume.

Following Steinhoff's brief engagement with some questions pertaining to autonomous weapons to close section 2, the third and final section of this volume is focused entirely on the ethics of "Autonomous Drones and the Future of Unmanned Weaponry." I mentioned already some of the moral objections and concerns that have been raised against autonomous weapons. I find many of these objections compelling, and, thus far in the debate, it is these voices that have held the most sway. Indeed, I have deep ethical reservations against the possibility of autonomous weapons. But, as I stated already, my aim in this volume is to move the debate forward. Hence, the last two chapters of this book offer two significantly different approaches to grappling with the morality of autonomous weapons. Each represents a major challenge in its own right to the current orthodoxy against the moral permissibility of autonomous weapons among ethicists.

In chapter 11, "Engineering, Ethics, and Industry: The Moral Challenges of Lethal Autonomy," George Lucas argues that much of the debate over "autonomous" weapons is largely confused and wrongheaded. This is because we make a mistake, he insists, when we try to assign any kind of ethical behavior, good or bad, to so-called autonomous weapons. Rather, we must treat them like the tools (or potential tools) that they are and test them to ensure that they can meet certain standards of performance compliance, just as we do in domestic liability law. If Lucas's view is correct, much of the present debate over autonomous weapons is misplaced and unnecessary.

Stephen Kershnar also counters the prevailing views on autonomous weapons in chapter 13, "Autonomous Weapons Pose No Moral Problem." He makes the definitive case that there is no intrinsic problem with autonomous weapons, and he directly engages all of the various arguments that have been offered to the contrary. These include arguments that people have a right not to be attacked by nonmoral agents and that autonomous weapons pose an inevitable accountability problem. Kershnar claims to show that these and all others like them fail. If he is right, then there is no moral barrier, in principle, to developing and using autonomous weapons, and they should be morally evaluated under the same conditions as all other weapons.

2

Just War Theory and Remote Military Technology: A Primer

MATTHEW W. HALLGARTH

1. Introduction

For as long as there have been human communities there have been conflicts between them. When these conflicts are between groups that have a publicly recognizable political identity, as in tribe, state, nation, or empire, the word "war" is deployed to describe these conflicts. A survey of human history suggests that wars are a de facto reality for human beings and will continue to be utilized to settle political disputes deemed significant enough to warrant recourse to military violence. Of course the causes of wars are numerous and diverse, subjective and objective, aggressive and preventive, trivial and substantial, and varied by time, place, methods, and social morays. Modern political entities almost unanimously use trained professionals to project military force, whether citizen volunteers, conscripts, or mercenaries. Military operations always use violence or the threat of violence to decide which political entity has authority over some matter or territory, such as what ideals prevail or who gets to control resources, riches, trade routes, borders, and powerful institutions like banks, key industries, and education content.

Historically, when political entities have resorted to military operations to settle or prevent disputes, these entities have sought the tactical and strategic advantages that superior technology provides. Every political group that engages in military operations seeks to gain something. What gain is sought varies with the objectives, but winning is always the goal, even if winning constitutes demonstrating power to prevent attack, to restore honor, or to set the scene for negotiations on some other issue. With the exception of superior leadership and training, as well as superior numerical and logistical advantages, technological superiority has always been a crucial element to military success. Historically, it is easy to describe technological superiority as constitutive of the difference between victory and defeat. Horses, stirrups, long bows, gunpowder, and repeating firearms are a few of the older examples; radar, faster jet planes, carrier battle groups, and laser guided weapons are newer ones. The recent development and deployment of unmanned military vehicles of various types is a newer one still, following a long historical trend of seeking and utilizing the advantages of superior technology for military operations. These technological advances are particularly important in nations like the US, nations fortunate to have excellent resources, mild government, and a system of economic incentives that releases the energies of a vibrant, intelligent, and technically innovative class yet a lack of available recruits. For the US, technological advantages overcome limits in manpower.

The language of military conflict is the language of justification. Military conflicts kill people and destroy property, causing every kind of imaginable harm in immense quantities. To do these things without any reason is madness. To do these things with bad reasons is unjustifiable. To do these things with good reasons may be unjustifiable if the same goals could be accomplished by other means with much less death and destruction. Modern military conflicts have greatly magnified these harms, and, as such, the burden of justification has grown to comport with these graver consequences. While what counts as an adequate justification for modern military operations is subject to vigorous scholarly debate, the burden of justification persists, and is indicative of a broad, though not universal, acknowledgment that military operations are subject to moral scrutiny and as such must be justified. As with previous technological advances, the development and deployment of unmanned military vehicles does nothing to change this justificatory burden. Use of these unmanned vehicles in military operations fits with earlier developments like repeating rifles and radar, developments that contribute to mission accomplishment for the side that has them, but developments that do not significantly alter the moral landscape of military operations per se. Unmanned military vehicles are tools; conscientious moral analysts must carefully analyze how to use these new tools in ways that are morally justified. It is plausible that the introduction of these weapons in the battle space may justify certain military missions that otherwise would be unjustified.

For moral agents that regard war as a very serious business that must be justified, the just war tradition, with its modern grounding in international law, persists as the best time-tested framework for thinking critically and morally about the justificatory burdens associated with resorting to military force. This justificatory burden includes criteria with respect to when to use force, how to apply it, and in the latest iterations how to manage the aftermath. The tradition persists because it works. It has been rigorous enough to be morally demanding. The tradition adequately captures our intuitions about crucial things to consider regarding the moral justifiability of particular military operations. It is adequately supported by and has substantially influenced the development of laws, oaths, codes, regulations, and rules of engagement. It has demonstrated abiding flexibility to adapt to changes in political models and technological developments without losing explanatory power. The development and use of unmanned military vehicles in military operations is something the just war tradition can accommodate and successfully assess, albeit with certain caveats. These caveats will be addressed at length in the remaining chapters of this book.[1] In what follows, I'll provide a perfunctory description of the just war framework to acquaint or reacquaint readers with its core precepts. My description captures the basics of the tradition as it stands today, even though the just war tradition has and continues to evolve over time. My core position, that the just war tradition can and will continue to be useful for assessing the moral justifiability of using unmanned military vehicles in particular military operations, is twofold. First, the specific criteria of the tradition hold up as useful tools for morally assessing their use. However, even if one or more criteria were to lose their explanatory and evaluative power with the introduction of these new weapons, that fact by itself wouldn't undermine the tradition's usefulness as a flexible and potent assessment model. Second, military history is a history of technological invention that provides clear advantages to the side that has them. Technologies are invented, exploited, and then properly scrutinized by thinkers seeking to rightfully limit their use to morally justifiable purposes. The introduction of unmanned military vehicles into the modern battle space isn't sufficiently different from the past introduction of new technologies to merit announcing the impending demise of the just war tradition. To close this essay, I'll briefly describe the main historical and contemporary opponents to the just war tradition. The introduction of unmanned military vehicles, I argue, won't change the nature of military operations enough to motivate them to change their views.

2. Just War Theory: A Brief Synopsis

Earlier I stated that the language of war and military operations other than war was the language of justification. The burden of justification for military activities are ancient and modern, religious and secular, customary and legal, reflecting a historical evolution of the language of justification to comport with the evolution of technology, strategy, and tactics. The just war tradition broadly refers to an amorphous and diverse historical literature on the justification for

---

[1] And, indeed, some of the contributors to this book will disagree with my argument here and argue that traditional just war theory cannot properly accommodate the use of unmanned military vehicles. Thus, the tradition needs to be revised to properly handle the new problematic ethical issues they now raise.

going to war and what counts as justifiable conduct within it. Michael Walzer captures this broad amorphous nature well, referring to the just war tradition as the "articulated norms, customs, professional codes, legal precepts, religious and philosophical principles, and reciprocal arrangements that shape our judgments of military conduct."[2] While this language of justification has, of late, been intentionally melded with international law, to include conventions, treaties, international watchdog agencies, and the use of tribunals of various types, this focus has been a relatively recent development.

An ancient reference to this burden of justification can be found in Deuteronomy 20:19–20 of the Hebrew Bible. Here the Torah recognizes war as a fact of life but nevertheless one subject to the burden of moral justification. With respect to sieges, this passage forbids cutting down an enemy's fruit trees to build siege works. The moral implication here is that, while battles are inevitable, battles are subject to moral assessment. This passage prohibits destroying an enemy's food sources to wage war. Since soldiers and innocent civilians both must eat, destroying food sources is morally unjustifiable because it doesn't discriminate between combatants and noncombatants.

The historical dialogue on the language of justification for military operations transcends Western moral and religious traditions as well. For example, in the sixth century B.C. the *Hindu Laws of Manu* specified, "When the King fights with his foes in battle, let him not strike with weapons concealed in wood, nor with barbed, poisoned, or flaming arrows."[3] This ancient restriction on weapons from a subcontinent source sanctions weapons for which the added cruelty is not militarily necessary for victory. A modern-day equivalent on this score would be contemporary restrictions on the use of certain kinds of bullets or the inclusion of hard-to-locate nonmetallic shrapnel in grenades and mines. Since both glass and metal effectively remove combatants from the battle space, metal should be used to make the shrapnel visible to x-ray machines or metal detectors.

The historical dialogue that became the modern just war tradition was influenced by intellectual titans such as Plato and Aristotle, Cicero and Augustine, and Aquinas, Gratian, Suarez, and Vitoria. Each thinker largely responded to contextual historical conditions and events that suggested the need for moral restraints in military conflicts. The specific criteria that came to form the content of the contemporary tradition coalesced over time in response to a few key developments. The first of these was the growth of larger and more stable political monopolies over territory and the subsequent use of violence for

---

[2] Michael Walzer, *Just and Unjust Wars: A Moral Argument with Historical Illustrations* (New York: Basic Books, 1977), 44.

[3] Georg Buhler, trans. *The Laws of Manu*, Chapter 7, verse 90, http://hinduism.about.com/library/weekly/extra/bl-lawsofmanu7.htm.

political purposes. Rules evolved, for example, to protect emissaries, to limit military violence to redressing certain injustices, and to punish these injustices with a severity appropriate to the crime. Rules on broader procedures coalesced around new political realities too, such as a requirement for vested political authorities to formally declare their violent intentions. Offensive and defensive war came to be distinguished as well. Defensive wars to protect life, property, and honor were thought easily justified and receive scant attention in the older Western literature. Offensive wars were understood intuitively to be more difficult to morally justify.

A second historical development to influence the development of concrete just war criteria was the gradual secularization of the justificatory apparatus for interstate military conflicts, a move that was first grounded in an ethics of natural law. This shift hinged on the growing realization that pagan peoples, such as the natives that Spain conquered in the new world, deserved the same moral protections as Christian opponents. Pagans came to be viewed not as subhuman savages to be treated with impunity but as moral agents created in the image of God. The moral rules of military conflict must be applied to human beings generally.

A third development in the just war tradition in the West was the solidification of the concept of national sovereignty following the Treaty of Westphalia in 1648. The brutal Thirty Years' War between reformers and Catholics over theological supremacy on the European continent exhausted the peninsula with punitive conflicts and reprisals directed at the idealistic and otherworldly goal of theological hegemony. States weary of brutal religious wars came painfully to accept mitigated religious diversity, agreeing in their exhaustion that counterproductive wars for pure orthodoxy were not a legitimate moral justification for war. While the Westphalia treaty solidified the primacy of national sovereignty, it also encouraged more secular thinking in the West with respect to the language of moral justification for going to war and how properly to fight it. Europeans beyond the mere academic set began to see the language of justification for military violence as including war generally, not simply war between like-minded believers. Grounding the language of military violence in natural law principles preserved God as the source of the moral order but severed the hubristic belief that God took sides in denominational feuds. The language of justification for war came to be theologically neutral though still morally rich, such as responding to unjust interstate aggression, maintaining balances of power, and righting moral wrongs associated with real or perceived violations of territorial integrity and political sovereignty.

The just war tradition today comprises a reasonably terse set of generally accepted criteria for entering a just war and how to behave in it. The following lists capture these criteria for readers unfamiliar with the tradition's basic tenets. After each, I provide a short justification for their relevance to the moral justifiability of military operations. Note that the lists emphasize criteria for a justified decision to go to war and principles to govern morally justified conduct in it. A third category, *jus post bellum*, justice after war, is a relatively recent category that some contemporary moral theorists argue ought to be included in the totality of moral justification for military operations.

Jus ad bellum (the decision to go to war): Since war is a very serious and destructive business that causes untold amounts of every kind of harm, the decision to go to war must be morally and legally justified. War shouldn't be entered into lightly, flippantly, or without serious consideration.

1. *Legitimate authority*: War can be declared only by agents of political leadership with that authority. These can differ from nation to nation. In the US, a Secretary of Defense or an ambassador cannot declare war. That authority is reserved for the Congress by Article One, Section Eight of the US Constitution.

2. *Just cause*: Largely viewed as the backbone of the *jus ad bellum* criteria, war that is entered into for unjustified reasons is immoral, even if the war is fought with moral restraint. Generally accepted "just causes" include, but are not necessarily limited to, resisting external attack, defending others from the same, protecting innocent humans from genocides and egregious brutality, and distributing punishment for grievous rights violations. The United Nations equates just causes with defensive words like "resisting aggression," "peacekeeping," and "security." Walzer focuses on resisting aggression, a category that may include preemptive and preventive attack in certain contexts.[4] Even if each of the other criteria for *jus ad bellum* is met, the cause must be just to morally justify the campaign.

3. *Declaration:* A sovereign that opts for war ought to announce that decision to the community of nations, but particularly to one's foe. A declaration of war may be the last opportunity to stop a war from commencing. Declaring war provides one last opportunity for a solution short of it.

4. *Last resort:* Since war is terribly destructive in so many ways, it's incumbent on political authorities to use measures short of war if there is a reasonable possibility that they may effectively resolve the issue. Contemporary examples of measures short of war include, but are not excluded to, economic sanctions, blockades, freezing aid disbursements, appeasement, and diplomacy. With last resort, leaders do have to make judgments as to whether continued efforts to use measures short of war have a reasonable chance of being effective. For that reason, there's often disagreement on whether this criterion has be satisfied in a particular case.

---

[4] Walzer, *Just and Unjust Wars*, 51–53.

5. *Reasonable chance of success:* If a war is very unlikely to successfully resolve the issues that measures short of war were unable to resolve, then the war is imprudent. This criterion is meant to avoid fruitless, pointless, and self-indulgent wars, even if a just cause can be articulated. Still, this criterion is open to a number of provisos. For example, occasionally circumstances such as an invasion by a superior foe justify putting up a military fight in the face of likely military defeat. This type of resistance can preserve important values and signal as much to the community of nations.

6. *Right intention:* This criterion presumes that war should be fought with the right motives. While motives are difficult to determine, they are best viewed as linked to the backbone principle of just cause. A right intention for war is the intention to fight specifically for the justice of the cause. Fighting for malice, spite, or ethnic hatred is immoral. Fighting for the love of war itself or to get reelected is unjustified. Fighting to distract a citizenry from deep domestic problems is unjust as well. Morally justified wars are fought to right an injustice and then to restore peace.

7. *Proportionality:* The last criterion customarily included in the *jus ad bellum* category is proportionality. Proportionality with respect to the decision to go to war requires that the benefits of a war be juxtaposed with the immense costs of war. Trivial injustices rarely, if ever, justify the cost and sacrifice that war entails. To start a war over a minor treaty violation is imprudent. To start a war because a neighboring nation initiated a massive invasion of one's home territory is most likely prudent. Proportionality shouldn't include merely a nation's expense in fighting a war. The potential damage to the adversary, as well as the probable long-term damage to international relations, global public opinion, and the possibility of festering resentments at home and abroad, is included.

Jus in bello (just conduct in war): Whether or not specific military operations are morally justified has a tenuous relationship at best to whether the hostilities are conducted in a morally justifiable way. The *jus in bello* criteria describe the moral responsibilities of those who execute the wars their leaders decide to pursue. When hostilities commence, the current just war tradition brackets morally justifiable military violence with two broad criteria: *discrimination* and *proportionality*. First, violent military action has to discriminate between combatants and noncombatants. Second, the costs of particular military action have to be proportional to the objectives sought. The thread running through both criteria is the moral requirement that particular military missions be reasonably assessed as militarily necessary to achieve justified goals of the conflict. Missions may discriminate and may demonstrate appropriate proportionality yet not contribute to achieving justified goals couched under the broad auspices of resisting aggression. These missions are wasted.

The two main criteria of discrimination and proportionality are supplemented with other *jus in bello* rules to specify what these principles should include in practice. These supplementary criteria charge fighters with obeying international laws that ban certain weapons. For example, a combatant in military hostilities who can be killed, cannot, in virtue of that fact, be killed with virulent biological agents or chemical weapons. Fighters also must provide benevolent quarantine to prisoners of war. The argument for this rule is that prisoners are no longer a threat to do harm and, as such, regain their noncombatant immunity, a right not to be killed. *Jus in bello* restrictions in the just war tradition also prohibit practices deemed evil in themselves. These include, but aren't necessarily limited to, mass rape campaigns, ethnic cleansing, genocide, and acts of treachery that erode respect for moral standards, such as executing a ruse by pretending to be a Red Cross worker. Some argue that justified conduct in war prohibits reprisals to incentivize an enemy to obey *jus in bello* rules more faithfully. The justification for this prohibition is the empirically controversial view that reprisals don't work. If reprisals don't work, then they are wantonly cruel and merely vengeful. Finally, some argue that the *in bello* criteria ought to include rules requiring states to maintain rights protections for their own citizens during war. The principle here is that a state at war must maintain reasonable respect for the human rights of its citizens, their property, and the legal system that provides minimally just institutions and rights protections.

The tenuous relationship between the *jus ad bellum* criteria and the *jus in bello* criteria for going to war is dependent on the long-held view that soldiers on both side of a military conflict are morally equivalent. Soldiers fighting for a just cause may fight unjustly, while soldiers fighting for an unjust cause may fight justly. This irony is easy to understand in practice. Unjust invaders who demonstrate proportionality and respect the combatant–noncombatant distinction in their violence are behaving justly under the auspices of an unjust invasion. Defenders of an unjust invasion who do not demonstrate proportionality and indiscriminately kill innocent civilians in their war of defense behave unjustly despite having a just cause. This irony is not a terminal problem since military conflicts are a fact of life. Regardless of which side of a conflict has a just cause, both sides share a justificatory burden how they behave during hostilities. At the level of national conflicts, citizen volunteers or draftees generally don't choose the wars they fight, and soldiers on both sides are likely to be propagandized as to the justice of their nation's cause. And most soldiers are likely to, or at least want to believe that their nation has right on its side. It is also the case in many conflicts that a clear bearer of the just cause is unclear. In both clear and unclear cases, the language of justification still falls on the violent executors of national objectives to fight with proportionality and discrimination, with reasonable adherence to rules of engagement that spell out what these broad categories mean in the actual practice of fighting in particular cases.

The view that soldiers on both sides of a conflict are morally equivalent has come under criticism in recent years. Jeff McMahan has argued that moral equivalency fails because soldiers fighting for a just cause haven't given up their right not to be killed. Fighters in an unjust war cannot claim self-defense any more than a bank robber can claim self-defense for shooting the armed guard defending the bank he's trying to rob. His argument is nuanced and convincing on many levels, and if anything at least puts a chink in the orthodoxy of moral equivalency.[5]

Whether the contemporary, generally acknowledged just war criteria are all necessary conditions for classifying a war as a just war, or whether a subset of them may be sufficient, is a topic for scholarly debate. How to interpret the criteria can be controversial. I hesitate, though, to call these criteria mere rules of thumb. Nevertheless, there's general consensus within the tradition that a justified decision to go to war requires a just cause, proper authority, be a last resort, and have aims appropriately proportional to its destructive costs. A just cause is almost certainly a necessary condition, for the other criteria lose most of their moral force if the chief reason for deciding to fight in the first place is unjustified.[6] While the *jus ad bellum* criteria remain a fruitful topic for scholarly debate, these debates within the tradition reflect abiding belief that resorts to military violence are and should be subject to moral assessment using the language of moral justification. The just war tradition provides this justificatory language. Debates within the tradition usually concern what the criteria mean, how the criteria ought to be applied in particular cases, and whether the criteria should be augmented or reduced to account for the influence of new realities, such as the introduction of nuclear weapons.

Briefly I add that, in recent years, some just war scholars, notably Brian Orend, have argued for the need to supplement the just war tradition with criteria for morally justifiable management of the *jus post bellum*, the aftermath of war. Debate in this new category is fluid and controversial, though rightly extolling the importance of ending wars properly. Orend's insight here is that, while to victors go the spoils, to victors also go moral responsibilities to those they vanquish. Do victors owe their vanquished enemies a Marshall Plan of sorts, or are initiatives like these merely charitable things that are only nice to do? This insight is based on the observation that excessively punitive treatment of

[5] McMahan's challenging critique of the moral neutrality thesis for combatants on both sides of a conflict can be found in his *Killing in War* (New York: Oxford University Press, 2009).

[6] Some have recently argued, in fact, that all other traditional criteria of *jus ad bellum* actually fall under and are internal to a proper understanding of "just cause." A good explanation of this position can be found in Jeff McMahan, "Just Cause for War," *Ethics and International Affairs* 19 (2005): 1–21.

a vanquished enemy is merely vindictive, that those who win the war must also win the peace. Winning the peace mitigates the potential for lasting animosity that may lead to future wars. This evolving set of criteria seems to depend on the capacities of the victors to assist in restoring losers to the community of nations, as measurable rehabilitation efforts are more likely to restore lasting and peaceful relations with vanquished enemies. Criteria proposed here include a fair peace settlement that's not excessively punitive. Rights violated by the war should be restored and their defense improved if possible. Postwar indictments should be appropriately targeted to discriminate between leaders, soldiers of varying ranks, and innocent civilians to avoid sweeping social economic sanctions that punish a nation en masse. If the enemy has committed egregious rights violations, proper war crimes trials for civilian and military leaders are appropriately consistent with due process and international law. Financial restitution should be deftly dealt with to avoid impoverishing the vanquished into bitter eagerness for a future fight. Finally, victors who respect human rights and the fair rule of law should, where possible, influence the reformation of decrepit institutions in the country of the vanquished, that they may rejoin the rights-respecting community of nations with renewed vigor. Some of these criteria are vulnerable to the charge of imperialism if not deftly instigated and depend, for their success, on the enemy's view that the victor's motives are reasonably honorable and just.[7]

Admittedly, *jus post bellum* criteria can put a heavy burden on victors in a number of ways, and the criteria are subject to broad interpretive latitude. Their uses depend also on fluid contextual facts. One brief example illustrates this point, though further research is warranted. If a vanquished enemy had corrupt institutions, how much time and treasure are victors required to invest to reform those institutions? These efforts may take decades and may depend, in part, on the willingness of the vanquished to internalize the changes. Japan after World War II was a success story for reforms of this type. Other initiatives like the North Atlantic Treaty Organization's (NATO's) efforts in the Balkans have had mixed results and seem to require a permanent presence there. Some reform efforts will likely fail too. Efforts in Afghanistan and Iraq are likely failures, though the jury is still out on these initiatives.

3. Just War Theory and Unmanned Military Vehicles

As with bullets and bombs, satellites, swords, and ships, unmanned military vehicles are inanimate objects. They are tools. Moral responsibility applies to

---

[7] For a fuller explanation of *jus post bellum* as a category, see Brian Orend, *The Morality of War* (Toronto: Broadview Press, 2006).

moral agents and not tools. The language of justification for military operations focuses the burden on whether and how moral agents can use these tools. The tools of war may be used if the conflict is justified by the "articulated norms, customs, professional codes, legal precepts, religious and philosophical principles, and reciprocal arrangements that shape our judgments of military conduct."[8]

If we consider the just war tradition, it should be apparent that the introduction of unmanned military vehicles could conceivably change the justificatory support for certain military missions or conflicts. Thus, it's clearly possible that the introduction of unmanned military vehicles could change a formerly imprudent and morally unjustified military campaign into a prudent and justified one. For example, aerial drones are much cheaper than manned aircraft, and they also provide their operators with much greater security than manned airframe pilots enjoy. It's quite possible, even likely, that some proposed military operations that would otherwise be too risky and costly without the availability of aerial drones would be made sufficiently safe and cost-effective merely because of the addition of these drones, enough to justify an otherwise unjustified military conflict or specific mission. The same argument could be made with respect to some urban conflict situations that would be too risky and costly to undertake without robot help. The development of urban robot drones to reconnoiter buildings and other ambush points, it seems, really could change some conflicts and their associated missions from imprudent and unjustifiable to prudent and justifiable ones.

This argument can be fortified by juxtaposing unmanned military vehicles with the specific just war criteria. With respect to the *jus ad bellum* criteria, the introduction of unmanned military vehicles doesn't seem to appreciably alter the moral justification for just cause, legitimate authority, declaration, and right intention in decisions on whether or not to go to war. The availability of drones, though, could provide relevant reconnaissance and other capabilities in such a way as to affect, for example, the timing of a specific declaration of war by a legitimate authority in response to a defensible just cause. With the other *jus ad bellum* criteria, unmanned military vehicles can have a significant influence on assessments of last resort, reasonable chance of success, and proportionality. The availability of aerial drones could influence perceptions about, for example, when a last resort threshold is reached. There's a rub here, for unmanned military vehicles could provide capabilities that give war a more distant last resort threshold if used to restrain or reconnoiter a potential foe, or an earlier one, if the addition of these vehicles make war less costly and risky and thus easier to commit to. With the criteria of reasonable chance of success, unmanned military vehicles clearly can influence how these determinations are made. While I find it difficult to consider how unmanned military

---

[8] Walzer, *Just and Unjust Wars*, 44.

vehicles could be a liability to the side that has them, they do certainly seem to provide a plethora of advantages in cost savings, reconnaissance, and amelioration of risk. As such, possessing these machines in some cases would likely make some missions and campaigns that would otherwise not have a reasonable chance of success into missions or campaigns that do have one. That likelihood introduces the problem that in some cases military violence could be used with drones when it would be imprudent to do so without them. This problem, however, cannot be generalized to the point of condemning these weapons, for unmanned military vehicles could just as easily open up military options that justice demands, missions that would otherwise be avoided due to higher costs and risks but that really ought to be pursued.

With respect to the *jus in bello* criteria, the introduction of unmanned military vehicles into the battle space can influence how assessments of proportionality and discrimination are made. For example, let's revisit my earlier example of utilizing reconnaissance robots in urban combat environments. These robots can provide numerous positive results. Urban combat is a stressful and close quarters environment. Using robots can locate and distinguish between combatants and civilians in particular structures. They can prevent unnecessary and wasteful destruction of lives and property. These machines don't make impulsive decisions under stress; they don't react violently to uncertainty. In short, these robots can provide war fighters with crucial information at a distance, information that facilitates better decisions that are more consistent with proportionality and discrimination. Urban reconnaissance robots will properly eliminate some destructive and unnecessary missions while more accurately revealing missions that otherwise might not be done but should be. Or these robots will help war fighters complete missions in ways that better protect innocent lives and property. Note that when I describe these urban robots, I'm assuming that a human operator controls these machines. The possibility of fully autonomous unmanned military vehicles exposes other problematic issues that will be addressed in other chapters of this volume of essays.

My presumption thus far has been that unmanned military vehicles are useful tools that the just war tradition can accommodate. The previous examples should how this can be true. Yet if we suppose that these vehicles actually were tools of a specific type so that the just war tradition en toto would condemn them, then these tools, it seems, would be more like chemical and biological agents. That is, they would have to be tools or weapons that were somehow evil in themselves. They would be tools that add nothing but gratuitous harm to a military conflict. But unmanned military vehicles are not like chemical and biological agents or other similar weapons. They are not, per se, tools that merely add gratuitous harm. Used correctly, they prevent great amounts of harm. Thus, since unmanned military vehicles are not evil in themselves, they aren't condemned by the just war tradition. Two more examples provide additional empirical support to this argument. One type of unmanned military vehicle recently developed is a walking robot that can carry supplies with a cadre of troops over difficult terrain. If these robot "mules" are more dependable than living mules, don't require rest and forage, are more useful in tough terrain than wheeled vehicles, then using them as tools is certainly morally justified, perhaps required in some cases. These vehicles could mean the difference between success and failure in a mission that passes the justificatory burden of the just war tradition. If these "mules" are used in support of a just cause and they measurably help troops to successfully execute militarily necessary missions that satisfy the proportionality and discrimination criteria of *jus in bello*, then using them is morally justified. These "mules" could save lives, might even enable troops to cleanly stop genocide in a remote area. Admittedly, these robot "mules" could conceivably be used to perpetrate gross injustices, such as carry biological or chemical agents to kill innocent civilians. Still, these robots are not evil in themselves the way a canister of saran gas is. These mules are militarily indistinguishable from pickup trucks, which can carry torture devices or life-saving vaccines. Moral responsibility applies to moral agents. Individuals and groups of people who operate remote control military vehicles are subject to moral judgment for immoral actions they perpetrate with unmanned robots, just as they would be subject to moral judgment for using some other acceptable military weapon to kill innocent civilians in a pogrom.

Or take another example. Some unmanned military robots have been developed to disarm improvised explosive devices (IEDs) safely. For consistency purposes, let's assume these bomb diffuser robots are used in military conflicts and subject to the strictures of the just war tradition. These robots are useful "human-controlled" machines that achieve justifiable goals (bomb diffusion and reconnaissance) with the benefit providing added safety for friendly troops. If a conflict is justified by a just cause and the troops fight consistent with the justificatory burdens of discrimination and proportionality, then utilizing these tools is certainly justified, perhaps required in certain cases. These robots are not evil in themselves, even if they could possibly be used for evil purposes that would merit moral condemnation. Again, moral responsibility applies to moral agents and not to the tools they use.[9] It's possible that these machines could be used to more safely enable a cadre of troops to carry out a grossly immoral genocidal mission or detonate a time-delayed dirty nuclear device in a crowded city. These immoral missions don't render the robots evil in themselves. The robots, like a handgun, can be tools used to do evil deeds. These bomb-diffusing robots aren't morally equivalent to dirty bombs.

[9] The argument that the moral duties surrounding bomb-disarming robots can be used analogously to shed light on the moral duties of unmanned aerial vehicles (UAVs) is made at length in Bradley J. Strawser, "Moral Predators: The Duty to Employ Uninhabited Aerial Vehicles," *Journal of Military Ethics* 9:4 (December 2010): 342–368.

An aside is worth addressing here, since it exposes a perplexity I have with extensive concern about these unmanned machines of late. Our use of the phrase "unmanned military vehicles" is somewhat confusing and, to my recollection, recent. Smart weapons guided by satellites or certain types of missiles guided by pilots or other delivery sources seem to be unmanned military vehicles as well, yet we haven't talked about them in those terms in recent years. These older guided weapons are remotely controlled, they are useful tools, they protect friendly forces from risk, and they are accepted as legitimate delivery vehicles. If they are used in conflicts that are supported by a just cause augmented by careful attention to the other *ad bellum* criteria and they are deployed with due care given to the *in bello* principles of proportionality and discrimination, then their use is morally justified. These older laser- and satellite-guided weapons clearly aren't evil per se but may be used in evil ways if deployed by ignoble moral agents that intend immoral objectives. Apparently, remote control machines have now achieved a new level of complexity that is leading people to rethink the moral justification for these types of weapons. The greatly advanced sophistication of more recent unmanned military vehicles permits even more remote operation and many hours of sustained deployment over time. These advances, however, do not make bomb-diffusing robots, urban reconnaissance machines, and even aerial attack drones different in kind from laser-guided bombs and other older vehicles guided from remote planes and satellite links. Sophisticated remote control vehicles and weapons have been around longer than many are inclined to think. Advances in technology improve their capabilities and increase their deployment time a great deal. Nevertheless, the use of these unmanned vehicles is only as good or as evil as the moral agents controlling them.

Conscientious moral theorists are ruminating over what the growing sophistication and increasing use of unmanned vehicles mean for the future of military conflicts. This is important work for those who persist, rightly I think, in viewing military operations as serious moral business. Concerns about deploying these vehicles are numerous, nuanced, developing, and diverse and reflect the ongoing view that the methods and means of war require the language of justification. Many of these concerns will be fleshed out at length in subsequent chapters in this volume. I point out, though, that these concerns with unmanned military vehicles tend to be associated not with their general use but with the methods and means of using them to deploy lethal force. I have found no one that objects in a serious way to using robots in safe ways to diffuse IEDs or reconnoiter a building that may contain enemy forces. Rather, objections usually take other forms, such as using these vehicles to deliver offensive lethal firepower against an enemy position.

While just war theorists accept military conflict as a fact of life and as subject to the language of moral justification, conscientious just war theorists generally do not want this technology to make the military option easier, to make it more tempting, to allow it to coarsen the moral sensibilities of deciders and users, or to make moral accountability for immoral use more difficult to ascertain. Conscientious just war theorists do not want this new technology to mitigate the need to strive for conflict resolution that avoids military alternatives. Still, this is not a unique problem for unmanned military vehicles either, as the introduction of new technologies has often made the military option more tempting for those who have these new technologies or have removed from them the painful reality of killing through the psychological insulation that distance provides.[10]

Concerns about deploying these vehicles mirror concerns raised by just war theory generally. Just war theorists analyzing the use of unmanned military vehicles have first to decide whether it is justified to use them in the deployment of lethal force and, if so, to assess the justified ways of using them consistent with recognized moral criteria. If a military operation isn't justified, using these vehicles to deploy lethal force isn't justified either. If a military option is justified, opponents to using them specifically to deploy lethal force must show that a military option is justified and deployment of unmanned vehicles is not. Since these vehicles are not evil in themselves, I think this burden cannot be overcome. However, technical limitations and concerns with these weapons can and should affect justifications for how and when to use them. If, for instance, an unmanned vehicle in a particular case has a reasonably increased risk of causing collateral damage to innocent people and property, say, in an urban environment, then it may be right to use other means to achieve a particular military end, even if military forces must bear some measurably higher risk to do those missions in more precise ways.[11] The mere fact that unmanned military vehicles, like aerial drones, are inexpensive and advantageous in a number of ways is not, ceteris paribus, a sufficient reason to use them at every opportunity.

Casuistic assessments are required in particular cases to assess using these vehicles in light of the evaluative criteria of just war theory. It has always been that way when the deployment of new weapons is subjected to moral assessment. The introduction of unmanned military vehicles into the projection of military force creates no paradigm shift in this debate. These are sophisticated technological tools the just war theory can accommodate. These tools are not evil in themselves, so they can be used. This means that moral judgments about their use in particular contexts will be ongoing and focused on unjustifiable uses for these tools, not on deeming them unjustifiable categorically.

---

[10] For a substantial discussion of the arguments in these last two paragraphs, see Strawser, "Moral Predators." Also see chapter 3 of this volume for a debate over some of these points. Uwe Steinhoff argues against some of Strawser's claims regarding the generalizability of this "lowering the threshold" worry against UAVs to other kinds of weaponry in chapter 9 of this volume.

[11] On this and related points see chapters 7 and 8 in this volume; on the debate over military forces bearing higher risk to protect noncombatants, see chapter 3.

4. Just War Opponents and Unmanned Military Vehicles

At this point I've briefly surveyed the terrain of just war theory and provided a glossy overview of the tradition and the generally accepted criteria as they evolved to exist today. My argument thus far has been to show that the introduction of unmanned military vehicles is not a game changer for the just war tradition. The tradition has been flexible with technological innovations in the past, has evolved to meet the moral complexities entailed by these technological changes, and has retained a core set of principles grounded in the irony of war as a fact of life with the moral statuses associated with innocent humans' rights to life and property. So while unmanned military vehicles can and does changes the situational variables used to make particular moral decisions with regard to military conflicts and the operations within them, these weapons don't render the just war tradition obsolete. Indeed, I think the tradition has ample moral assessment horsepower to accommodate the introduction of these weapons. But even if it doesn't accommodate the introduction of unmanned military weapons in some particular way, the just war tradition is sufficiently flexible to adapt to these conundrums by adding, subtracting, or fleshing out existing just war principles in novel ways.

In what remains, I want to expose the reader to the fact that just war theory is not held universally as a moral assessment tool for war and other military conflicts. The two broad views that have historically rejected the just war tradition as a moral assessment guide for war are broadly known as realism and pacifism. Each of these two categories can be further subdivided into types. Briefly I want to acquaint the reader with the philosophical underpinnings of these two categories and their chief (though perhaps not all) subcategories. The point I want to argue here is as follows: those who reject the just war tradition as the best time-tested moral assessment tool for decisions to go to war and conduct in war will most likely not be motivated to change their views merely because of the introduction of unmanned military vehicles into the battle space. In fact, I consider the introduction of unmanned military vehicles to be largely irrelevant to these viewpoints, since these new machines don't alter the philosophical underpinnings of realism and pacifism at all. This is an important section to include here for the following reason. It is one thing to argue that the just war tradition can accommodate these new machines without losing explanatory power. It is another thing to argue that the two chief opponents to the just war tradition won't change their positions vis-à-vis war because of the introduction of these new machines. This later conclusion leads me to infer that substantive moral analysis of the ramifications of introducing these weapons will come from within the just war tradition, not from outside it. As we'll see, realists will see these new machines more as tools to exploit. And pacifists will remain pacifists with or without these weapons added to the mix.

4.1 Realism

The view that wars and lethal military operations other than war are or should be subject to moral scrutiny is not universally held, despite the ubiquitous historical use of justificatory language to analyze these operations. Some thinkers vigorously argue that moral categories either do not or should not apply to war and related military operations. While I disagree with these thinkers, their views merit at least brief attention, as they are fundamentally related to and bracket the application of the just war tradition to the deployment of unmanned military vehicles. These opponents to the just war tradition are historically categorized as either realists or pacifists, though there are varieties of each with nuanced differences in both.

Realism has a long tradition of its own and includes such notables as Thucydides, Machiavelli, and Hobbes as well as contemporaries like Kissinger, Niebuhr, Mao, and Truman. The view is powerful among political scientists and among many scholars and bureaucrats involved in international relations. While realists do hold and defend some sophisticated and nuanced doctrines, their foundational assumptions are fairly easy to describe. Realists argue that the concept of "moral war" is inconceivable. With respect to the actions of states in the international context, realists argue that what does, or what should, influence state behavior are nonmoral considerations such as national security, self-interest, and power. For some realists, talk about morality and international relations is idle chatter, a category mistake, for even if it would be preferable to apply moral categories here, that is just not how states make decisions to deploy military force. It is a descriptive fact for these realists that states make decisions with respect to other states based on the aforementioned nonmoral considerations.

Some realists argue against such a deterministic view, holding that, while states could apply moral categories to their deliberations and decisions in the international sphere, they are better served if they don't. Using moral categories in the climate of international anarchy will only make you weaker, hinder you, and make you subject to exploitation. Thus, at the international level states *should* restrict themselves to act militarily only for national interests' sake.. It is important to note that realists of this stripe are not necessarily restricted from using moral language to describe their rationale for utilizing war and other military missions to accomplish state purposes. As long as the final determinant for state action at the international level is based on calculations of interests, moral language may be subsumed and utilized under this broader nonmoral category. A realist can, I think, consistently argue that states *should* or *ought* to put interests, security, and power first. They can argue as well that unwise decisions to deploy military force that do not further a state's measurable interests, security, and power are immoral ones. This distinction is important, for it gives these realists access to moral language and arguments without the charge of inconsistency. Here the words and arguments are merely prudential and may serve a number of nonmoral purposes, such as establishing mutually agreed on rules like conventions motivated toward preventing suffering and damage inconsistent with the enhancement of national interests on either side. Here the rules would be like those in a game, only here a more complicated and dangerous one.

Realists have deployed a few additional arguments to support their views, and I mention them briefly here. Some realists promote a psychological defense for their views, arguing that applying moral categories to war and other military applications of international violence only makes common soldiers more inclined to suffer. The crux of this view is that a realist position reduces guilt for the soldier who is better served thinking that war is somehow a "'stepping out'" of the normal moral domain. I am dubious about the argument's truth; nevertheless, it is largely dependent on empirical psychological investigation. Even if this argument were true, that empirical fact would not in itself be sufficient justification for removing moral justifications from decisions to use military force. Another realist argument holds that morality in war is a set of empty and impotent platitudes, since there is no enforceable international positive law to persuade and restrict the actual behavior of military professionals. These arguments are not particularly convincing, as many people behave according to moral principle without the force of law to guarantee their obedience. And many people obey existing laws even when they are reasonably sure they will not be caught, within the confines of military service and in human life generally. The last and perhaps more interesting argument of some realists is the view that there is no morality at all. Such realists take a nihilist position about morality generally. If there is no morality at all, then there is no morality in military operations either. These realists would argue that the justificatory language of all morality is a veneer over struggles for security, interests, and power, whether at the international, intrastate, or individual levels.

This discussion of the realist rejection of a moral basis for talking about war and other violent military operations is pertinent to discussions about the use of unmanned military vehicles to project military power. To the realist, if these vehicles contribute to a state's security, interests, or power, then they will be or should be used. Using these vehicles is a prudential consideration alone. If, for example, these vehicles are effective, reliable, and cheap to operate or if they protect crucial interests, deter opponents, provide quality intelligence, and so forth, then the wise realist will or should use them. In fact, under certain conditions, unmanned military vehicles do all of these things quite well. A realist can even argue that using unmanned military vehicles is morally required, at least preferred, if they contribute substantially to the primary goals of maintaining or enhancing a state's security, interests, or power. In this regard, a wise realist would justify the use of unmanned military vehicles in the same way he would justify using radar. Both provide your side with distinct advantages to achieve state objectives with military might.

4.2 Pacifism

Pacifism is the antiwar position, but it can be more than that. Pacifism has an eerie conceptual relationship to realism in that both groups think moral justifications for or during war are category mistakes. While realists eschew using moral justifications for war and other violent military operations for a variety of reasons already mentioned, realists nevertheless accept war as a de facto inevitable and necessary human activity. Pacifists likewise eschew using moral justifications for war, not because they are irrelevant but because war is so terrible as to never be morally justified by the principles just war proponents embrace. Pacifists often take a utilitarian stance to justify their views, arguing that the consequences of war, especially of modern war, are so grave that no moral justification for it can overcome the immense harms that military operations cause to people and property. A few deontological pacifists argue that war, for some pacifists all violence, is inherently an unjust violation of fundamental rights, regardless of the purported justification for fighting.

Critics in both the realist and just war camps charge that pacifist arguments are excessively wedded to the idea of avoiding "'dirty hands,'" for surely some wars are strongly justified and persuasive counterfactuals could be given to show that aggressive responses result in less harm than noninvolvement. Even here though, pacifists reject getting involved, preferring their nonviolent approach even if the position removes them from qualification to hold certain political positions, particularly at times when internal and external threats make a martial response a self-preservation necessity.[12]

Like the realists, pacifists have their varieties. St. Augustine, a private pacifist, argued that private citizens had no right to self-defense but held that some conditions justified state-sanctioned fighting on behalf of the city of man to resist evil or to punish an egregious wrongdoing. As much as I appreciate St. Augustine as a seminal thinker, this argument never seemed persuasive: the view that I cannot resist a mugger but can, under certain conditions, fight

---

[12] For an interesting and informative look at how pacifist views caused a group's political power to wane, see Peter Brock, *The Quaker Peace Testimony: 1660 to 1914* (Syracuse: Syracuse University Press, 1990). The Quakers were squeezed by two things: new and numerous immigrants didn't share their pacifist views; and the French–Indian War highlighted a community's need to use force to protect itself from external threats.

for purposes of state. Other pacifists take the opposite position: that resisting a mugger is morally justified as an act of self-defense but that wars of state are so lethal and destructive that they are never morally justified. If practically implausible, this position has a measure of intuitive appeal grounded in the right to self-defense and the acknowledgment that state-sponsored violence is egregiously lethal and destructive. Still others argue from the purist perspective, holding that any violence against human beings is immoral, whether private or state sanctioned. Mohandas Gandhi fits this category. Proponents of this version of pacifism are criticized with the charge that they are selfish or hopelessly idealist, since some morally good actions require violence given the facts of human existence. The pacifist, indeed Gandhi's response, is that people can resist aggression effectively by a coordinated and organized campaign of nonviolent civil disobedience. And while this objection is hard to refute in principle, it fails for its impractical otherworldliness. For some situations simply require political violence to resist aggression. And it seems false to claim that nonviolence resistance will always work if it is done correctly. In Gandhi's case, his success is owed as much to the nature of the British regime he resisted and to British financial exhaustion after WWII. Britain's political system had implicit respect for human rights and the value of self-determination, despite its colonial abuses. Another imperial power, like the Mongols, lacking the same respect for rights, would have interpreted Gandhi's efforts as weakness and most likely crushed it.

The moral argument against pacifism, and one that sides with the just war tradition, describes violent resistance to wrongful aggression as something for which the resistor is not morally responsible. While aggressors have their own statuses as moral agents, they and their lackeys forfeit the right not to be harmed as moral agents precisely because of their wrongful aggression. It may be hard for individual moral agents to process, but violently resisting aggression can be interpreted as avoiding the same dirty hands problem that pacifists badly want to evade. Aggressors are responsible for the retribution they receive by moral agents defending their life and property against violent opportunists. Conscientious just war theorists are just as alarmed as pacifists at the death of innocent people. The just war principle of noncombatant immunity covers those who have not forfeited their rights not to be harmed in military operations while preserving a moral justification for resisting those who mean to violently harm you, your property, and your cherished traditions and values.

This discussion of pacifism has moral import as well for discussing the justification for using unmanned military vehicles to conduct violent military operations. Pacifists who reject war as never morally justified will presumably not become just war proponents because of the introduction of unmanned military vehicles, just as pacifists who eschewed war with arrows and axes were not convinced to adopt a prowar stance after the introduction of guns. Pacifists do not object to the tools of war, which can be used for many peaceful purposes but to the consequences of war or, ceteris paribus, to the injustice of it. I can imagine that some pacifists might be mildly pleased that these new vehicles remove some human beings from unnecessary risk or wrongful harm. But they might also be mildly alarmed that removing our own people from unnecessary risk and harm makes military options more tempting. Pacifists will likely remain unconvinced by the argument that unmanned military vehicles make military violence sterile enough to be a palatable alternative to resolving international disputes.

Private pacifists of the Augustinian sort who approve of state-sanctioned military action under conditions of resisting evil or punishing a wrong will likely accept the introduction of unmanned military vehicles, so long as using these vehicles comports with their justificatory criteria for resorting to military violence in general. If violent military action is morally justified, then that action won't now become unjustified because unmanned military vehicles are now utilized to resist evil or punish a wrong. However, if military action were to be avoided due to cost and risk and those costs and risks are mitigated by the introduction of unmanned military vehicles in particular cases, then perhaps private pacifists would lament that more military responses are now a plausible alternative. That may be a concern, though I don't think a weighty one, since there are times when it is cost-prohibitive to use military violence in cases where military violence really ought to be used. If justice demands a military response in some cases, then unmanned military vehicles are a positive good if they make an otherwise cost-prohibitive operation a cost-acceptable one.

4.3 Epilogue

In the mid- to late nineteenth century, military forces found that they could use hot air balloons for four distinct purposes: aerial bombing, reconnaissance, communications, and transport. Early deployments were ineffective, though in time technological refinements made their use as military tools distinctly advantageous, even if in limited ways. Balloons could achieve measurable benefits that included the following: they could make hitherto inaccessible targets accessible; they mitigated troop risk by making enemy troop movements more transparent to decision makers; they improved communication between units; they were cost-effective; and they could be used to make the enemy change his tactics to his disadvantage. Modern remote control military vehicles are used today for the same reasons, albeit with exponentially higher levels of sophistication and payoff. The time-tested, morally potent tenets of the just war tradition were useful in assessing when and how to use the balloons in military operations. The formidable explanatory power of that same tradition can and should be used to morally assess when and how to use balloon's sophisticated technological cousins as well. Balloons and modern remote control military vehicles aren't bad in themselves. They are bad when used by intentionally and unintentionally bad or ignorant people to accomplish morally unjustifiable purposes. You can say the same about kitchen knives and hand drills.

3

Distinguishing Drones: An Exchange

ASA KASHER AND AVERY PLAW

1. (Kasher)

The purpose of the present chapter is to exchange views with respect to several ethical and moral aspects of killing by remote control, in particular by usage of what have been dubbed unmanned aerial vehicles (UAVs).

We start by pointing out the major conceptual elements of the notion of *killing by remote control by usage of a UAV*:

1. Operation of a weapon involves an operator, a weapon, and a target. When a pistol is being used, the operator and the weapon are in the same place, and the target is nearby. When a helicopter is being used, the operator and the weapon are also in the same place, but the target is not nearby. When a UAV is being used, the operator and the weapon are far from each other, as are the weapon and the target.
2. Killing by a usage of a UAV is done by bringing an explosive to the proximity of the target.
3. The weaponry involved in killing by a usage of a UAV is accurate: chances are very high that the explosive device hits the intended coordinates of the target.
4. The explosive device involved in killing by a usage of a UAV will cause death or injury to people in a certain range around the target.

Consequently:

1. Killing by a usage of a UAV does not involve any significant jeopardy to the life of the operator of the UAV.
2. Killing by a usage of a UAV can cause collateral damage.
3. Killing by a usage of a UAV does not involve significant harm to the military equipment used in the operation.

Facing a new type of weaponry or a new type of usage of familiar weaponry, a discussion of the ethical, moral, and sometimes legal aspects of the emerging usage of the weaponry is required that would provide answers to the following major questions, on grounds of some general ethical, moral, and legal conceptions:

1. Under what circumstances is it allowed to use the new weaponry or put the familiar weaponry to a new use?
2. Under what circumstances is it strictly forbidden to do it?
3. What are the conditions imposed on doing it, when it is allowed, that are new restrictions and not simple consequences of familiar restrictions imposed on usage of weaponry in general?

The required delineation of circumstances is expected to be couched in terms familiar from the relevant ethical and moral traditions of just war theory and the related international conventions and customary international law. However, a need for new concepts and principles may arise and is perhaps even expected for two major reasons. First, though a framework of concepts, values, and principles can be deep, rich, and successful and usually is applicable to new circumstances, some such circumstances may turn out to require new concepts for depicting them and new principles of guiding activity in them. A simple example would be the usage of nuclear weaponry compared with conventional weaponry. Second, human experience shows that general frameworks, be they ethical, moral, or legal, are never perfect. There is always ample room for improvement. When new circumstances are under consideration, such improvement may take place, with respect to both the given novelty and the general framework. An example we will, I assume, meet later is the attitude toward the life and dignity of combatants, where I take present practices to be deeply flawed.

2. (Plaw)

Kasher's thoughtful introduction to the ethical examination of UAVs as weapons of war draws attention to their novelty. In light of this novelty he suggests that "a need for new concepts and principles may arise and is perhaps even expected." I want to suggest the opposite. In the next few paragraphs I will do two things. First, I will challenge the novelty of UAVs with an eye to undermining the expectation that their appearance warrants a departure from the traditional ethical principles regulating the conduct of war. Second, I will suggest that there is good reason to be cautious about such departures in general.

To begin with, UAVs are not so new. The first experimental models of UAVs appeared in 1917. The first serious "assault drones" were developed by the US Navy starting in 1941, and by October 19, 1944, they "were used for the first time in...formation, dropping bombs on targets on Ballale Island, south of

Bougainville."[1] The Navy again experimented with the use of assault drones in the Korean War, while the Air Force experimented with BGM-34 Firebees armed with the AGM-65 Maverick missile and Paveway laser-guided bombs in the final years of the Vietnam War.[2] And of course UAVs have been employed widely for combat reconnaissance from WWII onward. During all of this time UAVs have been subject to the same legal rules and ethical norms that are commonly understood to apply to the general use of weapons in combat (e.g., the principles of necessity, distinction, proportionality, humanity). So it is not obvious why we should expect new principles and concepts to arise now.

Moreover, UAVs are part of a larger class of weapons with an even longer and more extensive history. Kasher points out that, when drones are used for attack, the operator is usually far from the weapon and the weapon is some distance from the target. This contrasts with the use of pistols and helicopters, for example, where the user is close to the weapon and not excessively distant from the target. But UAVs are hardly the only weapons whose use involves these twin types of distance. Consider certain classes of guided missiles such as the preprogrammed cruise missile and remotely operated smart missiles. Here the user is far from the weapon, and the weapon is, at least initially, far from the target. As Steven Zaloga, a military historian specializing in aerospace technology, aptly remarked, "Guided missiles differ from UAVs in [only] one crucial respect: UAVs are designed to return to base after their mission, while guided missiles explode when they impact their target."[3] But there is no obvious reason to think that this difference is ethically salient and therefore that it warrants new ethical norms for the use of drones in combat.

Finally, I want to emphasize the need for caution in departing from established ethical principles for the conduct of warfare. Kasher stresses that the ethical frameworks that are conventionally applied to a complex phenomenon like armed conflict are never perfect and that there is always room for improvement. He remarks that he finds some present practices "deeply flawed," particularly in relation to the customary "attitude toward the life and dignity of combatants." But even if principles of just war theory and humanitarian law can be shown to be imperfect, the burden of proof on those proposing reforms remains substantial. In regard to the principle of distinction, for example, Jeremy Waldron argued forcefully in a recent working paper on drone strikes that "to revise it or reformulate it . . . involves considerable risk."[4] Principles like

---

[1] Steven Zaloga, *Unmanned Aerial Vehicles: Robotic Air Warfare 1917–2007* (New York: Osprey Press, 2008), 4, 7–8, 40.

[2] Ibid., 40.

[3] Ibid., 4.

[4] Jeremy Waldron, "Can Targeted Killing Work as a Neutral Principle," NYU Public Law and Legal Theory Working Papers, March 1, 2011, 13, available at http://papers.ssrn.com/sol3/papers.cfm?abstract_id=1788226.

distinction have become established over centuries (during which time weapons have evolved quite a bit), in part because they capture enough that is common among diverse perspectives to gain acceptance and in part because they have proved reasonably enforceable. They have now been effectively internalized by most soldiers. As Waldron notes, they now represent "one strand of proven normativity (in an otherwise normative-free zone)."[5]

Naturally, they also represent a permanent invitation for philosophers to tinker. But Waldron argues, I think with great force, that philosophical tinkering is often "reckless," because we wind up championing a principle that is "tidier" but that is not similarly capable of "anchoring itself in habit, ethos and discipline in the midst of the conduct of war."[6] The result is to weaken the only decent if imperfect bit of normativity we have in areas of supreme danger and violence.

The point here is not to preclude reform of basic humanitarian principles like distinction, for the principles have been adapted over time and some adaptations have proven beneficial and there is no reason to discount this possibility in the future. It is simply to stress that, just as the dangers attendant on change are substantial, so is the burden of proof on those proposing reform.

3. (Kasher)

"Facing a new type of weaponry or a new type of usage of familiar weaponry," I claimed, "a need for new concepts and principles may arise and is perhaps even expected." An example I mentioned was the introduction of nuclear weaponry. The concept of deterrence has played a major role in moral and ethical discussions of it, even though it could hardly be found in the traditions of just war. No principle of proper deterrence is simply derivable from the classical principles of just war theories. Plaw raises a two-tier objection: (1) entrenched principles should not be reformed; and (2) there is nothing new in the usage of drones and therefore there is no reason for raising the possibility of some revision of principles. I do not accept any part of the objection.

3.1 Norms

First, the family of norms that guides or should guide a person in military uniform is much oversimplified when reference is made just to some principles of just war such as distinction or proportionality. The family of norms that guides a combatant, whether a sergeant or a lieutenant, is multilayered. It includes

---

[5] Ibid., 12.
[6] Ibid.

principles of several kinds, doctrines, standard operating procedures, rules of engagement, and commands. Even if some abstract principle does not have to be revised as a result of the introduction of new weaponry or a new usage of it, the soldier is expected to be in need of some revision in the guiding family of norms, not only on the self-evident levels of commands and rules of engagement but also on the level of doctrines. An example is fighting terrorism.[7]

An example of another type of revision is the introduction of a ban on antipersonnel land mines. It would be implausible to depict the history of norms related to the usage of such mines as if nothing changed on some high level of the related guidelines when more than 150 states signed and ratified the Ottawa Treaty.

Even principles may undergo a revision, sometimes disguised as being just a new interpretation of given principles. The 1977 International Committee of the Red Cross (ICRC) Protocols I and II, additional to the Geneva Conventions, constitute a chapter in the history of the Principle of Distinction. The ICRC itself point out the "innovations" included in the protocols.

Conservatism with respect to norms verges on fundamentalism. A firm resistance to put principles under moral scrutiny is never justifiable. A firm resistance to consider moral improvements of principles that guide or should guide crucial activities is immoral.

Plaw quotes Jeremy Waldron's claim that "to revise [a principle] or reformulate it…involves considerable risk." Maybe so, maybe no, but, be it as it may, what if the continued application of the principle involves considerable risk too? Claiming with Waldron that the risk stems from an alleged inability of a revised norm of "anchoring itself in habit, ethos, and discipline in the midst of the conduct of war" is making two significant mistakes. First, the test of instant anchoring "in the midst of the conduct of war" ignores all forms of instruction, training, and education used for introduction of new norms into practice. Second, it ignores the roles played by doctrines, standard operating procedures, rules of engagement, and commands, even "in the midst of the conduct of war," in revising practical guidelines. Examples abound.

I am not eager to revise principles and doctrines for the sake of novelty. I am interested in responsible moral advancement. I respect the wisdom of just war theories and the contribution of their implementation to alleviating the calamities of war. However, the ordinary attitude shown in many of these theories toward the human dignity and life of the combatants is morally unjustifiable. If one claims that the principle of distinction, as stated in customary international law, for example, is morally justifiable, I don't see why the burden of proof is on me rather than on whoever claims it is morally impeccable. It seems not less than ludicrous to use the term "humanitarian" for the present family

[7] Asa Kasher and Amos Yadlin, "Military Ethics of Fighting Terror: An Israeli Perspective," *Journal of Military Ethics* 4:1 (2005): 60–70.

of norms pertaining to combatants. Given the marginal respect they manifest to the human dignity and life of combatants, the term "civilarian" rather than "humanitarian" would fit them better.

3.2 Novelty of UAVs

According to a 2005 US Congressional Research Service report, "UAVs have traditionally been used for reconnaissance and surveillance, but today they are being employed in roles and applications that their designers never envisioned... Congress may have to contemplate the replacement of a significant portion of the manned aircraft fleet with unmanned aircraft that have yet to be designed."[8] Such circumstances should not be ignored by anyone who is seriously engaged in conceptual, ethical, moral, or legal analyses of present and possible usages of drones in warfare. A thorough scrutiny of applications is required and usually takes place under such circumstances. It would be utterly implausible to avoid such systematic evaluation of usages on grounds of some fundamentalist faith in the conceptual breadth and moral quality of a given family of norms of a certain kind.

According to the same report, "UAVs range from the size of an insect to that of a commercial airliner."[9] Plaw quotes Steven Zaloga, who remarked that "guided missiles differ from UAVs in [only] one crucial respect: UAVs are designed to return to base after their mission, while guided missiles explode when they impact their target." Does it make sense to compare guided missiles to much of what appears in the variety of drones on the spectrum of sizes from an insect to an airliner and then draw the conclusion that the norms intended to guide usage of missiles are sufficient to guide all usages of drones? I don't think so. Here are two brief arguments.

First, it has been reported that the US Federal Aviation Administration "is considering rules that will allow police departments to start using [drones] within the next few years."[10] Unlike guided missiles drones are expected to be able to do more than just fire and return, for example, be of a small size, enter a place, identify a person, fire without causing collateral damage, and return.[11] There is no reason to assume that the portion of police ethics that would guide

---

[8] Elizabeth Bone and Christopher Bolkcom, "Unmanned Aerial Vehicles: Background and Issues for Congress," Report for Congress, April 25, 2003, 8, available at http://www.fas.org/irp/crs/RL31872.pdf.

[9] Ibid., 3.

[10] Christian Caryl, "Predators and Robots at War," *New York Review of Books*, September 29, 2011, 55, available at http://www.nybooks.com/articles/archives/2011/sep/29/predators-and-robots-war/?pagination=false.

[11] Note: this is compatible with our earlier understanding of *killing by remote control by usage of a UAV*.

the usage of drones is going to be the portion of military ethics that guides the usage of guided missiles. The portion of military ethics that would guide such drones will probably be different from either.

Second, consider the possibility of "swarms" of drones, clouds of small drones "that would share their intelligence, like a hive mind, and have the capability to converge instantly on identified targets."[12] There is nothing in the realm of guided missiles that is on a par with such a swarm. Conceptual, ethical, moral, and legal aspects of a given usage of drones have to be analyzed according to the intended usage and not on a general level that puts guided missiles and drones into the same category of military weaponry.

4. (Plaw)

I have argued that there are good reasons to be cautious about trying to adapt the ethical norms that currently regulate the conduct of war in the light of the increasing use of drones in combat operations today. I've suggested two reasons for such caution. First, drones aren't as new as some sensational accounts may suggest. Indeed, their first use as combat weapons dates back more than sixty years. Moreover, I suggest that they mark more of an incremental rather than radical change in the technology of war, especially compared with certain (cruise and smart) missiles. Second, I argued more generally that seeking to alter, or make exceptions to, norms governing the conduct of war is a dangerous business. This is because we might all too easily destabilize the rules that have been gradually embraced and internalized over centuries of actual combat with superficially improved rules that fail to attain similar authority or that prove less enforceable in the field. These considerations are not of course intended to foreclose the possibility of beneficial reform to existing norms and laws of war. But I think that they help to show why we should be cautious—why we should want to be thoroughly convinced of both the deficiency of the established ethical norms and the anticipated benefits and practicability of proposed changes.

Kasher, by contrast, is impressed by the novelty of combat drones and the new tactics they make possible. In response to my first argument that drones aren't so new he points, for example, to some of the cutting-edge developments in drone technology, particularly reports of drones of very different sizes (from insects to jumbo airliners). He also points to new tactical possibilities including the possibility of drones being used in "swarms" or "clouds."

Here I would offer two brief responses. First, a range of sizes is not unique to drones. It is also notably characteristic of cruise and smart missiles (which I noted earlier are also similar to drones in both of the ways Kasher suggested

---

[12] Caryl, "Predators and Robots at War," 56.

drones are distinct from other weapons). The Central Intelligence Agency is reported, for example, to be employing scorpion missiles, which are 21.5 inches long, weigh 35 pounds, and can be guided remotely, in drone attacks in Pakistan in an effort to minimize civilian casualties.[13] By contrast, consider the Tomahawk TLAM-E Ground Launched Cruise Missile (with booster), which is 20 feet 6 inches long, weighs around 3,500 pounds, and is capable of carrying a 1,000-pound nuclear warhead.[14] So, just as cruise and smart missiles share the two features Kasher initially identified as distinguishing drones, they also share drones' diversity of size and capability. Again, it is not obvious why different rules need apply.

Second, the tactics potentially permitted by drones, like deployment in a swarm or cloud, are also not so terribly unique. For example, missiles can also be used in "swarms" or "clouds" (albeit usually only once). Indeed, this was exactly the point of multiple independent targeted reentry vehicles (MIRV) missile technology developed in the 1960s and 1970s. This technology permitted a single missile in flight to rapidly launch multiple nuclear warheads. Part of the idea was to suddenly engulf the enemy in a cloud or swarm of incoming warheads and thus to overwhelm any potential missile defenses. At the level of conventional attacks, US defense contractors have developed miniature air-launched decoy guided missiles that permit the user to "deploy cloud-like swarms of the smart, man-sized missiles."[15] So again it is not clear that these tactics are unique to drones or that they call for amendment of the existing ethical norms of war.

Still, my "drones aren't so new or unique" argument is intended only to temper this particular reason for expecting that new ethical norms for the conduct of war will be necessary, not to decisively establish whether they are or are not. New norms could be required for other reasons even if combat drones are neither as new as is sometimes thought nor as different from other weapons. The ethical norms in question may have been flawed since their adoption for reasons unconnected with these weapons systems. Indeed, reading Kasher's harsh description of the "family of norms pertaining to combatants," and in particular their "unjustifiable" attitude "toward the human dignity and life of the combatants," one has the impression that his dissatisfaction long predates and goes beyond the increasing use of drones in combat over the last decade. To

[13] Joby Warrick and Peter Finn, "Amid Outrage over Civilian Deaths in Pakistan, CIA Turns to Smaller Missiles," *Washington Post*, April 26, 2010, available at http://www.washingtonpost.com/wp-dyn/content/story/2010/04/25/ST2010042503646.html?sid=ST2010042503646; US Navy, "United States Navy Fact File: Tomahawk Cruise Missile," April 23, 2010, http://www.navy.mil/navydata/fact_display.asp?cid=2200&tid=1300&ct=2.

[14] US Navy, "United States Navy Fact File."

[15] David Axe, "Decoy Swarm Could Overwhelm Enemy Defenses," *Wired*, June 1, 2011, http://www.wired.com/dangerroom/2011/06/decoy-swarm-could-overload-enemy-defenses/.

assess the force of his criticism, however, we need a more specific description of how current ethical norms fail to properly protect the dignity and life of combatants and what preferable alternatives are available. Here drones may be useful as a convenient means of dramatizing the perceived deficiency of current ethical norms even if they are not as new or unique as is sometimes thought. Let me demonstrate what I mean. I'll use drones to illustrate one of the broad criticisms I take Kasher to make of contemporary just war principles.

In each of his entries in this exchange, Kasher has singled out the principle of distinction as a potential object of criticism (as indeed he has elsewhere).[16] The objection he raises is that, as currently understood, this principle fails to adequately respect "the human dignity and life of combatants." This is a potentially important charge because the principle of distinction is often seen as the fundamental core of humanitarian law as well as just war theory.

So is Kasher right? What we need to know to start to assess the force of Kasher's charge is what the principle of distinction as currently understood requires and what is problematic about it. The principle of distinction is nicely summarized in Article 48 of the First Additional Protocol to the Geneva Conventions (1977). It requires that, in conducting military operations:

> Parties to the conflict shall at all times distinguish between the civilian population and combatants and between civilian objects and military objectives and accordingly shall direct their operations only against military objectives.

In essence, military force should be deliberately directed only against military targets and never civilian targets. Thus far, distinction seems unobjectionable in relation either to drones or other combat operations. We don't want armies deliberately targeting civilian population centers.

Kasher's real objection, if I'm correct, arises with the way this principle is currently applied to planning specific military operations, including drone strikes. Just war theorists often read distinction as implying an obligation of "due care."[17] Michael Walzer, in particular, influentially interpreted the principle of distinction to involve not just a requirement not to target civilians but also "a positive commitment to save civilian lives."[18] Walzer argued, in essence, that the state must not only limit itself to legitimate military targets but also *minimize* the unintended harms to civilians attendant on such attacks. One important implication of this reading is that where there is a tactical trade-off

---

[16] Asa Kasher, "The Principle of Distinction," *Journal of Military Ethics* 6:2 (2007): 152–167.

[17] Alex Bellamy, *Just Wars: From Cicero to Iraq* (Malden, MA: Polity Press, 2006), ix, 125, 191; Michael Walzer, *Just and Unjust Wars* (New York: Basic Books, 1977), 155–157, 217.

[18] Walzer, *Just and Unjust Wars*, 156.

between increased danger to combatants and civilians, the *increased risk must be borne by the combatants*: "if saving civilian lives means risking soldier's [sic] lives, the risk must be accepted."[19] This view of distinction is also reflected in international humanitarian law (albeit with less explicit reference to the risk to be borne by soldiers). For example, Article 57(2)(ii) of the First Additional Protocol of the Geneva Convention (1977) imposes the following requirement:

> Those who plan or decide upon an attack shall: take all feasible pre-cautions in the choice of means and methods of attack with a view to avoiding, and in any event to minimizing, incidental loss of civilian life, injury to civilians and damage to civilian objects.

Of course, if risk to civilians must be minimized, risk to soldiers will often be heightened.

Kasher's objection here, if I'm right, is that the "due care" requirement radically devalues soldiers' lives in relation to civilian lives. Certainly there is truth in this charge. Imagine a scenario where military planners are confronted with two possible means to achieve the same legitimate objective, one that endangers no civilians but puts hundreds of soldiers at risk and one that endangers one civilian but also puts only one soldier at risk. Taken very literally, Article 57(2)(ii) would seem to require that planners choose the first option although it puts hundreds of soldiers unnecessarily at risk (because this would protect the life of one civilian and hence minimize incidental loss of civilian life).

Combat drones dramatize this concern. For drones provide a means of attack that, as Kasher notes in his first entry, "does not involve any significant jeopardy to the life of the operator of the UAV." So risk to the attacking side's soldiers can often be reduced literally to zero. At the same time, however, the risk to civilians on the ground will sometimes be heightened compared with a ground operation that does put soldiers at risk. One effect of the growing use of drones in combat may thus be to persistently raise Kasher's concern with the duty of "due care" and to cast it in its most dramatic light—where there is a real possibility of eliminating the risk to soldiers entirely, which is (perhaps needlessly and even immorally) precluded. The key question is thus cast into sharp relief: "Should the principle of distinction be read as prohibiting drone strikes which safeguard soldiers' lives if they increase the danger to civilians (compared with alternatives)?"

I believe that Kasher will want to say no, at least in some cases, because such a principle fails to respect "the dignity and lives of combatants." If I'm right, I'd be interested in learning what restriction, if any, Kasher would favor on drone operations that entail a comparatively high risk to civilians.

[19] Ibid.

For my part, while recognizing the force of Kasher's point, I'd still say yes to at least a moderate version of the duty of "due care" (Walzer, for example, wants soldiers to assume "some" additional risk, not all of the risk).[20] I believe that there are several strong reasons for upholding this duty. For one thing, the consequences of abandoning it may be very bad. If we say that it is ethically permissible for military planners and officers in the field to shift risk onto civilians, they are likely to do so and to do so as much as they can. After all, soldiers have the same interest as anyone else in protecting their own lives and those of their comrades. Moreover, they may well be tempted to carry out more operations that endanger civilians once the restraint of having to assume the balance of risk themselves is removed. Indeed, if we add that there is a natural tendency for hostility to develop between opposing sides in war, we may well worry that endangering enemy civilians will become a positive temptation. In essence, the argument is that abandoning the expectation of due care is likely to greatly increase the risks, and consequent harms, to civilians.

A second argument is that the increased risk to civilians attendant on abandoning the duty of "due care" is especially unfair because it shifts risk and harm onto the defenseless. Civilians, after all, do not have the right fight back, to defend themselves and their families, in the way that soldiers do. Civilians are generally expected to refrain from participating in combat. In exchange, they receive "immunity," or protection, from attack under humanitarian law and just war theory. Shifting risk from soldiers onto civilians violates their immunity without giving them the right to fight in their own defense.

There is of course much more to be said in support of preserving the duty of due care and the principle of distinction as currently understood. But I hope that this will be at least enough to get the conversation started. So I'll close simply by observing that the issue is not a new one (Walzer's controversial illustration of what due care requires dates from WWI).[21] Also it is raised equally dramatically by the possibility of using cruise or smart missiles (which can also wholly eliminate the risk to soldiers on the launching side) rather than sending in soldiers on the ground.

5. (Kasher)

During the present exchange, Plaw has argued (1) that common norms intended to guide states, military forces and persons in military uniform, when they take active part in armed conflict, should not be discarded or even amended; (2) that drones do not constitute a new type of weaponry and therefore their prevalent

[20] Walzer, "Response," *Journal of Military Ethics* 6:2 (2007), 170; Walzer, *Just and Unjust Wars*, 156.
[21] Walzer, *Just and Unjust Wars*, 152.

usage in warfare should not give rise to any suggestion that norms be revised; and (3) that what is taken to be my own major norm in moral need of revision, namely, the principle of distinction, is morally justifiable and therefore should not be revised, let alone discarded. To advance the present exchange, for which I am grateful to Plaw, I add some brief clarifications and arguments with respect to each of the three issues.

5.1 Issue (1)

Norms are not sacred. The norms that governed the institution of slavery were eradicated, in a successful attempt to extend the realm of protected human liberties. Some norms that governed royal regimes were revised, in a successful attempt to enhance justice and democracy. Norms that are intended to be morally justifiable ought to be considered afresh whenever it seems we have new conceptions or novel presentations of the moral point of view or new contexts in which the norms have to be successfully applied. Norms that are meant to be politically prudent and militarily practical and professional ought to be scrutinized when the political structure changes in a radical way or when the nature of military activity is significantly transformed. Norms of international law and principles of just war doctrines are no exception.

A policy of strictly guarding the status quo in a realm of norms obstructs improvement of military activity on the developing grounds of moral, political, and professional standards. Guarding the status quo means not allowing revisions in any direction, that is, not allowing a norm being replaced by another one, whether it means extending some domain of permissible activity or rather narrowing it. A simple example would be the protection of psychotherapists, who are not physicians, in military uniform. If the norm is that just physicians ought to be protected, it means psychotherapists should not be treated on a par with physicians; therefore, if they are in military uniform they are not immune from direct military attack on them, which means they are not going to be able to render combatants humanitarian services on a par with physicians. This is, indeed, an undesirable result of the policy of guarding the status quo.

The same logic should be used in the case of drones. Since drones can be used more accurately than missiles, their usage is expected to cause much less collateral damage than the usage of missiles. A revision of some prevalent norms that would result in a new norm that requires accurate weaponry be used, say, for targeted killing in an urban area, rather than a bomb or a missile ought to be accepted as a moral improvement of the given norms. Conservative reluctance to revise any norm is, therefore, morally as well as politically and professionally unjustifiable.

5.2 Issue (2)

Plaw has repeatedly argued that drones do not constitute an utterly new type of weaponry and are rather similar to missiles of certain types. The suggested similarities seem to be dubious, but I won't indulge myself in a detailed comparative discussion, since I think looking for similarities is wrongfully headed toward retaining related norms intact. More fruitful than a search for similarities would be a search for dissimilarities, because revealed significant differences might trigger movement toward morally improved practices as guided by appropriately revised norms. Since drones are more amenable than other types of weaponry to accurate remote control, and thus involve significantly lower risks of causing disproportionate collateral damage, they should perhaps become the required legitimate means for obtaining certain legitimate ends in accordance with strict requirements of proportionality. Ethical doctrines of drone usage should replace ethical doctrines for usage of prevalent weaponry usage that is significantly more harmful.

5.3 Issue (3)

Plaw is right in thinking I take a major merit of the usage of drones to be the protection it provides their operators from hostile fire. He is also right in ascribing to me a negative attitude toward the principle of distinction, as it is commonly understood and practically applied. However, several clarifications have to be made to enable our readers to grasp the major elements of our positions.

First, notice that the body of norms intended to regulate activity under circumstances of armed conflict often appears under the title of international humanitarian law. Whatever one takes to be the literal meaning of "humanitarian," it definitely means an attitude toward human beings as such, not toward a certain group of people. However, the principle of distinction is actually a "civilarian" law rather than a humanitarian one. It shows no interest in combatants and is strictly restricted to protection of noncombatants, where every person in military uniform presumably belongs to the former group and only the wounded, the shipwrecked, as well as physician, chaplains, and a few others presumably belong to the latter one. There is a world of restrictions imposed on military activity meant to protect noncombatants, and there is no field of significant manifestation of respect for the human dignity of combatants in the broad sense of men and women in military uniform.

Second, the starting point for moral consideration of the right attitude toward persons in military uniform should be neither international law nor a just war doctrine but rather the constitutional principles of a democratic regime. Assuming that every such constitution cherishes respect for human dignity, whether it uses the term or not, a compelling justification is required for a state allowing itself to commit some of it citizens to participate in activities that significantly jeopardize them and thus seem to involve breaching the fundamental duty of protecting their human dignity, which includes protecting their life. In Israel these persons are conscripts who are entitled to demand a moral and constitutional compelling justification. Where such persons are volunteers, the required justification is not provided by their being volunteers. A democracy is not going to tolerate an institution of voluntary slavery; why should it tolerate an institution of voluntary jeopardy? Of course there are circumstances of collective self-defense under which some jeopardy is a military necessity. This, however, does not mean that a democracy may tolerate an immoral practical distinction between persons in military uniform and other persons.

Third, a democratic state owes its citizens in military uniform a special justification for jeopardizing their life when they do it not for the relatively simple reason of defending their fellow citizens but when they are required to do it for the sake of saving the life of enemy citizens who are noncombatants. The moral challenge is particularly strong when the latter persons are not under the effective control of the state, live in the vicinity of legitimate military targets, and have been effectively warned that they jeopardize their life by not moving away for a while. In a sense, such persons become close to having rendered themselves voluntary human shields of a military target. A person in military uniform of a democratic state is, then, entitled to challenge its state: "What justification do you have for jeopardizing my life to save the life of a voluntary human shield of an enemy military target?"

There are indeed well-known attempts to answer what I elsewhere called "the soldier's question," but they all fail in showing a compelling moral justification for the creation of the jeopardy under consideration. Some answers are begging the question, for example, when the person in military uniform is told the jeopardy is required for the sake of the state acting morally. The person's question is exactly this: why is it moral for the state to thus jeopardize my life? The challenge posed in the question is thus left unmet. Other attempts, such as the forfeiture theory, do not fare better. Not only are they dissociated from the attitudes of a person toward one's own service in military uniform, but also they do not amount to a justification on compelling moral grounds. Why is it morally justifiable to tolerate an institution that requires forfeiture of life and liberty?

The usage of drones circumvents such difficulties. A full-fledged ethical and moral doctrine for drone usage is still required, but significant parts of the benefit of their usage are already quite clear: diminished risk of operators, less collateral damage. The latter benefit is most welcome; not less so is the former one, morally and ethically.

6. (Plaw)

Kasher as always makes some forceful points, but his overall case is not persuasive. Let me start by briefly restating and clarifying my prior points, and then I'll explain why Kasher's case falls short. My first point was that we should be cautious in attempting to rewrite long-standing principles of humanitarian law and just war theory. In other words, we should expect to see a compelling case for clear and substantial moral gains before we open this can of worms and risk destabilizing established norms. The second point is that drones are neither as new as is sometimes suggested nor as radically different from some other weapons systems (like smart missiles) that have been effectively regulated by the existing laws of armed conflict. This is not to say that there is nothing novel, or interesting, or challenging about the widespread employment of weaponized drones but only that we need not rush to the conclusion that their proliferation calls for new laws of war. My third point—and here I think the clash with Kasher is clearest and most significant—is this: the specific moral case for a loosening the principle of distinction to permit the wider employment of weaponized drones in counterterrorist operations is not sufficiently compelling to warrant revision of the conventional principle of distinction.

Kasher thinks that I exaggerate my first and second arguments to set an impossibly high threshold for him to meet in arguing for a revision of the principle of distinction. I don't think that the standard is either impossible or unreasonable or that the underlying arguments are exaggerated. But let's set the matter aside for now to focus on the key point: does the principle of distinction withstand the potent critique Kasher launches at it with regard to combat drones?

The core of Kasher's case is the claim that the conventional principle of distinction gives too much weight to civilian lives and too little to soldiers' lives—and hence would be best described as "civilarian" law rather than "humanitarian" (i.e., giving equal protection to humans as such). He points out that this bias is especially troubling in certain types of counterterrorist operations, for example, where the terrorists are operating from foreign territory, surrounded by sympathetic civilians who act virtually as "human shields." Putting soldiers in danger just to reduce the collateral risk to such civilians is arguably to treat their lives with contempt. Insofar as states' first responsibility is to the safety of their own citizens, the principle of distinction might be argued to demand that states betray their highest duty in such cases. Armed drones, on the other hand, offer the possibility of conducting counterterrorist operations without endangering soldiers at all.

Kasher ends his last contribution by observing that in many cases armed drones can in fact reduce the risk not only to the attacking state's soldiers but also to civilians in the target zone who might be endangered by other types of military operations. This is of course true, but in such cases the principle of distinction will not only permit the use of drones but also in many cases require it. By consequence, such cases pose no challenge to principle of distinction. The most important cases here are those in which the use of drones diminishes (or eliminates) the risk to soldiers but increases the risk to civilians around the target (relative to other tactics that would pose a lower risk to civilians but entail a higher risk to soldiers). It is these strikes that a conventional reading of the principle of distinction (buttressed by the duty of "due care") would forbid but that Kasher thinks may be justifiable (because equal or greater weight should be given to the lives of soldiers).

I've already suggested two reasons for upholding the principle of distinction's prohibition of tactics that impose an elevated risk to civilians in the vicinity of targets (relative to alternative tactics). Here I will defend those reasons against Kasher's objections.

The first reason I mentioned was consequentialist. As it exists, the principle of distinction restrains states' natural bias toward the protection of their own forces over enemy civilians. Removing this restraint and validating states' natural bias to protect their own and transfer risk onto the enemy civilians is likely to lead to a great deal of risk and harm being imposed on enemy civilians. Indeed, once the practice is established, the harm to civilians may well wind up well out of proportion to any plausible military goal—or the punishment of civilian populations may itself become the goal.

My second argument was that civilians are defenseless in the sense that they lack the combatant privilege to fight back and consequently are supposed to have immunity from attack. The point here is that there is an important moral difference between asking combatants with the means and training and right to defend themselves to assume risk and imposing it on those who generally lack the means, training, and right to defend themselves. Kasher seeks to undermine this distinction by suggesting that the civilians in question may be sympathetic to the terrorists and may deliberately remain, or place themselves, where they'd be endangered by counterterrorist strikes (and hence may be morally complicit in terrorist operations). That is of course true. But some could equally hate the terrorists, resent their presence in the midst of their community, but lack the means to immediately expel them (and hence would not be morally complicit). But Kasher ignores this distinction and seems prepared to assume the guilt of all local civilians or to permit states to do so. Moreover, this deficiency is not easily corrected, for even if one wanted to it's not obvious how the sympathies and intentions of individual local civilians could be determined with adequate confidence to separate out the terrorist sympathizers for diminished protection.

Fortunately, conventional humanitarian law already contains a proviso addressing at least some of the concerns Kasher raises but does so consistent with the conventional principle of distinction. Specifically, Article 51 of the First Additional Protocol to the Geneva Conventions asserts that civilians can lose their immunity from attack if "and for such time as they take a direct part in hostilities." The scope of this exception is detailed in the recent International Committee of the Red Cross's "Interpretive Guidance on the Notion of Direct Participation in Hostilities under International Humanitarian Law" and includes a range of specific, observable support functions (such as driving an ammunition truck to supply an active firing position) that entail a loss of immunity.[22] While these rules are no doubt imperfect, I suggest that they more reliably track our moral intuitions than a general reduction of the duty to protect civilians in target zones (relative to the targeting state's soldiers).

Kasher suggests that these two arguments in support of the conventional principle of distinction, as with others that have been offered, are unpersuasive. Many such arguments, he suggest, fall into one of two categories (although these categories are clearly intended as exemplary rather than exhaustive). The arguments are either question begging or rely on a forfeiture theory (i.e., soldiers forfeit the expectation that their state will prioritize their protection when they join the army) that he thinks is indefensible. I don't think that either of the arguments I've offered fits neatly into either of these categories.

Neither of my arguments is question begging, at least in the conventional sense of simply assuming an answer to the question they address so that a critical examination of the argument winds up returning to the question with which it began. They offer a reasoned answer to the question of whether an adequate moral justification can be offered for imposing the preponderance of risk in counterterror operations on soldiers, each anchored in a strong independent moral intuition (although one could certainly ask questions about the roots of these intuitions). In the first case, the argument appeals to the common intuition that there is something especially objectionable about killing someone who is defenseless (as opposed to killing someone say in a battle or a duel) and the expectation that one should be prepared to take extraordinary measures to avoid committing so heinous an act. The second argument is anchored in the commonsense intuition that the shedding of less blood (especially of the defenseless), however bad, is better than the shedding of more blood. By consequence, an act that is likely to lead to less blood being shed (especially by the defenseless) is better than one that is likely to lead to more.

Similarly, neither argument need rely, or at least rely strictly, on a forfeiture theory. The second argument, for example, hangs not on the moral status of soldiers in general but on the moral preference of less blood to more. The state's

---

[22] Nils Melzer, "Interpretive Guidance on the Notion of Direct Participation on Hostilities under International Humanitarian Law," International Committee of the Red Cross 2008, 56, available at http://www.icrc.org/eng/assets/files/other/icrc-002-0990.pdf.

expectation that soldiers should be prepared to assume risk when necessary to save many civilians is not different in kind from what is expected, for example, from first responders or even from ordinary citizens in jurisdictions with Good Samaritan laws to prevent harm coming to defenseless victims.

My first argument *could* be framed in terms of a general forfeiture theory but need not be. It could equally turn either on features of the counterterror operation or on the types of soldiers typically asked to conduct such operations. For example, since counterterror strikes are characteristically preemptive attacks whose purpose it is to safeguard *potentially* threatened civilian lives, it makes sense that planners and soldiers should be expected to take special precautions and assume risk to protect civilian lives *actually* endangered by the operation. Moreover, the soldiers asked to carry out such operations are typically not conscripts or average soldiers but members of highly trained special operations teams who have not only volunteered for this type of work but also have done so in full knowledge of the kinds of high-risk operations involved (indeed, in some case *because* of those high-risk operations). It is therefore justifiable to ask these soldiers in particular to assume the preponderant risk in counterterror operations and not to rely on drones where they impose an unnecessary and disproportionate risk to civilians. So while I personally would endorse some version of what I take Kasher to mean by a forfeiture theory, this position isn't necessary for the arguments I've offered for applying the conventional principle of distinction to counterterrorist drone strikes.

In conclusion, while Kasher raises some serious and troubling concerns, I don't think that his case against the conventional principle of distinction is, as yet, convincing on balance. By implication, it does not meet the high standards (of a clear and substantial moral gain) that in my first argument I suggested should be met before attempting to actually rewrite a core principle of customary international humanitarian law.

7. (Kasher)

In conclusion, let me briefly illustrate the differences between Plaw's positions and my own by pointing out three foci of my disagreement with the points made in the previous section. Many other arguments and counterarguments will have to be left for future exchanges.

First, Plaw claims that "validating states' natural bias to protect their own and transfer risk onto the enemy civilians is likely to lead to a great deal of risk and harm being imposed on enemy civilians." Actually, Plaw's claim is just another beautiful example of begging the question. The soldier's question is a challenge: why does my state, come what may, prefer enemy civilians over myself? One does not meet the challenge by claiming that otherwise risk and harm would be imposed on enemy civilians. One does not meet a challenge by sending it back as an answer.

Second, Plaw argues that "increased risk to civilians attendant on abandoning the duty of 'due care' is especially unfair because it shifts risk and harm onto the defenseless." To be sure, nothing in my position is tantamount to abandoning the duty of due care. Carving due care in a way that is significantly different from the way Plaw does it is far from abandoning the duty to alleviate calamities of war among civilians. Moreover, under the circumstances we have had in mind during the present exchange, civilians are never directly attacked. They can be jeopardized when they are at the close vicinity of a terrorist. Under such conditions the neighbors of the terrorist, more often than not having rendered themselves human shields of the terrorist, are not defenseless. When they are on their own, really defenseless, they are never attacked.

Finally, here is a moral test that common systems of norms of armed conflict have failed. The fact that drones usually create much less collateral damage than previously usual weaponry is justifiably counted as commendable from the point of view of those common norms. However, the fact that drones diminish casualties among their operators has so far not been counted as such within the framework that presents itself as "humanitarian," not just "civilarian." As long as common systems of norms show such disrespect for the human life and dignity of people in military uniform they ought to be regarded as having failed one of our fundamental moral tests.

PART TWO

THE ETHICS OF DRONE EMPLOYMENT

4

Drones and Targeted Killing: Angels or Assassins?

David Whetham

Targeted killing is certainly not a straightforward subject to discuss, as the chapter heading "Murder, Self-Defence, or Execution? The Dilemma of Assassination" in Michael Gross's book *Moral Dilemmas of Modern War* suggests.[1] Perhaps the complication is because targeted killing might not be easily categorizable under just one discrete heading. Indeed, what if targeted killing is actually all of these things simultaneously? Even if it is not, does it *really* matter if we don't have a specific definition for this type of activity?[2]

The association of targeted killing with drones is clearly embedded in the public consciousness. Of course, as with most kinds of military technological development, there is no reason that it has to be used only in one specific way—as other chapters in the volume attest, drones can be employed in a dizzying variety of roles, from covert surveillance or overt reassurance (with a visible presence over voting booths) all the way through to a precision strike deep into an opponent's territory. However, it is in the role of "stealthy assassin" that the unmanned aerial vehicle (UAV) has caught the public imagination. Since 2002, when the man thought to be responsible for the bombing of the *USS Cole* two years previously was targeted and killed in Yemen by the adaptation of a UAV surveillance craft into an ad hoc offensive missile platform, drones have offered an effective way of employing deadly force from afar.[3] The possibilities of this new technology were enthusiastically embraced as the centerpiece of US counterterrorism operations by President Barack Obama, who hugely expanded their use in an effort to "take the fight to al Qaeda."[4] There seems no stopping the rise of this now ubiquitous weapon system, but what does it mean for the existing rules and practice of warfare? Does the ability to carry out

---

[1] Michael L. Gross, *Moral Dilemmas of Modern War: Torture, Assassination and Blackmail in an Age of Asymmetric Conflict* (Cambridge: Cambridge University Press, 2009).

[2] The views expressed in this chapter are the author's own and should not be taken to represent any official position or institution.

[3] "CIA 'Killed al-Qaeda Suspects' in Yemen," *BBC*, http://news.bbc.co.uk/1/hi/2402479.stm.

[4] "State of the Union Address," January 28, 2010. http://news.bbc.co.uk/1/hi/8484451.stm.

targeted killing in a way never before available upset the War Convention, and what does this mean for the way war is understood and practiced?

Let us start with the basics: what actually is the war convention? In normal life there is a general prohibition on murder; murder is something that is considered wrong. However, that doesn't mean that all killing is considered murder. An individual acting in legitimate self-defense may kill an attacker; however, as long as that action was necessary and the force employed was not excessive in relation to the perceived threat, that killing is not regarded as murder (although I appreciate that the test may be applied in different ways in Texas or London). When lethal force is used on behalf of a state or political community in a war, it too is generally not regarded as murder. We accept that it is excusable or even sometimes worthy to kill in such situations. Of course, that doesn't mean that all killing in war is justified—it is still possible to commit murder within a war: for example, deliberately targeting a noncombatant or a surrendering combatant would be considered both murder and a war crime. This commonly held idea that in war it is possible to use deadly force in a legitimate way is informed by our understanding of the War Convention. Contemporary just war scholar Michael Walzer helpfully explains for us that the War Convention is "a set of articulated norms, customs, professional codes, legal precepts, religious and philosophical principles, and reciprocal arrangements that shape our judgements of military conduct."[5] So can the War Convention accommodate targeted killing? If it can, what would it look like, and what would the potential implications be?

The war convention is clearly a complicated idea and is therefore a little hard to pin down. Being such a complex set of norms, customs, and codes, it can be found in positive international law, but because of the way that this gets determined and agreed upon this is also not the only place to look for it. Professional soldiers often understand this best. For example, in the UK it is telling that the British military were apparently reluctant to directly target Muammar Gaddafi, even though the politicians were much happier to publicly consider this. This led to what appeared to be an embarrassing split between the chief of the Defence Staff, General Richards, and the UK government at the very start of the 2011 Libya campaign (which the press enjoyed immensely).[6]

In a debate in June 2007, before the election, then presidential candidate Barack Obama was keen to distinguish between assassination and something called targeted killing in response to a question about pursuing US enemies into other people's countries: "I don't believe in assassinations, but

---

[5] Michael Walzer, *Just and Unjust Wars: A Moral Argument with Historical Illustrations* (Basic Books, 2000), 44.

[6] For example, see "Is Gaddafi a Legitimate Target: Fox and Hague Slapped Down by the Generals after Suggesting that Gaddafi Could Be Personally Targeted," *New Statesman*, March 21, 2011. http://www.newstatesman.com/blogs/the-staggers/2011/03/gaddafi-generals-hague-fox.

Osama Bin Laden has declared war on us, killed 3,000 people, and under existing law, including international law, when you've got a military target like Bin Laden, you take him out. And if you have 20 minutes, you do it swiftly and surely."[7] Obviously, while legitimate self-defense is something any responsible leader needs to practice, "we" don't do assassination. It was back in the 1970s that President Gerald Ford formally banned assassination as a tool of US policy in the embarrassing aftermath of the uncovering of various plots against international leaders that were considered unfriendly to US interests. This helps explain the careful use of language by current US attorney general Eric Holder when he made clear that the current drone strikes against targets in Yemen and Pakistan were categorically not assassinations: "They are not, and the use of that loaded term is misplaced," he insisted.[8] "For reasons that are often difficult to articulate, assassination evokes particular revulsion," but why should this be?[9] What is actually wrong with assassination?

Historically, there is a certain unease associated with the use of "underhanded" tactics; after all, one picks out a victim rather than a genuine adversary in either an ambush or an assassination. Killing another person under such circumstances appears "unsporting or even cowardly."[10] Such qualms are certainly not new, being seen in the writings of Homer, Herodotus, and Thucydides. Euripides sums these feelings up: "A brave man thinks it unworthy to kill his enemy by stealth; he meets him face to face ... Do not praise the clever spear of one who *steals* victory."[11] Cicero records how the Roman senate refused to countenance the assassination, or "treacherous murder," of even a powerful enemy—one who was waging an unprovoked war.[12] One can even find references in the Bible: Deuteronomy 27:24 states, "A curse on him who smiteth his neighbour in secret."

Kant explains this apparently pervasive attitude in practical terms in his pamphlet *Perpetual Peace*, where he argues that acts of hostility that make a mutual confidence "impossible during a future time of peace"—such as the use of assassins, poisonings, breach of surrender, and the instigation of treason—all

---

[7] Quoted in Adam Entous, "Special Report—How the White House Learned to Love the Drone," *Reuters.com*. http://www.uk.reuters.com/article/2010/05/19/uk-pakistan-drones-idUK TRE64H5U720100519?pageNumber=3.

[8] The US Department of Justice, "Attorney General Eric Holder Speaks at Northwestern University School of Law," Northwestern University, Chicago, March 5, 2012. http://www.justice.gov/iso/opa/ag/speeches/2012/ag-speech-1203051.html.

[9] Gross, *Moral Dilemmas*, 101.

[10] David Whetham, *Just Wars and Moral Victories: Surprise, Deception and the Normative Framework of European War in the Later Middle Ages* (Leiden: Brill, 2009), 2.

[11] Euripides, *Rhesus*, 510–511. See also Homer, *Iliad*, 6.242–243 and 11.384–395; Herodotus 1.212.2, and Thucydides 4.86.6.

[12] Cicero, *De Officiis*, {39} XIII.

destroy the minimum level of trust required to achieve a stable peace at war's end.[13] It is related reasoning that leads Walzer to argue:

> The killing of political leaders is ruled out in international law even (or especially) in wartime—and ruled out for good reason—because it is the political leaders of the enemy state with whom we will one day have to negotiate the peace.[14]

It is one of the peculiarities of the War Convention that it might be acceptable to kill thousands in a conventional conflict but not just target, assassinate, or execute the leader who sends them to war against you. However, Walzer does also suggest:

> There *are* obvious exceptions to this rule—no one, no moral person, would have objected to an Allied effort to assassinate Hitler; we were in fact not prepared to negotiate with him—but ordinary leaders are immune.[15]

As such cases demonstrate, there may, of course, be a very real cost in allowing someone who is carrying out particularly heinous crimes to continue with his or her policies.[16] The Acts and Omissions doctrine suggests that there *is* a moral difference between things you directly do and things that happen though you might have prevented them.[17] Thus, the additional deaths caused by a tyrant are his responsibility, not ours when we choose not to intervene. However, it would also seem true that culpability can reside 100 percent with one party yet that another party might still bear some responsibility for not preventing something bad happening when they could have intervened to stop it. When the acts are related to genocide, choosing to watch the perpetrator down the barrel of a gun without pulling the trigger would be a stark test.[18]

---

[13] Immanuel Kant, "Perpetual Peace," quoted in G.M. Reichberg, H. Syse, and E. Begby (eds.), *The Ethics of War: Classic and Contemporary Readings* (Oxford: Blackwell, 2006), 521.

[14] Walzer, "Five Questions about Terrorism," *Dissent*, Winter 2000: 5–16.

[15] Ibid.

[16] Although it appears that one of the main reasons for not assassinating Hitler in the latter stages of the war was because it was considered that his replacement might be more competent at prosecuting the German war effort. See "The secret plan to kill Hitler," *BBC News*, July 23, 1998. www.news.bbc.co.uk/1/hi/uk/137570.stm. Accessed February 29, 2012.

[17] See Jonathan Glover, *Causing Death and Saving Lives* (Penguin Books, 1990), 92–112.

[18] The author of this chapter has interviewed military personnel who have had to do precisely this while gathering evidence for the international community to make a decision about intervening or not (regrettably, in this particular case, the international community chose not to act despite the clear evidence that had been gathered and presented to them).

If some of the critics of targeted killing are right, why not just be honest and bite the bullet—just as not all killing is murder, perhaps not all assassinations are actually bad? In some situations, why not kill the tyrant? Angelo Codevilla argues, "Often...there is no quarrel with the enemy country, only with its chief. In such cases, it is both futile and immoral to demolish a country in the hope that this will persuade the tyrant to give way."[19] If such an argument is indeed convincing (and it does appear hard, given the alternatives, to reject the core idea out of hand), why wouldn't you extend such reasoning to the terrorist who has killed civilians before and is planning to do it again? Because terrorists don't respect those rules anyway, and that minimum level of trust is lacking from the start—this makes it easier, surely? Their lack of respect for the rules of war and therefore the lack of any sense of reciprocity from terrorists makes assassination a very tempting tool, and don't we have a duty to protect our own people? As long ago as 2004, the US executive director of Amnesty International pointed out in a carefully balanced piece that the victims of terror attacks also possessed human rights and that these victims were perhaps not being sufficiently considered in the human rights discussions taking place in the nongovernmental organization community.[20] However, are these considerations sufficient for a new norm to be adopted by civilized states? Because the cannibals eat missionaries, should the missionaries also eat cannibals?[21]

Rather than abandoning the rules against assassination completely perhaps there are more satisfying rationales to be found in the existing principles of self-defense or protecting the innocent. What does the law of armed conflict say on the matter? The current British Manual states at 5.13 that while there is no rule dealing specifically with assassination, the following rules would be applicable to help determine whether or not the killing of a selected enemy individual was lawful in a given situation:

a. Attacks may not be directed against civilians...
b. Attacks must be limited to military objectives, including enemy combatants...
c. Only combatants have the right to participate directly in hostilities.
d. Enemy combatants may not be killed by resort to perfidy [i.e., treachery— abuse of the rules of war to gain an advantage].[22]

---

[19] Angelo Codevilla, "Get Rid of Saddam Hussein Now: The Moral Justification." *Wall Street Journal*, February 25, 1991. Quoted in David L. Perry, *Partly Cloudy: Ethics in War, Espionage, Covert Action, and Interrogation* (Lanham, MD: Scarecrow Press, 2009), 184.

[20] William F. Schultz, "Security Is a Human Right Too," *New York Times*, April 18, 2004. http://www.ngo-monitor.org/article/_security_is_a_human_right_too_.

[21] Father Gillis, quoted in A. C. Grayling, *Among the Dead Cities: Was the Allied Bombing of Civilians in WWII A Necessity or a Crime?* (London: Bloomsbury, 2006), 202.

[22] UK Ministry of Defence, *The Manual of the Law of Armed Conflict* (Oxford: Oxford University Press, 2004), 62.

The next paragraph (5.14) makes clear that one cannot legally put a bounty on an enemy's head or ask for them "dead or alive."[23] Of course, all of this needs to be cross-referenced with the very clear direction in 5.3.2:

> A civilian is a non-combatant, protected from direct attack and is to be protected against the dangers arising from military operations. He has no right to participate directly in hostilities. If he does so, he loses his immunity.[24]

For those who support targeted killing as legitimate policy option, it is this last statement that is so important in differentiating it from other, illegitimate activities. So as long as you are not putting a price on someone's head or using treachery or perfidious methods, you may target a specific combatant. As long as they are not injured or otherwise hors de combat, this can be done when and where you like (within the other rules of war pertaining to, e.g., proportionality, of course). But you cannot target any civilians at any time unless they have made themselves liable to attack through their actions.

This framework gives us two effective options. First, stating that "person x is a member of a group that we recognize as combatants and against whom we are at war" would permit military action against that person at any time in the same way that actions against any member of the rest of that group can be justified at any time. As long as no treachery is involved and other norms are applied (e.g., proportionality, military necessity), such an action would simply be a standard military operation, not really targeted killing at all (although this term might still appear applicable as a description when the person who is being targeted is not a member of the military forces but rather is being designated as a combatant anyway). Under this understanding, a civilian planting an improvised explosive device (IED) on the roads in Helmand Province would obviously be directly participating in hostilities and would therefore join that group of combatants. Presumably, if his brother gives him a lift to do this, he too is directly participating at that time, therefore they both can now be considered firmly in the category of combatant regardless of whether they have ever worn a uniform or even carried a gun. However, is this designation forever? For other members of the class of combatant, the war convention is quite clear: "soldiers are subject to attack at any time (unless they are wounded or captured)."[25] If that is true, and both the planter of the IED and his car-owning

---

[23] The preceding paragraph (5.12) also makes clear that the use of snipers in warfare is a long-established practice, not prohibited by the law of armed conflict, but that the other provisions of the law still apply equally to snipers (e.g., not firing at civilians).

[24] Ibid.

[25] Walzer, *Just and Unjust Wars*, 138.

brother are legitimate targets until the end of hostilities, presumably the same applies to the husband in Nevada who one day gives his drone-operating wife a lift to the Air Force base on the way to do the school run. Does he too become a combatant forever liable to be targeted at any time? Doing a neighborhood carpool suddenly seems very dangerous if one of the dads is considered a legitimate target forever because he once gave the mom a lift to work when her car was in the garage.[26]

When really examining the implications of such a determination in this way, it no longer seems quite as obvious that this is going to be the right approach from a practical perspective for many people involved on the periphery of military or terrorist planning and operations. There are also political and moral implications of labeling certain people into groups in this way that states may wish to avoid. For example, the UK refused to recognize the Provisional Irish Republican Army as anything other than criminals—the country did not want to dignify terrorists who deliberately targeted noncombatants with the title "combatant" for it was thought that this would be to give their struggle and perhaps even their actions a degree of legitimacy.[27]

One can therefore see why states might prefer an alternative option in some cases or for some individuals for whom it is inappropriate to identify as a member of a combatant group in an ongoing sense. Here, we can act against specific individuals who pose a threat. They are still regarded as civilians, but as long as they are in the process of posing that threat they lose their protected status as a noncombatant. Here, the man planting the IED is a civilian who loses his protected status while setting up the device, planting it, and waiting for it to detonate. His brother is liable to attack while acting as a chauffeur and can also be targeted at that time. By extension, the husband in Nevada can also be targeted while acting as chauffeur, but not once his wife is safely at work, flying her drones, and actually using deadly force against her country's enemies, because he is no longer involved. Some suggest that targeted killing applies really only in this type of situation. Georgetown law professor Garry Solis provides one such definition that might be useful here. According to Solis, targeted killing is:

> The intentional killing of a specific civilian or unlawful combatant who cannot reasonably be apprehended, who is taking a direct part

---

[26] See David Whetham, "Remote Killing and Drive-By Wars," in D. Lovell and I. Primoratz (eds.), *Protecting Civilians during Armed Conflict: Theoretical and Practical Issues during Violent Conflict* (London: Ashgate, 2012).

[27] For some history, see "Provisional IRA: War, Ceasefire, Endgame?" *BBC*, http://news.bbc. co.uk/hi/english/static/in_depth/northern_ireland/2001/provisional_ira/.

in hostilities, the targeting done at the direction of the state, in the context of an international or non-international armed conflict.[28]

The targeted killing must take place during an armed conflict; otherwise, it is just a homicide (or possibly an act of domestic law enforcement—see following), but the designation is not applicable to "normal" military targets or against conventional enemy armed forces because these would rather be straightforward examples of acts of war. Solis is also very clear that this cannot simply be a routine activity but is special in the sense that it requires very high-level authorization.

Even though we are talking about civilians rather than military personnel here, this is still commensurate with the core idea found in all codifications of basic human rights—while there is an absolute right not to be arbitrarily deprived of life, the use of lethal force against an individual can still be justified if it is absolutely necessary for the defense of another person from an act of unlawful violence by that individual.[29] That "absolutely necessary" qualification is why arrest of that civilian must be impossible—if an arrest can be attempted with a reasonable prospect of success, clearly using lethal force as a first response cannot be considered absolutely necessary. In the case of a conflict situation, where a civilian takes up arms, plans an attack, or builds an IED, he has forfeited his protection; put another way, he has forfeited his right not to be targeted for the period relating to the carrying out of that activity. Clearly, seeking to arrest somebody during an armed conflict is rarely an easy thing to do. A terrorist leader, well protected and constantly moving from safe house to safe house in contested or hostile territory, may simply be impossible to apprehend in such a way. If an opportunity presents itself for a state to prevent ongoing acts of harm from such an individual with a drone strike or other similar method, if the evidence is extremely clear, and if authorization is granted by somebody suitably high up in, or even above, the normal chain of command, that would be a case of targeted killing carried out in self-defense.

Careful definitions such as Solis's attempt to make a clear distinction between targeted killing carried out for the right reasons and straightforward acts of murder or extrajudicial execution. The latter can be defined as "killings committed outside the judicial process by, or with the consent of, public officials, other than as necessary measures of law enforcement to protect life or as

---

[28] Gary Solis, *The Law of Armed Conflict: International Humanitarian Law in War* (Cambridge: Cambridge University Press, 2010), 538.

[29] For example, see section 2(2) of the European Convention of Human Rights. That is why a police officer who kills a bank robber who is threatening the lives of the general public is not violating the rights of the robber (although this would not be a case of targeted killing as this is in a domestic setting rather than in that of an armed conflict).

acts of armed conflict carried out in conformity with the rules of international humanitarian law."[30]

Clearly, without an imminent threat to trigger an act of legitimate self-defense, a government using the military means at its disposal to eliminate people it dislikes is not practicing targeted killing but rather is employing the military tools of the state to carry out something akin to extrajudicial executions. Such killings might demonstrate a state policy to kill the enemies of that state "not for operational or self-defence purposes, but as a means to punish opponents of the State."[31] Thus, the death in London of former KGB agent Alexander Litvinenko in 2006, poisoned by a lethal dose of Polonium 210, was clearly not a targeted killing in the sense already outlined but appears instead to have been a case of extrajudicial execution.[32] Litvinenko was an outspoken critic of the Russian government and joins the long list of dissidents and journalists who have met grisly ends after alleging links between Vladimir Putin's rise to power and FSB[33] involvement in acts of domestic terrorism. Compare this with the killing of Abu Musab al-Zarqawi, "the mastermind behind hundreds of bombings, kidnappings and beheadings" in Iraq in 2006, where two 500-pound laser-guided bombs were dropped on his head while he was meeting with other insurgent leaders in what he thought was a safe house.[34] Six others died in the same attack; however, given the degree of ongoing threat posed by Zarqawi and the impossibility of launching a successful detention operation, this was obviously considered a proportionate cost. This was a targeted killing. Therefore, the clear distinction is that the act is neither punishment for past actions nor reprisal but rather a preventive act taken in self-defense.

The problems, both moral and legal (and indeed practical), of acting to prevent future threats while retaining the status of defending party are well-known and have been discussed at length.[35] Genuine self-defense requires that a threat is not distant but rather immediate and pressing. The scope of legitimate self-defense can be seen in the classic formulation articulated in 1837 by US secretary of state Daniel Webster in correspondence relating to

[30] Nigel Rodley, *The Treatment of Prisoners under International Law*, 2d ed. (Oxford: Clarendon Press, 1999), 182.

[31] Amos Guiora, "Targeted Killing as Active Self-Defense," *Case Western Reserve Journal of International Law* 36 (Spring 2005): 319, 329.

[32] Luke Harding, "Alexander Litvinenko Poisoning: Move to Extradite Second Murder Suspect," *Guardian*, February 29, 2012. http://www.guardian.co.uk/world/2012/feb/29/alexander-litvinenko-polonium-suspect-charged.

[33] Federal Security Service of the Russian Federation.

[34] Ellen Knickmeyer and Jonathan Finer, "Insurgent Leader Al-Zarqawi Killed in Iraq," *Washington Post*, June 8, 2006. http://www.washingtonpost.com/wp-dyn/content/article/2006/06/08/AR2006060800114.html.

[35] For example, see the excellent work by Henry Shue and David Rodin, *Preemption: Military Action and Moral Justification* (Oxford: Oxford University Press, 2010).

the destruction of the *Caroline*. Only where there is a concrete imminent threat can it be said that there is a "necessity of self-defence, instant, overwhelming, leaving no choice of means, and no moment for deliberation."[36] This imminence is what gives the necessity criteria its validity.[37] However, it is also easy to imagine how this imminence of the threat criteria required when acting in self-defense might get gradually pushed farther and farther into the future due to the understandable fear of not being able to act in time and therefore being, at least in part, responsible for innocent deaths in the terrorist attack that was not averted. The greater the potential threat, for example, the activation or detonation of a weapon of mass destruction, the less imminent that threat needs to be to justify preventive action right now, at least as far as most people would consider. However, this well-meaning responsibility to protect idea, grounded in genuine fear for the safety of others, can still end up eroding the legitimacy of the action, particularly as applied to threats well short of the weapon of mass destruction–type example: "He will plant the IED in the morning" leads to "He will give a lift to the UAV operator at the weekend" leads to "He is planning something in the next couple of years" leads to "He did it once, we're sure he'll do it again."

Also, we have to accept that the problem with any norm is that it doesn't get used just by "nice people." When we defend establishing a targeted killing norm, we imagine it being used for the world's benefit against someone like Osama Bin Laden or another high-level terrorist leader. We understandably think of the nastiest individuals or regimes and think about how much better the world would look without these people doing harmful deeds. But if it becomes a norm, it becomes a norm for everyone, and there is no reason to suppose that the careful rules that Solis or anyone else proposes will not be abused by some actors also claiming to be acting in self-defense.

To give just three examples of how a norm could be abused are as follows. In response to the UN-supported intervention to protect the Libyan people in 2011, Muammar Gaddafi proclaimed, "You are terrorists... This is an unjustified aggression."[38] Robert Mugabe branded members of the international press as "terrorists" in November 2001 along with the entire Opposition Movement for Democratic Change (including fifty-seven members of Parliament) for challenging or even reporting on his disastrous governmental policies.[39] Finally, police on the Nigerian Delta are known as "kill and go" by the local population due to their execution of anyone who is perceived to be a threat or obstacle to

---

[36] "The Caroline Case," 29 *British Forces and State Papers* (1841), 1137–1138.

[37] For an interesting discussion on this area, see Seth Lazar, "Necessity in Self-Defence and War," *Philosophy and Public Affairs* 40.1 (Winter 2012): 3–43 .

[38] "The West Are Terrorists," *MSN News,* March 20, 2011. http://news.uk.msn.com/articles.aspx?cp-documentid=156584494.

[39] *World Press Freedom Review* (International Press Institute, 2002), 61.

the corruption and flow of oil money.[40] Legitimizing their actions by enabling them to call it targeted killing seems perverse. It is such reasoning that leads some to fear that even if targeted killing can be justified in rare situations, the supposed relaxation of the normal standards of human rights it requires itself presents a greater risk than the international terrorism that it seeks to protect us from. It will be abused by the Gaddafis and Mugabes of this world, who will then be able to turn around and say, "We have followed your rules—what we are doing is therefore legitimate."

Do we care as long as no one is using it on us? As long as someone like Gaddafi can't follow up the rhetoric with the means to do anything about it, why should we care? After all, we in the West have an enormous asymmetric advantage over nearly every potential opponent at the moment due to the technologically advanced military tools at our disposal. Michael Gross suggests we might be able to go down this track and think about reestablishing a norm against assassination or targeted killing if our opponents ever do generate the same kind of capabilities that we now have at our disposal.[41] Until hostile drones are a real threat over UK airspace or a US president can be targeted while driving to a state banquet, this is not something that we really need to worry about. However, a norm that works only as long as the other side cannot or will not adopt it doesn't seem to be a very sustainable one, nor does it seem to be a morally correct one on even the most basic notions of moral reciprocity. Once the genie is out of the bottle, it will be very hard to put back in again.

Unfortunately, it might even be too late already—for example, in summer 2006, Russian security forces were given the legal power to hunt down and kill terrorism suspects overseas if so ordered by the Russian president.[42] The Russian state certainly has access to the same advanced technology and also appears to possess the will to use it. However, even if another state wanted to apply the same careful protocols that would make such a norm more palatable, what are they?

In 2006, small but significant steps were taken toward providing some of this much-needed clarity when the Israeli High Court was asked to rule on whether targeted killing was permissible. The judges ruled that it was impossible to determine in advance that "every targeted killing is prohibited according to customary international law, just as it cannot be determined in advance

[40] John Vidal, "Nigeria's Agony Dwarfs the Gulf Oil Spill: The US and Europe Ignore It," *Guardian*, May 30, 2010. http://www.guardian.co.uk/world/2010/may/30/oil-spills-nigeria-niger-delta-shell.

[41] Gross, *Moral Dilemmas*, 120.

[42] Peter Finn, "In Russia, a Secretive Force Widens," *Washington Post*, December 12, 2006. http://www.washingtonpost.com/wp-dyn/content/article/2006/12/11/AR2006121101434_2.html.

that every targeted killing is permissible."[43] While determining that each case needed to be judged individually, Justice Aharon Barak made clear that, while there was always a duty to minimize any harm to the civilian population, specific civilians who had lost their protected status by virtue of taking a direct part in hostilities could be legitimately targeted. This group was seen to include those who used or bore arms, those who were traveling to or from an attack, those who planned such attacks, or those who enlisted, guided, or sent others to carry out such attacks.[44] While this provided a useful marker for debate, it also prompted a whole plethora of questions about what this might actually mean in practice. For example, how serious must the act be for a targeted killing to be considered a proportionate response? How much evidence is enough? How much involvement is enough? How far up and down the terrorist hierarchy can one go? When is the last acceptable window of opportunity to prevent a future act and how much risk is acceptable?

The UN Special Rapporteur noted in 2010 that, to date:

> No State has disclosed the full legal basis for targeted killings... Nor has any State disclosed the procedural and other safeguards in place to ensure that killings are lawful and justified, and the accountability mechanisms that ensure wrongful killings are investigated, prosecuted and punished.[45]

Given that we keep our own safeguards and legal justifications for targeted killing secret, it is difficult to see how any other actor can live up to our expectation, even if they did have any intention of doing so. Besides, and importantly, we in the West don't actually have a very good track record on this. There is little doubt that the extensive Phoenix Program of political assassinations against the thousands of village leaders in southern Vietnam would have been legitimized as targeted killings had the term been around at the time.[46] It is also very easy to imagine how if the term had been around in the 1970s, the British government would have used it to eliminate IRA and Sinn Fein leaders, including quite a few who are currently in government and subsequently participated

---

[43] HCJ 769/02 The Public Committee against Torture in Israel v. The Government of Israel— Summary of Judgment, *Summary of Israeli Supreme Court Ruling on Targeted Killings*, December 14, 2006. http://www.jewishvirtuallibrary.org/jsource/Politics/sctassass.html.

[44] Aviram Zino, "High Court: Targeted Killing Permissible," *Ynetnews*, December 14, 2006.http://www.ynetnews.com/articles/0,7340,L-3339905,00.html.

[45] Philip Alston, *Report of the Special Rapporteur on Extrajudicial, Summary or Arbitrary Executions: Addendum, Study on Targeted Killings* (United Nations Human Rights Council, May 28, 2010). http://www2.ohchr.org/english/bodies/hrcouncil/docs/14session/A.HRC.14.24.Add6. pdf.

[46] "Vietnam: Policy and Prospects 1970," Hearings before the Committee on Foreign Relations, United States Senate (Washington, DC: US Government Printing Office, 1970).

in the Northern Ireland Peace Process.[47] "Well it's self defence, innit?" Jeremy Waldron points out that anyone can propose "protective" death squads on that basis.[48] Using drones instead of hooded assassins really makes little difference to the principles at stake. The genuine contribution that lawyers and ethicists and military people can make to this debate is to "remind the public how much our acceptance of certain principles in law (including self-defense) is bound up with legal process."[49] Only by having public disclosure can the parameters of any norm be properly established. The US has recently taken some steps in this direction with the US Attorney General's address in May 2012 setting out a minimal framework for targeted killing so the American people could be "assured that actions taken in their defense are consistent with their values and their laws."[50] He was referring specifically to the targeting of a potential US citizen who was also a senior operational leader of al Qaeda or affiliated forces and was known to be actively engaged in planning attacks on Americans. He argued that the "due process clause" in the Fifth Amendment of the US Constitution would not be violated if:

> First, the U.S. government has determined, after a thorough and careful review, that the individual poses an imminent threat of violent attack against the United States; second, capture is not feasible; and third, the operation would be conducted in a manner consistent with applicable law of war principles.[51]

Whether the same principles he sets out should or would also apply when considering the targeting of non-US citizens under the self-defense rubric was not made explicit here, but one assumes so. However, he did make clear that the US considered the use of force overseas consistent with international legal principles if conducted, for example, "with the consent of the nation involved—or after a determination that the nation is unable or unwilling to deal effectively with a threat to the United States."[52]

While this is hopefully the start of real public-policy level engagement by the US in this area and may help to influence the emerging norm, it still raises as many questions as it attempts to answer. What still concerns many people about targeted killing is who exactly takes these decisions and determines if an

---

[47] Jeremy Waldron, "Can Targeted Killing Work as a Neutral Principle?" *New York University Public Law and Legal Theory Working Papers, Paper 267* (2011), 7.http://lsr.nellco.org/nyu_plltwp/267.

[48] Ibid., 9.

[49] Ibid.

[50] "Attorney General Eric Holder Speaks."

[51] Ibid.

[52] Ibid.

individual poses a "significant threat" or if state y is really "unable or unwilling" to respond to a threat perceived by the United States?[53] What if state x adopts this norm but for security reasons cannot or will not share the intelligence it has regarding the threat posed by an individual in state y? If state y refuses to simply act on trust, does that mean that state x can then carry out a targeted killing in state y's territory anyway? If the answer to this is considered to be yes right now by the US government (and current activities in the area of Pakistan bordering Afghanistan would suggest something not too far from this interpretation), what if in the future the uncooperative state is actually the US itself? If state x is Russia seeking to protect itself from an alleged dangerous terrorist but refusing to share the evidence to support this view, does that make a Russian precision strike in Chicago acceptable? If the norm has been firmly established in other parts of the world, how is one to step back and say that suddenly it doesn't apply anymore? Or are we back to the untenable moral and legal exceptionalism that these particular rules apply only to everyone else's backyard rather than on the soil of the remaining superpower?

The public debate into what acceptable practice looks like has well and truly started and that has got to be a good thing.[54] Without transparency as to why an individual has been killed, a targeted killing carried out anywhere for the best of reasons and in the most careful, conscientious, and professional way might as well be considered an assassination or just plain murder. As the Alston report suggests, this type of transparency combined with genuine accountability may ultimately be the best safeguard of them all.[55]

Obviously, the context means that a public trial with the expectation of full disclosure of all information is never going to be realistic or even necessarily desirable. There will inevitably be genuine security concerns attached to the release of certain types of sensitive security information. However, states need to give an idea as to the nature of the threat that the dead person represented, how imminent the threat was, and so forth as far as is possible: "without disclosure of the legal rationale as well as the bases for the selection of specific targets (consistent with genuine security needs), States are operating in an accountability vacuum."[56] If a state is not prepared to provide any of that information at all or any reason or justification for a killing, then we should refrain

---

[53] My thanks to Stephen Coleman for posing these questions and pointing me towards this discussion of the inner working of a government decision: Laura Blumenfeld, "In Israel, a Divisive Struggle over Targeted Killing," *Washington Post*, August 27, 2006. http://www.washingtonpost.com/wp-dyn/content/article/2006/08/26/AR2006082600917.html?sid=ST2007112401542.

[54] As this chapter is going to print, a valuable contribution to the targeted killing debate has just been published. See Finkelstein, Ohlin, and Altman (eds.), *Targeted Killings: Law and Morality in an Asymmetrical World* (Oxford: Oxford University Press, 2012).

[55] Alston, *Targeted Killings*, 27.

[56] Ibid.

from calling such an action targeted killing and instead call it what it effectively becomes—an execution.

Although contentious, targeted killing is already well on the way to becoming a norm. It is certainly likely to be used increasingly as the number of boots on the ground decline through the draw down in Afghanistan and people are replaced with drones to provide continued support for our Afghan National Army allies with a lower political cost attached.[57] Perhaps the best we can do is demand clarity over what is being done in our names in the hope that this too becomes part of that norm.

---

[57] For a discussion of the political costs of military action using stand off weapons, see Whetham, *Remote Killing and Drive-By Wars.*

5

War without Virtue?

Robert Sparrow

1. Introduction

According to the homepage of the US Marine Corps, "The values that define a Marine are: Honor; Courage; and Commitment."[1] Of honor, we are told, "Marines are held to the highest standards, ethically and morally. Respect for others is essential. Marines are expected to act responsibly in a manner befitting the title they've earned." Of courage, "Courage is not the absence of fear. It is the ability to face fear and overcome it. It is the mental, moral, and physical strength ingrained in every Marine. It steadies them in times of stress, carries them through every challenge and aids them in facing new and unknown confrontations." The Marine Corps webpage also explains to page visitors—and potential recruits—that the US Marine Corps motto, *Semper Fidelis* (Latin for "always faithful") "...distinguishes the Marine Corps bond from any other. It goes beyond teamwork—it is a brotherhood and lasts for life." Finally, we are told that "becoming a Marine is a transformation that cannot be undone, and *Semper Fi* reminds us of that. Once made, a Marine will forever live by the ethics and values of the Corps."

As a number of authors have observed, these statements—and others like them, which may be found in the self-descriptions of many armed services around the world—set out a distinctive "role morality" for members of the armed services—a "warrior code."[2] The emphasis on the lasting transformation of character involved in becoming a Marine, alongside the list of the traits

[1] US Marine Corps, "Principles and Values." http://www.marines.com/main/index/making_marines/culture/traditions/core_values.

[2] Shannon E. French, *The Code of the Warrior: Exploring Warrior Values, Past and Present* (Lanham, MD: Rowman & Littlefield, 2003); Renee Moelker and Peter Olsthoorn, "Virtue Ethics and Military Ethics," *Journal of Military Ethics* 6:4 (2007): 257–258; Peter Olsthoorn, *Military Ethics and Virtues: An Interdisciplinary Approach for the 21st Century* (London: Routledge, 2011); Bradley C. S. Watson, "The Western Ethical Tradition and the Morality of the Warrior," *Armed Forces and Society* 26:1 (1999): 55–72. For similar statements of sentiments as those contained on the Marine Corps webpage cited in note 1, see, for instance, the United States Army page, http://www.army.mil/values/; and the British Army page at http://www.army.mod.uk/join/25736.aspx.

that define a Marine, suggests that this code is best understood as a virtue ethics consisting in a list of "martial" or "warrior" virtues and an account of how they relate to each other.[3] A "good warrior" is a person who cultivates and exercises these virtues.

There are, of course, grounds for cynicism about what any large organization says about its ethics. There is perhaps even more reason to be cautious about the claims that the military make about their ethics, given the extent to which the struggle to influence perceptions, both at home and overseas, has become an essential part of modern warfare.That power of ruling elites to defend their interests depends upon their ability to convince the poor to serve in their armies provides further reason for caution. It may well turn out that accounts of warrior virtues are essentially ideological, in that their primary role is to ensure that ordinary people continue to support the military rather than to accurately describe the motives and behavior of those who go to war. Nevertheless, even if this were the case, accounts of military virtue would continue to play an important role in mediating the relationship between the armed forces and the larger society. Indeed, ideas about warrior virtues could play this ideological role only if many people in the military themselves actually believe in them. To insist that ideas about martial virtue are largely ideological, then, would not be to deny that they play a real social role.

It seems likely, of course, that notions of martial virtue *do* play a real role in shaping behavior in modern military organizations as well as an ideological role in sustaining support for the military. While military life is often replete with rules and regulations, the military confronts as a profoundly practical dilemma two classical philosophical criticisms of rule-based systems for guiding action: the fact that every rule requires interpretation to be applied; and the fact that the application of complex sets of rules is often too time-consuming to be practical. Converting rules into actions therefore requires a faculty of judgment, the development of which in turn presupposes extensive practice. That is, it requires the cultivation and exercise of good habits. Shaping the character of service personnel is therefore the best way to promote the values encoded in military rules and regulations, including both military efficiency and ethical ideals.[4]

Yet recent developments in the nature of modern warfare seem to call into question the extent to which it is either necessary or possible for many combatants to cultivate or exercise "martial virtues." While long-range killing has been a feature of war since the invention of the spear and the sling, the advent of long-range teleoperated robotic systems such as the Predator and Reaper

---

[3] Jamison Yi, "MCMAP and the Marine Warrior Ethos," *Military Review* 846 (2004): 17–24.

[4] Reed R. Bonadonna, "Above and Beyond: Marines and Virtue Ethics," *Marine Corps Gazette* 78:1 (1994): 18–20.

drones fielded by the US arguably marks a significant quantitative—and perhaps even qualitative—change in the nature of military combat. Traditional conceptions of military virtue have typically relied on an account of the distinctive moral circumstances of "warriors" who are risking their lives for the sake of the political community. By transforming combat into a "desk job" that can be conducted from the safety of the home territory of advanced industrial powers without need for physical strength or martial valor, long-range robotic weapons call the relevance of such accounts into question. This chapter will therefore investigate the implications of these developments for conceptions of military virtue and for the future of the armed forces.

2. Remotely Piloted versus Autonomous Weapon Systems

Before I begin, I need to say a little bit more about the robotic technologies that pose the most dramatic challenge to the need for martial virtues. What are popularly understood as robot weapons are properly divided into two categories that raise different sets of ethical issues. Much of the popular and philosophical literature has focused on the prospects for—and ethics of—autonomous weapons systems (AWSs), which, as the appellation suggests, are systems that are capable of playing a role in combat without any human guidance. In reality, however, almost all of the "robotic" weapon systems that are being developed and deployed at the current moment require a human operator to make key decisions: they are remotely operated or unmanned military systems (UMS) rather than autonomous systems. These latter systems include unmanned aerial vehicles (UAVs) such as the Predator, Reaper, and Global Hawk, which have been used extensively in Afghanistan and Iraq, as well as remote control submersibles, ships, tanks, trucks, and artillery pieces. They are robots insofar as they are unmanned (do not have a pilot onboard), typically possess some capacity for autonomous action (e.g., the Reaper is capable of flying between waypoints without a human operator), and, because the popular conception of robots does not distinguish clearly between autonomous systems and remote control machines.

The prospect of the development and deployment of *autonomous* weapons systems capable of wielding lethal force without the intervention of a human operator raises a distinctive set of ethical issues, concerning the extent to which they may lower the threshold of conflict, the responsibility for deaths caused by these systems, and the possibility that autonomous weapons may turn on those who have designed them, which I (and others) have dealt with elsewhere.[5]

---

[5] See, for instance, Peter Asaro, "How Just Could a Robot War Be?" in Philip Brey, Adam Briggle and Katinka Waelbers (eds.), *Current Issues in Computing and Philosophy* (Amsterdam:

The presence of the human "in the loop" means that remotely operated systems do *not* raise the latter two issues: I have dealt with the implications of UMS for the threshold of conflict in a previous publication.[6]

My concern here, then, is with the ethics of remotely piloted vehicles (RPVs) or "unmanned" systems and their implications for the martial virtues. A number of contemporary dynamics suggest that such weapons are likely to play an increasingly important role in future wars. Foremost among these is the fact that the publics of many First World nations appear increasingly casualty shy—at least in the context of the wars of choice-rather-than-necessity that their governments have wanted to fight. Unmanned systems hold out the hope to governments that they may conduct military campaigns without risk of their citizens seeing their sons and daughters come home in body bags. In theory at least, by providing real-time video of the areas they survey, drones also allow lethal force to be used more precisely and with fewer civilian casualties, thus further reducing the risks of political backlash both domestically and internationally.[7] Finally, many militaries are under budgetary pressure and unmanned systems are also generally held to be cheaper than the systems they replace.

These are all—roughly speaking—political virtues of UMS, but of course these systems also have a number of important military–strategic virtues that are driving their uptake. The relative cheapness of unmanned compared with manned systems is also an important consideration for military commanders, who must also hoard their resources during wartime. UMS greatly reduce the fog of war, which allows military operations to be coordinated more efficiently and force employed with greater precision. Robotic weapons—and drones in particular—greatly accelerate the tempo of battle, which in turn places pressure on rival militaries to adopt these systems to be able to operate at the necessary pace.[8] Last—but by no means

IOS Press, 2008), 50–64; Gary E. Merchant et al., "International Governance of Autonomous Military Robots," *Columbia Science and Technology Law Review* 12 (2011): 272–315; Noel Sharkey, "Cassandra or False Prophet of Doom: AI Robots and War," *IEEE Intelligent Systems* 23:4 (2008): 14–17; Robert Sparrow, "Killer Robots," *Journal of Applied Philosophy* 24:1 (2007): 62–77; Robert Sparrow, "Robotic Weapons and the Future of War," in Jessica Wolfendale and Paolo Tripodi (eds.), *New Wars and New Soldiers: Military Ethics in the Contemporary World* (Surrey, UK: Ashgate, 2011), 117–133.

[6] Robert Sparrow, "Predators or Plowshares? Arms Control of Robotic Weapons," *IEEE Technology and Society* 28:1 (2009): 25–29.

[7] As I have argued elsewhere (Sparrow, "Predators or Plowshares?") these "virtues" of drones also make it more likely that governments will resort to violence. The assessment of the overall impact of the development and use of drones on levels of casualties, both civilian and military, is therefore more complex than first appears and must take account of casualties in incidents that would not have occurred were it not for the capacity drones provide for governments to wield force across national borders with little risk of casualties in their own armed services.

[8] T. K. Adams, "Future Warfare and the Decline of Human Decisionmaking," *Parameters: US Army War College Quarterly* (Winter 2001): 57–71.

least—unmanned systems can help keep warfighters out of "harm's way" and therefore assist commanders both in husbanding the strength of their forces and in fulfilling their moral duty to—as much as is militarily possible—safeguard the lives of those under their command. For all these reasons, most commentators are predicting a greatly increased role for unmanned systems in the future of the armed services.[9]

3. Desk Jockey Warriors?

At first sight, at least, there is something profoundly disturbing about the idea of a war conducted by computer console operators, who are watching over and killing people thousands of kilometers away. In fact, it is harder than initially appears to justify this intuition, especially in the context of a realistic appreciation of the weapons that UMS such as the Predator replace. The argument that new weapons render war immoral by making it too easy to make the decision to take human life is hardly new. Indeed, it is at least as old as the crossbow—which was condemned for making it possible for peasants to kill armored knights—and perhaps even as old as the sling. In an age of long-range artillery, cruise missiles, and high-altitude bombing, it may appear perverse to single out remote control weapons for making possible "killing at a distance." Many warfighters who fire weapons in the services of high-tech industrial powers now never set eyes on the people they intend to kill. Moreover, modern heavy weapons systems typically disperse responsibility for their effects amongst multiple parties: for instance, an artillery spotter calls in the target, a commander orders the attack, and a gunner fires the howitzer or cruise missile.

Yet there remains an element of risk in each of these activities: spotters may themselves be spotted and fired upon, bombers may crash or be shot down, commanders and artillery gunners may themselves be shelled or killed when weapons malfunction catastrophically. Long-range unmanned systems such as Predator and Reaper have succeeded in removing the operators from the theater of operations entirely, allowing them to "fight" wars in complete safety from the air-conditioned comfort of their command modules. The absence of risk to life and limb, the geographical distance between the operators and those they affect, and the technological dynamics driving the development of these systems call into question both the need for a number of important warrior virtues and the capacity of those whom we might call "desk jockey warriors" to exercise them. Most fundamentally, the operators of remotely operated weapons have no need

---

[9] Peter W. Singer, *Wired for War: The Robotics Revolution and Conflict in the 21st Century* (New York: Penguin Books, 2009).

for courage and no opportunity to develop or exercise it. They may also, I will argue, have a reduced capacity to develop or exercise other important martial virtues.

4. The Martial Virtues

To assess the likelihood that the advent of remote control weaponry threatens to undermine or transform the martial virtues, we first need to have a better account of precisely what these virtues consist in and why they are important. A precise classification and full discussion of the martial virtues is beyond the scope of this chapter.[10] Moreover, different armed services offer slightly different lists of virtues and emphasize different virtues even when they offer the same list. Nevertheless, a brief survey and discussion of a number of virtues, along with an understanding of why they are important, will be of considerable assistance in evaluating the challenge posed by the robotics revolution in warfare.

4.1 Courage

The first and most important martial virtue is courage.[11] To be capable of pursuing goals amidst the chaos of battle, a warrior must possess a "willingness to face fear and overcome it." Discussions of courage typically note the importance of both *physical* and *moral* courage. Physical courage is the willingness to face fear of bodily discomfort, injury, and death. Moral courage is the willingness to face and overcome fear of the social and personal sanctions that may be incurred by doing what is right rather than what is popular, expected, or prudential.

The relationship between physical and moral courage is controversial. Peter Oolsthorn even argued that they are only weakly—if at all—correlated and that military training should be reoriented to emphasize moral rather than physical courage.[12] On the other hand, much military training proceeds as though there *is* a relationship between physical and moral courage and in the belief that the strength of will necessary to overcome physical challenges will

---

[10] The most extensive discussion to date that I am aware of is provided in Olsthoorn, *Military Ethics and Virtues*. The first three virtues that I discuss each merit a whole chapter in Olsthoorn's book.

[11] Hilliard Aronovitch, "Good Soldiers: A Traditional Approach," *Journal of Applied Philosophy* 18:1 (2001): 13–23, at 17.

[12] Peter Olsthoorn, "Courage in the Military: Physical and Moral," *Journal of Military Ethics* 6:4 (2007): 270–279.

also assist individuals in confronting moral dangers.[13] In part, I suspect this is because physical courage *can* be trained while it is unclear whether or not moral courage can be trained. More importantly, it is the nature of war that having the courage of one's convictions is not enough to guarantee success— the willingness of one party to resort to violence to settle a dispute requires the other to have the capacity to summon physical courage as well.[14] Indeed, ultimately a warrior must be prepared to risk his (or her) life for the cause in which he (or she) fights.[15] Someone who is paralyzed with fear at the thought of suffering or (even) his own death may find it impossible to summon moral courage when he most needs it. For this reason, I suspect that physical courage will remain at the heart of any viable "warrior code" for the foreseeable future.

4.2 Loyalty

Loyalty is the other virtue that is absolutely central to military service. In war—and in preparation for war—soldiers must be willing to place themselves at risk, indeed to sacrifice themselves, for the sake of the larger objectives of the unit, and ultimately the nation. As it will almost never be in the interests of individuals to risk their lives for the sake of the collective, both the nation and the military unit must appeal to motivations of their members other than their self-interest. The two main traits that the military relies on in this context are honor (which will be discussed in the next section) and loyalty. Loyalty involves a willingness to bear risks and make sacrifices for the sake of that to which one is loyal. In military contexts, this usually means a willingness to suffer physical hardships and even to risk death for the sake of the other members of a combat unit, and its commander, and much military training is dedicated to achieving the small group cohesion that generates such commitment.[16] However, loyalty to larger institutions (e.g., "the Marines," the "Commander in Chief," the nation, or the constitution) and values (e.g., the traditions of the Corps, liberty, democracy) also plays a crucial role in promoting discipline, encouraging ethical behavior, and reducing the threat of military coups or other forms of social disorder that flow from military forces being willing to use or threaten violence outside of wartime.

---

[13] Yi, "MCMAP and the Marine Warrior Ethos."

[14] Olsthoorn, "Courage in the Military," 274.

[15] Ryan R. Gorman, "War and the Virtues in Aquinas's Ethical Thought," *Journal of Military Ethics* 9:3 (2010): 257–258, at 254.

[16] For some observations about how loyalty to one's immediate comrades can promote both ethical and unethical behavior, see Steven M. Silver, "Ethics and Combat: Thoughts for Small Unit Leaders," *Marine Corps Gazette* 90:11 (2006): 76–78.

4.3 Honor

Related to loyalty, but distinct from it, is the virtue of honor. A sense of honor is the concern for how well one lives up to one's chosen ideals.[17] Honor is vital insofar as it plays a crucial role in helping motivate warriors to risk life and limb for the sake of the cause in which they fight and in motivating them to live up to ethical ideals. In particular, a sense of honor plays a vital role in encouraging warfighters to abide by the principles of *jus in bello*. "Warriors" fight wars with honor and with the desire to test their skills against other warriors: they do not target civilians, and they use force only proportionate to their goals in discriminating fashion. A sense of honor also helps warfighters resist the various temptations to immoral behavior, such as looting and raping, to which they are likely to be exposed in war.[18] Finally, insofar as ideas about what it means to be an honorable warrior provide intellectual and spiritual resources to reconcile a history of violence with a return to peace and social order, they may also assist with reintegrating returned servicemen into civilian life.[19]

Notoriously, honor is a social virtue. It is social in two senses. First, the dictates of honor are inevitably, to a certain extent at least, a function of the culture and understandings of social group. How a "good warrior" comports himself or herself is, to a large degree, determined by the example of role models and the behavior of peers. Thus, for instance, to be a good Marine is to live up to the traditions of the Marines.[20] Second, a sense of honor is reflexive in structure and involves a concern for the judgment of others, especially our peers.[21] To gauge our own worth, we ask ourselves how we appear to others. To bolster our own resolve, we imagine how we will appear to others if we fail to live up to our standards. The virtue of (a sense of) honor consists in a large part, then, in being able to pick out the appropriate group of people whose opinions should matter to us. This in turn inevitably requires an evaluation of the activities and character of those around us, which itself will be partially determined by the appropriateness of their responses to our own activities. For this reason, a sense of the value of one's own life and choices is also a prerequisite for a sense of honor. There is "no honor among thieves" both because

[17] As Paul Robinson, "Magnanimity and Integrity as Military Virtues," *Journal of Military Ethics* 6:4 (2007): 259–269, points out, strictly speaking, "honor" itself is not a virtue but, rather, what one acquires from exercising other virtues. A *sense* of honor, on the other hand, may constitute a virtue in an important range of cases.

[18] Not only are these activities now understood to be evil in themselves, but they are also inimical to winning "hearts and minds" in counterinsurgency warfare and to maintaining domestic support for military campaigns in the context of modern media-saturated warfare.

[19] French, *The Code of the Warrior*, 4–7, 10.

[20] Ibid., 15; Silver, "Ethics and Combat," 76.

[21] Peter Olsthoorn, "Honor as a Motive for Making Sacrifices," *Journal of Military Ethics* 4:3 (2005): 183–197.

stealing from others is nothing to be proud of and because an honorable person does not allow his own sense of worth to be shaped by the opinions of those who steal.

4.4 Mercy

The final virtue I wish to mention is mercy.[22] Mercy typically does *not* appear in the list of virtues on the webpages and in statements of the values of national armed services. Nevertheless, there are good reasons to think of mercy as an important virtue, the exercise of which is facilitated by military service and which plays a constitutive role in what it means to be a warrior.[23] To be merciful is to refrain, out of compassion, from killing or causing suffering when one is both able and would be justified in doing so. Those who have the power to kill therefore also have the opportunity to show mercy. Not all warriors are merciful, but those who are play a crucial role in showing how the warrior's code is indeed an *ethical* code and not merely a tradition. The cultivation and demonstration of mercy is one of the main things that distinguish warriors from mere "killers." In showing mercy, warriors demonstrate their respect for human life even in the midst of war.[24]

While the idea that combat is an arena that makes mercy possible is a familiar one, for many people there will be an element of cognitive dissonance in thinking of warriors as having a merciful *character*. Rather, we typically think of warriors as being trained to *overcome* their sympathetic impulses to be capable of killing in the pursuit of victory. This dissonance should disappear when we remember that a "warrior code" defines a "role morality" and that the form and place of particular virtues in an ethical life may be different in different roles. Mercy in a warrior will take a different form to mercy in a doctor but is possible nevertheless.

5. Virtues as Character Traits

It is worth emphasizing that all of these virtues consist in more than simply a disposition to act in the way that is most obviously associated with the virtue.

---

[22] To write of mercy as a virtue is slightly clumsy. However, the more grammatically correct "mercifulness" is even clumsier.

[23] One place where ideas about mercy do clearly play a key role in determining what it means to be a warrior is in regards to expectations concerning the treatment of prisoners of war. My thanks to Catherine Mills for drawing this to my attention.

[24] As French, *Code of the Warrior*, demonstrates, the content of "warrior codes" has differed across history and cultures—and not every warrior code has valued mercy in the way I have described here. Nevertheless, the idea that warriors kill only reluctantly—and consequently value mercy—is, I would submit, central to the warrior codes of modern militaries that understand war within the framework of just war theory, which insists that we should fight wars only reluctantly and—even then—subject to constraints determined by the need to minimize the concomitant loss of human life.

Virtuous actions flow from the character of an agent, and that character consists in a larger set of dispositions to behave in accordance with the particular virtue.[25] Thus, for instance, persons who possess the virtue of courage will not only overcome their fear but will also do so in a certain spirit, in a manner appropriately sensitive to context, and (arguably) only in a just cause; they will also respond to other acts of courage and cowardice and to courageous and cowardly people in particular ways. This will be important to the argument that follows because, while it may be possible for the operators of remotely piloted weapons to act in ways that would appear to be in accordance with various virtues, it is less clear whether they can develop the larger set of dispositions that are necessary for them to have a virtuous character.

6. Desk Jockey Warrior Virtues?

Armed with this brief discussion of a number of important martial virtues and a sense of why they are important, we are now in a better position to evaluate the impact of the advent of remotely piloted and robotic weaponry. I will discuss each of these virtues in turn and argue that the advent of remote control warfare poses a significant threat to the relevant virtue. Because an obvious question in any discussion of the ethical implications of UMS is the extent to which alleged impacts are actually unique to these systems, I will also offer some observations on this matter in each case.

6.1 Courage

Most obviously, UMS operations call into question the need for courage by those who operate them. Courage, understood as "the ability to face fear and overcome it," requires cause for fear for its exercise. Yet long-range UMS pilots control these systems from thousands of kilometers away, beyond the reach of enemy action. They will not be killed or injured if the systems they are operating crash or if the weapons they are firing explode. They are, in fact, completely safe and consequently have no cause for fear—or need for courage. Indeed, there is no need for operators to be physically fit or even able-bodied, as long as they are able to operate the controls of the weapon.

It might be argued that a form of courage is still necessary to be able to pilot UMS: moral courage. Pilots of these systems must be willing to make life-or-death decisions, including the decision to kill another person, in circumstances where making the wrong decision may lead to the death of other warfighters. Thus, piloting drones is not for the fainthearted.

---

[25] Rosalind Hursthouse, *On Virtue Ethics* (Oxford: Oxford University Press, 2001), 10–12.

The problem with this line of argument is that it fails to distinguish UMS operators from ambulance drivers, pharmacists, surgeons, paramedics, police, and rescue workers. Members of these professions must also make life-or-death decisions, and thus working in these roles also involves moral courage. Indeed, given that members of these professions will be physically present in situations where people may die as a result of their choices, they arguably require *more* courage than UMS operators.

In response, it might be claimed that while all these roles do involve life-or-death decisions, they do not involve the deliberate decision to kill, which UMS operators must be willing to make. This is true, as far as it goes, although one would also note that police officers are occasionally required to make the decision to use lethal force and that members of these other professions are occasionally required to make a deliberate decision to sacrifice—if not directly kill—the lives of one or more people to save others. However, the idea that the decision to kill requires moral courage relies crucially upon a folk-psychological account of the nature and psychological consequences of killing that in turn relies upon the idea that the person who kills and the person who is killed are physically present to each other. Indeed, the common intuition that there is something morally suspect about long-range or remote control killing arises precisely because of a concern that the geographic and psychological distance between killer and killed makes killing too easy. That is, the idea that it takes moral courage to fire a missile at—and kill—someone who one has seen as only pixels on a screen is precisely what is under dispute in debate about the morality of killing via UMS.[26]

Unless it can be shown that UMS operators are typically reluctant to kill and fear the moral and psychological implications of doing so, the argument that it requires moral courage to operate the systems will be unconvincing. What little, largely anecdotal, evidence I have been able to gather from the literature is ambiguous on this question. Reports of posttraumatic stress disorder among the pilots of Predator and Reaper UAVs suggest that the decision to kill via these systems may exact a high personal toll and therefore properly requires moral courage.[27] On the other hand, I have seen reports that those who fly these UAVs are typically eager to attack targets, that they are excited when they do so, and that a key task in training the pilots of Predator and Reaper is reminding them that they are "killing people" and not just "shooting electrons"—suggesting that little moral courage is required to make the decision to fire.[28]

---

[26] For useful discussions, see David Whetham, "Remote Killing and Drive-By Wars," in David Lovell and Igor Primoratz (eds.), *Protecting Civilians during Armed Conflict: Theoretical and Practical Issues during Violent Conflict* (Ashgate, 2012); Jeff Sparrow, *Killing: Misadventures in Violence* (Carlton: Melbourne University Publishing, 2009).

[27] See, for instance, Singer, *Wired for War*, 346–347.

[28] See, for instance, Bryan Bender, "Attacking Iraq, from a Nev. Computer," *Boston Globe* April 3, 2005, A6; Noah Shachtman, "Drone School, a Ground's-Eye View," *Wired Magazine*, May 27, 2005. http://www.wired.com/science/discoveries/news/2005/05/67655.

One thing this discussion does reveal, however, is that to the extent that we are concerned with moral courage, then the operators of (some) remotely piloted weapon systems may require more of it than operators of other weapons that facilitate killing at a distance. UMS typically provide their operators with much *more* information about the battle space and the fate of those they fire upon than more familiar long-range weapons such as artillery, cruise missiles, and aerial bombardment.[29] The suggestion that it takes little moral courage to kill at a distance using UMS will therefore apply much more generally in modern warfare.

There is another set of circumstances that may require moral courage of UMS operators, which is when they receive an order that is immoral or illegal. For instance, a pilot may pay a high personal price for refusing to fire, when ordered to do so, on a target he or she believes is a civilian rather than a military target. Refusing such an order will therefore require the ability to overcome fear of the institutional sanctions that may result, which in a military context may include imprisonment.

Yet the operators of UMS are arguably much less likely to be called upon to execute illegal orders than are combatants in the field and are much better placed to resist them, both institutionally and psychologically. Because the telemetry from these systems and communication networks that support their operations is typically recorded, commanders are likely to be much more cautious about issuing illegal orders. For the same reason, operators can be confident that their behavior, and any reasons they provide for it will be documented if the matter comes to trial.[30] The operators of UMS are also much less likely to be influenced by terror or hatred or other strong emotions that may grip combatants who are under threat or in the midst of combat and that make it harder for combatants to find their moral compass when ordered to participate in war crimes. Finally, as I discuss later, the demands of loyalty are much weaker on UMS operators than on combatants physically located in the theater of operations, so they are also much better placed to resist peer pressure to carry out immoral acts.

The operators of UMS therefore have no need for physical courage and arguably have little need for moral courage. Indeed, they have no opportunity to exercise physical courage and arguably greatly reduced opportunities for moral courage. While the argument that they have little need (or opportunity) for moral courage may apply more generally to long-range killing in modern warfare, the argument that they have no need (and have no opportunity to demonstrate) for physical courage seems *almost* uniquely applicable to these new weapons systems.[31]

---

[29] For further discussion of the implications of fact, see Robert Sparrow, "Building a Better WarBot: Ethical issues in the design of unmanned systems for military applications," *Science and Engineering Ethics* 15:2 (2009): 169–187.

[30] Whetham, "Remote Killing and Drive-By Wars."

[31] I say "almost" because ever since the invention of the telegraph there have been small numbers of people directly involved in war who have been beyond the reach of enemy action.

6.2 Loyalty

The operations of remotely piloted weapons also pose a significant challenge to loyalty. As I noted already, what is required in traditional military service is loyalty to the members of a small combat unit as well as to the larger institutions of which they are a part. Operators of UMS may train and work alongside others, but they do not *fight* alongside them. Indeed, it is questionable whether they are ever in combat at all. As a result, they have little need for loyalty to their comrades, a greatly reduced capacity to demonstrate it, and little opportunity to develop and cultivate it.

Operators have little need for loyalty from their comrades because they are in no danger. Soldiers on the battlefield require loyalty from those alongside whom they fight because without such loyalty it is not reasonable to expect them to risk their lives for each other or for the military objectives of the group. Being safely located thousands of kilometers from the enemy, operators of UMS can carry out their duties without needing to worry about being let down by their comrades.

Interestingly, this argument about the reduced need for loyalty among the operators of UMS is *more* forceful than in the case of many of the other means of long-range killing with which they are often compared. Even the crews of B-52s bombing from out of the range of enemy antiaircraft defenses or gunners firing cruise missiles from a battleship hundreds of kilometers away from their targets rely upon the dedication and service of other members of the armed services, without whose diligence their own lives would be at risk from the weapons they employ. UMS operators face no such risks.

That the operators of UMS have a reduced capacity to demonstrate loyalty is more controversial but still seems to be the case. Loyalty requires the willingness to bear risks and to make sacrifices, yet UMS operators bear no risks and have a greatly reduced capacity for sacrifice in the course of their duties. They may, of course, work hard and diligently for long hours, but this seems hardly comparable to the sacrifices that soldiers may make for each other on the battlefield. Even if a Predator drone comes to the rescue of others by destroying an enemy who was threatening troops on the battlefield just in the nick of time, the operators will have shown no bravery and undergone little hardship. It is difficult to see what operators could do that *would* demonstrate loyalty.

If the pilots of remotely operated weapon systems struggle to demonstrate loyalty, then it follows that it will be difficult for them to develop and cultivate it, as virtues must be sustained through regular exercise. Another reason to think that UMS make the development of loyalty more difficult is the fact that those involved in the operations are scattered around the globe. The pilots who fly them are often on a different continent from those who launch, refuel, and maintain them. More importantly, the pilots may never meet or even speak to the people "alongside" whom they fight. Admittedly, war often involves fleeting cooperation between strangers in different services or even in the armed forces of different nations. Air support and indirect fire support often involve people fighting the same battle for many days without ever having the chance to meet. This latter dynamic is therefore hardly new. Nevertheless, the operations of UMS do seem to represent its apogee to date.

Of course, UMS operators may still demonstrate loyalty to the *institutions* within which they serve, with which they *will* have extended relationships. Again, though, we might wonder whether the reduced opportunities they have to make sacrifices impacts on the capacity to demonstrate loyalty. Trying hard to achieve set objectives, working long hours, or declining "better offers" from other potential employers out of loyalty to their particular armed service will not distinguish UMS operators from civilian workers. There is nothing distinctively "martial" about loyalty of this sort.

The absence of risk and the geographic separation between UMS operators and the theater of operations are therefore also a serious threat to the martial virtue of "loyalty." While UMS are not alone, among the technologies of modern warfare, in making loyalty less important and less likely to develop, the near-total absence of risk involved in the operations of long-range UMS does pose a distinct challenge to the need for loyalty.

6.3 Honor

It is clearly possible for UMS opeartors to be better or worse warfighters, both in a technical and an ethical sense. They were awarded decorations for airmanship when they demonstrated technical proficiency. It is also possible for them to operate these systems in ways that are more in accordance with or less in accordance with the principles of *jus in bello* and thus to aspire to behave in an ethically exemplary fashion. The operation of UMS is often difficult and— insofar as these weapons contribute to military victory, help preserve the lives of friendly warfighters, and reduce civilian casualties—worthwhile. These considerations suggest that operations involving UMS contain all the ingredients necessary for their operators to maintain a sense of honor.

There are, moreover, some reasons to think that UMS operators are more likely to behave ethically in "combat" than combatants located in the theater of operations. Fear of death or injury in battle can contribute to combatants violating the requirements of *jus in bello*. Since UMS operators have nothing to fear from their enemies, they are better placed to be able to pause and consider the consequences of their actions. The mediated nature of the relationship with events in the theater of operations also means that they are less likely to be gripped by other strong emotions—such as anger, aggression, or hatred—that may make it more difficult to think about and do what is right.

Nevertheless, there are three important challenges to the cultivation and exercise of the sense of honor by desk jockey warriors.

First—the flip side of the previous observations—if UMS operators face fewer challenges to acting ethically, they may have less reason to cultivate a sense of honor. I will discuss the possibility that this simply demonstrates that we should be prepared to trade honor for the use of weapons that produce better outcomes. For the moment, I simply want to note the tension between the claim that UMS operators are better placed to act ethically and the claim that they fight with honor. They may lack an honorable *character* even if particular actions meet a high ethical standard.

Second, the mediated nature of the relationship between the operators and those they kill may make it more difficult for them to respect—and to earn respect from—those against whom they fight and those who may kill. They may never set foot in the country in which they "fight" or meet any of the people against whom they fight. In the absence of any human relations with those who their actions will affect, warfighters may be less inclined to resist impulses arising out of fear, hatred, or anger where these emotions *do* arise.

Contra the previous claim, then, this would suggest that there may be a *greater* need for honor among those who pilot remotely operated weapons. Unfortunately, UMS pilots are alienated from two groups of people who should properly be an important resource for the development and maintenance of a sense of honor: enemy warriors and civilians in the territory where war is being fought. I noted already that honor is a social virtue with a reflexive structure. The first community to which warriors look to determine the standards to which they should adhere to and how well they are doing so is their immediate comrades. Yet "honor" that is affirmed only by one's comrades is always going to be fragile, especially if one's comrades are also engaged in the same behavior, the honor of which has come into question. Moreover, the "peers" of warriors would typically include enemy warriors—even if the assessment of the enemy is more often imagined than actually ascertained. UMS pilots will never meet their enemies, and it is hard to imagine their targets offering them respect for the honor with which they fight. When warriors look beyond their peers for evaluation of their activities, one place they would be well advised to look is the population among whom they fight, who, one would hope, might admire their commitment or value the care they take to avoid civilian casualties. UMS pilots are denied access to this resource as well. Once more, of course, these problems are not confined to UMS but will arise with any long-range weapon fired from outside of the territory in which war is taking place.

However, third, the more fundamental challenge that UMS pose to the sense of honor arises out of the thought that there is something inherently dishonorable about killing people one is observing on a video screen from thousands of kilometers away and who have no opportunity to return fire. The absence of danger to the operator, as well as the power of the sensors and weapons they command, seems to make killing too easy to be called honorable.

This is, I think, a widespread and powerful intuition, but it turns out to be remarkably hard to unpack. In particular, we need to be careful to avoid relying on an argument about chivalry here. War is not a game, and there is no reason that it should be fair. Indeed, there is some reason to believe that if a war is worth fighting—if one believes that one is fighting in a just cause—then it would be best if it were over quickly with as few losses on one's own side as possible. Certainly, there is a moral obligation on commanders to try to preserve, as much as is compatible with achieving military objectives, the lives of the troops under their command. Ensuring a (favorable) asymmetry of forces whenever their troops go into battle is one of the best ways to meet this obligation. In this context, UMS look like ideal weapons.[32] At the very least, they are no more or less "fair" than cruise missiles or high-altitude bombing.

On the other hand, the principles of *jus in bello* already place restrictions on the way wars may be fought, including those that prolong wars and make particular military victories harder to achieve. Nerve gases and dum-dum bullets are each useful weapons in some circumstances, but their use is nevertheless prohibited by the law of armed conflict. Firebombing the residential suburbs of cities might hasten an enemy surrender but would violate the requirement for discrimination in *jus in bello*. Roughly speaking, these sorts of prohibitions are justified by the belief that even though these weapons or strategies might be justified in some particular cases, the overall consequences of their use—or of allowing the ethics of their use to be assessed on a case-by-case basis—outweigh their military virtues.

My suspicion is that our intuitions about the honor of the use of UMS have a similar structure. That is, they arise from—and draw attention to—a concern that disassociating physical courage from a war would be disastrous in the long term. As long as courage is required to go into battle, then warriors will fight for causes only that (they believe) are worth fighting for. There is, of course, no guarantee that the causes that warriors think are worth fighting for are in fact worth going to war for: history is full of examples where, with the benefit of hindsight, we wonder why people ever cared so much about a pretext for war that they were prepared to kill or die for it. How many more wars would have been waged, though, if those who fought in them did not require courage to participate?

---

[32] An argument made forcefully in Bradley Jay Strawser, "Moral Predators: The Duty to Employ Uninhabited Aerial Vehicles," *Journal of Military Ethics* 9:4 (2010): 342–368.

Because *any* asymmetry will reduce the risks to warriors on the side with the superior forces and because of the obligation on commanders to protect their troops, I do not think this line of argument can serve to show that the use of unmanned systems is unethical *simpliciter*. Indeed, it may be ethically required to achieve maximum military advantage over an enemy in combat even though the result may be that there is little honor in any victory achieved. Moreover, the suggestion that the use of UMS lacks honor will generalize to other means of effectively risk-free killing that are now prevalent in modern warfare. Nevertheless, insofar as UMS represent the apogee to date of a logic of risk-free warfare and have become perilously close to achieving it, it is entirely appropriate that concerns about this logic should attach most forcefully to these systems.[33]

The implications of UMS for the extent to which those who operate them can plausibly maintain a sense of honor are complex and difficult to resolve. There is I think much more work, both philosophical and empirical, to be done on this topic. My initial investigations suggest, though, that the operations of UMS also pose a substantial challenge to this important martial virtue.

6.4 Mercy

Along with their power to kill, operators of remote weapon systems also have the option not to exercise this power even when they would be justified in doing so. At first sight it would appear, then, that there will still be a role for mercy in the character of those who operate UMS.

Yet again, there are reasons to be concerned that the exercise and cultivation of mercy may be threatened by UMS.

To begin with, the organizational and institutional context in which the operators of UMS "fight" arguably makes it harder for them to exercise discretion. Since the operators are not in any danger, it is more plausible to expect them to follow orders from other people who may be geographically distant and also to wait for orders to follow. The long loiter time and extensive reach of these systems also allow more opportunity for multiple parties to have input

---

[33] Strawser, "Moral Predators," criticizes this line of argument for implying that states should renounce any weapons that generate significant asymmetry of forces and as resting on unreliable judgments about future states of affairs. However, Strawser here confuses the ethics of unilateral disarmament with the ethics of arms control more generally. The fact that the widespread deployment of a particular class of weapons would lower the threshold of conflict is a traditional ground for arms control, and there is nothing especially controversial or difficult about the assessments of probability involved in judging that a given class of weapons does so. Moreover, we could be justified in pursuing arms control of new weapons even if existing weapons produce a similar or greater risk of war simply because it may be more plausible to establish an arms control regime for new weapons as they are developed and become controversial than it is to demand that states renounce their existing arsenals.

into decisions about what and when to attack.[34] Indeed, targeting "by committee" has increasingly become possible even for mobile targets now that drones can provide nearly continuous surveillance over a large territory.[35] If the role of UMS operators is merely to execute decisions made by others, then they may have little opportunity to show mercy.

However, there is a more fundamental challenge to the idea that mercy can play a role in the operations of UMS, owing to the geographic distance between the operators and the people whose lives they take or spare and the mediated nature of their engagement with them. Not every refusal to kill is plausibly described as an act of mercy, let alone as flowing from the virtue of being merciful. Virtue involves action for the right motives. In the case of mercy, it requires action motivated by compassion. Compassion is most fundamentally a response to the needs of the concrete other—to a particular person in a particular time and place. For instance, when a soldier refrains from killing an enemy because he or she sees a terror in the enemy's eyes, it may be an act of mercy (when such an action is consistent with and flows from the character of the soldier).

Yet we might wonder whether the sensor systems that guide the operations of UMS are capable of communicating the moral reality necessary to ground compassion. This concern may take two forms, which are easier or harder to assuage. It might be argued that current sensing technologies are incapable of transmitting enough of the humanity of their targets to allow genuine mercy but conceded that future sensors might overcome this limit. A more radical critique, though, would deny that *any* remote sensing system or spy camera is capable of communicating the *moral* reality of people half a world away. That is, even if UMS operators have access to images of the quality that one might have a mere meter away from someone, the relation between them and the person whose life they were sparing would not be capable of sustaining genuine compassion. This latter critique would rest on a thesis in media ethics about the moral difference between representation and reality, which seems plausible to me but which I am unable to defend, for reasons of space, here.[36]

---

[34] Singer, *Wired for War*, 348–353.

[35] Note that these effects of UMS also partially extend to include the operations of other combatants. Quite early in the debate about the impact of UAVs on military operations, a number of commentators drew attention to the way these systems posted a threat to the autonomy of battlefield commanders by making it possible for distant officers—or even for the civilian leadership—to exercise control over operations in real time. See, for instance, Jeffrey A. Harley, "Information, Technology, and Center of Gravity," *Naval War College Review* 50:1 (1997): 66–87, at 83–84; John A. Gentry, "Doomed to Fail: America's Blind Faith in Military Technology," *Parameters: US Army War College Quarterly* (Winter 2002): 88–103, at 100; Noah Shachtman, "Attack of the Drones," *Wired Magazine* 13:6 (2005). http://www.wired.com/wired/archive//13.06/drones_pr.html.

[36] For an early defense of this claim, see Jerry Mander, *Four Arguments for the Elimination of Television* (New York: Morrow Quill Paperbacks, 1978).

Once more, we must be mindful of a comparison with other forms of long-range killing. Those who fly bombers or fire cruise missiles or long-range artillery may never meet the people against whom they fight. Any compassion they have for their enemies must necessarily be abstract, which will also rule out genuine acts of mercy. There may, however, be a subtler and insidious threat to mercy involved in the operations of UMS arising from the inability to demonstrate mercy in circumstances where it would normally be appropriate. Unlike those who drop bombs from a great height, the operators of UMS may be able to watch terrified and helpless individuals being killed and maimed by the weapons they have unleashed. Yet even if they choose not to fire out of concern for the welfare of those they are surveying, their relation to their targets may be too abstract for this choice to count as merciful. Over time, this lack of opportunity to show mercy where it might otherwise be appropriate may contribute to a hardening of the heart among the operators and eventually to the development of the vice associated with a *deficiency* of mercy—callousness.

We don't typically think of mercy as a martial virtue. Yet, as I have argued, mercy plays an important role in distinguishing modern warriors from mere killers. The geographical and psychological distance between UMS operators and their targets suggests that it may be extremely difficult for the pilots of remotely operated weapons to demonstrate this important virtue.

7. The Future of the Martial Virtues

I have suggested here that the development and deployment of remotely operated weapon systems constitute a serious threat to current notions of martial virtue. However, the ultimate import of these findings, it might be argued, depends on the impact of robotic weapons on how wars are fought in the future and also on the response of the armed services to the challenges posed by remotely piloted operations.

7.1 Robotic Weapons and the Future of War

One good reason for downplaying the significance of this threat to martial virtues is cynicism about the extent to which future wars will in fact be fought remotely. Remotely operated weapons have undoubted utility in many roles and for this reason are likely to be continued to be deployed at an ever increasing intensity of operations. However, the idea that it will ever be possible to (successfully) fight a war without placing warfighters in roles that require traditional martial virtues looks to be a fantasy for at least two reasons.

First, the utility of remotely piloted weapons is heavily dependent on the technological capacities of their adversaries. To date, drones and their ilk have overwhelmingly been deployed in asymmetric conflicts against adversaries without robust antiaircraft (or antisubmarine) systems, with limited capacity to deploy electronic countermeasures or conduct cyber warfare, and certainly without the ability to launch kinetic attacks on the satellite and other communications infrastructure on which they depend. It remains to be seen how survivable and effective robotic weapons will be in combat with a technologically advanced adversary. For this reason, it would be extremely unwise for any nation to let its capacity to field a traditional (manned) military force decline too precipitously, let alone to commit to an entirely unmanned military.

Second, in asymmetrical wars of the sort currently being fought by the US in Afghanistan and North Africa, which are widely predicted to constitute a large percentage of future conflicts, victory will usually turn on achieving one of two objectives to which robotic weapons can make limited contributions. Accomplishing a lasting political settlement of the dispute that was the cause for war either requires directly controlling—traditionally, by occupation—activities in a territory or installing a friendly government. Occupying territory will require putting "boots on the ground." Achieving the influence required to install a friendly government will almost always involve cultivating sufficient political support among the civilian population by winning "hearts and minds," which is also likely to require a more robust engagement—both civilian and military—than UMS allow.

For these reasons it seems likely, that, for the foreseeable future, most wars will involve combat operations conducted by soldiers physically located in the theater of operations. However, if this is the case, then it may seem as though we have little reason to worry that the traditional military virtues will be undermined or transformed by the operations of UMS.

Yet the belief that the martial virtues will remain necessary is compatible with the argument that unmanned operations pose a profound threat to the martial virtues—indeed, it only makes the latter more pressing. The worry is not that the need for the martial virtues will disappear or even that the virtues themselves will not be realized by warriors when wars are fought but rather that the operations of UMS are inimical to these virtues so that when they *are* required they will be lacking.

Moreover, the political and military–strategic dynamics driving the uptake of UMS suggest that the threat to the martial virtues may be more pronounced than first appears. UMS are already the weapon of choice for governments seeking to prosecute wars in the face of concerns about domestic political opposition should friendly or civilian casualties occur. The expectations of risk-free war that these weapons encourage may eventually effectively force their use in an increasing number of roles. Thus, even if the martial virtues are threatened only among UMS operators, this will be a significant concern if this group comes to constitute an increasing proportion of those who see active service.

But it may also be difficult to confine the cultural impact of the operations of UMS to the operators themselves. The more the militaries of industrial societies aspire to risk-free warfare, the harder it may be to convince those in the armed services that they should aspire to the martial virtues.

7.2 Military Training and the Future of the Virtues

Most of the professional life of members of the armed services is not spent in combat. Similarly, combat operations are not the only place where virtues are learned or exercised or even the only place where they are necessary. Thus, perhaps even if particular martial virtues are no longer needed—or developed—in the operations of UMS, they may still be maintained in military culture and inculcated through training or in the day-to-day routines of those who operate them.

However, training to inculcate virtues that warriors are unlikely ever to be able to exercise is an uneasy compromise. Combat operations are the core function of the armed services—their raison d'être. Training exercises or military routines that do not contribute to combat effectiveness are likely to erode over time becuase it will be difficult to justify their presence. At best then, this approach might serve as a temporary stopgap to preserve the martial virtues from the implications of UMS in the short term.

8. Conclusion: War without Virtue?

It has not been my purpose here to determine whether the use of UMS is ethical or unethical. I have undertaken the smaller—but related—task of examining the impact of these weapons on the martial virtues. I have argued that the operations of UMS pose a significant risk to the place of the martial virtues within the organizational culture of the armed services and to current understandings of the ethics of war. For those who care about the future shape of armed conflict, this should be a disturbing prospect. Indeed, although I have not attempted it here, it may be that a longer and more ambitious argument could be made that the threat posed to the martial virtues by UMS gives us reason to reconsider current enthusiasm for them.

There would, admittedly, seem to be something paradoxical—if not downright implausible—in arguing that the fact that a class of powerful and effective weapons reduces the need for military virtues gives us any reason to refrain from employing them. If unmanned systems will save both friendly combatant and civilian lives (due to their capacity to allow more precise use of force), then so much the worse for the virtues. Soldiers may be more than happy to give up the martial virtues if doing so means they don't get their legs blown off by an improvised explosive device in a foreign country. Civilians in the area where the conflict is taking place may also prefer that industrious technicians use UMS rather than have warriors use the more destructive or less accurate manned systems that would otherwise serve in their place.[37]

There is some force in this thought. One certainly cannot rule out a priori the possibility that the evils of war would be reduced by trading the martial virtues for better weaponry. However, in closing, I will observe that we should be very cautious about giving up on the warrior virtues. As noted already, it is doubtful that wars will ever be fought entirely by weaponry that eliminates the need for the traditional martial virtues. However, perhaps more importantly, the traditions and ethics of the armed services, which have established their various "warrior codes," have developed and evolved over many years and through many conflicts. While war remains a ghastly business, where they are maintained, warrior codes function to reduce the horror of war and tame the worst excesses of young men sent out to kill strangers in foreign lands with weapons of terrifying power. Before we abandon the traditional martial virtues we would need to be very confident that whatever was likely to replace them would serve equally well in this demanding task. Given the powerful dynamics currently driving the development and deployment of UMS, it may be that this is a dangerous experiment that that we are about undertake.[38]

---

[37] See, for instance, the sentiments quoted in the penultimate paragraph of Pir Zubair Shah, "My Drone Wars," *Foreign Policy* March–April (2012). http://www.foreignpolicy.com/articles/2012/02/27/my_drone_war?page=full.

[38] My thanks to Catherine Mills, Jim Sparrow, Dirk Baltzly, and Bradley Strawser, all of whom read and commented on versions of this paper.

6

Robot Guardians: Teleoperated Combat Vehicles in Humanitarian Military Intervention

ZACK BEAUCHAMP AND JULIAN SAVULESCU

The drones will make the difference, God willing.
Libyan rebel Tareq Khalil Shihbani, April 25, 2011, on hearing
news that the US would be targeting government forces with
aerial Predator drones

1. Introduction

Perhaps the most common concern about the proliferation of teleoperated combat vehicles (or, as we will call them, drones) goes along these lines: because drones take humans out of combat situations, they decrease the costs of going to war, making the initiation of war by states equipped with drones more likely. There is limited evidence that currently existing drones have "lowered the threshold" to war any more than, say, cruise missiles or regular aircraft. However, it is reasonable to assume that, as the technology advances and as drones take on more and more combat roles today reserved for humans, this critique may gain some force. We suggest lowering the threshold is not, as commonly assumed, necessarily a bad thing. In at least one case, the bug is in fact a feature: drones have the potential to significantly improve the practice of humanitarian intervention, understood here the use of military force to protect foreign citizens from mass violence like genocide or ethnic cleansing.

We will defend this view by reference to each of the two core areas of just war theory: the morality of going to war, *jus ad bellum*; and the morality of waging war, *jus in bello*. We will argue that, on the assumptions made in the "lowering the threshold" argument, drones will both (1) make it more likely that states launch justified humanitarian interventions; and (2) improve the conduct, morally speaking, of such interventions once launched. We here aim to show (1) and (2) to be the case by reference to only some relatively noncontroversial standards in just war theory.[1]

Our argument will proceed in three parts. In Section 2, we will lay out several widely accepted principles of *jus ad bellum* and *jus in bello* and explain why empirical examples of humanitarian intervention have fallen short of this ideal mark. Section 3 breaks down the "lowering the threshold" argument into its component parts and explains why they must imply the conclusion that drones will morally improve, rather than worsen, the practice of humanitarian intervention by reference to the standards examined in Section 2. The final section responds to several objections P. W. Singer has prominently given to the morality using of drones in humanitarian intervention.

2. The Troubled Moral Reality of Humanitarian War

The philosophical debate about humanitarian intervention has uncomfortably straddled the divide between ideal and nonideal moral theory. Though war itself can happen only in nonideal circumstances (mass killing, after all, being no one's ideal solution to a problem), moral debate on its humanitarian subspecies often relies on idealized assumptions about how intervening parties conduct themselves.[2] We assume, for example, that intervening parties in humanitarian conflict are willing to subject their soldiers to maximum justifiable risk in protecting civilians even though, in practice, political leaders are either uninterested in doing so or constrained by public opinion. Soldiers in humanitarian conflict are exposed to lower risk with the consequence that more civilians die, perhaps most prominently in the Kosovo intervention (a case we will examine in some detail). The "ought" of just war theory often does not take into account the "can" of political and military reality.

Avoiding the messy reality of war through simplifying assumptions may be justifiable as a means to get at basic moral truths, but it creates difficulties when we attempt to apply theory to real cases of humanitarian intervention. Since states do not often live up to our moral expectations, abstract discussion of the morality of war often does not sit well in the discussion of empirical cases. The aim of this section is to illustrate three ways the reality of humanitarian intervention falls short of three generally accepted standards. The failings examined here are not intended to be an exhaustive list of moral problems in the practice of humanitarian intervention. Rather, we are picking out three acute deficiencies related to states' unwillingness to risk their own soldiers because,

---

[1] Aside from the idea that humanitarian military intervention can ever be justified, of course—a view that we must assume rather than argue.

[2] John Rawls, *Law of Peoples* (Cambridge, MA: Harvard University Press, 2001), 89–94.

as will be shown in Section 3, the "lowering the threshold" case against drones depends on the assumption that drones make war more likely by lowering the risk of casualties to the side employing them.[3] Since drones have been used only in one comparatively recent case of intervention (the 2011 war in Libya) and this section is concerned with historical problems in intervention, discussion of the impact of drones themselves will necessarily be limited.

The first problem with the current conduct of intervention occurs at the *ad bellum* level: states often fail to intervene when it is justified. Understanding why this is morally problematic requires clarifying the character of the justification for humanitarian intervention, which could be understood in three ways. First, third-party states could be morally *obligated* to get involved in the conflict and hence to blame if they decide against intervention. Second, humanitarian intervention could be *supererogatory* in the sense that it would be morally good for third-party states to intervene but not morally required. Third, intervention could be justified but neither obligatory nor supererogatory, morally acceptable but not especially an improvement over the moral status quo. Since it is hard to imagine what a case fitting the third account would look like (for reasons that should become apparent by the end of this section), we will accept that in all cases where intervention is justified, it is either morally obligatory or supererogatory. Indeed, the literature on the moral status of intervention is divided along obligatory versus supererogatory lines.[4]

If intervention is either obligatory or supererogatory in any case where it is justified, a world in which intervention does not take place is morally worse than a world where it does. This conclusion trivially follows if intervention is obligatory, but it also holds if intervention is supererogatory. Even though no one is ever obligated to intervene on the supererogatory view, it would still be morally *better* if a state chose to intervene, meaning that a world of nonintervention is morally worse than a world where intervention takes place. A world of nonintervention is in an important sense a morally defective world: a morally important end, stopping significant human rights abuses, is not being accomplished. Thus, even on the most minimalist view of the justification of intervention, it would be a significant moral good if more justified interventions took place. Indeed, if the costs of going to war were lowered, what was supererogatory might become erogatory: lowering the costs to humanitarian war may take away one of the principal motivations (the harm to the intervening agent) for making it supererogatory.

---

[3] This assumes that the other existing problems are not so severe as to render the entirety of humanitarian intervention unjustifiable. Since we cannot address every critique of the practice of intervention, we will assume other problems do not reach that level of severity.

[4] See Cécile Fabre, "Mandatory Rescue Killings," *Journal of Political Philosophy* 15.4 (2007): 363–384.

Unfortunately, the reality is that states fail to intervene when they should with depressing frequency. Since 1990, the two clearest cases of genocide—Rwanda in 1994 and Darfur from 2003 to 2007—were not met with international intervention.[5] The same holds for persistent conflicts that, while not involving genocidal extermination campaigns, have still caused extraordinary suffering (the long-running violence in the Democratic Republic of the Congo being a clear example). Even in most cases where intervention takes place, as in Kosovo in 1999, mass atrocities are allowed to go on for some time before triggering foreign interventions.[6] So why do we fall short of our moral ideal?

One clear reason is reluctance on the part of advanced democracies (the only states with both the capabilities and desire to conduct a successful intervention) to risk their own troops for foreign lives. There are varied reasons for their casualty aversion. Some leaders believe they have moral responsibilities to their own soldiers' and nation's interests that preclude intervention. Even those with different moral views may feel politically constrained by the prevalence of conflicting beliefs among the public or other political factions. While there is substantial evidence that views of the morality of intervention are shifting, neither political leaders nor their citizens have become full-on moral cosmopolitans willing to weight the lives of their soldiers equally with those of foreigners.[7] For now, the risk of loss of life among intervening forces appears to be a serious deterrent to intervention.

The clearest example of this effect at work is the American response to the 1994 Rwandan genocide. In 1993, seventeen US troops were killed during Operation Restore Hope, a UN sponsored humanitarian intervention in Somalia. These deaths, dramatized by photographs of the soldiers' mutilated bodies, convinced the Bill Clinton Administration that the risks of humanitarian intervention outweighed the benefits, producing new administration doctrine that erected significant barriers to the use of American troops for humanitarian objectives.[8] As this backlash was taking place, the evidence that the members of the Hutu ethnic group were systematically exterminating rival Tutsis in Rwanda was becoming increasingly unequivocal. The commander

---

[5] This cutoff point of 1990 is nonarbitrary because (1) 1990–2000 saw more humanitarian interventions than any other ten-year period in history and (2) modern understandings of humanitarian intervention have shifted considerably in the post–Cold War period. See Martha Finnemore, *The Purpose of Humanitarian Intervention: Changing Beliefs about the Use of Force* (Ithaca, NY: Cornell University Press, 2003).

[6] Libya 2011 is a rare exceptive case where intervention was premised on the imminent risk of mass atrocities rather than evidence of ongoing atrocities.

[7] For evidence that views of the morality of intervention are shifting, see International Commission on Intervention and State Sovereignty (ICISS), *The Responsibility to Protect* (Ottawa: International Development Research Centre, 2001).

[8] Thomas G. Weiss, "Overcoming the Somalia Syndrome—Operation Rekindle Hope?" *Global Governance* 1 (1995): 289–298.

of the weak UN peacekeeping force on the ground, Canadian General Romeo Dallaire, conveyed a message to Washington that a comparatively small deployment of international combat troops could have prevented the lion's share of the killing. Yet, as Samantha Power documents in her authoritative *A Problem from Hell*, the Clinton Administration chose not only to do nothing but also to actively obstruct international action:

> President Clinton did not convene a single meeting of his senior foreign policy advisers to discuss U.S. options for Rwanda. His top aides rarely condemned the slaughter. The United States did not deploy its technical assets to jam Rwandan hate radio, and it did not lobby to have the genocidal Rwandan government's ambassador expelled from the United Nations. Those steps that the United States did take had deadly repercussions. Washington demanded the withdrawal of UN peacekeepers from Rwanda and then refused to authorize the deployment of UN reinforcements. Remembering Somalia and hearing no American demands for intervention, President Clinton and his advisers knew that the military and political risks of involving the United States in a bloody conflict in central Africa were great, yet there were no costs to avoiding Rwanda altogether. Thus, the United States again stood on the sidelines.[9]

Indeed, as Power shows, not only did the administration itself become gun-shy after Somalia, but also the Republican opposition hammered the Clinton Administration on it, creating legislative and political roadblocks that limited (although not totally removed) the administration's ability to get involved in Rwanda. The Somalia-caused casualty aversion in the US precluded an intervention against the clearest case of genocide since the end of the Cold War.

The current practice of humanitarian intervention, then, falls well short of our ideal, as states often fail to intervene when they could do a great deal of good. While casualty aversion likely does not fully explain every case of nonintervention, it clearly plays a significant and at least occasionally determinative role in policymakers' decision not to intervene.[10] Were there a means by which the risk to intervening forces could be dramatically lowered or even

---

[9] Samantha Power, *A Problem from Hell: America and the Age of Genocide* (New York: Harper Perennial, 2003), 335.

[10] Casualty aversion, of course, would not directly explain failing to use impersonal means, such as sanctions and jamming radios. However, there is some evidence the administration might have viewed these as the "thin end of the wedge" that would then inevitably lead to the deployment of personnel.

eliminated, it seems likely that in at least some cases states would launch justified interventions in cases that they otherwise might not.

Even when states do manage to overcome the myriad barriers to intervention, casualty aversion can still hamper their ability to conduct the fighting in accordance with a central *jus in bello* rule: the necessity of preserving noncombatant life. There is an enormous unresolved debate in the literature over whether and when civilians may be killed in pursuit of military objectives. However, much of this discussion is not relevant in the case of humanitarian intervention for the simple reason that the core military objective in humanitarian intervention *is* the protection of civilians. In other wars soldiers have to weigh the moral value of, say, defending an invaded province or defeating an opposing force, against the potential cost in civilian lives. In contrast, the sole end-goal of a humanitarian intervention is protecting civilians and minimizing the loss of civilian life. In humanitarian intervention, there is thus no moral conflict between objectives whose moral importance is set by diffuse and difficult-to-weigh values but rather an empirical one: what strategies and tactics permitted by other *in bello* principles most effectively minimize the loss of civilian life?[11]

One might object that the goal of humanitarian intervention is not to protect civilian life in a roughly consequentialist sense but rather to end an ongoing crime against humanity. On this view, genocide and ethnic cleansing may be so morally heinous that it would be acceptable for more civilians to die in the process of ending a genocide than the genocidaires themselves would have killed if left alone. This claim would rest on an underlying theory that there is something uniquely terrible about genocide and other mass killings over and above the loss of life they cause.

While we cannot fully refute this argument here, it strikes us (and most proponents of humanitarian intervention) as deeply implausible.[12] Even granting there is something particularly bad about intentional mass murder, it seems hard to imagine that it would follow from this that states could knowingly pursue a course of action that is likely to create more innocent victims than the genocide itself would. To refer to an earlier example, the idea that international forces would be justified in launching an intervention that would result in the

---

[11] This caveat is necessary to rule out repugnant conclusions like "intervening states should assist in mass slaughter if that will best minimize civilian casualties."

[12] Indeed, it seems so clear that humanitarian intervention is principally about saving lives that it is generally taken as an analytic truth. For a philosophical example, see Thomas Pogge, "Preempting Humanitarian Intervention," in Aleksander Jokic (ed.), *Humanitarian Intervention: Moral and Philosophical Issues* (Peterborough: Broadview Press, 2003); for a more practical example, see ICISS, *The Responsibility to Protect*, 37. The latter is the founding document of the Responsibility to Protect doctrine, the principal means by which humanitarian intervention is justified in political debate today.

deaths of 900,000 Tutsis to prevent the Hutus from killing 800,000 seems repugnant. Further, since the notion of intervention itself is usually justified on the basis of the rights of those being slaughtered, it is hard to see how the principle that "genocide must be stopped" better protects the rights of the victims than the idea that the goal of intervention is minimizing the loss of civilian life.[13] We will then assume that all interventions have as their goal bringing about the end to the conflict that best minimizes civilian loss of life as compared to possible alternatives while employing only strategies and tactics that accord with all relevant *jus in bello* rules.

What does this discussion have to do with casualty aversion? Simply put, casualty aversion can seriously hamper the intervening state's ability to minimize the loss of civilian life. When states grant significant weight to minimizing casualties, they are more likely to fight in ways that result in significant—and preventable—loss of civilian life. This problem can manifest in a number of concrete ways, two of which we will spotlight here. First, intervening militaries often rely heavily on airpower and other standoff weapons capable of striking from a safe distance. Though this is not intrinsically problematic, there is often a tradeoff between distance and accuracy: the higher planes fly, for example, the harder it can be for pilots to ensure their bombs don't unintentionally hit civilian targets. The intervening states' understandable desire to protect one's own soldiers, then, can directly result in civilian death. Second, casualty aversion in intervening states can prolong wars, and by extension their casualty count, by causing the intervener to adopt suboptimal strategies for ending the fighting. Oftentimes, the quickest way to defeat enemy forces involves putting one's own soldiers at risk through necessarily casualty-prone means like massive ground invasions. High-altitude airpower alone, or ground deployments that avoid serious engagement with enemy forces, may still be enough to end to the fighting, but the goal might not be accomplished nearly as quickly as it would in a world where intervening forces took on more risk. The longer the fighting goes on, the higher the civilian casualty count is likely to be.

The 1999 Kosovo intervention is the clearest example of these two dynamics at work. To halt the mass murder of ethnic Kosovars by Slobodan Milosevic's Serbian army, the North Atlantic Treaty Organization (NATO) committed airpower assets to support the Kosovo Liberation Army (KLA)'s effort to drive Serbian forces out of Kosovo. In planning the war, NATO committed to a "zero casualty" doctrine that elevated the absolute safety of NATO pilots to the level of a side constraint on NATO war making.[14] Steps taken to comply

---

[13] On the notion that intervention is usually justified on the basis of the rights of those being killed see, for example, Michael Walzer, *Just and Unjust Wars: A Moral Argument with Historical Illustrations* (New York: Basic Books 2000; original ed. 1977), 108.

[14] Steven T. Hosmer, *The Conflict over Kosovo: Why Milosevic Decided to Settle When He Did* (Santa Monica, CA: RAND Corporation, 2001), 133–134.

with the doctrine included, but were not limited to, establishing a 15,000 feet altitude for bombers and keeping NATO troops far away from direct combat. The 15,000 feet bombing height significantly impeded pilot ability to verify their targets, which appears to have had significant consequences: according to Human Rights Watch, more than half of civilian casualties of the bombing campaign were caused by hits on "illegitimate or questionable" targets.[15] The refusal to use ground troops may also have allowed Milosevic to get away with a significantly accelerated rate of killing in the territory he controlled. Finally, it is not at all clear that NATO airpower was the decisive factor in this defeat. As Jean Bethke Elshtain put it in her assessment of the Kosovo war:

> The Serbian army could operate with impunity without any worry of facing its opponents on the ground. In the meantime, there was plenty of "collateral damage" to civilians going on. Once we had exhausted the obvious military targets, we degraded the infrastructure on which civilian life depends—this despite a disclaimer from President Clinton that we had no quarrel with the Serbian people for they, like the Iraqis under Saddam, were victims. Because one cannot eliminate atrocities on the ground by dropping bombs from an altitude that keeps airplanes safely out of range of any possible ground fire, although the Serbians had almost no ability to fight back, our ends were tainted by our means—means that will surely haunt us in the future.[16]

It is possible that the "zero casualty" tactics Elshtain castigates may be defensible. On some moral views, leaders have obligations to protect their soldiers that require exposing civilians to greater risk. But the fact that the choice between soldier and civilian has to be made is a serious problem for the practice of humanitarian intervention. If the goal of an intervention is to save lives, the fact that an intervention may (rightly or wrongly) end up killing many of those it intends to save must be seen as a serious concern.

There is a clear connection between this problem and the basic justifiability of any given intervention in the first place. It is a commonly accepted *ad bellum* principle that any just war must have a reasonable probability of achieving its objectives.[17] If we are correct in saying the objective of intervention is protecting civilians, then any intervention that seems likely to result in the deaths of

---

[15] It is possible that some of these attacks were intentional rather than accidental. This cannot be known with certainty, but, given the UN war crimes prosecutor found insufficient evidence to even commission a formal investigation, it seems likely that targeting mistakes are the more likely explanation in the majority of cases.

[16] Jean Bethke Elshtain, "The Third Annual Grotius Lecture: Just War and Humanitarian Intervention," *American University International Law Review* 17:1 (2001): 17–18.

[17] Walzer, *Just and Unjust Wars*, 107; ICISS, *The Responsibility to Protect*, 37.

more civilians than it saves seems likely to fail to achieve its objectives. Thus, the *ad bellum* principle of "reasonable prospects," as the aforementioned is commonly referred to, requires any intervention to have a reasonable chance of limiting civilian life compared with the status quo for it to be justifiably launched in the first place.

If this account of reasonable prospects in humanitarian intervention is accurate, then the *in bello* casualty aversion problems previously discussed create a serious *ad bellum* concern about humanitarian intervention. Supposing casualty aversion does, as we have suggested, cause states to select strategies that prioritize the protection of their own soldiers at the expense of civilian life, then the chances that any given intervention manages to improve on the status quo for civilians decreases. If intervening states are willing to consider strategies oriented only around low-risk tactics like high-altitude bombing, then it may be that there is no strategy acceptable to potential intervening states that protects more civilians than it would cause to die. At the very least, the intervention would fail to maximally minimize civilian casualties. The value states place on protecting their own could make them incapable of effectively protecting others.

This third problem, together with the other two outlined, suggests that casualty aversion creates serious problems for the practice of humanitarian intervention. The desire to protect their own soldiers causes states to (1) fail to intervene when they should, (2) intervene using strategies that are likely to cause more harm to civilians than necessary, and (3) potentially fall prey to (2) to the extent that (1) may no longer be the case—that is, cases where intervention would be justified if states were to pursue the right strategies might not be justified in reality given the constraints imposed by casualty aversion. How drones can ameliorate all three problems will be the subject of the next section.

3. The Promise of Humanitarian Drones

Drones, we are often warned in severe tones, make war more likely. By lowering the costs, drones give states an incentive to fight wars that they might not otherwise. That is presumed to be a bad thing. However, as was made clear in the last section, sometimes the wars states do not fight are the ones they most ought to. Is there any chance that drones' supposed propensity to increase the likelihood of going to war might improve the flaws in the current practice of humanitarian intervention?

We will argue that, if we accept the internal logic of the lowering the threshold argument, the answer to that question is likely yes. Our argument will proceed by fully spelling out the almost always unstated premises at work in the threshold argument (as we will refer to it) and then showing that they imply drones could very well better or altogether solve all three of the problems with humanitarian intervention created by casualty aversion.

The basic structure of the threshold argument can take two forms: one fully empirical, merely describing the causal logic by which drones make war more likely; and another normative, which adds moral premises to arrive at the conclusion that the increase in the likelihood of war is a morally bad consequence of drone technology. The basic structure of the empirical argument, as applied to any given advance in drone technology or set of drone technologies, is as follows:

(P1) Development and use of drone system Y by state Z's military uniquely eliminates or significantly ameliorates negative consequence X (cost X, for short) of going to war.
(P2) The existence of cost X is both a necessary and sufficient condition to prevent state Z from initiating war in one or more imaginable cases.
(C1) State Z developing drone system Y for military use will cause it to go to war in one or more cases where it otherwise would not have.

Adding one premise gives the argument the desired normative force:

(P3) The war or wars in (C1) are likely, for reason R, to be unjust wars.
(C2) The development and use of drone system Y will cause state Z to launch unjust war(s) that it otherwise would not have, a morally bad outcome.

There are two important unclarities in this formulation. First, "cost X" is undefined. Without knowing what cost drones lessen, it is hard to evaluate whether that cost, in fact, deters states from going to war. Second, "reason R" is also undefined. This is critical, needless to say, because wars could be unjust in a variety of ways. One could imagine drones enabling unjust wars on either *jus ad bellum* or *jus in bello* grounds—that is, drones might cause states to launch wars that are necessarily unjust, or drones might alter their conduct in wars in such a way as to render otherwise justifiable wars entirely unjust. Thus, both cost X and reason R must be further specified to evaluate the validity of the threshold argument.

Cost X seems unlikely to be uniquely eliminated by a particular drone system unless it refers to *human* costs. Drones are different from other sorts of standoff weapons (like aircraft and artillery) not because they move humans further away from the enemy, but because they can remove humans from the battlefield altogether. The ability to fully replace humans in combat is the only *necessary* difference between drones and, say, better artillery, rifles, or manned aircraft. If the threshold argument is to be accepted without implausibly strong assumptions about the political, legal, or financial implications of nonexistent drone systems, then the argument must hinge on the one quality that qualitatively distinguishes drones from other sorts of military technology.[18] Thus, "cost X" must refer to the risk of human casualties; drones make war more likely by limiting the risk to which soldiers of casualty-averse states are exposed.

If we take the only distinguishing feature of drones to be their capability to remove humans from the battlefield, it follows that the reason drones make *unjust* wars more likely (reason R) must have something to do with this capability. Absent an assumption that making war more likely must mean making unjust war more likely, there must be something specific about the wars that drones make more likely that makes drone-fueled wars peculiarly likely to be unjust. Given that what distinguishes these wars from others is that that they would not have been launched without drones, it is likely that the unique property of drones, removing humans from the battlefield, must be the source of the propensity to being unjust. There could be a number of ways to concretize this claim—for example, it might be that leaders are more likely to go to war as a first rather than last resort without the threat of casualties or that soldiers removed from the battlefield are more likely to commit atrocities. For the moment, we will remain agnostic on the specific mechanism at work in reason R but take it to generally refer to the idea that removing soldiers from the battlefield makes unjust wars more likely.

We can now reconstruct the full argument with more clarity:

(P1) Development and use of drone system Y by state Z's military uniquely eliminates or significantly ameliorates the risk of state Z's soldiers being killed in war.

(P2) The risk of casualties removed by drone system Y is both a necessary and sufficient condition for keeping state Z from initiating war in one or more imaginable cases.

(C1) State Z developing drone system Y will cause it to go to war in cases where it otherwise would not have.

(P3) The war or wars that (C1) shows will be caused by drone system Y are likely, as a consequence of removing state Z's soldiers from the battlefield, to be unjust wars.

(C2) The development and use of drone system Y will cause state Z to launch unjust war(s) that it otherwise would not have, a morally bad outcome.

---

[18] It is generally assumed, however, that currently existing combat drones such as the Predator and Reaper systems are cheaper than manned equivalent, that is, (1) disputed among experts, and (2) not guaranteed to be the case with all drone systems.

With this argument in hand, we can now move to the central contention of this section: namely, last section's discussion of humanitarian intervention gives us reason to doubt (P3) and (C2) if we accept the rest of the threshold argument. If casualty aversion is a significant reason why humanitarian interventions are often either not launched when they ought to be or conducted poorly, then we may have significant reason to believe that drones make just humanitarian interventions more likely if we accept the logic of the threshold argument.

Our argument is purely internal to the logic of the threshold argument. It is possible, as some have argued, that proponents of the threshold argument are mistaken. There may never be drone systems that significantly lower the threshold to war. Our argument assumes, rather than accepts, the claim that drone technology will eventually reach that point. Thus, we will make only minimal references to existent or developing drone systems, as the aim of the argument is to critically examine the implications of a certain projection of the future rather than to advance our own positive view.

Recall the three problems for humanitarian intervention created by casualty aversion: (1) interventions do not get launched when they should; (2) once launched, strategic and tactical choices made to protect soldiers end up costing civilian lives; and (3) interventions may end up killing more than they save as a consequence of (2). If the threshold argument is empirically correct, it is quite simple to see how drones will solve problem (1): they take humans away from risk, eliminating the risk of casualties to the intervening state in an intervention to stop mass atrocities. The moral and political concerns with putting one's soldiers in the field are removed when you no longer have to put troops in the field, yet the pro-intervention argument—that mass killing is a moral evil that must be stopped—is no weaker. The development of more advanced drone systems thus shifts the decision calculus in favor of intervention, assuming asymmetric acquisition of drones.

This claim does not depend on the strong assumption that drones can remove humans entirely from the battlefield. Rather, the logic is linear: the riskier combat roles that drones can fill, the easier intervention becomes. Even if drones will always require on the ground support from humans, the less humans are exposed to risk, the lower the risk of human casualties. More to the point, since ours is an internal argument, the threshold argument *demands* the conclusion that drones make humanitarian intervention more likely even if there may be empirical reason to doubt drones can ever fully replace humans. If drones reduce risks to humans enough for the threshold argument to have force, it must follow that wars to which casualty aversion is a particularly important barrier (like humanitarian interventions) are among the most likely to be triggered by the threshold effect.

One might object that the level of casualties publics will accept in humanitarian intervention is significantly lower than in other wars and, hence, that marginally lowering the threshold is more likely to make nonhumanitarian wars more likely than to encourage humanitarian intervention. This is theoretically possible but, given the research on the causes of wars, improbable. Even if we grant that states are more willing to tolerate casualties in wars waged with self-interested rather than humanitarian goals in mind, it does not follow that lowering the threshold makes self-interested wars more likely. States often refrain from going to war for all sorts of reasons—for example, nuclear deterrence,[19] economic interdependence,[20] or shared democratic institutions.[21] There is little reason to suppose that lowering the casualty threshold would have much of an effect on these other barriers to war.

By contrast, the cases of intervention considered in this paper—Somalia, Rwanda, and Kosovo—demonstrate that policymakers willing in principle to conduct humanitarian intervention can be uniquely deterred by casualty aversion. The same US administration made the decision to intervene (or not) in all three cases. It is hard to point to any serious international, political, or financial deterrent that militated against intervention in Rwanda but allowed for it in both Somalia and Kosovo. Post-Somalia casualty aversion, and the "zero casualty" character of Kosovo, is the most coherent explanation for the differences between the cases. It seems that there is at least prima facie evidence that humanitarian interventions are more likely to be principally deterred by fear of casualties than other kinds of war.

This conclusion comports with what we know more broadly about humanitarian intervention. Most recent cases of wars explicitly billed as interventions involve strong, democratic states intervening against comparatively weak autocratic states or factions in anarchic "failed states"—in other words, cases where the intervener has overwhelming military superiority and hence can plausibly adopt casualty-averse strategies. By contrast, there has never been a case of humanitarian intervention where a state intervened against a foe with rough military parity certain to inflict heavy casualties to the intervening forces. This history suggests, again, that the decision to intervene on humanitarian grounds is much more sensitive to the risk of casualties on the part of the intervening state than other sorts of war.

This evidence is suggestive rather than conclusive. Proving conclusively that intervention is uniquely casualty sensitive is outside the scope of this paper. The goal of this brief discussion, rather, is to show that we have at least some

---

[19] Thomas Schelling, *The Diplomacy of Violence* (New Haven, CT: Yale University Press, 1964).

[20] Jack S. Levy and William R. Thompson, *Causes of War* (West Sussex: Wiley-Blackwell, 2010), 69–77.

[21] Bruce Russett, *Grasping the Democratic Peace* (Princeton, NJ: Princeton University Press, 1993).

reason to think that, if the next waves of drone technology lower the threshold to war, the most *likely* sort of war to be enabled is humanitarian war. At a minimum, we have no reason to believe drones are likely to lower the threshold only for nonhumanitarian wars. The empirical record gives no reason to doubt our conclusion about the logic of the threshold argument.

But how could we be sure that the humanitarian interventions drones enable will not be plagued by *in bello* strategy problems? If we have rightly identified the cause of those problems—casualty aversion—then the answer is simple: by taking over combat roles from humans, drones will allow generals and policymakers to select strategies oriented around minimizing civilian deaths rather than their own casualties. Drones that significantly lowered the threshold to war would have to significantly reduce the need for humans in risky combat roles. The risk to humans would otherwise still be too large for drones to significantly ameliorate the effect of casualty aversion on policymakers and military leaders. If drones are effective enough in combat that militaries are willing to use them in lieu of humans, then drones could be effectively deployed in humanitarian interventions, allowing for the development of a strategy for protecting civilians with fewer constraints imposed by the risk of human casualties. Problems like the zero casualty doctrine would be resolved.

One does not have to imagine future drone systems to evidence this claim. The unmanned combat aerial vehicles (UCAVs) currently in use, most prominently Predator and Reaper drones, have already demonstrated their utility for humanitarian intervention in Libya. Military journalist Tom Ricks details the reasons:

> We have seen Qaddafi's forces adapting to the presence of NATO aircraft overhead, for example, moving from tanks to pickup trucks. So closer observation is needed before striking. That requires getting down low, but that can sucker a NATO aircraft into getting hit. Drones are a good answer to this tactical problem. Likewise, they can get down under clouds in bad weather, taking away from Qaddafi's goods [sic] the advantage of attacking under overcasts. Plus, drones can "loiter" over a target, which helps both with observation and deterrence.[22]

On Ricks's telling, UCAVs are well suited both for distinguishing between enemies and civilians and engaging ground troops in ways that might risk the lives of pilots in manned aircraft. These are precisely the two tactical roles in which manned aircraft were ineffectively (from the standpoint of civilian

---

[22] Tom Ricks, "A Rare Disagreement with Ignatius, on the Deployment of Armed Predators to Libya," *Best Defense*, April 22, 2011. http://ricks.foreignpolicy.com/posts/2011/04/22/a_rare_disagreement_with_ignatius_on_the_deployment_of_armed_predators_to_libya.

protection) deployed in Kosovo and other interventions. Though a comparatively miniscule number of drones were used in Libya, they were deployed to
"hit targets that are close to civilians or inside dense urban areas."[23] Militaries
thus not only already recognize UCAV effectiveness in minimizing civilian
casualties but also have already started employing them toward this end. As
UCAV technology improves, it has the potential to significantly improve the
conduct of the airpower-heavy interventions we see today.

It is true that drones employed to assassinate suspected al Qaeda targets
in Pakistan, Afghanistan, and Yemen have been associated with considerable
civilian casualties. Might not this be a similar problem in humanitarian intervention? There are several responses. First, drones will presumably not conduct
"signature strikes," the attacks on potential terrorists identified only by patterns of behavior (rather than specific target intelligence) that appear to cause
many of the unintended casualties in the US counterterrorism campaign.[24]
Second, no intervention is without costs, and we must compare the costs of
this strategy to others available, such as the use of conventional bombing or
ground troop deployment. Third, drones would be used for different purposes,
given that the goal of the campaign is to protect civilians rather than kill terrorist leaders. Military leaders would thus be incentivized to avoid, rather than
risk, civilian death as a consequence of their mission.

The utility of drones for humanitarian intervention will by no means be limited to UCAVs. The threshold argument, of course, must assume significantly
more advanced drone technology than what we have already have if it is to be
seen as an argument against expanding drone technology. In all likelihood,
the systems that would significantly lower the threshold are not UCAVs—they
are ground drones (or unmanned combat ground vehicles [UCGVs]). Not only
are UCGVs increasingly feasible technologically (in fact, one of the first models was deployed to Iraq as early as 2007), but they are also the most plausible
means of lowering the threshold.[25] Ground troops make up by far the largest
percentage of casualties in the past seventy years of warfare. Even in World
War II, which saw the most sustained aerial and naval engagements of the
modern era, deaths on the ground overwhelmingly outnumbered those in the
air or at sea. Unless one can make a case that reducing the risk of aerial and
naval casualties alone will lower the threshold, which seems unlikely given

[23] Julian Barnes and Charles Levinson, "US Drones Hit Targets in Libya," *Wall Street Journal*,
April 25, 2011. http://online.wsj.com/article/SB10001424052748704489604576282703009692
640.html.

[24] Adam Entous, Siobhan Gorman, and Julian Barnes, "U.S. Tightens Drone Rules," *Wall Street
Journal*, November 4, 2011. http://online.wsj.com/article/SB10001424052970204621904577013
982672973836.html.

[25] Noah Shachtman, "First Armed Robots on Patrol in Iraq (Updated)," *Wired Online*, August 2,
2007, http://www.wired.com/dangerroom/2007/08/httpwwwnational/.

both (1) the aforementioned casualty distributions among service branches and (2) the particularly troop-intensive character of recent wars, then it seems like some form of ground drones are necessary for the threshold to going to war to be meaningfully lowered.

Drones capable of operating like conventional infantry and tanks could immensely improve intervention. Research on the use of airpower suggests that bombing can be highly effective in shifting the military balance in favor of a ground force but oftentimes cannot succeed alone.[26] The interventions discussed already where airpower was the principal military instrument employed by the intervener—Kosovo and Libya, most prominently—relied heavily on local ground forces to accomplish their objectives. Of course, not all victims of genocide or ethnic cleansing campaigns have their own ground force, let alone one strong enough to protect civilian populations even with air support from international forces. Intervening states' casualty-averse reticence to deploy significant ground forces, then, makes interventions less likely to protect civilian life. If drones replace humans in most or all significant ground combat roles, this problem could be fixed.

Ground drones' advantages extend beyond the superior efficacy of fighting on the ground. Commanding generals would be free to devise strategies with comparatively little weight given to their own losses. If, for example, civilians would be best protected by heavy deployments to ambush-prone jungles or by block-to-block city street fights, military leaders would be free to engage in either without concern for their own losses. This suggestion is not errant speculation—militaries are already open to the idea of using drones to replace humans in combat-intensive humanitarian interventions. The Project on National Security Reform, a 2008 blue-ribbon American panel reporting directly to the president, envisioned a future of drone-dominated humanitarian intervention into high-intensity combat zones in one of its scenarios for the future of American warfare in 2040.[27]

Using drones in this fashion could also improve intelligence gathering, enabling more precise targeting. Though it may be difficult for armies to find trained soldiers with language and cultural competencies to deploy in risky zones, it would be easier to find experts who could observe from remote drone operating bases. Drones equipped with cameras or voice-over-internet software (à la Skype or Google Voice) would allow experts to remotely translate relevant conversations and otherwise help separate legitimate targets from

---

[26] Robert Pape, *Bombing To Win: Air Power and Coercion in War*, Ithaca and London: Cornell University Press, 1996.

[27] Chris Waycoff and Matthew Russell, "The Nine Post-Reform Scenarios," in Sheila R. Ronis (ed.), *Project on National Security Reform Vision Working Group Report and Scenarios* (Carlisle: Strategic Studies Institute, 2010), 54–57.

noncombatants. Ground drones, then, could reduce the risks to civilian life created by bad intelligence about whom to target.

This section has shown three things. First, the argument that drones make war more likely by lowering the cost of going to war (the "threshold" argument) makes little conceptual sense unless the cost being lowered is the cost in human lives. Second, it is possible that improved drone technology will increase the likelihood of humanitarian interventions as opposed to other kinds of war. Third, humanitarian intervention will be morally improved by the use of drones (according to the metrics set up in Section 2) because (1) intervention will be more likely in cases where it is appropriate and (2) drones improve the conduct of intervention by lowering the risk that generals will develop plans oriented around protecting their own troops rather than saving civilian life. The next section will address several potential objections raised to these arguments.

4. Singer's Objections

P. W. Singer's *Wired for War* is the both the most comprehensive and popular book to date on military robotics. In it, he very briefly touches on the technology's implications for humanitarian intervention, noting some of the potential advantages of the technology mentioned here but principally raising serious qualms about its use. His treatment is brief. His first objection presents an epistemic skepticism about the efficacy of humanitarian intervention that we will consider in our conclusion (it is itself only two sentences long). This section will first expand on, and then rebut, Singer's critique of the use of drones in humanitarian war.

Singer's greatest concern is that drone-driven war undermines the democratic legitimacy of even the best wars. For Singer, wars waged by democratic states are morally justified only if they have been approved by legitimate legal channels and with significant public input. Otherwise, "the already tenuous link between the public and its foreign and defense policy, the whole idea of a democratic process and citizenship is perverted."[28] Making war costless takes the public out of the loop by giving it no reason to care about the decision to go to war. This effect takes away the public's crucial role in deliberating about and then consenting to the decision to start a war, rendering the war necessarily unjust. Thus, even the most just interventions are illegitimate if they are waged principally with drones that eliminate the costs to the intervening (democratic) state.

Singer appears to be relying on a supercharged version of the standard "right authority" *ad bellum* principle. Broadly, right authority holds that only

[28] P. W. Singer, *Wired for War* (New York: Penguin Books, 2009), 323.

militaries given a certain sort of authoritative approval to fight may wage war permissibly. For militaries attached to states, this authorization usually must come from domestic legal codes or the United Nations. In the American domestic context, for example, right authority could be conferred by a congressional declaration of war or compliance with the War Powers Act, which specifies the conditions under which the president may deploy force without an explicit congressional declaration.

Singer appears to want to modify the standard understanding of right authority to extend beyond compliance with formal legal statutes to a broader public deliberative standard. On the standard view, it does not matter how invested the public is in any given decision to go to war so long as proper *formal* legal authority for war exists. For Singer, this is not enough. War must, in his view, be authorized by deep involvement by the public writ large in the decision to go to war:

> Wars without costs can undermine the morality of even "good" wars. When a nation decides to go to war, it is not just deciding to break stuff in some foreign land. As one philosopher puts it, the very decision is "a reflection of the moral character of the community who decides." Without public debate and support and without risking troops, though, the decision of war may only reflect a nation that doesn't give a damn.[29]

Call this view *substantive* right authority, understood as the principle that a certain threshold of public attention, deliberation, and buy-in is, in addition to formal legal authorization, necessary to confer right authority on a war. Because drones take troops out of combat, they remove the public interest and buy-in created by the risk to soldiers, rendering any subsequent war illegitimate.

Some version of substantive right authority may be an improvement over formal right authority, but any variant strong enough to rule out the use of drones in humanitarian warfare entirely is almost certainly wrong. First, it is morally bizarre to include the requirement that "soldiers' lives must be at risk" as a necessary component of right authority. This principle would require states to unnecessarily sacrifice the lives of their soldiers solely to get across the point that war involves people dying to its other citizens. Take the following example: state A has the military capability to prevent the genocide of people B. It can do so by either (1) deploying a traditional infantry brigade with air support, which would result in the deaths of 400 of A's soldiers and 400,000 of B's civilians, or (2) deploying an all-drone brigade that precludes any casualties on A's part and results in the deaths of only 20,000 of B's civilians. Because right authority

[29] Ibid.

is a deontological principle (if it is not satisfied, a war is necessarily unjust), accepting substantive right authority would imply that option (1) might be justified whereas option (2) never could be. This seems on-face perverse. For what reason could it conceivably be morally acceptable to get soldiers and civilians killed to improve the quality of public discourse about war?

Suppose the "risking soldiers" requirement was removed, and substantive right authority was concerned only by the fact that drones diminish the public's awareness and concern with military affairs. Formulated in this fashion, the principle is extraordinarily broad—hallmarks of modern armies like all-volunteer militaries, cruise missiles, and stealth aircraft all lower the population's awareness of war by lowering the risks associated with war. Arguments identical to Singer's have been made about such things. But surely substantive right authority could not in principle rule out going to war using any of these technologies. Why do drones cross the line?

Singer might object that the very thesis argued for here—the casualty aversion/threshold argument about intervention—proves that there is something unique about drones in terms of lowering public investment in war. However, saying that drones make war more likely by lowering casualty counts is not the same thing as saying they coarsen public discourse or lessen interest in military affairs. Given that Western states have launched zero casualty wars in Kosovo and Libya, one of two conclusions is inescapable: either current technology already has already fatally weakened public debate about war, or else something other than the risk of casualties in a war is the key factor in determining the appropriate level of public involvement by the standards of Singer's substantive right authority principle. In either case, there is little reason to see anything uniquely problematic about drones. There is, at best, very weak evidence to suggest the damage done to public debate is enough to outweigh the immense amount of harm drones could preclude. What is the problem is public participation in democratic deliberation, not drones.

Singer's other theoretical argument is hard to take as seriously. He writes:

> Even if the nation acts on a just cause, such as the motivation to stop genocide, war can be viewed as merely an act of selfish charity. One side has the wealth to afford high technologies and the other does not. The only message of "moral character" a nation sends out is that it alone gets the right to stop bad things, but only at the time and place of its choosing, and, most important, only if the costs are low enough. While the people on the ground being saved may well be grateful, even they will see a crude calculation that cheapens their lives.[30]

---

[30] Ibid.

It is hard to see what sort of moral principle is being appealed to here. Humanitarian intervention is not, or at least should not be, about sending out "moral messages;" it should be about saving the lives of people in dire need. It strains credulity that any victim of any genocide would care enough about the species of their savior to make them prefer to be murdered. While one might construe Singer's argument as a criticism of the motivations behind a drone intervention, even he admits that a "selfish charity" (itself a nigh-oxymoronic term) intervention is still conducted for altruistic reasons. This position, rather than appearing to be a truncated version of a complex moral argument, is simply mystifying.

Singer's final worry—rooted in a skepticism that any war can be conducted without significant unintended consequences for the people it is ostensibly protecting—taps into a broader truth about the debate over drones. Given that the most advanced drone technologies are still yet to be developed, any discussion over the implications of their development, moral or otherwise, is still in a certain sense speculation. We cannot know anything about the future of drone technology with certainty, other than the fact that the technology is advancing at an astonishing pace.

However, by critically examining our theories about the future of drone warfare, we prepare ourselves for a confusing ethical future. This was the goal of our argument in this chapter. We have attempted to identify various ways drones could be used to make more and more effective humanitarian interventions. We have not evaluated in detail the risk that they will cause more unjust war or be deployed for other immoral means. We have not attempted an overall evaluation of their development. What we have attempted to show is that the simple argument that drones lower the threshold for war can have advantages in humanitarian conflict. When, where, and how drones could ethically be deployed will depend on the details of their capacities and limitations and the nature of any specific conflict.

7

Counting the Dead: The Proportionality of Predation in Pakistan

AVERY PLAW

1. Introduction

Between June 2004 and the end of 2011, the Central Intelligence Agency is widely reported to have carried out about 300 covert drone strikes in Northwest Pakistan that have killed more than 2000 people, some of whom were civilians.[1] Not surprisingly, these strikes have been harshly criticized. One important charge is that the strikes have resulted in elevated and even disproportionate numbers of civilian deaths—the latter term connoting a breach of the international law of armed conflict (ILOAC), which requires that military operations be planned to avoid disproportionate civilian harm. Senior US officials, by contrast, have claimed that civilian casualties have been low. They have also argued that the strikes are compliant with ILOAC, including the proportionality requirement. This chapter explores the proportionality of the civilian casualties of drone strikes, drawing on a range of sources including the four most rigorous and transparent databases tracking the impact of the drone strikes.

This question of the proportionality of drone strikes is an especially important one because it goes straight to the legality and morality of a tactic that has become increasingly central to the US counterterrorism strategy, especially under President Barack Obama. Since his inauguration, Obama has overseen more than five times the total number of strikes carried out during President George W. Bush's two terms in office. Such drone strikes are also credited with having eliminated more than half of al Qaeda's senior leadership.

In this chapter I argue that the best available empirical evidence suggests that drones strikes have resulted in a comparatively moderate to low rate of civilian casualties and that their accuracy appears to have significantly improved over the last two years. While this does not entail that all US operations have

---

[1] I would like to thank Matthew S. Fricker, Carlos Colon, and Aaron Cardoso for their assistance in researching this chapter.

complied with the requirement of proportionality, it does suggest that violations have not been very widespread or systematic.[2] Consequently, the issue of
proportionality does not appear to provide a basis for claiming that US drone
strikes in general are either unethical or illegal (although this does not preclude such claims on other grounds).

That said, a couple of reservations are in order. First, these conclusions
should be regarded as no more than provisional. Although the data used in this
chapter are the best available, it still suffers from a degree of uncertainty due
to the nature of reporting in the Federally Administered Tribal Areas (FATA) of
Pakistan. Second, this chapter does not support all the claims advanced by US
officials. In particular, it shows that some of their claims about the accuracy of
the drone strikes are exaggerated.

2. The Drone Debate

Charges that the Central Intelligence Agency (CIA) drone campaign has killed
an excessive number of civilians have emanated from a number of quarters. The Pakistani press has been particularly outspoken. The following are
only a few prominent examples.[3] On March 11, 2011, the *Pakistan Observer*
reported, "The US drones or the predator planes which have been on the killing spree in Pakistan's northern belt since August 2008 and have so far killed
over fourteen hundreds people with the big majority as the innocent civilians
(as admitted by the international watch dogs) . . . have paced up attacks after a
relative pause of a month or so [sic]."[4] A March 26, 2011, report in Pakistan's
the *Nation* insisted that "there is mounting evidence that those killed are
ordinary Pakistani citizens, and the Al-Qaeda masterminds thus killed are
few and far between."[5] Along similar lines another Pakistani daily, *Dawn*,
reported in January 2010 that "of the 44 predator strikes carried out by US
drones in the tribal areas of Pakistan over the past 12 months, only five were
able to hit their actual targets, killing five key Al-Qaeda and Taliban leaders,

[2] In particular, civilian casualty counts aggregate effects across time, whereas the legal and
ethical requirement for proportionality is calculated on an operation-by-operation basis. So a low
overall casualty count does not preclude the possibility that some specific operation may have
violated the proportionality requirement. But it does suggest that the number of operations that
have done so is probably relatively small.

[3] The following examples are drawn from Avery Plaw, Matt Fricker, and Brian Glynn Williams,
"Practice Makes Perfect? The Changing Civilian Toll of CIA Drone Strikes in Pakistan," *Perspectives
on Terrorism* 5 (2011): 5–6, 57–58.

[4] Tariq Saeed, "Drone Strikes Kill 6 in NWA," *Pakistan Observer*, March 12, 2011. http://pako-
bserver.net/detailnews.asp?id=80509.

[5] "Ending Drone Attacks," *Nation*, March 26, 2011. http://www.nation.com.pk/
pakistan-news-newspaper-daily-english-online/editorials/26-Mar-2011/Ending-drone-attacks.

but at the cost of over 700 innocent lives. . . . For each Al-Qaeda and Taliban terrorist killed by US drones, 140 innocent Pakistanis also had to die."[6] In April 2009 the Pakistani daily the *News* published an article by terrorism expert Amir Mir reporting that Predator strikes had killed only fourteen high-value al Qaeda targets but were responsible for 687 civilian casualties (that is, 98% of total casualties).[7] On February 1, 2010, Mir added that in January 2010 alone 123 Pakistani civilians had been killed in ten errant CIA drone strikes, while only three al Qaeda targets had been eliminated (a civilian casualty rate of 97.6%).[8]

Similar charges appear regularly in the Western press in both newspapers and professional journals. For example, a July 27, 2011, report in the *Guardian* disputes claims that there have been few civilian victims of the drone strikes, quoting a local Pakistani source as follows: "For every 10 to 15 people killed, maybe they get one militant."[9] Similar claims appear in professional journals. For example, in an article titled "Death from Above: UAVs and Losing Hearts and Minds," in the May–June 2011 issue of *Military Review* (a publication of the United States Army Combined Arms Center), Dr. Jeffrey A. Sluka argued that "The drone strikes have already caused well over a thousand civilian casualties, have had a particular affinity for hitting weddings and funerals, and appear to be seriously fueling the insurgency."[10] A May 2009 *New York Times* editorial titled "Death from Above, Outrage from Below," written by David Kilcullen (a former senior counterterrorism adviser to General David Petraeus) and Andrew Exum (who served as an Army Ranger in Iraq and Afghanistan) has been especially influential. Kilcullen and Exum argued forcefully for "a moratorium on drone strikes into Pakistan" in part because this tactic "often kills more civilians than militants" and stokes "public anger" against a "faceless

---

[6] "Over 700 Killed in 44 Drone Strikes in 2009," *Dawn*, January 2, 2010. http://archives.dawn.com/archives/144960.

[7] Amir Mir, "60 Drone Hits Kill 14 Al-Qaeda Men, 687 Civilians," *News*, April 10, 2009; see also Brian Williams, "Pakistani Responses to the CIA's Predator Drone Campaign and Al Qaeda and the Taliban," *Terrorism Monitor* 8.7 (2009): 3–5.

[8] Amir Mir, "US Drones Killed 123 Civilians, 3 al-Qaeda Men in January," *News*, February 1, 2010. http://www.infowars.com/us-drones-killed-123-civilians-three-al-qaeda-men-in-january/.

[9] Saeed Shaw and Peter Beaumont, "US Drone Attacks in Pakistan Claiming Many Civilian Lives, Says Campaigner," *Guardian*, July 17, 2011. http://www.guardian.co.uk/world/2011/jul/17/us-drone-strikes-pakistan-waziristan; see also George Monbiot, "With Its Deadly Drones the U.S. Is Fighting a Coward's War," *Guardian*, January 30, 2012. http://www.guardian.co.uk/commentisfree/2012/jan/30/deadly-drones-us-cowards-war.

[10] Jeffrey A. Sluka, "Death from Above: UAVs and Losing Hearts and Minds," *Military Review*, May–June 2011. http://usacac.army.mil/CAC2/MilitaryReview/Archives/English/MilitaryReview_20110630_art012.pdf.

enemy" that is "blowing up people's houses from the air." In particular, Kilcullen and Exum cite the following statistics:

> Press reports suggest that over the last three years drone strikes have killed about 14 terrorist leaders. But, according to Pakistani sources, they have also killed some 700 civilians. This is 50 civilians for every militant killed, a hit rate of 2 percent—hardly "precision."[11]

While allowing that these reports may slightly exaggerate civilian casualties, Kilcullen and Exum stress that "every one of these dead noncombatants represents an alienated family, a new desire for revenge, and more recruits for a militant movement that has grown exponentially even as drone strikes have increased." Kilcullen also advanced these arguments in congressional testimony, in his book *The Accidental Guerilla*, and in a high-profile report for the Center for New American Security.[12]

Legal critics of the drone campaign have drawn on the numbers disseminated by Kilcullen and Pakistani sources to charge that drone strikes violate ILOAC. Probably the most persistent and influential of these critics is Mary Ellen O'Connell, the Robert and Marion Short Professor of Law at Notre Dame Law School. O'Connell has repeatedly charged that the CIA drone strikes violate the central ILOAC principle of proportionality. In testimony before Congress in April 2010, for example, she argued that of the many ways that the CIA drone strikes in Pakistan violate the laws of war, "most serious of all, perhaps, is the disproportionate impact of drone attacks."[13] In a paper titled "Unlawful Killing with Combat Drones: A Case Study of Pakistan, 2004–2009," circulated in 2009 and due to be published in 2012, she quoted Kilcullen at length and infers that CIA drone attacks in Pakistan have resulted in "the disproportionate loss of civilian lives.... Fifty civilians killed for one intended target is a disproportionate result by anyone's calculation." Indeed, she argues that this illegal outcome was inevitable given the environment and the weapons being used: "In Western Pakistan missile strikes are inevitably going to kill far more unintended than

---

[11] David Kilcullen and Andrew Exum, "Death from Above, Outrage from Below," *New York Times*, May 16, 2009. http://www.nytimes.com/2009/05/17/opinion/17exum. html?pagewanted=all&_r=0.

[12] David Kilcullen, *The Accidental Guerilla* (New York: Oxford University Press, 2009), 230–232; Andrew Exum, Nathaniel Fick, Ahmed Humayun, and David Kilcullen, "Triage: The Next Twelve Months in Afghanistan and Pakistan," Center for a New American Security, June 2009, 18. http://www.cnas.org/files/documents/publications/ExumFickHumayun_TriageAfPak_June09.pdf.

[13] Mary Ellen O'Connell, "Lawful Use of Combat Drones," Testimony before the House of Representatives Subcommittee on National Security and Foreign Affairs, April 28, 2010, 5. http://www.fas.org/irp/congress/2010_hr/042810oconnell.pdf.

intended targets."[14] In another paper titled "Drones under International Law," which appeared in October 2010 as part of the Whitney R. Harris World Law Institutes International Debate Series, O'Connell again cites Kilcullen's testimony and argues as follows:

> Most strikes are associated with one person's name. Yet, every strike kills a number of persons. It is difficult to make the argument that killing 30, 12, or even six persons is proportional in the killing of one person.... So in conclusion, we see that U.S. use of drones is failing the relevant tests of the lawful use of force. It is failing... under the principle of proportionality.[15]

For O'Connell and some other leading scholars of international law, the implication is clear. O'Connell ended her article by approvingly quoting the following assessment from Kenneth Anderson, professor of law at the American University's Washington Law School: "the international law community does not accept targeted killings even against al Qaeda... [A] strategic centerpiece of U.S. counterterrorism policy rests upon legal grounds regarded as deeply illegal... by large and influential parts of the international community."[16]

By contrast, US officials have argued that in conducting drone strikes the CIA rigorously adheres to ILOAC standards including proportionality. For example, in the most extensive official comment on drone strikes to date (albeit it does not mention Pakistan by name), Harold Koh, a legal adviser to the State Department, argued on March 26, 2010:

> In my experience, the principles of distinction and proportionality that the United States applies are not just recited at meetings. They are implemented rigorously throughout the planning and execution of lethal operations to ensure that such operations are conducted in accordance with all applicable law.[17]

US officials have also been unofficially claiming for several years that the effects of the strikes have been very accurate and proportional. For

---

[14] Mary Ellen O'Connell, "Unlawful Killing with Combat Drones: A Case Study of Pakistan, 2004–2009," Notre Dame Law School Legal Studies Research Paper 09–43, 20. https://webspace.utexas.edu/rmc2289/LT/Mary%20Ellen%20OConnell%20on%20Drones.pdf.

[15] Mary Ellen O'Connell, "Drones under International Law," Whitney R. Harris World Law Institute, October 8, 2010, 8. http://law.wustl.edu/harris/documents/OConnellFullRemarksNov23.pdf.

[16] Ibid., 8–9.

[17] Harold Koh, "The Obama Administration and International Law," speech at the American Society for International law. http://www.state.gov/s/l/releases/remarks/139119.htm.

example, in an article in *Foreign Affairs* in July–August 2011, Peter Bergen and Katherine Tiedemann report US government representatives claiming that between May 2008 and May 2010 the drone program produced "fewer than 30 civilian deaths."[18] In an earlier article in *Foreign Policy* in April 2010, the same authors reference a US official in December claiming that "just over 20" civilians had been killed in the prior two years while "more than 400" fighters had been eliminated, a ratio of just under twenty militants killed per civilian killed.[19] Similarly, a July 22, 2010, BBC story reported a senior US official claiming that under Obama 650 militants had been killed compared with about twenty civilians—a ratio of militant to civilian casualties of 32.5 to 1.[20]

US officials' claims concerning the accuracy of drone strikes have recently become bolder. In an article published on Bloomberg on January 31, 2011, an unnamed US official is reported to have claimed that "the 75 strikes launched in the ungoverned tribal region since the drone program accelerated in mid-August have killed several hundred militants without causing any deaths among civilian non-combatants"—that is, without any collateral casualties whatsoever.[21] Similarly, John Brennan, the US deputy national security adviser for Homeland Security and Counterterrorism and Obama's chief adviser on counterterrorism, recently stated:

> One of the things President Obama has insisted on is that we're exceptionally precise and surgical in terms of addressing the terrorist threat. And by that I mean, if there are terrorists who are within an area where there are women and children or others, you know, we do not take such action that might put those innocent men, women, and children in danger. In fact I can say that the types of operations that the US has been involved in, in the counter-terrorism realm, that nearly for the past year there hasn't been a single collateral death

---

[18] Peter Bergen and Katherine Tiedemann, "Washington's Phantom War: The Effects of the U.S. Drone Program in Pakistan," *Foreign Affairs*, July–August 2011, 13.

[19] Peter Bergen and Katherine Tiedemann, "The Year of the Drone: an Analysis of U.S. Drone Strikes in Pakistan 2004–2010," *Foreign Policy*, April 26, 2010. http://www.foreignpolicy.com/articles/2010/04/26/the_year_of_the_drone; original article Scott Shane, "CIA to Expand use of Drones in Pakistan," *New York Times*, December 3, 2009. http://www.nytimes.com/2009/12/04/world/asia/04drones.html?pagewanted=all.

[20] Aleem Maqbool, "Mapping US Drone and Islamic Militant Attacks in Pakistan," *BBC News South Asia*, July 22, 2010. http://www.bbc.co.uk/news/world-south-asia-10728844; Ken Dilanian, "CIA Drones May Be Avoiding Pakistani Civilians," *Los Angeles Times*, February 22, 2011. http://articles.latimes.com/2011/feb/22/world/la-fg-drone-strikes-20110222.

[21] Tony Cappacio and Jeff Bliss, "U.S. Said to Reduce Civilian Deaths after Increasing CIA Pakistan Strikes," *Bloomberg*, January 31, 2011. http://www.bloomberg.com/news/2011-01-31/u-s-said-to-reduce-civilian-deaths-after-increasing-cia-pakistan-strikes.html.

because of the exceptional proficiency, precision of the capabilities that we've been able to develop.[22]

Brennan made this claim on June 29, 2011, so his assertion that there have been no civilian casualties resulting from US counterterrorism operations in almost a year would extend back from that day to close to the middle of 2010.

The president himself also recently chimed in on this issue, albeit in notably more cautious language. In a forum on Google+ on January 30, 2012, Obama answered questions from six selected citizens, including one on the prudence and legitimacy of CIA drone strikes in Pakistan. The president answered the question with unusual directness, given that the strikes in Pakistan are covert operations that the government has avoided officially acknowledging. He acceded that "a lot of these strikes have been in the FATA."[23] In defense of the policy, he pointed out that the only people targeted were "people who are on a list of active terrorists." Moreover, many of these are "al-Qaeda suspects who are up in very tough terrain along the border between Afghanistan and Pakistan," and "for us to be able to get them in another way would involve probably a lot more intrusive military action than the ones we're already engaging in." Finally, and most importantly for present purposes, Obama insisted that drones had "not caused a huge number of civilian casualties," adding that it was "important for everybody to understand that this thing is kept on a very tight leash."[24]

The defenses of the drone program and its accuracy advanced by US officials have also received corroboration from respected scholars who have independently researched the campaign's impact. C. Christine Fair, for example, professor at Georgetown University and an expert on Pakistan who has researched the strikes, characterized them as "the product of meticulous planning among lawyers, intelligence officers, and others who scrupulously and independently confirm information about potential enemies, working to establish a rigorous 'pattern of life' to minimize the deaths of innocents." She argued that the strikes "are usually accomplished with minimal civilian deaths" and described the statistics on which critics like Kilcullen and O'Connell base their arguments as "simply bogus."[25]

There is clearly an important debate here with serious implications for US counterterrorism policy in Central Asia, which in turn sets a precedent for the security policies of other countries. Are CIA drone strikes producing large and

[22] "Obama Administration Counter-Terrorism Strategy." C-Span. June 29, 2011, available at http://www.c-spanvideo.org/program/AdministrationCo (accessed October 14, 2011).

[23] "Obama Defends US Drone Strikes in Pakistan," *BBC News*, January 31, 2012, available at http://www.bbc.co.uk/news/mobile/world-us-canada-16804247 (accessed February 25, 2012).

[24] "Obama Defends US Drone Strikes in Pakistan," *BBC News*.

[25] C. Christine Fair, "Drone Wars," *Foreign Policy*, May 28, 2010. http://www.foreignpolicy.com/articles/2010/05/28/drone_wars?page=0,0.

perhaps disproportionate numbers of civilian casualties? This chapter moves toward a resolution of this question through an investigation of the most rigorous independent databases tracking the drone strikes. It focuses primarily on the issue of proportionality because it is not otherwise obvious exactly what kind of standard could be used to measure whether the number of civilian casualties are excessive (i.e., compared with what?) or exactly what such a determination would entail. By contrast, proportionality provides a standard of assessment (however awkward) and carries well-established legal and ethical implications.

3. The Proportionality Calculus

The principle of proportionality is an especially important standard against which to measure the CIA drone strikes because it is a core requirement of contemporary ILOAC as well as of just war theory (JWT), the most prevalent ethical framework for evaluating the conduct of war.[26] Both JWT and ILOAC allow that it is unreasonable to expect that civilians will never be killed in the conduct of armed conflict. Therefore, they seek not to prohibit civilian harms entirely but rather to minimize unnecessary harm. The degree of civilian harm that may be justified in both JWT and ILOAC is regulated by the principle of proportionality. The principle is articulated, for example, in the Statute of the International Criminal Court, which prohibits the following:

> Intentionally launching an attack in the knowledge that such an attack will cause incidental loss of life or injury to civilians or damage civilian objects...which would be clearly excessive in relation to the concrete and direct overall military advantage anticipated. (8(2)(b)(4), see also the First Additional Protocol to the Geneva Conventions, 51(5)(b) and 57(2)(iii) and (iv))

Such a prohibited attack would constitute a war crime under the ICC statute.[27]

In the recent omnibus study of *Customary International Humanitarian Law* published by the International Committee of the Red Cross (ICRC), the authors identify the principle of proportionality as undoubtedly constituting customary international law binding on all states.[28] They stress that it is explicitly

---

[26] See, for example, Alex Bellamy, *Just Wars: from Cicero to Iraq* (Cambridge: Polity Press, 2006), 124–125.

[27] See Jean-Marie Hencaerts and Louise Doswald-Beck, *Customary International Humanitarian Law* (Cambridge: Cambridge University Press, 2006), 47.

[28] Ibid., 46–49.

entrenched in many international conventions in addition to those cited already, relating both to international and noninternational armed conflicts, and that it finds expression in many military manuals and in some countries is also explicitly enshrined in domestic legislation. It has also been repeatedly recognized by international courts as constituting customary law binding on all states in both international and domestic conflict.[29] They formulate the customary principle as follows:

> Launching an attack which may be expected to cause incidental loss of civilian life, injury to civilians, damage to civilian objects, or a combination thereof, which would be excessive in relation to the concrete and direct military advantage anticipated, is prohibited.[30]

A comparison between the ICC Statute articulation and this customary formulation suggests that the language in which proportionality is defined is fairly consistent. The key points are that expected "incidental" harm to civilians must not be "excessive" in relation to anticipated "direct military advantage."

The key issue then in determining whether the civilian casualties produced by CIA drone strikes in Pakistan breach the ethical and legal standard of proportionality is whether planners should reasonably have expected them to be "excessive" in relation to anticipated "direct military advantage." Before turning to that key issue in the next section, however, it will be helpful to clarify an issue that often gives rise to confusion in such discussions and to recognize a few unavoidable limitations of such analysis.

The point requiring clarification is that two forms of proportionality are often conflated in discussions of civilian casualties but should be clearly distinguished. Specifically, there are important differences between what is sometimes called "macroproportionality" and the standard of "microproportionality," which is the focus here. Macroproportionality is a *jus ad bellum* criterion that is concerned with when resort to military force is justified. Microproportionality is a *jus in bello* criterion concerned with how military force can legitimately be deployed in the context of armed conflict. Macroproportionality turns on the question of "whether the overall harm likely to be caused by the war is less than that caused by the wrong that is being righted."[31] In the present instance, this question weighs the entire harm al-Qaeda and the Taliban have wrought against the entire military response to this harm and its effects. While important, this

---

[29] For example, see the International Criminal Tribunal for the former Yugoslavia, *Kupreskic Case (Judgment of 14 January 2000)*, paragraph 524.

[30] Hencaerts and Doswald-Beck, *Customary International Humanitarian Law*, 46.

[31] Bellamy, *Just Wars*, 123.

question is beyond the scope of this chapter. The focus here is strictly on the tactic of drone strikes in Pakistan and the controversial question of whether these operations violate the *jus in bello* criterion of microproportionality—that is, do they kill an excessive number of civilians in relation to the anticipated direct military benefits of specific operations?

Some important limitations of microproportionality analysis also warrant attention, particularly in relation to ongoing covert operations. Three stand out. First, it is important to acknowledge that the following analysis is at best partial and suggestive. Unfortunately, an assessment of microproportionality involves some issues that cannot be settled given the limited data that are currently publicly available. For example, the proportionality calculus compares the expectations of operational planners concerning risk to civilians and direct military advantages. But the operations being examined here are secret, and there is no way to know with certainty what operational planners knew about the risks of operations to civilians or exactly what military goals they anticipated such operations would achieve. Of course, we can make informed guesses, especially where we can identify persistent patterns in the data. But it must be emphasized that the provisional conclusions here are based on no more than informed guesses.

Second, microproportionality is intended to be measured on an operational basis. As the definitions already introduced both stressed, it is addressed to "any attack," and any one attack that violates its criterion constitutes a war crime, regardless of whether the overall pattern of attacks is excessively harmful to civilians or not. However, in light of the limited data available, this chapter will have to rely on aggregate data and identify patterns in it that reflect the tactic's proportionality over time. It therefore relies on the idea that these general patterns tell us something about how individual operations are going, at least most of the time. In essence, it assumes that a higher civilian fatality rate over time suggests a greater likelihood that some individual operation violated the standard of proportionality. By contrast, a lower average civilian fatality rate lends support to the view that strikes are generally proportionate. Admittedly, this inference is crude and the picture it provides imperfect, but it's not clear that there are better alternatives. Moreover, this approach may permit some rough insight even within the confines of a relatively short chapter.

Third and finally, it should be noted that the proportionality calculus itself poses some inherent challenges. In particular, while it does provide an independent basis for assessing the justifiability of the unintended civilian casualties resulting from a given operation, it does so by invoking a very different type of consideration, specifically anticipated direct military advantage. This poses a difficulty: in terms of what common units can foreseeable civilian casualties be measured against a direct military advantage? Or, to frame it another way, how many civilian lives is it worth to eliminate, for example, three low-level enemy militants or to seize a cache of arms or to interdict an important source of weapons and ammunition? The point here is that the proportionality calculus compares incommensurables—effectively apples and oranges—which cannot generally be measured in common units. The limits that such comparison of incommensurables imposes on rendering decisive judgments are a matter of continuing dispute, but a point of broad agreement is that such determinations must rely on practical, context-sensitive judgments rather than on the authoritative establishment of some universal rules (e.g., one low-level militant is worth one civilian life). This does not of course mean that one cannot make more or less convincing arguments that can convince more or fewer readers. It just means that such arguments are unlikely to overcome all reasonable disagreement with knockdown arguments.

4. Counting the Dead

The following section explores the proportionality of CIA drone strikes in Pakistan based on the best publicly available data on their impact. It brings together data from the four databases tracking the drone strikes that are (1) publicly accessible on the Internet; (2) comprehensive in scope (covering all strikes from 2004 to the end of 2011); and (3) transparent—that is, that permit readers to easily check their sources. These four databases have been compiled, respectively, by the New America Foundation (NAF), the *Long War Journal* (*LWJ*), the University of Massachusetts (UMass DRONE), and the Bureau of Investigative Journalism (TBIJ).

These databases differ in their reporting of the impact of the drone campaign, particularly in relation to the number of civilians being killed. Referencing them all in this chapter introduces a degree of uncertainty over the numbers. But such uncertainty is probably inescapable given the limited access of reporters to the FATA and especially to the locations of drone strikes and the resulting controversies that have arisen over what is really happening on the ground. The challenges of getting reliable numbers on the strikes are well captured by Farhat Taj, a research fellow at the University of Oslo who has written extensively about the drone campaign in Pakistan:

> After every attack the terrorists cordon off the area and no one, including the local villagers, is allowed to come even near the targeted place. The militants themselves collect the bodies, bury the dead and then issue the statement that all of them were innocent civilians.[32]

[32] Farhat Taj, "Drone Attacks," *Daily Times*, January 2, 2010. http://www.dailytimes.com.pk/default.asp?page=2010%5C01%5C02%5Cstory_2-1-2010_pg3_5.

Moreover, as Christine Fair notes, "The CIA will not even acknowledge the drone program exists, much less discuss its results," at least officially.[33] Press reports therefore usually draw on some local reporting or purported eyewitnesses or local officials contacted from the outside, supplemented by the accounts circulated by Pakistani and sometimes (unofficially by) American government officials. One result is that press reports often differ over the details of individual strikes. This situation poses two challenges to researchers: first, it is uncertain whether any of the reports are accurate; and second, even if some reports accurately reflect the reality on the ground, it is difficult to know which ones they are. The harsh fact is that there just are no simple answers to these challenges and hence no way to avoid some uncertainty over the actual impacts of drone strikes.

This chapter introduces the four databases as the fairest expedient given the inevitable uncertainty over the strikes' impacts. While the four databases do overlap in some of the sources on which they rely—notably Pakistani sources like *Dawn* and *Geo TV*, along with international sources like *the New York Times* and *BBC News*—they also employ rather different methodologies to overcome discrepancies. For example, the NAF database records the range of casualty figures across all of the reports and averages the reports to get approximate overall numbers. By contrast, the UMass DRONE database (in which I participated) selected in each case the most credible news account based on a number of factors—including level of detail provided and range of sources cited—and relied on the numbers provided in these accounts. The *LWJ*, by contrast, relies more on its own reports of the incidents, often informed by the wire services and US and Pakistani intelligence sources. Finally, TBIJ claims to have arranged teams on the ground in Pakistan that have investigated at least some strikes (although only a little of this source material is currently publicly available).[34] In short, an advantage of introducing all four databases is that a wide range of sources and methodologies are engaged.[35]

Table 1 summarizes the finding of the four databases from 2004 to 2011. Both NAF and the TBIJ present their estimates of total persons killed and possible civilians killed as ranges (for example, the TBIJ reports total casualties resulting from drone strikes in Pakistan to the end of 2011 as between 2,370 and 2,981). NAF also presents ranges for its year-to-year totals. In all these

---

[33] Fair, "Drone Wars."

[34] Chris Woods, "Witnesses Speak Out," Bureau of Investigative Journalism, February 4, 2012. http://www.thebureauinvestigates.com/2012/02/04/witnesses-speak-out/.

[35] At the same time, the obvious disadvantage that this entails of uncertainty over the numbers is at any rate an inescapable admission of reality—there just are no certain numbers. It is also perhaps worth noting that the four databases do encompass some opposed attitudes to the drone strikes. For example, the tone of the Bureau of Investigative Journalism's coverage of the "Obama Terror Strikes" is overtly critical, while the *Long War Journal*'s coverage of what it calls the "Air Campaign in Pakistan" is clearly more favorable. In neither case need this orientation be assumed to influence the data they collect on specific strikes, but any suspicion that it might should be mitigated by including both databases.

cases I have taken an average of these ranges to obtain a single number estimate (for example, in the foregoing case of TBIJ's estimate of total casualties 2675.5 total people killed) to facilitate calculation and comparison. For the purposes of the following discussion, I treat these averages as reflecting a rough best estimate based on the NAF and TBIJ data. However, I want to note that, when the TBIJ breaks out its data by year, it uses the number at the bottom of its ranges of both total and civilian casualties (rather than the average). I have included these low-end estimates in Table 1 but have supplemented them in the bottom two rows of Table 1 with the TBIJ's high-end estimates and resulting average estimates of total and civilian casualties resulting from drone strikes.

There are a number of immediately striking things about the numbers in Table 1. First, there are some quite significant divergences in the estimates of civilian casualties. Consider, for example, the differences over the proportion of total casualties identified as civilians. The LWJ and UMass DRONE are relatively low, at 6.03 percent and 3.86 percent, respectively, while the NAF and TBIJ present ranges of possible civilian casualties of

Table 1 **Four Databases' Reporting on Drone Strikes in Pakistan**

Source	Total Strikes	Total Killed	Estimate of Civilian Deaths	"Unknowns"	Civilian Deaths as Percentage of Total
New America[36] 2004–2007	9	101	9	– – – – – – – –	8.91
2008	33	294	145	– – – – – – – –	49.32
2009	53	547	163	– – – – – – – –	29.80
2010	118	800	40	– – – – – – – –	5.00
2011	70	457	26	– – – – – – – –	5.69
Total 2004–2011	**283**	**2199**	**383**	– – – – – – – –	**17.42**
LWJ[37] 2004–2007	11	215	20		9.30
2008	35	317	31	– – – – – – – –	9.78
2009	53	506	43	– – – – – – – –	8.50
2010	117	815	14	– – – – – – – –	1.72
2011	64	435	30	– – – – – – – –	6.90

(continued)

[36] See http://counterterrorism.newamerica.net/drones. The New America Foundation (NAF) presents its data in terms of high–low estimates. These numbers represent the average of those ranges, rounded off where necessary. NAF regularly updates its data in light of new information and analysis.

[37] See http://www.longwarjournal.org/pakistan-strikes.php. LWJ updates its data in light of new information and analysis.

Table 1 **(Continued)**

Source	Total Strikes	Total Killed	Estimate of Civilian Deaths	"Unknowns"	Civilian Deaths as Percentage of Total
Total 2004–2011	**280**	**2,288**	**138**	– – – – – – – –	**6.03**
UMass Drone[38] 2004–2007	10	166	14	17	8.43
2008	33	290	15	63	5.17
2009	54	582	39	86	6.70
2010	131	863	13	176	1.51
2011	64	481	11	107	2.29
Total 2004–2011	**292**	**2,382**	**92**	**449**	**3.86**
Bureau of Investigative Journalism[39] Low-End Estimates 2004–2007	12	161	108		67.08
2008	38	268	74	– – – – – – – –	27.61
2009	55	562	122	– – – – – – – –	21.71
2010	128	909	101	– – – – – – – –	11.11
2011	76	470	59	– – – – – – – –	12.55
Low-End Total 2004–2011	309	2,370	464	– – – – – – – –	19.58
High-End Total 2004–2011	309	2,981	812	– – – – – – – –	27.24
Average Total 2004–2011	**309**	**2,676**	**638**		**23.85**

which the averages are 17.42% and 23.85%, respectively. The range of divergence here is from around one in twenty-five of the casualties being a civilian to close to one in four.

These differences are all the more striking given that the databases rely on many of the same sources and that many of the other key numbers they report are fairly close, as are some patterns in the numbers. Some examples of similar numbers are

[38] See http://umassdrone.org. These data are regularly updated in light of new information and analysis.

[39] See http://www.thebureauinvestigates.com/2011/08/10/resources-and-graphs/. The year-by-year numbers in this table follow the TBIJ's convention of reporting only its low-end fatality totals on a year-by-year basis. However, the high-end and averaged results are also included in the last two rows of the table. TBIJ regularly updates these data on the basis of new information and analysis.

the total numbers of strikes, which vary only between 280 (*LWJ*) and 309 (TBIJ), and total casualties, which vary only between 2199 (NAF) and 2675.5 (TBIJ). Moreover, all of the databases show a very sharp decline in the proportion of civilian casualties from 2009 to 2010 before a smaller increase in 2011. For example, the proportion of civilians killed fell from 29.8 to 5 percent from 2009 to 2010 according to the NAF, from 8.5 to 1.72 percent according to the *LWJ*, from 6.7 to 1.51 percent according to UMass DRONE, and from 21.71 to 11.11 percent according to TBIJ.

All of this loose agreement throws the divergences over civilian casualties into sharp relief. A big part of the explanation is simply that the studies count civilian casualties differently. For example, as Spencer Ackerman aptly noted in the *Washington Independent*, "New America was more methodologically aggressive than [Brian] Williams [et al., in the UMass DRONE study] in counting as civilians all who could not be clearly identified as militants, which perhaps accounts for the variance in their results."[40] Indeed, the UMass DRONE study is unique among the four databases in that it created a separate category of "unknowns" into which it classified cases for which there was insufficient data to be confident about combatant–civilian status.[41] This strategy resulted in a lower count of civilians than the other databases. The TBIJ, by contrast, appears to follow a variant of the NAF approach of erring in the direction of counting problematic cases as "possible civilians": as they explain:

> Where accounts vary as to whether civilians or militants were killed, we report this and present a minimum and maximum reported number of casualties. We have also identified a number of cases where media sources refer only to "people" killed (and not the more usual "militant"). Here we indicate that civilian casualties may be possible.[42]

What this means in practice is that even when there are multiple credible reports and sources identifying those killed as militants or suspected militants, if there is at least one source in one report that characterizes them as "people" (or of course "civilians") then they are listed as possible

---

[40] Spencer Ackerman, "New Study Suggests Drone Strikes Don't Kill as Many Pakistani Civilians as Claimed," *Washington Independent*, May 28, 2010. http://washingtonindependent.com/85945/n ew-study-suggests-drone-strikes-dont-kill-as-many-pakistani-civilians-as-claimed.

[41] In August 2012, long after the text of this article was completed, NAF did a revision of its data and introduced a category of unknowns (perhaps following the lead of UMass DRONE).

[42] Drones Team, "Covert US Strikes in Pakistan, Somalia and Yemen—Our Methodology," Bureau of Investigative Journalism, August 10, 2011. http://www.thebureauinvestigates. com/2011/08/10/pakistan-drone-strikes-the-methodology2/; see also Alice Ross, "Untangling the Data," Bureau of Investigative Journalism, August 10, 2011. http://www.thebureauinvesti-gates.com/2011/08/10/drones-untangling-the-data/.

civilians.[43] This is a perfectly sensible approach if one is primarily concerned with making sure that one does not miss any civilian casualties. It is, however, open to concerns that it will often end up treating militant deaths as possible civilians. Finally, the *Long War Journal*, frequently relies on accounts offered by American and Pakistani officials, often conveyed through the Associated Press (AP), Reuters, or Agence France-Presse (AFP).[44] These government officials often have more information on strikes than would be available through independent reporting. However, their own interests and prejudices could skew the resulting data, possibly toward a lower civilian count.

Still, none of these approaches seems unreasonable. The unavoidable fact is that cases about which little is known present a problem of classification, and consequently for estimating proportionality, and there is no ideal solution. But we can at least say that the bulk of the differences between the databases' findings arise from their different (reasonable) ways of trying to address this problem. This point is well illustrated by comparing the lowest count of civilian casualties (UMass DRONE, 3.86 percent) and the highest (TBIJ, 23.85 percent) and observing that the difference is almost entirely accounted for by UMass DRONE's category of "unknowns" (18.85 percent of all casualties). That is, if you reclassify every single one of UMass DRONE's "unknowns" as a civilian, then UMass DRONE would go from the lowest reporting of civilians killed to virtually tied with the highest of the four estimates (with 22.71 percent compared with TBIJ's 23.85 percent). In view of the observation that the disagreement among databases arises mainly out of the irresolvable knot of how to report the unknown cases, and their reasonable albeit different ways of addressing the problem, I suggest that the best way to proceed is to put all the data on the table and see what can be inferred from it collectively.

So what can we plausibly conclude from these divergent accounts of the number and proportion of civilians killed in drone strikes? I think that we can reasonably infer at least three things.

---

[43] Drones Team, "Covert US Strikes." They also write, "We report all instances where civilians are reported to have been killed or injured." In addition to reflecting the priority that underlies their methodology, this affirms what is perhaps self-evident—that as with "people," where one source says "civilians" were killed even in contradiction to many others then TBIJ lists possible civilians killed (the same appears to apply to the term "tribesmen"). See, for example, strikes reported on October 8, 2010; October 15, 2010; January 7, 2011; March 8, 2011; April 13, 2011; June 6, 2011; June 27, 2011; July 11, 2011; and August 22, 2011.

[44] Some recent examples include reports on August 2, 2011; August 9, 2011; August 15, 2011; August 19, 2011; September 23, 2011; October 13, 2011 (twice); October 16, 2011; October 28, 2011; and November 17, 2011.

1. Since the databases reflect a diverse spectrum of plausible approaches, it
is reasonable to think that the actual civilian fatality number is probably
within the spectrum (that is, between 3.86 and 23.85 percent).

2. Despite their differences the databases agree on some key points even in relation to civilian casualties, and that gives us additional reason to take their
findings seriously. For example, all the databases show a very sharp drop in
both the absolute and proportional number of civilian casualties from 2009
to 2010 and a slight increase from 2010 to 2011 (although the numbers
remained well below those for 2004–2009).[45] So they all agree that civilian
casualties have decreased from 2009 to 2011.

3. However, the 2010 and 2011 civilian casualties reported by each of the
databases are still of sufficient quantity to cast doubt on deputy national
security adviser Brennan's claim that strikes have gone for close to a year
without a single civilian death (a point that is confirmed in month-by-month
breakdowns).[46] So US officials' claims of "no collateral deaths" appear to be
exaggerated.

5. Assessing Proportionality

All of the numbers examined in the last section were concerned with civilian casualties compared with the total casualties. However, the principle of
proportionality requires that the number of civilian casualties be compared
with a second factor—anticipated direct military advantages. So what direct
advantages have been obtained thus far? The general goal of drone strikes
is to disrupt enemy operations and to degrade enemy capabilities by killing
enemy operatives, especially leaders. Here the general goals (of disruption and
degradation) are difficult to measure, but success in the immediate goal (killing enemy operatives, especially leaders) can be quantified, although as with
civilian casualties some disagreement has arisen over precise numbers. The

---

[45] The TBIJ is a bit of an outlier in regard to the 2010 drop, showing a fall of just under one-half
from the 2009 proportion (21.7 to 11.1 percent), whereas *LWJ* and UMass DRONE show a drop
to one-quarter of the 2009 proportion (8.5 to 1.72 percent and 6.7 to 1.51 percent) and the NAF
shows a drop to one-sixth (from 29.8 to 5 percent). On the other hand, the *LWJ* is the outlier here
in relation to the 2010 to 2011 increase. Where the increase is marginal on the other counts (less
than 1 percent for NAF and UMass DRONE and less than 1.5 percent for TBIJ), *LWJ* shows just
over a 5 percent increase (from 1.72 to 6.9 percent), albeit still remaining considerably below the
2004–2009 proportions.

[46] See Plaw et al., "Practice Makes Perfect?" 60–61; also see Chris Woods, "US Claims of 'No
Civilian Deaths' Are Untrue," Bureau of Investigative Journalism, July 18, 2011. http://www.
thebureauinvestigates.com/2011/07/18/washingtons-untrue-claims-no-civilian-deaths-in-pak-
istan-drone-strikes/.

Table 2 **Suspected Militants Killed in Drone Strikes in Pakistan**[47]

	New America		Long War Journal		UMassDrone		Bureau of Investigation Journalism
	HVTs	LLM	HVTs	LLM	HVTs	LLM	Low End Militant
2004–7	3	89	4	191	4	131	53
2008	11	138	19	267	20	192	194
2009	7	377	16	447	16	441	440
2010	12	748	18	783	18	656	808
2011	6	425	10	395	13	350	411
Total	**39**	**1,777**	**67**	**2,083**	**71**	**1,770**	Low-End 1,906 High-End 2,169 **Average 2,038**

information on suspected enemy combatants offered by the four databases introduced in the last section are outlined in Table 2, with separate categories for leaders or high-value targets (HVTs) killed and low-level militants (LLMs) killed (except for TBIJ, which does not distinguish HVTs and LLMs).

Comparing the data on suspected LLM deaths in Table 2 and civilian deaths in Table 1 show that all three databases show at least about three times more suspected low-level militants are being killed than civilians (specifically, 3.19 times according to TBIJ's average numbers,[48] 4.64 times according to NAF's average numbers, 15.09 times according to *LWJ*, and 19.24 times according to UMass DRONE, with "unknowns" kept distinct). Moreover, these proportions do not account for HVTs being killed. On the UMass DRONE data, HVT deaths alone are 77.17 percent of the number of civilian deaths, on the *LWJ* numbers 48.55 percent, and on the NAF numbers 10.18 percent. Obviously when the HVTs are added to the proportion of LLMs to civilians, the results become more imbalanced toward suspected militants killed. So many times more suspected enemy combatants have been killed than civilians, and a significant number of them have been HVTs.

However, the "proportionality" calculus requires more than that the number of civilians killed is much smaller than the number of (suspected) enemy combatants killed. What is required is that the anticipated military advantage of an operation is greater than the foreseeable civilian harm. Again, the proportionality principle requires that this assessment be made on a case-by-case basis. Unfortunately, the covert nature of the strikes and the limited information

[47] For database sources see Table 1.

[48] TBIJ's high-end numbers indicate that 2.67 suspected militants are being killed for each civilian, while their low-end numbers suggest 4.19 suspected militants per civilian.

that has circulated unofficially make it impossible to reconstruct what direct military advantages planners did (and should have) expected in most individual operations and what danger to civilians they did (and should have) foreseen. Often, the primary goal of a strike has to be guessed from the facts reported. Moreover, even if the target can be guessed, it is difficult to know how much planners anticipated (and should have anticipated) that his killing would disrupt particular operations and degrade the enemy organization's capacities.

So in view of these challenges how can the "direct military advantage" that forms the back half of the proportionality calculus be assessed? In this section I'll pursue a three-part strategy. First, I'll fill in the classic considerations as much as available data permit. Unfortunately, this means looking at longer-term patterns of results rather than the operation-by-operation assessment of reasonable expectations that a strict analysis of proportionality requires. In particular, I'll consider the strikes' effectiveness in obtaining the immediate goal (killing enemy operatives and especially leaders). I'll also touch on the broader goal of degrading the enemy organization's capacities and examine whether, even in principle, this is plausibly proportionate to the harm produced by drone strikes. Here the challenge of incommensurability can be at least partially circumvented by focusing on one common feature of drone strikes and the actions of those targeted—that is, a trail of dead bodies. Specifically, we can compare the number of civilians that targets are killing and the number of civilians killed in targeting them to see which number is bigger.

In light of the limitations of the conventional approach to assessing proportionality, I will also pursue a second alternative. I will briefly compare the data on drone strikes outlined in the last section with some illuminating parallel cases—for example, data on a similar tactic employed in other circumstances. While not technically decisive in regards to proportionality, I think that such comparisons may prove instructive.

Finally, I will briefly consider the changing pattern of proportionality. For even if the principle was violated in some instances, or even possibly persistently over a period of time, that does not mean that it still is being violated. If the precision of the strikes has improved, it is at least possible that past violations could be redressed without prejudicing current operations.

Together, these three approaches may provide a crude general impression of overall proportionality. Nevertheless, it is important to emphasize that nothing in them meets the operation-by-operation assessment of reasonable expectations both of direct military advantage and of likely harm to noncombatants that the ILOAC and JWT principles properly require.

In regard to the first approach, much of the work has already been done in the second paragraph of this section. We saw that LLM deaths ranged from 3.19 to 19.24 times civilian deaths depending on which database was used. Along with

LLMs killed, between 39 and 71 senior leaders (of al-Qaeda and the Afghan and Pakistani Taliban) are reported killed. These leaders include Baitullah Mehsud, the leader of the Pakistani Taliban, and Atiyah Abd al-Rahman, al-Qaeda's number two after the death of Osama Bin Laden.[49] Indeed, Jane Mayer reported in 2009, before the drone campaign really ramped up, that "counterterrorism officials credit drones with having killed more than a dozen senior Al Qaeda leaders and their allies in the past year, eliminating more than half of the C.I.A.'s twenty most wanted 'high value' targets."[50] A strong case can thus be made that drone strikes are highly effective in eliminating enemy operatives, including key leaders, particularly when these HVTs are hidden in inaccessible and politically problematic locations like the FATA.

However, even if it is provisionally conceded that drone strikes are effective in their immediate goals, would even the clear attainment of their larger strategic goals warrant the associated harm to civilians? I suggest that a sober consideration of what al-Qaeda and the Taliban have already done supports a positive answer. According to the University of Maryland's Global Terrorism Database, al-Qaeda and its regional affiliates are responsible globally for 4,443 civilian deaths and 6,556 injuries (and 193 military deaths and 338 injuries).[51] Similarly, Table 3 provides an overview of UN reports on the civilian carnage wrought in Afghanistan from 2007 to 2011 by antigovernment elements (AGE), which are mainly composed of Afghan Taliban networks. The total civilians killed over the five years is 7,762.

Table 3 **UN Reported Civilian Fatalities in Afghanistan Insurgency**[52]

Years	Total Civilians Killed per Year	Civilians Killed by Antigovernment Elements (AGE)	Proportion of Civilians Killed Accounted for by AGE (%)
2011	3,021	2,332	77.19
2010	2,790	2,037	73.01
2009	2,412	1,533	63.56
2008	2,118	1,160	54.77
2007	1,523	700	45.96
Total	**11,864**	**7,762**	**65.42**

[49] Mark Mazetti, "C.I.A. Drone Is Said to Kill Al Qaeda's No. 2," *New York Times*, August 27, 2011. http://www.nytimes.com/2011/08/28/world/asia/28qaeda.html; Jane Mayer, "The Predator War," *New Yorker*, October 26, 2009. http://www.newyorker.com/reporting/2009/10/26/091026fa_fact_mayer.

[50] Jane Mayer, "Predator War."

[51] http://www.start.umd.edu/gtd/. These results are based on identifying al-Qaeda as the Perpetrator (it includes "al-Qaeda suspected" cases) and separating out the cases where the target type is military.

[52] Years 2009–2011: http://graphics8.nytimes.com/packages/pdf/world/20120204_afghan_civilians_deaths.pdf; years 2007–2008: http://unama.unmissions.org/Portals/UNAMA/human%20rights/UNAMA_09february-Annual%20Report_PoC%202008_FINAL_11Feb09.pdf.

The civilian carnage produced by al-Qaeda and the Taliban obviously dwarfs that produced by all of the drone strikes combined, even on the most unfavorable count, by many orders of magnitude. Taking the highest average estimate of civilian casualties from the four databases (638) and comparing it with the lesser of the al-Qaeda and the Taliban totals (i.e., al-Qaeda at 4,443), the al-Qaeda total is just under seven times larger, and the combined Taliban and al-Qaeda total (of 12,205 civilians killed) is over nineteen times larger.[53] By contrast, if you compare the Taliban and al-Qaeda totals with the lowest of the databases' estimates of civilian casualties (UMass DRONE at 92), their death toll is 132.7 times larger.

Faced with such a scale of atrocities, it would be difficult to argue against the proportionality of a planned drone strike if US officials had good reason to think that it would significantly damage al-Qaeda or Taliban capabilities (or disrupt imminent attacks) even if it posed a risk to a small number of civilians. The demonstrated viciousness of these organizations lends credibility to the view that such a strike might save more civilian lives than it costs. A February 25, 2012, statistical study by Patrick Johnson and Anoop Sarbahi, two Harvard research fellows, lends support to this view. Their analysis, which focused on the FATA, "suggests that . . . drone strikes are associated with decreases in both the frequency and lethality of militant attacks overall and in IED and suicide attacks specifically."[54] Further corroboration is provided by the apparent US success in reducing the number of major attacks orchestrated by al-Qaeda central command (AQCC) from its bases in Pakistan. Indeed, there are few reports of successful attacks orchestrated by AQCC after 2010, and an increasing number of experts in the last year have declared it severely weakened.[55] This likely means that more of the work of orchestrating attacks is being downloaded to regional franchise operations, like al-Qaeda in the Arabian Peninsula (AQAP), which are less likely to be significantly affected by CIA drone strikes in Pakistan. In this way, the US's very success in harming al-Qaeda's central command may be gradually undermining its rationale for continuing to use drones to hunt and kill its leaders in Pakistan. Still, as long as drone strikes are required to suppress al-Qaeda command and control in Pakistan, a plausible argument can be made that the scale of the threat

---

[53] Or, using TBIJ's high-end estimate of civilian casualty estimate of 812 alone (see Table 1), the combined al-Qaeda and Taliban death toll remains over fifteen times larger.

[54] Patrick B. Johnston and Anoop Sarbahi, "The Impact of U.S. Drone Strikes on Terrorism in Pakistan," Discussion Paper, Belfer Center for Science and International Affairs, John F. Kennedy School of Government, February 25, 2012, abstract. http://patrickjohnston.info/materials/drones.pdf.

[55] Eric Schmitt, "Intelligence Report Lists Iran and Cyberattacks as Leading Concerns," *New York Times*, January 31, 2012. http://www.nytimes.com/2012/02/01/world/intelligence-chief-sees-al-qaeda-likely-to-continue-fragmenting.html?_r=1&scp=2&sq=al%20qaeda%20fragment&st=cse.

that al-Qaeda poses to civilians and the support it can potentially extend to regional franchise operations conduces to the proportionality of CIA drone strikes.

In some ways, the same argument can be made regarding the Afghan Taliban. They appear to be responsible for an even greater scale of atrocities against civilians. When their imminent attacks are disrupted or their capacities are degraded, it is reasonable to think that one effect is to prevent attacks likely to have resulted in some civilian casualties (as well as military deaths of course). A complication arises, however, in applying this argument to the Afghan Taliban, for as Table 3 clearly shows both the number and the proportion of civilian deaths caused by AGEs has been steadily rising since 2007. What this suggests is that the Taliban strategy in Afghanistan is becoming increasingly vicious. Moreover, it seems plausible that the intensification of drone strikes on their bases in Pakistan may be helping to inspire this increased viciousness. If this is the case, then it could be argued that CIA drone strikes in Pakistan (with their own attendant civilian deaths) are also contributing to the increased Taliban targeting of civilians in Afghanistan. At any rate, it is certainly clear that they are not doing very much to reduce the overall number of civilians being killed. But this argument, while certainly troubling, seems to move beyond the ambit of the principle of proportionality, which takes consideration of only "direct military advantages" and not longer-term strategic shifts in the enemy's treatment of civilians (for which they are ultimately morally and criminally responsible). And this of course makes sense, since otherwise the proportionality calculus would be made permanent hostage to the threat that the enemy might be prompted to opt for more war crimes. So the calculus focuses quite narrowly on the tangible, immediate impacts on the ground, and if these are to prevent or reduce immediate attacks on civilians then this should be factored into the assessment of proportionality. So again there is reason to think that the lawless viciousness of Taliban conduct in Afghanistan tends to lend support to the proportionality of CIA drone strikes in Pakistan because that many more atrocities could be prevented and because weakening the Taliban is that much more urgent.

A second, albeit less conventional, approach to assessing the proportionality of CIA drone strikes in Pakistan is to compare their civilian casualty rates with other cases that are in some sense analogous. However, it must be stressed that such comparison is not part of the formal proportionality calculus, which focuses exclusively on expected civilian harm and anticipated direct military advantage. Still, such comparison may provide some useful perspective and may help to frame broad standards that can supplement the difficult comparison on which proportionality is exclusively based.

Table 4 lays out some illuminating comparative cases. To begin with, it shows that US non-drone operations in the FATA—for example, commando raids and

Table 4 **Civilian Death Rates in Comparative Campaigns**

	Total Fatalities	Civilian Fatalities	Proportion of Civilian Casualties (%)
Nondrone US Operations in FATA[56]	32	12	37.50
Pakistani Army Operations in FATA, April 2002 to March 2007[57]	1,440	451	31.32
Israeli Targeted Killings, 2000–2011[58]	427	175 (nontargets)	40.98
Estimated World Combat Average for the 1990s[59]			88.89

precision artillery strikes—have killed a much higher proportion of civilians than drones (at 37.5 percent as opposed to between 3.86 and 23.85 percent for the drone strikes). The nondrone operations also killed an unusually high number of "unknowns" (13 people, or 40.62 percent of the total), in addition of course to instigating a higher degree of anger in Pakistan. For example, the best-known US commando raid into the FATA occurred on September 3, 2008. Special Forces attacked an alleged al-Qaeda compound in South Waziristan but seem to have gotten pinned down in a firefight that attracted the attention of locals. Twenty Pakistanis were widely reported killed, at least seven of whom were identified as women and children noncombatants by the Pakistani

[56] Nondrone operations refer to preplanned strikes rather than hot pursuits or border incidents such as that of November 26, 2011, in Mohmand Province, in which US investigations suggest that US-led NATO forces responded to hostile fire from across the Pakistani border, resulting in the deaths of twenty-four Pakistani soldiers. The US strikes represented in this table occurred on March 12, 2008; September 3, 2008; and May 2, 2011. The first was a precision artillery strike, and the latter two were commando raids. For details see http://umassdrone.org.

[57] All of these statistics were compiled from various media sources by the Institute for Conflict Management, http://www.satp.org/satporgtp/countries/pakistan/Waziristan/timeline/2002.htm.

[58] B'Tselem Statistics, http://www.btselem.org/statistics, under "Fatalities" see the categories for "Palestinians killed during the course of a targeted killing" and "Palestinians who were the object of a targeted killing" for "until," "during," and "since" Operation Cast Lead.

[59] See, for example, Mark Osiel, *The End of Reciprocity* (Cambridge: Cambridge University Press, 2009), 143; Mary Kaldor, *New and Old Wars* (Stanford: Stanford University Press, 2001), 8.

government.[60] No HVTs are known to have been killed. The head of the Pakistani Army, General Ashfaq Kayani, harshly condemned the US operation and vowed that the Pakistani Army would resist such violations of sovereignty "at all costs."[61] In the next two weeks, Pakistani troops were reported to have fired warning shots at US helicopters and ground troops near the border.[62] By comparison, the costs and dangers of carrying out drone strikes seem modest.

Similarly, the Pakistani Army is reported to have killed a greater proportion of civilians than the drone strikes in their operations in FATA from April 2002 to March 2007 (31.32 percent as opposed to between 3.86 and 23.85 percent for the drone strikes). It should also be borne in mind that large-scale Pakistani military campaigns often result in thousands of refugees fleeing combat and extensive damage to homes and civilian infrastructure. They also result in casualties among soldiers that are generally avoided in the case of drone strikes. Again then, drone strikes appear to represent a far more proportionate option in terms of impact on civilians (as well as on soldiers and infrastructure). Indeed, of the available options to confront militants operating out of the FATA, drone strikes appear to be the most proportionate.

CIA drone strikes in Pakistan also look more proportionate than at least one recent counterterrorism campaign that is in some respects similar: the Israeli use of targeted killing in response to the second intifada. According to statistics assembled by the Israeli nongovernmental organization B'Tselem (which is itself highly critical of targeted killing), Israel's use of the tactic from 2000 to today resulted in the killing of 427 people including the unintended killing of 175 nontargets (for a 40.98 percent proportion of unintended killings). However, it must be emphasized that because someone wasn't an intended target doesn't mean that they were not a combatant, and if a very large portion of the unintended targets were combatants that might make the results of the Israeli campaign more comparable with the CIA strikes in Pakistan. Nonetheless, to reach the same level of proportionality of the CIA drone strikes (between 3.86 and 23.85 percent), around half of the Israeli nontargets would have to have been combatants, and reading the B'Tselem case-by-case descriptions of the incidents, this seems unlikely.

The final statistic provided for comparison in Table 4 is what appears to be the most widely cited estimate of the rate of civilian casualties characterizing

[60] "ISAF Troops Kill Seven Innocent Civilians in NWA: ISPR," *Associated Press of Pakistan*, September 3, 2008. http://www.app.com.pk/en_/index.php?option=com_content&task=view& id=51444&Itemid=2.

[61] Jane Perlez, "Pakistan's Military Chief Criticizes U.S. Over Raid," *New York Times*, September 10, 2008. http://www.nytimes.com/2008/09/11/world/asia/11pstan.html?scp=2&sq=kayani%20at%20 all%20costs&st=cse.

[62] "Pakistan Troops 'Repel' US Raid," BBC News, September 22, 2008. http://news.bbc.co.uk/2/ hi/south_asia/7628890.stm.

all conflicts in the 1990s—that is, eight civilian deaths for each combatant killed. Obviously this proportion of civilian casualties (88.89 percent) dwarfs that of the drone strikes (between 3.86 and 23.85 percent). But I suggest that this statistic, however popularly cited, be treated cautiously as I have not been able to find the supporting data. Moreover, a recent study (albeit offering an avowedly conservative assessment of civilian deaths) has at least partially challenged it. Drawing on Lacina and Gleditsch's (2005) dataset for battle deaths, Kristina Eck and Lisa Hultman (2007) found that over the 1989–2004 period at least, battle deaths exceeded deaths from one-sided violence (a rough indicator of civilian casualties) by a ratio of two to one.[63] Still, even on Eck and Hultman's conservative estimate, the apparent civilian deaths resulting from drone strikes (between 3.86 and 23.85 percent) is significantly lower than the norm for civilians killed for 1989–2004 (at 33.3 percent).

On all the comparisons examined then, the civilian casualty rate of the drone strikes looks significantly better than alternative actions. All things considered, it looks like the proportionate alternative if one is committed to going after dangerous militants operating in the FATA with military force (compared, for example, with US ground operations or Pakistani military campaigns). It also improves significantly on at least one similar counter-terrorist campaign (that is, Israel's targeted killing from 2000 onward)—although it should be noted that Israel has been widely criticized over these strikes.

The final perspective on proportionality that I will discuss is the changing precision of the program itself. As noted in the last section, all four of the major databases tracking the CIA drone strikes in Pakistan record a sharp reduction in civilian casualties in 2010—ranging from a drop of almost one-half according to the TBIJ to three-quarters for *LWJ* and UMass DRONE to almost five-sixths for NAF. Moreover, while all four databases show some increase in the proportion of civilian casualties in 2011, on three of the four it is relatively marginal, and even on the fourth (*LWJ*) it remains well below the rate before 2010.

Obviously this sharp reduction in civilian casualties significantly strengthens the case that the strikes are being conducted proportionately. But there is also evidence that this reduction reflects an improved commitment to the principle of precaution (or what is sometimes called "due care"), which, while not part of the proportionality calculus per se, is closely connected with it. In

---

[63] Kristine Eck and Lisa Hultman, "One-Sided Violence against Civilians in War: Insights from new Fatality Data," *Journal of Peace Research*, 44:2 (2007): 241; Bethany Lacina and Nils Gleditsch, "Monitoring Trends in Global Combat: A New Dataset of Battle Deaths," *European Journal of Population*, 21:2–3 (2005): 145–165.

the words of the ICRC study on *Customary International Humanitarian Law,* the principle of precautions in attack is defined as follows:

> In the conduct of military operations, constant care must be taken to spare the civilian population, civilians and civilian objects. All feasible precaution must be taken to avoid, and in any event to minimize, incidental loss of civilian life, injury to civilians and damage to civilian objects.[64]

Professor Alex Bellamy, in his *Just Wars: from Cicero to Iraq,* aptly defines due care as the requirement that "combatants must take positive steps to minimize the risk to non-combatants."[65] Precaution is an extrapolation of, and completion of, the principle of proportionality (which might otherwise permit parties to shift risk to civilians up to the point of actually violating the proportionality calculus).

Several explanations for the improved accuracy of CIA targeting have been suggested. Most importantly, there are said to be, in Bergen and Tiedemann's words, "increased numbers of U.S. spies in Pakistan's tribal areas" presumably producing more and better targeting information.[66] There are also reports of new and improved technology being introduced to improve the accuracy of drone strikes, most notably the use of "Pathrai" homing beacons. In addition, the CIA has begun to make increasing use of a new generation of killer drones known as Reapers, which are able to stay aloft longer than the smaller Predator drones and are better able to distinguish between innocent civilians and militants and to choose an opportune moment to engage the latter.[67]

There are also some indications that the CIA is being more careful to avoid attacks that might endanger civilians. For example, Ken Dilanian reported in a *Los Angeles Times* article at the end of February 2011 that, according to both US and Pakistani officials, "the CIA passed up a chance to kill Sirajuddin Haqqani, the head of an anti-American insurgent network…when it chose not to fire a missile at him from a Predator drone because women and children were nearby."[68] The article mentions two other opportunities to hit HVTs that were passed up for similar reasons. There are also separate reports that new safeguards have been introduced into the CIA program. In January 2011 US officials were already claiming that "each strike is approved by either CIA director Leon

---

[64] Hencaerts and Doswald-Beck, *Customary International Humanitarian Law,* 51.

[65] Bellamy, 191.

[66] Bergen and Tiedemann, "Washington's Phantom War."

[67] Plaw et al., "Practice Makes Perfect?" 61–63.

[68] Ken Dilanian, "CIA Drones May Be Avoiding Pakistani Civilians."

Panetta or his deputy, Michael Morell."[69] All of this suggests a heightened level of caution and restraint.

There are also reports that the CIA has shifted to using smaller, more precise missiles on its drones. Specifically, Joby Warrick and Peter Finn reported in the *Washington Post* in April 2010 that the CIA has shifted from relying primarily on 100-pound Hellfire missiles to carry out attacks to using more precise 35-pound missiles called "Scorpions," especially in urban settings, in a move that has "kept the number of civilian casualties extremely low."[70] Moreover, there does not seem any obvious reason to think that the use of smaller missiles, more restrictive approval procedures, homing beacons, and more intelligence collectors should not continue to have a positive impact on reducing the civilian toll of drone strikes.

These adaptations of drone targeting, and the latter two in particular, appear to reflect a serious commitment to exercising due care and to complying with the principle of precaution. This reflects a broader commitment to proportionality—not only to minimum compliance with the proportionality calculus but also to the underlying ethical imperative to protect civilians as much as possible. It may well be that a good part of the motivation for this commitment is practical rather than moral—fewer civilian casualties should generate less political backlash—but what matters most here is the action and the outcome.

6. Conclusion

On the critical and contested question of whether the CIA drone strikes in Pakistan are killing a disproportionate number of civilians in violation of the standards of JWT and ILOAC, the evidence examined here would suggest not. While there is some uncertainty over the real numbers, the best available evidence suggests that civilian casualties are moderate to low in relation to suspected militant casualties. Moreover, the scale of al-Qaeda and Taliban atrocities against civilians warrant assuming some risks in pursuit of the goal of weakening their capabilities. Drone strikes also compare favorably with military alternatives in the region, specifically American and Pakistani ground operations and Israeli targeting operations. Finally, the accuracy of drone operations has greatly improved in the last two years, seemingly as a result of a greater commitment to precaution and due care. None of this proves that every

---

[69] Tony Cappacio and Jeff Bliss, "U.S. Said to Reduce Civilian Deaths after Increasing CIA Pakistan Strikes," Bloomberg, January 31, 2011. http://www.bloomberg.com/news/2011-01-31/u-s-said-to-reduce-civilian-deaths-after-increasing-cia-pakistan-strikes.html.

[70] Joby Warrick and Peter Finn, "Amid Outrage over Civilian Deaths in Pakistan, CIA turns to Smaller Missiles," *Washington Post*, April 26, 2010. http://www.washingtonpost.com/wp-dyn/content/article/2010/04/25/AR2010042503114.html?nav=emailpage.

CIA drone strike has complied with the standard of proportionality. It remains perfectly possible that some strikes were (or should have been) expected to produce incidental loss of civilian life that would be clearly excessive in relation to the direct military advantages anticipated. But the analysis does suggest that violations have not been very widespread or systematic. It also suggests that, in terms of proportionality at least, drone strikes should at least provisionally be permitted more time to achieve their objectives and to prove how precise and effective they can become.

8

The Wizard of Oz Goes to War: Unmanned Systems in Counterinsurgency

REBECCA J. JOHNSON

> ...You may fly over a land forever; you may bomb it, atomize it, pulverize it and wipe it clean of life—but if you desire to defend it, protect it and keep it for civilization, you must do this on the ground, the way the Roman legions did, by putting your young men in the mud.[1]

1. Introduction

The military has witnessed the convergence of two disparate trends over the past decade—a resurgence of population-centric warfare and the proliferation of unmanned systems.[2] Since the attacks of September 11, 2001 drew the US into Afghanistan in October of that year, over 800,000 US service members have deployed to that country.[3] Over a million have deployed to Iraq between March 2003 and December 2011.[4] While not the target of lethal force, the

---

[1] T. R. Fehrenbach, *This Kind of War* (New York: Macmillan, 1963), 454.

[2] "Population-centric warfare" is the common military term for counterinsurgency or any type of conflict that identifies the population as the "center of gravity," or "the source of power that provides moral or physical strength, freedom of action, or will to act." *DoD Dictionary of Military and Associated Terms*, Joint Publication 1–02, 2008. These can include stability operations or reconstruction and stabilization missions, currently viewed as a matter of the US Department of Defense (DoD) directive on equal footing with major combat operations. In counterinsurgencies, insurgents and counterinsurgents both fight for the support and legitimacy of the population; defeating enemy forces is simply a means to that end. For that reason, counterinsurgencies are identified as population-centric. For a critique of population-centric warfare, see Gian P. Gentile, "A Strategy of Tactics: Population-Centric COIN and the Army," *Parameters* (Autumn 2009): 5–17.

[3] Jim Garamone, "Allen: Troops Will Accomplish Afghan Mission," *American Forces Press Service*, March 20, 2012. http://www.defense.gov/news/newsarticle.aspx?id=67611.

[4] Amy Belasco, *Troop Levels in the Afghan and Iraq Wars, FY2001-FY2012: Cost and Other Potential Issues*, R40682 (Washington, DC: Congressional Research Service, 2009), 9.

civilian populations of both countries have served as a critical focal point of US efforts. Unfortunately, this attention has come at a cost; at least 137,000 civilians have been killed in the two theaters as a direct result of the fighting.[5] While American service members go to great lengths to protect civilians from the harm of military operations, their enemy feels no such constraint.[6] American presence in villages draws insurgent fire directly into population centers. A common enemy tactic is to hide among the civilian population, forcing US troops into the nearly impossible position of trying to isolate combatants among a larger noncombatant community.

At the same time, the US has fielded thousands of unmanned systems into both theaters. The Army alone has logged over a million flight hours within the first decade following September 11.[7] While a number of these are equipped with bombs responsible for killing hundreds in Afghanistan alone, these systems also provide critical intelligence, surveillance, and reconnaissance (ISR), improvised explosive device (IED) detonation, and close air support. In combination, these capabilities help reduce the threat to the warfighter and improve accurate targeting of the enemy.

The combination of these two trends—the resurgence of population-centric warfare and the deployment of unmanned systems—has created a counterinsurgency environment where the population has become an inextricable part of the battle space at precisely the same time that the warfighter is becoming increasingly protected from the threats and dangers of war.[8] In today's wars noncombatants are inextricably part of the battle space at all times and, thus, simultaneously threatened (though not targeted) by the violence produced by all sides at all times. Yet, ironically, the warfighters—counterinsurgents and insurgents alike—have the ability to remove themselves from the battle space, utilize even rudimentary technology for lethal effect, and use that technology to improve their understanding of the battle space and enemy for improved lethality and force protection. American counterinsurgents clearly have superior technological capability for the purposes of maximizing lethality while improving force protection, but the sheer effectiveness of the Taliban's use of IEDs for targeting and cell phones

[5] Neta C. Crawford, "The Cost of War since 2001: Afghanistan, Iraq, and Pakistan, Executive Summary," *The Costs of War Project* (Providence, RI: Watson Institute for International Studies, 2011), 4. Crawford's analysis offers an assessment of the multiple casualty estimates from Iraq and Afghanistan and provides a very useful evaluation of the different methodologies employed by the various estimates. The numbers included here are her calculation of the most reliable minimum number of civilian deaths.

[6] See Chapter 7 in this volume.

[7] Kris Osborn, "Army Surpasses 1 Million Unmanned Flight Hours," April 29, 2010. http://www.army.mil/article/38236/army-surpasses-1-million-unmanned-flight-hours/.

[8] Rebecca Johnson, "Doing More with More: The Ethics of Counterinsurgency," International Symposium of Military Ethics, San Diego, January 2010. http://isme.tamu.edu/ISME10/isme10.html.

for communicating US troop movements demonstrates that even basic technology provides combatants on both sides improved security relative to the population.

While this new dynamic of warfighters on both sides fighting remotely while simultaneously threatening noncombatants raises a wide range of important ethical questions, this chapter will explore only the role played in this dynamic by the employment of unmanned systems by American counterinsurgents. Specifically, do unmanned systems have a defensible place in counterinsurgency operations, or do they exacerbate the problem of exposing noncombatants to higher levels of lethality?[9] To the extent any weapons system enables service members to discriminate and target belligerents with greater accuracy, free them to focus on building relationships rather than provide security, and therefore support rather than replace service members in the battle space, they reinforce traditional efforts to protect civilians from the horrors of war. To the extent unmanned systems are used to reduce the presence of US service members while increasing the lethality of combat, they subvert the intention that underlies noncombatant immunity and proportionality of means.[10]

First I will outline some of the specific moral challenges of counterinsurgency—focusing on the difficulties of defining combatancy (identifying who may be targeted with lethal force), maintaining effective discrimination (targeting only legitimate combatants), providing meaningful noncombatant immunity (protecting noncombatants from intentional harm), and enforcing proportionality of means. It is in this context that the following section will evaluate the effect unmanned systems may have on either facilitating or hindering service members' ability to uphold these restraints while effectively reaching their goal of solidifying popular support for the government.[11] The conclusion will provide

---

[9] There are a host of other important moral questions surrounding the use of autonomous systems in combat, but the most common current employment of unmanned systems includes remote operators in the targeting decision loop. Hence, I leave discussion of autonomous weapons out of the present focus. For a defense of lethal autonomous systems, see Ronald Arkin, "The Case for Ethical Autonomy in Unmanned Systems," *Journal of Military Ethics* 9 (2010): 332–341.

[10] Avery Plaw offers a very useful comparison of collateral damage rates in attacks conducted by unmanned systems, ground forces, and manned aircraft in Chapter 7 of this volume.

[11] The chapter focuses exclusively on the moral implications of unmanned systems deployed by military personnel in counterinsurgency operations. For a thorough and thoughtful discussion of the legal and moral considerations surrounding civilian government officials utilizing unmanned systems, see Human Rights Institute, Columbia Law School, "Targeting Operations with Drone Technology: Humanitarian Law Implications" (Background Note for the American Society of International Law Annual Meeting, March 25, 2011), 25–36. In essence, there is no meaningful moral distinction: civilian government officials may utilize lethal force in conflicts. Legally, they will be designated as "materially participating in hostilities" and legitimately may be targeted in response. They are not afforded the protections granted lawful combatants, such as POW status, if captured.

some guidance for how to better facilitate the use of unmanned systems in counterinsurgencies for the purpose of building government support and reducing insurgent strength.

2. The Moral Significance of Counterinsurgency

Before evaluating the specific moral concerns surrounding the use of unmanned systems, we should first be clear about the moral constraints on the use of lethal force generally, and the particular requirements for the moral use of lethal force in counterinsurgencies specifically. Only once we understand the conditions under which states may fight counterinsurgencies justly can we judge whether and what role unmanned systems may play in their just prosecution. Most statesmen, soldiers, and citizens recognize that there are times when waging war is both legitimate and necessary. At the same time, states agree to fight those wars within certain limits intended to minimize the destructive power of war and facilitate the transition back to a state of peace. The purpose of following just war principles is to limit the scope and pain of war, which as Michael Walzer points out "is hell even when the rules are observed, even when only soldiers are killed and civilians are consistently spared."[12] In fact, "war is so awful that it makes us cynical about the possibility of restraint, and then it is so much worse that it makes us indignant at the absence of restraint."[13] It is with ambivalence concerning our ability to constrain the horrors of war that we commit ourselves to these restraints; it is our way of recognizing that we are both justified to use lethal force against another people and aware of the price that people will pay for our pursuit of justice.

An understanding of limited war, then, contains two related elements: "(1) a specific justification for sometimes killing another human being; and (2) severe and specific restrictions upon anyone who is under the hard necessity of doing so."[14] These restraints are what allow soldiers "to distinguish their life's work from mere butchery."[15] *Jus in bello* criteria governing the just conduct of war are dearly held.[16] The just conduct of war centers on discriminating between combatants and civilians, refraining from targeting noncombatants in battle, and ensuring that the collateral damage done by battle does not outweigh the legitimate military objective. These criteria are codified in international law through the Geneva Conventions and domestically in the US by the Uniform Code of Military Justice.

[12] Michael Walzer, *Just and Unjust Wars* (New York: Basic Books, 2006), 30.

[13] Ibid., 46.

[14] Paul Ramsey, *The Just War: Force and Political Responsibility* (Lanham, MD: Rowman & Littlefield, 2002), 144.

[15] Walzer, *Just and Unjust Wars*, 45.

[16] Colin Kahl, "In the Crossfire or the Crosshairs: Norms, Civilian Casualties, and U.S. Conduct in Iraq," *International Security* 32:1 (Summer 2007): 7–46.

Counterinsurgency poses a unique dilemma for those committed to fighting justly.[17] While conventional war focuses military actors and means against military targets, counterinsurgencies are characterized by the proliferation of targets, tools, and actors.[18] This is because the population determines counterinsurgents' success or failure. Ignore the population and the insurgents win—civilians provide protection and material support that are essential to insurgents' victory. Attack the population and the insurgents win—targeting them with the same military tactics applied to the insurgents merely serves to alienate the population and increase support for the insurgency. Win the support of the population and the insurgents lose—without the material support, cover, and legitimacy provided by the population the insurgents cannot survive.[19]

Why spend time discussing the moral requirements of counterinsurgency? The character of counterinsurgency is sufficiently unique as to demand specific constraints and restraints on the use of force.[20] This fact is recognized in military doctrine: FM 3–24, *Counterinsurgency*, dedicates an entire chapter to "Leadership and Ethics for Counterinsurgency" in an effort to prepare junior leaders for the amplified ethical challenges they will face:

> Ethically speaking, COIN environments can be much more complex than conventional ones. Insurgency is more than combat between armed groups; it is a political struggle with a high level of violence. Insurgents try to use this violence to destabilize and ultimately overthrow a government. Counterinsurgents that use excessive force to limit short-term risk alienate the local populace. They deprive themselves of the support or tolerance of the people. This situation is what insurgents want. It increases the threat they pose. Sometimes lethal responses are counterproductive. At other times, they are essential. The art of command includes knowing the difference and directing the appropriate action.[21]

[17] Steven Metz and Raymond Millen, *Insurgency and Counterinsurgency in the 21st Century: Reconceptualizing Threat and Response* (Carlisle Barracks, PA: Strategic Studies Institute, U.S. Army War College, 2004); John Nagl, *Learning to Eat Soup with the Knife: Counterinsurgency Lessons from Malaya and Vietnam* (Chicago: University of Chicago Press, 2005); Austin Long, *On "Other War": Lessons from Five Decades of RAND Counterinsurgency Research* (Santa Monica, CA: RAND, 2006); Angel Rabasa, Lesley Anne Warner, et al., *Money in the Bank: Lessons Learned from Past Counterinsurgency (COIN) Operations* (Santa Monica, CA: RAND, 2007); Daniel Marston and Carter Malkasian (eds.), *Counterinsurgency in Modern Warfare* (New York: Osprey Publishing, 2008).

[18] United States Army, *Field Manual (FM) 3–24: Counterinsurgency* (Washington, DC: US Government Printing Office, 2006), 1–1.

[19] Walzer, *Just and Unjust Wars*, 184.

[20] In military doctrine, a "constraint" is defined as a requirement (something that must be done), while a "restraint" is defined as a prohibition (something that cannot be done).

[21] Department of the Army, *FM 3–24: Counterinsurgency* (Washington, DC: Department of the Army, 2006), 7–5.

The concerns are real: Our accepted interpretation of just war fighting (known as *jus in bello*, or just conduct in war) prohibits "total war," or a war that focuses the entire force of the state against the entire population of the enemy because it destroys noncombatant immunity and enlarges the battlefield to include the political, social, and economic spheres. To characterize their actions in combat as just, troops must demonstrate restraint by restraining their use of lethal force to combatants and military targets alone. When wars are purely kinetic, this approach to just war fighting may make sense. It breaks down in counterinsurgency.

Counterinsurgency is characterized by both a proliferation of targets, including the entire population that serves as the conflict's strategic center of gravity, and a proliferation of the tools of warfare, including the political, economic, and social elements necessary to win the population's support for the government rather than the insurgency. While the entire population does not become the literal target of lethal force, (1) the challenge of distinguishing between combatants and noncombatants in counterinsurgency increases the risk of being targeted by lethal force by increasing the pool of potentially targetable individuals to the entire population, and (2) regardless of whether civilians are targeted by lethal force, they are functionally targeted by insurgents and counterinsurgents alike. A bullet may cause a civilian to stop breathing, but the political, social, and economic pressure combatants on all sides place on civilians in an effort to sway their (potentially coerced) support can effectively end that civilian's life and way of life just the same. The proliferation of targets and tools results in an expanded battlefield that leaves the population no opportunity to escape from the conflict and no way to return to their former lives once the war ends.

To put it another way, the just war tradition tells us that the only intention appropriate when undertaking war is to recreate the conditions necessary for the life and well-being of the political community. Wars may be fought only because these conditions have been threatened by another. In counterinsurgency the conditions for life and well-being of the community are threatened by insurgents who seek to undermine the ability of the state to provide its core functions to the population: the provision of security, political stability, and conditions for economic well-being.[22] In response, the only intention the state may pursue in countering the insurgent threat is to maintain or reestablish its ability to provide those conditions to the population. In moral philosophy, an "intention" is the state of affairs one is trying to bring about. It is contrasted to one's "motive" or why one is trying to

[22] George Kennan, "Morality and Foreign Policy," *Foreign Affairs* 64 (Winter 1985–1986): 205–218.

create that particular state of affairs.[23] In the context of counterinsurgency, it is morally irrelevant why the state seeks to be the agent responsible for providing the population's security, political stability, and conditions for economic well-being; the only morally significant factor is whether the state is—in fact—trying to provide those services. Defeating the insurgency is simply a means to that end.

While this intention remains the same regardless of the type of threat (the state would also be trying to retain control of its ability to provide security, political stability, and the conditions for economic well-being in the face of an external invasion), the necessary means differ. The insurgency seeks to defeat the state by eroding the population's belief in the state's will and capacity to provide security, political stability, and the conditions for economic well-being. The state defeats the insurgency by convincing the population that it possesses both the will and the capacity to govern legitimately. The insurgents defeat the state by convincing the population that the state lacks either the will to govern legitimately by adopting overly harsh tactics that punish the population for the insurgents' actions or the capacity to govern in the face of growing insurgent power. Either of those roads leads to insurgent victory.

This means that counterinsurgents have a particular challenge to minimize harm done to noncombatants in their efforts to defeat insurgents who live and fight among the population. They likewise have a particular challenge to act in such a way that communicates to the population that they retain the ability to govern legitimately in the face of insurgent attacks. It is not enough to minimize collateral damage in a literal, body count, sense; US forces have the additional responsibility of minimizing the effect their presence has on the fabric of the civilian population to protect the population's ability to return to a state of peace following the war.

Demonstrating the will and capacity to govern legitimately while defeating an insurgent threat is no small feat. It requires an even greater commitment to the traditional moral requirements of combat. The remainder of this chapter will detail the specific moral challenges of counterinsurgency: the challenge of defining who is a combatant (and may therefore be targeted with lethal force); the challenge of targeting only legitimate combatants in an environment where insurgents and civilians are virtually indistinguishable; and the challenges of protecting noncombatants from intentional and disproportionate harm in an environment where insurgents collocate with the civilian population. In exploring these challenges, it will evaluate the effect unmanned systems have on service members' ability to honor these limits on the conduct of warfare.

[23] Fernando Teson, "Eight Principles for Humanitarian Intervention," *Journal of Military Ethics* 5 (June 2006): 99–101.

3. The Challenge of Determining Combatancy

Counterinsurgency is often referred to as "graduate-level warfare."[24] This is equally true of the moral requirements this type of combat brings. In a politically focused war where all sides compete for popular support, the line between combatant and noncombatant can blur.[25] The following section will discuss the challenge of defining combatancy—or who may be targeted and killed legitimately. We must first identify the group of people we characterize as combatants before we can literally identify the specific individuals who fit in that group (the principle of distinction). Distinction becomes possible only once combatancy is settled. In the context of counterinsurgency (or population-centric warfare generally), these dual tasks of defining combatancy and then distinguishing between combatants and noncombatants are—to some—virtually impossible.[26] The second half of this section evaluates the effect of unmanned systems on determining combatancy. In the final analysis, unmanned systems improve the intelligence collection capability of counterinsurgents in a way that improves their ability to conclude with evidence and confidence that those individuals targeted with lethal force are, in fact, combatants acting in a "continuous combat function" or individuals who meet the targeting threshold through their "direct participation in hostilities."[27] Unmanned systems improve the difficult process of determining combatancy in an environment where belligerents intentionally blend with noncombatants. On this ground, their use should be embraced, not shunned.

There are important distinctions in international humanitarian law concerning appropriate restraints on the use of lethal force between what are considered to be international armed conflicts (IACs) and noninternational armed conflicts (NIACs). As will be discussed in greater detail, Geneva Convention III, Art. 4.A provides the commonly accepted definition of "combatant" in IACs. There is no legally accepted equivalent in NIACs, only criteria for determining when civilians may be targeted on the basis of their material participation

---

[24] *FM 3–24: Counterinsurgency*, 1–1. For a contrary view, see Dave Maxwell, "Is COIN the Graduate Level of War?" *Small Wars Journal Blog*, July 20, 2008. http://smallwarsjournal.com/blog/is-counterinsurgency-the-graduate-level-of-war.

[25] ICRC, "Interpretive Guidance on the Notion of Direct Participation in Hostilities under IHL," *International Review of the Red Cross* 90 (2008): 991–1047; Sarah Kreps, "The Second Lebanon War: Lessons Learned," *Parameters* 37 (2007): 72–84.

[26] Anisseh van Engeland, *Civilian or Combatant? A Challenge for the 21st Century* (New York: Oxford University Press, 2010); Michael Gross, *Moral Dilemmas of Modern War: Torture, Assassination, and Blackmail in an Age of Asymmetric Conflict* (Cambridge: Cambridge University Press, 2010), Part II; Richard Arneson, "Just Warfare Theory and Noncombatant Immunity," *Cornell International Law Journal* 39 (2006): 101–126; Paul Ramsey, *The Just War: Force and Political Responsibility* (New York: Rowman & Littlefield, 2002), chapter 18.

[27] Both of these concepts will be discussed more fully herein.

in the conflict.[28] Though the conflict includes international participation, US action in Afghanistan and more broadly against al-Qaeda, the Taliban, and their affiliates has been characterized as a noninternational armed conflict, which legally denies combatant status for nonstate material participants.[29] This chapter sacrifices technical legal precision for simplicity and uses the term "combatancy" to refer to both groups of individuals.

As this section will demonstrate, unmanned systems do not replace the human determination of who warrants engagement as a combatant. While there is some legitimate concern that the targeting ability of unmanned systems may tempt decision makers to rely on technology over their own judgment, we lack evidence to demonstrate that decision makers employ questionable targeting criteria. The debate concerning the morality of signature strikes is a real and pressing one, but not one that has anything to do with unmanned systems as a technology. It has to more to do with the political decision of what actions qualify as identifiers of combatancy status. What is more, the surveillance ability of unmanned systems undeniably improves the military's ability to identify members of armed groups and civilians who are participating materially in hostilities. These capabilities are critical to determining combatancy in an environment where combatants blend in with the population. It is hard to imagine an asset more capable than unmanned systems in determining combatancy in population-centric conflicts.

In conventional warfare, combatants refer to those individuals who fight on behalf of the state. Traditionally, soldiers have been recognizable by wearing uniforms.[30] The practice not only aids in identifying one's countrymen to reduce friendly fire incidents but also draws enemy fire to those in uniform, away from those who are not. This intentionally increased risk on the part of soldiers has traditionally been seen as part of the nobility, part of the honor of the profession of arms. The practice had become so standardized that the Geneva Conventions have codified the formal requirements for combatancy in terms of these visible indicators of combatant status (and thus guaranteeing the right to prisoner of war, or POW, status):

1. Being commanded by a person responsible for his subordinates
2. Having a fixed distinctive emblem recognizable at a distance

---

[28] Marco Sassoli and Laura M. Olson, "The Relationship between International Humanitarian Law and Human Rights Law Where It Matters: Admissible Killing and Internment of Fighters in Non-International Armed Conflicts," *International Review of the Red Cross* 90 (2008).

[29] Human Rights Institute, "Targeting Operations with Drone Technology," Part IA.

[30] David Whetham, *Just Wars and Moral Victories: Surprise, Deception and the Normative Framework of European War in the Later Middle Ages* (Boston: Brill Press, 2009).

3. Carrying arms openly
4. Conducting their operations in accordance with the laws and customs of war.[31]

This traditional "status-based" approach to determining combatancy is challenged in conflicts that include nonstate actors of any stripe. On one end of the spectrum are groups like the Kosovo Liberation Army (KLA)—that clearly fought as the agent of a group that claimed de facto legitimacy (and thereby approximated a state's military); wore the fixed, distinctive sign; demonstrated a weak but functional chain of command; and sporadically abided by the laws and customs of war. It gets a little murkier with fighters from the Northern Alliance. They can still claim to represent a segment of Afghan society; they fought openly, though without any identifying marks; and arguably followed the laws and customs of war when fighting alongside US Special Forces troops.[32] It gets harder still when talking about private security contractors. They are not fighting as agents of a state; they are agents of their companies and are providing security for individuals in return for personal profit.[33] At the far end of the spectrum lie individuals (including children) who run supplies for or provide intelligence to the insurgency. The question of material participation becomes essential for understanding when and under what conditions these individuals become legitimate targets. This is where we have seen the tradition evolving the past decade—from a status-based conception of combatancy, where anyone in uniform is a legitimate target at all times—to a conduct-based conception of combatancy, where only those participating materially in hostilities may be targeted while they are participating.[34]

In 2009, the International Committee of the Red Cross (ICRC) published *Interpretive Guidance on the Notion of Direct Participation in Hostilities under International Humanitarian Law* in an effort to clarify when civilians may be targeted during ongoing hostilities either through their serving in a continuous combat function (CCF) or through their direct participation in hostilities (DPH). The

---

[31] International Committee of the Red Cross (ICRC), "Convention (III) Relative to the Treatment of Prisoners of War," *International Humanitarian Law—Treaties and Documents*, 1949, http://www.icrc.org/ihl.nsf/FULL/375.

[32] Doug Stanton, *Horse Soldiers: The Extraordinary Story of a Band of US Soldiers Who Rode to Victory in Afghanistan* (New York: Scribner, 2009); Andrew Alexandra, Deane-Peter Baker, and Marina Caparini (eds.), *Private Military and Security Companies: Ethics, Policies and Civil-Military Relations* (London: Routledge, 2008).

[33] Markus Hehdal, "Blood and Blackwaters: A Call to Arms for the Profession of Arms," *Journal of Military Ethics* 8 (2009).

[34] Of course, material participation does not extend rights of combatancy in terms of POW status. For greater fidelity on this discussion of the moral status of combatants, see the extended discussion of Jeff McMahan's views in *Killing in War* (Oxford: Clarendon Press, 2009) by Gerald Lang, Michael Otsuka, and Bradley Jay Strawser in the various articles offered in the symposium in *Analysis* 71 (2011): 511–559.

most challenging designation, and the one most similar to traditional notions of combatancy, is the continuous combat function, which applies only to members of nonstate armed groups.[35] According to the ICRC's *Interpretive Guidance*, "…under IHL, the decisive criterion for individual membership in an organized armed group is whether a person assumes a continuous function for the group involving his or her direct participation in hostilities (hereafter: 'continuous combat function')."[36] Those avowed members of the Taliban—not farmers by day, insurgents by night, but core Taliban members and fighters—meet the CCF standard. That means that just like regular members of state militaries, they may be targeted permissibly at any time even while not actively prosecuting military objectives.

While there are important moral questions concerning the parameters of CCF, members of known armed groups are relatively straightforward from a combatancy perspective. The more difficult moral question concerns when it becomes legitimate to target those individuals who would reasonably be considered civilians. Individuals cross this threshold from protected noncombatants to targetable actors when they participate materially in the conflict.

The *Interpretive Guidance* provides three key criteria to determine when a civilian has crossed the line to material participation (thereby becoming eligible for targeting).

To qualify as direct participation in hostilities, a specific act must meet the following cumulative criteria:

1. The act must be likely to adversely affect the military operations or military capacity of a party to an armed conflict or, alternatively, to inflict death, injury, or destruction on persons or objects protected against direct attack (threshold of harm).
2. There must be a direct causal link between the act and the harm likely to result either from that act or from a coordinated military operation of which that act constitutes an integral part (direct causation).
3. The act must be specifically designed to directly cause the required threshold of harm in support of a party to the conflict and to the detriment of another (belligerent nexus).[37]

Philip Alston, the UN's special rapporteur on extrajudicial, summary, or arbitrary executions, notes the limiting factor of DPH:

> The key, however, is to recognize that regardless of the enemy's tactics, in order to protect the vast majority of civilians, direct participation

---

[35] ICRC, *Interpretive Guidance*, 69.

[36] Ibid., 33.

[37] ICRC, *Interpretive Guidance on the Notion of Direct Participation in Hostilities under International Humanitarian Law* (Geneva: Red Cross, 2009), 16.

may only include conduct close to that of a fighter, or conduct that directly supports combat. More attenuated acts, such as providing financial support, advocacy, or other non-combat aid, does not constitute direct participation.[38]

This means that the DPH enables targeting only when individuals are engaged in military operations. There are those in the Western just war tradition, like Paul Ramsey, who would disagree with this more exclusive interpretation of direct participation. According to Ramsey, collaboration is sufficient to convey combatancy:

> In contemporary insurgency, the fact is that a peasant is often a civilian by day and a combatant by night. Others are close cooperators all or some of the time, and therefore technically combatants also. In short, the decision of the insurgents to conduct war by selective terror results in a situation in which a whole area is inhabited mainly by "combatants" in the ethically and politically relevant sense that a great number of the people *are* from consent or from constraint the bearers of the force to be repressed.... *The insurgents themselves* have enlarged the target it is legitimate for counter-insurgents to attack, so far as the principle of discrimination is concerned; and it is therefore mainly the principle of proportion that limits what should be done to oppose them.[39]

This argument follows the "They Started It" line of moral reasoning. Through their efforts to hide among the population, the insurgents themselves and those individuals who are sympathetic to or cooperative with the insurgents are morally responsible (to at least some degree) for enlarging the population that may be legitimately targeted, not the counterinsurgents. Counterinsurgents are simply operating within a military environment that contains the enlarged target area and are not then culpable for failing to discriminate between combatants and noncombatants.

Richard Arneson pushes the point further, arguing that civilians carry a responsibility for carving out their own noncombatant position by withdrawing from areas where the insurgency is being fought, passing intelligence on to the counterinsurgents, and providing other assistance to those battling the insurgents. "If civilians support an unjust guerrilla warfare effort, they may

---

[38] Philip Alston, *Report of the Special Rapporteur on Extrajudicial, Summary or Arbitrary Executions: Addendum Study on Targeted Killing.* A/HRC/14/24/Add.6 (May 28, 2010), 19.

[39] Paul Ramsey, *Just War*, 435, italics in original.

be culpable for doing so, and culpability may erode the moral of traditional noncombatant immunity."[40]

Walzer seems to agree with the argument of an enlarged target area, though he fails to draw the same conclusion as Ramsey and Arneson that counterinsurgents need not discriminate in their operations as a result. According to Walzer, insurgents have enlarged the target area in two ways:

> First, their day-to-day existence is much more closely connected with the day-to-day existence of the people around them than is ever the case with conventional armies. . . . And second, they fight where they live; their military positions are not bases, posts, camps, forts, or strongholds, but villages. Hence they are radically dependent on the villagers, even when they don't succeed in mobilizing them for "people's war."[41]

In his seminal work on counterinsurgency, David Galula rejects the premise that insurgents and their supporters enlarge the target area. "The complicity of the population is not to be confused with the sympathy of the population; the former is active, the latter inactive, and the popularity of the insurgent's cause is insufficient by itself to transform sympathy into complicity."[42] For this, as well as for pragmatic reasons ("antagonizing the population will not help"), Galula argues that harm done to the population at large should be kept to a strict minimum during counterinsurgencies, and any misdeeds should be "punished severely and even publicly . . ."[43]

This disagreement surrounding the appropriate conception of direct participation—conduct-based combatancy—is meaningful for understanding appropriate limits on the use of lethal force in counterinsurgencies. Rules of engagement (ROE) have varied over time in Iraq and Afghanistan concerning what acts constitute DPH over what time frame. These have varied from very strict interpretations similar to those advocated by the *Interpretive Guidance* to more permissive rules that allowed targeting all orange and white cars in Iraq.[44]

Drones can play an important role in identifying material participation and membership in armed groups. The improved ISR capacity of drones allow for a substantially improved ability for operators to monitor an individual's movements for days at a time to determine periodic instances of material participation or actual membership in an armed group. What is more, current technology

[40] Richard Arneson, "Just Warfare Theory and Noncombatant Immunity," *Cornell International Law Journal* 39:3 (2006): 118.

[41] Walzer, *Just and Unjust Wars*, 184.

[42] David Galula, *Counterinsurgency Warfare: Theory and Practice* (New York: Frederick A. Praeger, 1964), 50.

[43] Ibid., 108–109.

[44] http://www.aaanet.org/press/an/0207/thu.html.

allows for individuals to be followed by a Reaper (and similar unmanned systems) until such time as the individual is away from noncombatants.[45]

Some, like Sarah Kreps and John Kaag, question the usefulness of this ability. They write, "True, these technologies provide militaries with more information with which to distinguish a combatant from a civilian. They also allow militaries to pinpoint and target some individuals, while sparing others. The weapons, however, do not ensure that a selected target is a legitimate target."[46] Given the current utilization of these systems (with a human responsible for validating targets and pulling the trigger), that is an obvious but morally insignificant point in examining human-controlled drones compared with other weapons. Until such time as targeting and launching strikes are conducted by an autonomous system without a human in the loop, a human will be responsible for determining whether a target is a legitimate target. There is no moral difference between a Reaper pilot and a Strike Eagle pilot in this regard, except that the Reaper pilot has a greater ability to track and monitor a potential target. Certainly, Kreps and Kaag are correct that the greater information provided by unmanned systems does not "ensure that a selected target is a legitimate target," but that is the case for *any* strike by *any* weapon system and thus is not a relevant consideration for drones qua drones.

The larger moral question surrounding combatancy is not the result of unmanned systems, though it is facilitated by them in important ways. The decision to employ signature strikes rather than personality strikes marks a significant expansion of the number of individuals considered to be "combatants." Allow me to explain. "Personality strikes" are strikes authorized for specific individuals. They represent "by-name" targeting—once an individual has been identified as a member of an armed group (and may therefore be targeted at any time, not exclusively while in the act of participating in hostility) he is added to a list of viable targets. Once the individual can be positively identified, he may be targeted by ground forces or air assets.[47] Morally, the use of personality strikes is unproblematic, provided appropriate scrutiny is utilized in determining who may be considered members of an armed group.[48] Unmanned systems

[45] John Brennan, "The Efficacy and Ethics of U.S. Counterterrorism Strategy," Woodrow Wilson Center, April 30, 2012. http://www.wilsoncenter.org/event/the-efficacy-and-ethics-us-counterterrorism-strategy.

[46] Sarah Kreps and John Kaag, "The Use of Unmanned Aerial Vehicles in Contemporary Conflict: A Legal and Ethical Analysis," *Polity* 44 (2012): 261.

[47] Adam Entous, Siobhan Gorman, and Julian Barnes, "U.S. Relaxes Drone Rules; Obama Gives CIA, Military Greater Leeway in Use against Militants in Yemen," *Wall Street Journal*, April 26, 2012, http://online.wsj.com/article/SB10001424052702304723304577366251852418174. html?mod=WSJ_World_MIDDLENewsIntl.

[48] There are those who argue for greater military transparency in the targeting process. Alston, *Study on Targeted Killings;* Human Rights Institute, "Targeting Operations with Drone

can assist in this designation, and this contributes to their significance in the moral conduct of counterinsurgency operations.

Signature strikes are something different. Signature strikes are strikes authorized against individuals who fit particular behavioral profiles, for example, transporting weapons or engaging in opium production.[49] The concerns with signature strikes are that there may be legitimate reasons for an individual to engage in suspect behaviors (transporting weapons for personal protection vice arming militants). Also, depending on the criteria incorporated into the behavioral profiles, senior leaders may be authorizing targeting on the basis of behavior that is seen to be indirect support to the insurgency, not direct participation in hostilities, as in the case with targeting those involved in opium trafficking.[50]

Again, this concern is amplified by the ease with which unmanned systems can act on signature strikes. This fear is amplified as the military moves toward fully autonomous systems that use computer algorithms to evaluate a target, identify threat, and potentially launch a lethal strike without a human trigger puller. At present, this capacity has yet to be fielded. What is more, the decision to use signature strikes and the decision of what behaviors may legitimately be covered by signature strikes have nothing to do with unmanned systems in particular. Ground forces may be provided the same targeting permissions to use while conducting foot patrols and fighter pilots may use signature strikes as part of flying manned sorties. The concern is more accurately focused on the potentially inappropriate implementation of an overly permissive ROE; it is not an indictment of unmanned systems themselves. Frankly, this enlarges the seriousness of the indictment of the use of signature strikes, since it broadens the number of ways they may be employed by the military, but focusing on their use by unmanned systems obscures the real moral question—whether it is acceptable to target an individual based on a pattern of life rather than actually observed combatant behavior.

Furthermore, criticisms of signature strikes stem more from fear of their inappropriate application than evidence that they have, in fact, been applied inappropriately. Any of the *jus in bello* criteria can be manipulated to the point of being meaningless. Unless one is to forsake the use of force entirely, the question is not whether inappropriate behavior *may* occur but whether it *has* occurred and how it is dealt with when it does occur.[51]

Technology." While the desire is understandable, it is practically unreasonable. The protection of intelligence gathering procedures and products necessarily precludes open discussion of the evidence used to determine who would be targetable through personality strikes.

[49] Entous, "U.S. Relaxes Drone Rules"; Alston, *Study on Targeted Killings*, 21.

[50] Ibid.

[51] The White House's Counterterrorism Advisor, John Brennan, notes in a Fox News Sunday interview that strikes are conducted with the consent of the countries involved. He does not

4. The Challenge of Distinction

The constraints concerning who qualifies as a combatant is made by higher-level leadership and communicated down the chain of command to those who will come in contact with potential combatants. These individual service members must use their judgment in applying leadership's constraints in specific circumstances to determine whether a specific individual is a member of an armed group, participating materially in combat, complicit in insurgent actions, or simply located within the battle space. This determination is a moral requirement of just conduct in war and is known as the principle of distinction. According to Article 48 of the Protocol Additional to the Geneva Conventions (AP1), "In order to ensure respect for and protection of the civilian population and civilian objects, the Parties to the conflict shall at all times distinguish between the civilian population and combatants and between civilian objects and military objectives and accordingly shall direct their operations only against military operations."[52] This section will explore the challenges counterinsurgents face in distinguishing between combatants and noncombatants. It advances the argument that unmanned systems improve, rather than hinder, service members' ability to positively identify legitimate targets. This increases lethality without increasing the potential for collateral damage. If anything, the ability to track potential targets while verifying combatancy allows drone operators to wait until both (1) positive confirmation of either CCF or DPH is made and (2) the now validated target is away from noncombatants.

Discrimination becomes particularly challenging in counterinsurgencies for precisely the same reasons determining combatancy is challenging.[53] Insurgents consciously take actions to blend in with noncombatants, operate out of civilian areas, and rely on noncombatant complicity—motivated by either general fidelity or fear of retribution—to evade counterinsurgents.

---

go so far as to state that the US shares targeting criteria with host national governments, but other reports indicate the US shapes its targeting practice in light of host national requirements. "John Brennan Talks War on Terror," Fox News Sunday, April 29, 2012. http://www.foxnews.com/on-air/fox-news-sunday/2012/04/29/john-brennan-talks-war-terror-joel-and-victoria-osteens-message-hope?page=2. For evidence of the US shifting targeting policy in response to host national requests, see David Rohde, "The Obama Doctrine," *Foreign Policy* (March–April 2012).

[52] Protocol Additional to the Geneva Conventions of August 12, 1949, and relating to the Protection of Victims of International Armed Conflicts (Protocol 1), June 8, 1977. While the US is not a signatory of the Additional Protocol, it considered binding under customary international law. The doctrine of distinction is articulated clearly in US military law. See DoD Directive 2311.01E, May 9, 2006.

[53] Kahl, "In the Crossfire or the Crosshairs;" LTC Tony Pfaff, "Ethics in Complex Contingencies: New Demands on the Warrior Ethic," paper presented at the 2004 JSCOPE Conference. http://isme.tamu.edu/JSCOPE04/jscope04.html. Some just war theorists have argued that the impossibility of discrimination in counterinsurgency removes the obligation from combatants. See Paul Ramsey, *The Just War: Force and Political Responsibility* (New York: Rowman and Littlefield, 2002), chapter 18; Jean Bethke Elshtain, *Just War against Terror* (New York: Basic Books, 2004).

At the same time, it is pragmatically and morally essential to distinguish accurately.[54] Pragmatically, the whole purpose of counterinsurgency operations is to build popular support for the government while eroding popular support for the insurgency. Angering the population by mistakenly targeting them and their families is not an effective route to building the perception that the government has the will and capacity to provide the population's security. General Stanley McChrystal's Tactical Directive of July 2009 made his recognition of this fact clear:

> We must fight the insurgents, and will use the tools at our disposal to both defeat the enemy and protect our forces. But we will not win based on the number of Taliban we kill, but instead on our ability to separate insurgents from the center of gravity—the people. That means we must respect and protect the population from coercion and violence—and operate in a manner which will win their support.[55]

Pragmatism is not the only reason forces distinguish between combatants and noncombatants. The members of the community of states have bound themselves to the traditional just war principle that, while combatants forsake their rights to life and well-being, noncombatants have not forsaken that right, and just warfighters treat them differently because of it. Even if our adversary has failed to commit itself to this obligation, we have. We have so committed ourselves, that is, if we aim to fight justly. A just soldier is bound to restrain intentional violence to combatants even when it is inexpedient or difficult.

This makes the use of signature strikes particularly concerning: what level of moral risk is a service member and nation willing to accept? According to the *Interpretive Guidance*, "In practice, the principle of distinction must be applied based on information which is practically available and can reasonably be regarded as reliable in the prevailing circumstances."[56] The moral question at hand is whether unmanned systems improve or hinder service members' ability to distinguish between those identified as members of armed groups and participating materially in hostilities. In the context of counterinsurgency, this includes an important manpower question. It is true that analyzing the video streams from unmanned systems is labor intensive, but using these systems for

[54] Geoffrey Corn and Chris Jenks, "Two Sides of the Combatant COIN: Untangling Direct Participation in Hostilities from Belligerent Status in Non-International Armed Conflicts," *University of Pennsylvania Journal of International Law* 33 (2011), 315.

[55] *Tactical Directive* (unclassified), released July 6, 2009. www.nato.int/isaf/docu/official.../ Tactical_Directive_090706.pdf.

[56] ICRC, *Interpretive Guidance*, 35.

the purposes of identifying combatancy frees ground forces to focus on their primary mission of securing the population's support for the government. They may be involved in capturing individuals who have been identified as legitimate targets but retain intelligence potential, but they can devote their attention to conducting the sort of operations that are necessary to build popular support and leave a portion of the missions focused on weakening insurgent strength to those with better visibility.[57]

It is easy to conceive of patterns of behavior that would indicate direct participation in hostilities; indeed, they are the same patterns of behavior that are used by ground forces. Unmanned systems simply serve to increase visibility of behavior and better enable tracking of those individuals who fit the identified patterns of combatancy.[58] Yes, this increases lethality, but it also improves the ability to distinguish between legitimate combatants and civilians. To quote from President Barack Obama's counterterrorism adviser, John Brennan:

> Targeted strikes conform to the principle of distinction—the idea that only military objectives may be intentionally targeted and that civilians are protected from being intentionally targeted. With the unprecedented ability of remotely piloted aircraft to precisely target a military objective while minimizing collateral damage, one could argue that never before has there been a weapon that allows us to distinguish more effectively between an al-Qa'ida terrorist and innocent civilians.[59]

In fact, as has been the case with precision guided munitions, one can make the argument that as the ability to more reliably determine behavioral patterns that indicate material participation and armed group membership, ground forces could face increased pressure to target only those individuals who have been verified through overhead surveillance to fit into either the DPH or CCF categories. This would reduce their ability to render judgment in the absence of secondary positive identification but would also further reduce the potential for collateral damage. At the very least, overhead surveillance could be

[57] John Brennan, "The Efficacy and Ethics of U.S. Counterterrorism Strategy," Remarks at Woodrow Wilson Center, April 30, 2012. http://www.wilsoncenter.org/event/the-efficacy-and-et hics-us-counterterrorism-strategy.

[58] Alston, *Study on Targeted Killings*, 24. Also, Phillip Meilinger, "Precision Aerospace Power, Discrimination, and the Future of Warfare," *Aerospace Power Journal* 15 (2001); Harold Koh, "The Obama Administration and International Law," *Annual Meeting of the American Society of International Law* (Washington, DC: United States Department of State, 2010); Michael Schmitt, "Precision Attack and International Humanitarian Law," *International Review of the Red Cross* 87 (2005).

[59] John Brennan, "The Efficacy and Ethics of U.S. Counterterrorism Strategy," Remarks delivered at the Woodrow Wilson Center, April 30, 2012. http://www.wilsoncenter.org/event/ the-efficacy-and-ethics-us-counterterrorism-strategy.

incorporated into the reviews of firefights to ensure any kills were "clean." This would meet requests for accountability in targeting, though there are equally significant moral concerns with potential Monday morning quarterbacking of military action conducted under fire.

This increased accountability aspect of unmanned systems should not be minimized. Unmanned systems provide a truly unprecedented ability to review battlefield decisions. In the words of David Whetham, "... Every movement of a UAV's joystick, every frame of camera footage and therefore every decision (or indeed hesitation or omission) of the operator is recorded and can be poured over at great length following any incident."[60]

5. The Challenge of Protecting Noncombatant Immunity

This improved ability to distinguish between combatants and noncombatants in an environment where insurgents have sought to hide within the civilian population improves the military's ability to protect noncombatant immunity. Service members distinguish between combatants and noncombatants in order to protect noncombatants from the horrors of war. Stated broadly, the norm of noncombatant immunity holds that soldiers may not intentionally target non-combatants in the prosecution of their legitimate war aims. Their immunity derives from the fact, discussed already, that while soldiers may forfeit their rights to life and liberty while in combat, noncombatants do not—their rights are to be protected, even in times of war.[61] While soldiers are allowed to kill in the prosecution of legitimate war aims and individual soldiers are allowed to kill in self-defense, so long as noncombatants do not threaten soldiers directly, it is wrong for soldiers to target them intentionally.[62] This section will analyze the specific challenges to honoring noncombatant immunity in counterinsurgency. It will then examine the ways unmanned systems might reduce rather than amplify the potential for collateral damage in the particular context of counterinsurgency warfare. While there are reports of civilians killed by drone

[60] David Whetham, "Remote Killing and Drive-By Wars," in D. Lovell and I. Primoratz (eds.), *Protecting Civilians during Armed Conflict: Theoretical and Practical Issues during Violent Conflict* (London: Ashgate, 2012).

[61] Walzer, *Just and Unjust Wars*, 136.

[62] Brian Orend, *The Morality of War* (Orchard Park, NY: Broadview Press, 2006), 106–107. For a discussion of how to deal with the obvious difficulty of assessing whether individuals are true noncombatants or whether they may pose a threat to soldiers see Pauline Kaurin, "When Less Is *Not* More: Expanding the Combatant/Noncombatant Distinction," in Michael Brough, John Lango, and Harry van der Linden, *Rethinking the Just War Tradition* (New York: State University New York Press, 2007), 115–130; Tony Pfaff, "Ethics in Complex Contingencies: New Demands on the Warrior Ethics," Joint Services Conference on Professional Ethics 2004. http://www.usafa.edu/isme/JSCOPE04/Pfaff04.html.

strikes, the smaller size of munitions carried by many unmanned systems, the improved capacity to identify noncombatants in the vicinity of legitimate targets, as well as the track record of trigger pullers waving off targets because of the presence of noncombatants should give confidence that unmanned systems enhance the counterinsurgents' ability to target lethality at legitimate targets while protecting noncombatants from the harm of war. No weapons system is perfect, but the best evidence available to date suggests that unmanned systems are a clear improvement.[63]

The commitment to noncombatant immunity is grounded in the premise that civilians do not forfeit their right to life simply because their governments have chosen to wage war. They are seen as being innocent of the state's war making. This serves as one of the moral differences between soldiers and civilians. On traditional just war theory, soldiers have no presumptive right to life—the conduct of their profession eliminates it.[64] This is why killing a soldier in the legitimate conduct of war fighting is not murder, while killing a solider in cold blood is. Unless a civilian acts as a soldier by participating materially in the conflict, she never loses her right to life, regardless of her proximity to the battle.

Legally, this sentiment has been codified in the Hague Conventions of 1907, which prohibited "the killing and wounding treacherously" of those not participating in conflict, and in the Geneva Conventions, which defines noncombatants in its "Common Article 3"—one of the articles common to each of the Conventions. Common Article 3 defines noncombatants as "Persons taking no active part in the hostilities, including members of armed forces who have laid down their arms and those placed 'hors de combat' by sickness, wounds, detention, or any other cause."[65] What does this mean in practice? Noncombatants "shall in all circumstances be treated humanely, without any adverse distinction founded on race, colour, religion or faith, sex, birth or wealth, or any other similar criteria."

Common Article 3 goes further to proscribe:

> To this end, the following acts are and shall remain prohibited at any time and in any place whatsoever with respect to the above-mentioned persons:
>
> (a)   violence to life and person, in particular murder of all kinds, mutilation, cruel treatment and torture;
> (b)   taking of hostages;
> (c)   outrages upon personal dignity, in particular humiliating and degrading treatment;

---

[63] For a more detailed discussion of the civilians killed by drone strikes, see Chapter 7 in this volume.

[64] For deeper debate of this issue, see McMahan, *Killing in War* and the reviews in *Analysis* (2011) noted already.

[65] Geneva Convention (III) Relative to the Treatment of Prisoners of War (1949), art. 3.

(d) the passing of sentences and the carrying out of executions without previous judgment pronounced by a regularly constituted court affording all the judicial guarantees which are recognized as indispensable by civilized peoples.

The fact that noncombatants may be harmed unintentionally in the normal course of pursuing a legitimate military target (with a proportional use of force) does not violate the norm of noncombatant immunity, provided that (1) the noncombatants were not the (intentional) target of the operation, and (2) reasonable steps were taken to minimize noncombatant harm (even if this means combatants assuming greater risks themselves).[66]

It is not merely that noncombatants retain their right to life in times of war; they retain their right to live unmolested by conflict—they retain the right to their livelihood. Any action that intentionally targets noncombatants' ability to live their lives normally violates noncombatant immunity. Forced detention, curfews, curtailment of speech, and other denials of individual autonomy all fail to honor the distinction between combatants and noncombatants and fail to honor the norm of noncombatant immunity.

This is one reason that the American military refrains from targeting religious centers, museums, hospitals, and schools. One could conceive of attacking any of those facilities in a way that would eliminate civilian casualties (attack the museum at night when it is empty, for instance), yet these facilities are among the most difficult targets to clear, even when the enemy uses them as a base from which to launch attacks. Why? Because targeting them is seen as targeting the people. Regardless of the physical harm (or lack thereof) that may be done to a civilian population, this action is seen as wrong. If the original understanding of noncombatant immunity stems from the status of an individual and a common acceptance that her rights to life and livelihood is not forfeited in times of war, then the "no harm no foul" principle still fails to honor the norm of noncombatant immunity, though it may pass the test of proportionality.[67]

This factor stands in tension with the rights-vindicating aspect of the counterinsurgents' mission. As I have argued elsewhere:

Counterinsurgents must strike a balance between the obligation to leave *individual* noncombatants outside the battlespace and the

---

[66] Walzer, *Just and Unjust Wars*, 155.

[67] Oliver O'Donovan, *The Just War Revisited* (New York: Cambridge University Press, 2003), 43; Frederick Kaufman, "Just War Theory and Killing the Innocent," in Michael Brough, John Lango, and Harry van der Linden (eds.), *Rethinking the Just War Tradition* (New York: State University New York Press, 2007), 99–114.

obligation to vindicate *all* noncombatants' right to be left outside the battlespace. In this equation, vindicating the right takes precedence over protecting the individual. First, vindicating the right is the only way to ensure that individuals collectively will be protected. Second, violating a right is worse than infringing it. It is undeniable that collateral damage prevents a specific person from exercising his right to be left unmolested by war, but it does so by affirming that the right both exists and is worthy of defense in the first place. Collateral damage is the *exception*, not the norm.[68]

Efforts necessary to successfully repair the population's ability to live unmolested by war—"aggressive saturation patrolling, ambushes, and listening post operations"[69]—are necessary to protect the population from insurgents who clearly intend to violate civilians' right to life. There is no other way to vindicate the right to life and livelihood that has been intentionally and systematically violated by the insurgency. At the same time, those actions jeopardize the lives and livelihoods of specific civilians at specific moments.

It is on this point that the use of unmanned systems has garnered the greatest controversy. Accounts vary wildly concerning the number of civilians killed in drone strikes since 2001. Estimates indicate that roughly 11 percent of those killed in strikes in Pakistan in 2011 were civilian (down from 17 percent from 2004 to 2010).[70] Total estimates of civilians killed from drone strikes in Pakistan range from 293 to 471 from 2004 to 2012.[71] Collateral damage—while a distastefully antiseptic term for unintentional civilian deaths—is considered to be an unfortunate but morally tolerable reality of an otherwise morally prosecuted war. Efforts to minimize, if not eliminate, collateral damage lay at the foundation of restrictive ROE that forbid targeting near population centers—even during the provision of close air support to reinforce troops under fire.[72]

---

[68] Rebecca Johnson, "Fight Right to Fight Well: General McChrystal's Approach to Preserving Noncombatant Immunity," *Small Wars Journal* 6 (April 2010).

[69] U.S. Army, *FM 3-24: Counterinsurgency* (Ft. Leavenworth, KS: Army Field Manual, 2006).

[70] New America Foundation, "The Year of the Drone," *Counterterrorism Strategy Initiative*, 2013. http://counterterrorism.newamerica.net/drones#2012chart.

[71] Ibid. Estimates of civilians killed by drones in Afghanistan are not publicly available, thought the United Nations Mission in Afghanistan (UNAMA) estimates that 187 Afghan civilians were killed by aerial attacks in 2011 (including fixed wing, rotary wing, and unmanned aircraft). "Progovernment forces" were responsible for 410 civilian combat-related deaths in 2011. This compares with 2332 civilian combat-related deaths attributes to "antigovernment elements" that same year. United Nations Mission in Afghanistan, *Afghanistan Annual Report 2011: Protection of Civilians in Armed Conflict*, (Kabul: United Nations, 2012), 2.

[72] *Tactical Directive*. To see the policy in action, see Jonathan Landay, "'We're Pinned Down: 4 U.S. Marines Die in Afghan Ambush," McClatchy News Service, September 9, 2009. http://www.

According to Brennan, in discussing strikes by unmanned systems:

> ...We only authorize a strike if we have a high degree of confidence that innocent civilians will not be injured or killed, except in the rarest of circumstances. The unprecedented advances we have made in technology provide us greater proximity to targets for a longer period of time, and as a result allow us to better understand what is happening in real time on the ground in ways that were previously impossible. We can be much more discriminating and we can make more informed judgments about factors that might contribute to collateral damage.[73]

The US most senior counterterrorism adviser continues:

> I can tell you today that there have indeed been occasions when we have decided against conducting a strike in order to avoid the injury or death of innocent civilians. This reflects our commitment to doing everything in our power to avoid civilian casualties—even if it means having to come back another day to take out that terrorist, as we have done.[74]

Chris Mayer agrees with this level of restraint, arguing that "military forces should use weapons that can precisely target" the insurgents. "Only this type of precise targeting respects NCI [noncombatant immunity] and the people whom it protects, and recognizes the strength of the noncombatant's rights."[75] It seems clear, then, that if unmanned systems are more precise in their targeting abilities and resulting abilities to respect noncombatant immunity and the rights of noncombatants, then they are morally preferred, in at least this regard. Insofar as this is true of them, they should be viewed as weapons of choice for counterinsurgency operations. Plaw's research suggests this is the case in Pakistan, though a more thorough review of the lethal use of unmanned systems elsewhere would be needed before reaching a definitive conclusion.[76]

mcclatchydc.com/227/story/75036.html; "DoD News Briefing with Geoff Morrell at the Pentagon Briefing Room, Arlington, VA," September 9, 2009. http://www.defenselink.mil/transcripts/transcript.aspx?transcriptid=4475. For a demonstration of the effect of ROE on collateral damage in Pakistan, see Chapter 7 of this volume.

[73] John Brennan, "The Efficacy and Ethics of U.S. Counterterrorism Strategy," Remarks at Woodrow Wilson Center, April 30, 2012. http://www.wilsoncenter.org/event/the-efficacy-and-ethics-us-counterterrorism-strategy.

[74] Ibid.

[75] Chris Mayer, "Nonlethal Weapons and Noncombatant Immunity: Is it Permissible to Target Noncombatants?" *Journal of Military Ethics* 6:3 (September 2007): 227.

[76] See Chapter 7 in this volume.

In counterinsurgency, however, there is an additional moral benefit to using unmanned systems for lethal strikes. Remember, insurgents target civilians in areas surrounding US forces. They do this out of their own perception of civilian complicity, and they find villages convenient locations to hide while planning and launching attacks. To the extent that unmanned systems can allow ground forces greater standoff from civilian populations, then they also reduce the inadvertent targeting of civilians that comes from insurgents using their communities as bases of operations. Certainly, greater use of lethal unmanned systems cannot eliminate the enemy's use of population centers, but they allow a greater ability to draw lethal action out of villages into less populated areas.

To be clear on this point, so long as US forces meet the proportionality, discrimination, and noncombatant immunity criteria of the law of armed conflict, they are not culpable for civilian casualties in counterinsurgency. At the same time, unmanned systems allow for an even higher level of fidelity to each of these moral and legal requirements, demonstrating clear value added in the moral prosecution of war. While it may seem counterintuitive to recommend removing US troops further from the population in an effort to better protect the population, the increasing employment of unmanned systems in this regard over the past decade demonstrate their benefit.

6. Conclusion

Any introduction of new technologies in combat should be scrutinized to ensure that their use comports with accepted restraints on the just conduct of war. At the same time, there is an important difference between being reflective and being reactionary. Decisions concerning combatancy are political decisions that make their way to commanders on the ground for implementation. Concerns that the existence of unmanned systems hastens decision makers down a slippery slope toward targeting civilians for acts of complicity both ignores the widespread use of similar practices throughout history and ignores the very real scrutiny both personality and signature strikes receive before they are authorized. Decisions regarding combatancy are made without consideration of the *means* used to prosecute targets—ground forces prosecute signature strikes the same as drones.

Unmanned systems do play a decisive moral role in their ability to facilitate distinction and noncombatant immunity. The ability to loiter on target, verify targets by multiple pilots and analysts, and review strikes after the fact improves both the ability and the incentive to distinguish combatants from noncombatants in a way that is simply superior to other methods. While the improved technological ability lowers the bar of acceptable levels of collateral damage, civilian deaths attributed to unmanned systems in a counterinsurgency environment remain low. Additionally, while there are multiple avenues to building popular support for the government, armed insurgencies must be countered with force. It is the only way to vindicate the rights to civilians' life and livelihood violated by the insurgents. Unmanned systems allow for the use of smaller missiles than fixed wing aircraft and provide greater flexibility to the ground forces they support.

Providing this support enables ground forces to focus on their primary tasks—building the relationships with the population necessary to understand and address the grievances that have created the fissures with the government that spurred the insurgency in the first place. So long as the humans guiding and prosecuting the war remain committed to the principles of combatancy, distinction, and noncombatant immunity—and at present we have no indications to the contrary—unmanned systems improve civilians' and military personnel's ability to prosecute counterinsurgency effectively and morally.

9

Killing Them Safely: Extreme Asymmetry and Its Discontents

UWE STEINHOFF

1. Introduction

Are there any special ethical problems with the use of automated weapons systems, of "killer robots," in war? Is there a special problem with killing by remote control? I will first argue in this chapter that this is not the case; however, I will also argue that there is a general problem with generating extreme military superiority and that the use of automated weapons and of "remote control killing" is part of this more general problem.

I will present my argument by critically engaging opposing views and arguments of philosophers Robert Sparrow, Suzy Killmister, and Bradley Jay Strawser. This selection is almost inevitable since at the time of writing there are virtually no other sustained *philosophical* discussions of the issues in question and in any case the contributions of these authors are exemplary in that they ask all the right questions—even if, in my view, they do not give all the right answers.

2. Sparrow on Killer Robots

Robert Sparrow offers the following argument against autonomous weapon systems, that is, against weapon systems that are "artificially intelligent" and can make "decisions" for themselves, for example decisions regarding whom to attack and in which way:

1. Premise: "It is a fundamental condition of fighting a just war that someone may be held responsible for the deaths of enemies killed in the course of it. In particular, someone must be able to be held responsible for civilian deaths. The responsibility at issue here is moral and legal responsibility and not mere causal responsibility."[1]

---

[1] Robert Sparrow, "Killer Robots," *Journal of Applied Philosophy* 24:1 (2007): 63–77, at 67.

2. Premise: There are many "acts" an automated weapon system might commit, including instances of the killing of innocent people, for which neither the programmer of the weapon, nor the commanding officer, nor the machine itself can (justly) be held responsible.[2]

3a. Conclusion: Therefore "it will be unethical to deploy autonomous systems involving sophisticated artificial intelligences in warfare."[3]

3b. Conclusion: "The deployment of weapon systems controlled by artificial intelligences in warfare is therefore unfair either to potential casualties in the theatre of war, or to the officer who will be held responsible for their use."[4]

(I distinguish these two conclusions because they are not equivalent, contrary to what Sparrow might think.)

This is, no doubt, an interesting argument, but there are a couple of problems with it. To begin with, the fundamental condition Sparrow mentions has never (as far as I am aware) been proposed by any just war theorist (besides Sparrow, that is). Thus, he introduces this principle for the first time. This, of course, would in itself not be a problem, but he would at least have to give an argument as to why we should accept that principle. He does not, however.[5] Thus, his argument lacks any firm grounding.

More importantly, the first premise is not only unsupported by argument but also wrong or at least too weak to get the desired conclusion. To see this, consider an example. The peaceful tribe of the Psychondos is threatened by colonialists who want to kill them all. The Psychondos, it is worth mentioning, all suffer from a rare disease: in the face of mortal danger, a Psychondo will suffer a psychotic break. Thus, when the colonialists attack, the Psychondos suffer psychotic breaks, perceive the bloodthirsty human colonialists as demons from hell trying to kill them, and defend themselves vigorously, so that enough colonialists are killed to convince the rest of them to retreat. Was the defensive war of the Psychondos against the colonialists unjust only because the Psychondo

---

[2] Ibid., 69–74.

[3] Ibid., 74.

[4] Ibid., 75.

[5] Sparrow refers to Thomas Nagel, "War and Massacre," *Philosophy and Public Affairs* 1 (1972): 123–144, esp. 133–142. However, first, and with all due respect to Nagel: one article about just war theory does not make one a just war theorist. Second, if Sparrow's interpretation of Nagel were correct, then my criticism would apply to Nagel too (so that we would at best have two exceptions within the just war theory: Sparrow and Nagel). Third, Sparrow's interpretation is not correct. Nothing Nagel says implies, let alone explicitly states, the "fundamental condition" Sparrow is talking about. Nagel can at best be interpreted as saying that *if* war is waged between persons, *then* those persons should treat each other *as persons*. He nowhere says that war *should* be waged between persons on both sides or that on each side, whether persons are involved or not, someone *must* be responsible.

fighters were nonresponsible while fighting? (By "unjust" I indeed mean unjust and not only "lacking just cause." Just cause is only *one* condition that must be fulfilled for a just war.) It does not seem so.

One might object here that there is a distinction between acting justly and acting not unjustly as well as between acting unjustly and not acting justly. For example, if lightning kills an innocent person, the lightning does not kill the innocent person unjustly, at least not in a certain sense of "unjustly." In this sense, only *responsible* agents can act justly or unjustly, and lightning is not a responsible agent. It seems not to make much sense to attribute "unjust behavior" or "just behavior" to it. However, the Psychondos, due to their psychotic breaks, were *ex hypothesi* also not responsible agents when they killed the attacking colonialists, and therefore they did not act justly or unjustly. A precondition for acting justly, namely, moral responsibility, was lacking.

Note, however, that if Sparrow were to take this line of defense, it would not much help him. For the defensive war of the Psychondos is not a war that is merely *excused*. Someone, let's say Catherine, who suffers a psychotic break and in this condition, due to her hallucinations, kills an *innocent* person, is only excused; but killing an innocent person would still be wrong under domestic law and certainly deplorable from a moral perspective. It is something the person *should not have done*. This can also be seen with regard to third-party intervention: a third party who is able to stop Catherine's attack on the innocent person by taking away her gun should do so.

This, however, is not the situation with the Psychondos. It is *good* that they manage to kill enough aggressors to thereby save their own tribe. One should *not* stop them from fighting the aggressor. Thus, even if their warfare against the aggressors were not just (in the sense described two paragraphs previous), their warfare against the aggressors is nevertheless not deplorable and is not one that should be stopped (the colonialists are the ones that should be stopped). Instead, we should wish them good luck.

Thus, even if we accepted this interpretation of "just" and "unjust," the desired conclusions would not follow. For if we say that being unjust or just requires moral responsibility on the part of the agent, we cannot suddenly interpret "unethical" in conclusion (3a) in a different way. In other words, to be coherent one would have to say that for an act to be unethical or ethical it has to be committed by a responsible agent. However, since the defensive war waged by the Psychondos against the unjust aggressors *ex hypothesi* lacks responsible agents, this war cannot be unethical.

The same is true for conclusion (3b). In addition, it should also be noted that for independent and quite obvious reasons the unjust aggressors cannot complain of being treated unfairly by the Psychondos or of being wronged by them. Since they attack the Psychondos unjustly, they have lost their right not to be attacked by them. There is no such thing as a right of an unjust aggressor not to be defensively attacked by a defender who is not morally responsible for his actions.

A further problem with premise (1) is that its formulation could suggest that a war can be just only if for each and every death that is produced by the war there is someone who can be held responsible for that death. But if that is really what is meant, it is obviously wrong not only in light of the Psychondos example but also in light of the trivial fact that the acts of some responsible agent can cause death without the agent being morally responsible for it. If I detonate a firecracker on New Year's Eve in my own courtyard and a jumpy neighbor falls off his ladder and breaks his neck, I am not really morally (or legally) responsible for that. And if an innocent person falls off his ladder (and breaks his neck) because the sound of a bomb detonating far away frightens him, then the people who dropped that bomb on a legitimate military target can, in my view, not plausibly be held morally responsible for it. Furthermore, it is intuitively quite implausible to assume that a just war becomes unjust the moment a single person is killed in a way that does not confer moral responsibility on anyone. If, however, the first premise is *not* meant to claim that for each and every death someone must be accountable, then Sparrow's argument cannot refute the view that at least the use of *some* automated weapons in war (as a supplement to human combatants) can be justified.

The second premise is correct. However, it is much too weak, with the effect that the conclusions do not logically follow from the conjunction of the first and the second premise (not even if the first premise is interpreted as saying that for each and every death someone must be accountable). After all, the first premise claims only that "someone" must be responsible for the casualties on the enemy side. Yet the programmer of the weapon, the commanding officer, and the machine are not the only persons or objects that are suitable candidates for responsibility. Hence, ruling out only them doesn't quite do. Other obvious candidates for responsibility are, after all, readily available in the form of *politicians*.

Let me illustrate this with a variation of the Psychondos example. We are now considering another peaceful tribe, the Phobicondos, who, as it happens, are also threatened by an unjust, genocidal aggressor. The Phobicondos all (but one) suffer from a rare affliction: in the face of mortal danger, they all freeze, completely unable to act—so they would fall easy prey to the aggressors. Fortunately, however, the chief of the tribe does not suffer from this affliction and is therefore also the bearer of the Holy Whistle. The effect of blowing into the whistle with all his might is that the Phobicondos will suffer a psychotic breakdown combined with enormous bravery and extreme aggressiveness. The genocidal aggressors come, the Phobicondos freeze, the Chief blows the whistle, the Phobicondos unfreeze and kill the unjust aggressors.

Obviously, there is now someone responsible for the deaths of the unjust aggressors: the chief of the Phobicondos. He is responsible for those deaths in the same way as politicians who decide to introduce automated weapons systems are responsible for the deaths caused by those weapons systems. Thus, the problem Sparrow sees is not really there.

Nothing changes in this respect if we consider not only unjust aggressors but also innocent victims. Let us assume there were, for whatever reasons, some innocent people among the aggressors. The Phobicondos, due to their condition, did not distinguish between the guilty aggressors and the innocent people, and so they killed the few innocents too. Were these innocents wronged or treated "unfairly" (the word Sparrow uses in conclusion 3b) by being killed? Of course they were. Not necessarily by the Phobicondon fighters (who are not responsible) but also by the chief. And if he could foresee that those innocent people would be killed by his fighters, he is responsible for this "collateral damage" (or, as I prefer to say, concomitant slaughter)—and, nevertheless, could still have been justified in inflicting it, due to proportionality considerations.

There is no difference here between the relation of the chief to the deaths of the civilians caused by his psychotic fighters and the relation of politicians to the deaths of civilians caused by automated weapons systems. In fact, the psychotic fighters *are* automated weapon systems in the sense that they can make their own targeting and fighting decisions *and* are not responsible for them.

In addition, there is also no morally relevant difference between the politician's relation to the deaths caused by automated weapon systems and his relation to the deaths caused by soldiers who can be held accountable. Moreover, there is also no difference between the politician and a commanding officer here. This brings us to a further problem with premise (2): why is the commanding officer not responsible, according to Sparrow? He says, and it is worth quoting him at length:

> If the autonomy of the weapon *merely* consists in the fact that its actions cannot always be reliably predicted and therefore that it may sometimes kill people whose deaths were not intended, then the analogy with existing weapons may be close enough. Employing AWS [Autonomous Weapon Systems], then, is like using long-range artillery. The risk that shells may land off target is accepted when the decision to fire is made. If they do kill people other than their intended targets, responsibility for the decision to fire remains with the commanding officer.
>
> However, this is a peculiar way to treat what are advertised as "smart" weapons. It implies that there is no fundamental moral difference between them and more ordinary "dumb" weapons. This way of resolving the problem therefore sits uneasily with the original claims

about the "autonomy" of such systems. What distinguishes AWS from existing weapons is that they have the capacity to choose their own targets....

So, the autonomy of the systems cannot be captured by the mere fact that they are unpredictable....At this stage of my discussion it will have to suffice to note that the autonomy of the machine implies that its orders do not determine (although they obviously influence) its actions. The use of autonomous weapons therefore involves a risk that military personnel will be held responsible for the actions of machines whose decisions they did not control. The more autonomous the systems are, the larger this risk looms. At some point, then, it will no longer be fair to hold the Commanding Officer responsible for the actions of the machine. If the machines are really choosing their own targets then we cannot hold the Commanding Officer responsible for the deaths that ensue.[6]

I think this reasoning is mistaken on a number of points. First of all, the last sentence of the quote is clearly wrong. Obviously, a commanding officer is not off the hook only because a soldier or machine he deploys can make its own targeting decisions. Consider an officer who knows that Private Hinks prefers killing civilians to killing combatants. In fact, just on the last mission Private Hinks committed atrocities against civilians. If the commanding officer continues deploying Hinks in this knowledge, he will be co-responsible for the further atrocities Hinks might commit against civilians. It will not do if the officer afterward says, "You know, I did not tell Hinks to kill the civilians. Indeed, I even told him not to. Of course, I knew that there was a very significant risk of him committing atrocities against civilians, but the *choice* to do so was his, not mine." As far as excuses go, this is a lame one, and no judge or jury with a modicum of decency will be impressed. By using the murderous Hinks, the commanding officer is grossly negligent at the very least, if not guilty of aiding and abetting murder.

This, however, is not different in the case where the commanding officer uses an automated weapons system he knows to sometimes target innocent civilians. If he uses it anyway, he is grossly negligent at the very least and can thus be justly held responsible for the (disproportionate) civilian deaths that occur.

This also reveals another mistake in Sparrow's argument. Sparrow seems to assume that because the autonomy of the automated weapon does not merely consist "in the fact that its actions cannot always be reliably predicted" there must be "a fundamental moral difference" between the automated weapons

---

[6] Ibid., 70–71.

and the "more ordinary 'dumb' weapons." But as far as the responsibility of the commanding officer is concerned, this assumption is entirely unwarranted. To wit, the fact that the *autonomy* of automated weapons or soldiers does not consist in their alleged unpredictability in no way conflicts with the fact that the degree to which the commanding officer is *responsible* for the actions of automated weapons or soldiers *is* dependent on the predictability or unpredictability of their behavior.

Thus, when Sparrow says that "at some point...it will no longer be fair to hold the Commanding Officer responsible for the actions of the machine" he is certainly right, but not in the way he thinks. After all, at some point it will also no longer be fair to hold him responsible for the actions of one of his soldiers. This point will be reached when the commanding officer could not reasonably *predict* that there was a sufficiently significant risk that the soldiers, the dumb bombs or the smart automated machines would act in the atrocious way they actually did act. If, however, he could or even did predict that, then the autonomy of the soldiers or weapons will not absolve him from his (at least co-) responsibility. Thus, contrary to what Sparrow suggests, "employing AWS, then, is like using long-range artillery." There is no special moral problem, no "fundamental moral difference" involved.

One final remark: I have already distinguished conclusions (3a) and (3b). The reason for this is that they do not quite say the same thing. To see this better, note that there is a distinction between just acts and justified acts. On this distinction, a *just* act (by a responsible agent, let's say) is an act that does *not wrong* anybody, does *not violate anybody's rights*. However, in law and in morality there is the so-called necessity defense or necessity justification: sometimes it can be *justified*, all things considered, to violate someone's rights, to wrong someone, if this is necessary to prevent something much worse from happening. This necessity justification is of course also used to justify "collateral damage" in war: while the rights of the innocent civilians are violated if they are foreseeably killed as a side effect of an attack on a military target, killing them might still be justified if it is not disproportionate compared with the good (like the destruction of an ammunition factory and in consequence, let us assume, the saving of many innocent people) that is being achieved by the attack.

Now, traditionally people talk about "just war theory" although just war theory actually is justified war theory. A war is really *just* only if it does not wrong anybody. A war in which the innocent defenders kill guilty aggressors only in necessary and proportionate self-defense would qualify as such a just war. A war in which innocent people die as a side effect of military measures would not. However, such a war could still be *justified* if one takes necessity justifications into account.

Now, I take it that Sparrow actually wants to argue for conclusion (3a), that is, for the conclusion that "it will be unethical to deploy autonomous systems involving sophisticated artificial intelligences in warfare." I think it is safe to assume that "unethical" means "unjustifiable" here. What about conclusion (3b) then? Well, although (3b) appears as a conclusion at the end of the paper, presumably derived from the first two premises, it is, when reading Sparrow's article, difficult to avoid the impression (and I hope I am not being unfair here) that (3b) is also used in the other direction, namely, as something supporting Premise (1). In other words, I had the impression that Sparrow considers the responsibility principle of Premise (1) as somehow based on an obligation not to treat people unfairly; and killing them in a way that confers on nobody responsibility for the killing would allegedly be unfair. Or, somewhat simplified, it seems that Sparrow derives (3a) with the help of (3b).

But such a derivation is not possible. (3b) states, as we saw, that "the deployment of weapon systems controlled by artificial intelligences in warfare is…unfair either to potential casualties in the theatre of war, or to the officer who will be held responsible for their use." However, for all intents and purposes unfair can be interpreted as unjust here. In any case, as with unjust action, unfair actions too can sometimes be *justified*, namely, by a necessity justification. Thus, showing that the deployment of automated weapons systems is *unfair* does not yet show that it is also *unethical* or *unjustified* all things considered.

There is even a deeper problem, which in fact might amount to a *reductio ad absurdum* of Sparrow's argument. To wit, he tells us that it is unfair if people get killed in war without anybody being responsible for it. However, *who* is then responsible for this unfairness? Who is the target of Sparrow's criticism? Metaphorical contexts aside ("Life has treated him unfairly"), occurrences of unfairness need somebody who is being unfair; they need an agent of the unfairness. That agent, of course, could also be a collective or perhaps an organization, like a state or a company (thus, there need not necessarily be one specific individual who is personally responsible, and persons can also be responsible to different degrees), but it cannot be nature. Nature is not an actor. Unfairness exists only where responsible actors (alone or collectively) cause or allow the unfairness with their acts or omissions.

Thus, if it were really true that nobody is responsible for civilian deaths caused by automated weapons systems, then it is quite difficult to see how those deaths beyond responsibility can be the result of anybody's being unfair. However, if they *are* the result of some people's being unfair, how can it then possibly be that those very same people are *not* responsible for the very deaths that result from their unfairness? Thus, it seems that Sparrow's argument is not only wrong but also conceptually or logically incoherent.

In a more recent article, Sparrow is more hesitant and tentative about his conclusions, which, as we just saw, is appropriate, for his argument does not succeed. While he alludes to the argument I have just criticized, he also offers an additional one, trying to show that robot weapons, if they lead to massive asymmetry, as of course they could, would make war immoral. The argument goes like this:

> To begin with, note that there are no morally relevant features that distinguish those it is permissible to directly kill (combatants) and those it is not (non-combatants) other than their membership in these groups....
>
> They [the warfighters from both sides] stand in a relationship of "mutual threat" and their "license to kill" stems from their right to self defence....
>
> However, if threat plays a role in establishing warfighters' "license to kill" then, as Kahn argues, should the armed forces of one side of a conflict be rendered incapable of posing a threat to the other, then the warfighters of the more powerful side will no longer have a justification for targeting the armed forces of the other. Instead, the moral permissions and obligations of war are replaced by a more limited right to self defence alongside the permissions and demands of policing.[7]

The problem with this argument is that Sparrow is making two assumptions here that, apart from a diminishing number of Walzerians, few prominent just war theorists would subscribe to. There are good reasons for this. First, there actually *are* morally relevant features that distinguish those it is (morally) permissible to directly kill and those it is not; however, membership in the group of combatants and in the group of non-combatants, respectively, is *not* one of them, for in contrast to what Sparrow suggests with the brackets, the group of combatants does not coincide with the group of legitimate targets, and the group of noncombatants does not coincide with the group of illegitimate targets.

Why is that? Let me explain.[8] There are four serious approaches one might use in distinguishing illegitimate human targets from legitimate ones, that is, those who cannot be justly killed, maimed, or injured from those who can be thus treated, or, in other words, those who have a right not to be killed, maimed, or otherwise be subjected to severe violence from those who have not.

---

[7] Robert Sparrow, "Robotic Weapons and the Future of War," in Paolo Tripodi and Jessica Wolfendale (eds.), *New Wars and New Soldiers: Military Ethics in the Contemporary World* (Farnham: Ashgate, 2011), 117–133, at 128.

[8] These brief explanations draw heavily on Uwe Steinhoff, "Killing Civilians," in Hew Strachan and Sibylle Scheipers (eds.), *The Changing Character of War* (Oxford: Oxford University Press, 2011), 381–394, at 381–385. For a more elaborate discussion, see Uwe Steinhoff, *On the Ethics of War and Terrorism* (Oxford: Oxford University Press, 2007), ch. 4; see there also for further references.

These approaches are the *moral guilt theory,* the *convention theory,* the *self-defense theory,* and the *justifying emergency theory.*

The *moral guilt theory,* which dominated just war theory after the Church father Augustine for at least a thousand years,[9] claims, roughly, that those who bear responsibility for an unjust war are liable to attack. But since it is entirely clear that civilians can bear responsibility for unjust wars (e.g., the billionaire industrialist lobbying his state into an aggressive war to get his hands on the neighbor state's resources or the influential ideologue calling for a genocide), the moral guilt theory cannot exclude civilians as legitimate targets of attack.

According to the *self-defense theory* of the distinction between legitimate and illegitimate targets, immediate aggressors would be legitimate targets of violent countermeasures (and thus, in the technical sense of the principle of self-defense, "non-innocent," that is, *harming,* from the Latin verb *nocere*), irrespective of whether one could morally blame them for their aggression. Conversely, individuals who are not immediate aggressors would even then be illegitimate targets if they were morally (co-)responsible for the aggression, for example, by supporting, or goading on, the immediate aggressor. Thus, Robert K. Fullinwider, who has given this theory its perhaps paradigmatic expression, claims that if mobsters coerce Smith (for instance, with terrible threats against his family) into unjustly trying to kill Jones, the mobsters are not legitimate targets of the defender Jones, since they do not pose the immediate threat, while Smith, who has started shooting, is. The problem with this approach, however, is, first, that it is entirely unappealing from a moral point of view and, second, that it seems not even to be true that the principle of self-defense allows defensive measures only against the immediate threats or aggressors. As Lawrence A. Alexander remarks:

> May Jones invoke the Principle of Self-Defense to kill the mobsters instead of Smith if by doing so he will cause Smith to relent? Of course he may....Jones not only could, but should, kill the mobsters rather than Smith if killing them would be no riskier than killing Smith and would remove the threat to Jones by removing Smith's motive for killing him.[10]

This is directly applicable to war. If the civilian cabinet of Aggressor Nation issues military orders to conscript by force children between eight and fourteen years of age and to send them off to invade Defender Nation, and Defender

[9] Colm McKeogh, "Civilian Immunity in War: From Augustine to Vattel," in Igor Primoratz (ed.), *Civilian Immunity in War* (Oxford: Oxford University Press, 2007), 61–83, at 66.

[10] Lawrence A. Alexander, "Self-Defense and the Killing of Noncombatants: A Reply to Fullinwider," in ed. Charles Beitz et al. (eds.), *International Ethics: A Philosophy & Public Affairs Reader* (Princeton, NJ: Princeton University Press, 1990), 98–105, at 99.

Nation could as easily end the invasion by mowing down the children (who pose the immediate threat) as by blowing up the civilian cabinet of Aggressor Nation, it seems morally outrageous to opt for the former strategy instead of the latter. The situation is not much different if we are talking not about politicians but about, let us say, an enormously influential group of clergy or tycoons who stand to profit from the invasion. If the conscription of the children and the unjust invasion is due to the unholy doings of these groups behind the scenes and could be stopped by giving *them* a taste of war instead of giving it to the innocent children, one could and should, all else being equal, do exactly that.

While the self-defense theory, narrowly interpreted, focuses on immediate or imminent threats or attacks, it makes sense to take into account less immediate threats and dangers as well. This is done by what I call, inspired by the German justifying emergency statute (*rechtfertigender Notstand*), the *justifying emergency theory*. For example, a sleeping soldier does not pose an immediate threat and of course is not currently attacking anyone; thus, on a narrow interpretation of self-defense (which is in fact suggested by the wording of Western self-defense statutes in some domestic jurisdictions and by some pacifists),[11] he cannot be liable to defensive countermeasures. However, it seems intuitively clear that one can also be justified in using violence against a danger that does not express itself in an *immediate* attack or threat. Consider, for example, a father camping with his family in the wilderness, who learns over radio that he and his family is being followed by five murderers who have already killed all campers they have encountered on their way. The attempt to flee with his children would be hopeless, the murderers would reach them by tomorrow night in any case, and law enforcement will not be able to save the family in time. To be caught by the murderers in unprotected terrain would mean certain death. So the family father takes his rifle, marches in their direction, finds an excellent place to lay an ambush, and once the murderers are in the right position he opens fire on them, killing them all, including two of them who attempted to flee after the first shots (if he allowed only one of them to escape, this might still result in the death of his family). This seems justified under the circumstances, but it is not strictly speaking justified as self- (or other-) defense.

Thus, the justifying emergency theory, in contrast to the self-defense theory (narrowly construed), can nicely explain why sleeping soldiers can be liable to attack. But of course, like the self-defense theory it does not exclude attacks on civilians. On the contrary, in the cases of the aforementioned tycoons or clergy, it allows attacks on these people too if this could avert the danger to innocent people.

---

[11] See, for instance, David Carroll Cochran, "War-Pacifism," *Social Theory and Practice* 22 (1996): 161–180, esp. at 169.

The *convention theory*, as formulated by George I. Mavrodes, argues that non-combatant immunity must be interpreted as a useful convention.[12] The convention restricts the brutality of war in the interests of the warring parties. As another author, Michael Green, formulates it:

> ...Nations will wish to limit war so that the possibility of their nation being totally destroyed is minimised, or at least significantly reduced. Most will wish that enough of their country remains so that their country can be rebuilt and their way of life continued after hostilities. A nation will wish to preserve its cultural, educational, and religious sites, its reproductive capacity (traditionally represented by women and children), and its non-military economic assets.[13]

But if the goal is to limit destruction, would not a single-combat convention, according to which, for example, the leaders or two other representatives of the warring nations should settle their differences in single combat, be much more useful?[14] The answer is no. One must not forget that war damage is not to be avoided *at any price*. Many find at least some things valuable enough to risk some degree of destruction. Mavrodes himself does not see this point clearly enough, since he finds the single-combat convention attractive (though utopian). Yet the idea that, in a clash that would normally have led to war, "whatever territory, influence, or other price would have been sought in the war"[15] should instead simply be handed over to the winner of individual combat is not as appealing as it might at first look. If the winning nation is out to rape, enslave, or murder the population of the other country, one can hardly expect—whether psychologically or morally—the threatened side to be willing to settle the matter by arm wrestling. This is also true if "only" its freedom and self-determination is threatened. Thus, the single-combat convention is actually not preferable to the civilian-immunity convention.

However, it is worth noting that the civilian-immunity convention cannot be seen merely as a contract whose binding force rests on reciprocity. That would imply that as soon as one side in a conflict starts to disregard it, the other side is entitled to do the same. A stronger interpretation of the convention theory bases it rather on the rule-utilitarian principle, which states roughly that those rules should be adopted and followed that maximize human happiness. If this

---

[12] George I. Mavrodes, "Conventions and the Morality of War," in Beitz et al., *International Ethics*, 75–89.

[13] Michael Green, "War, Innocence, and Theories of Sovereignty," *Social Theory and Practice* 18 (1992): 39–62, at 57.

[14] This is a question posed by Richard Norman, *Ethics, Killing and War* (Cambridge: Cambridge University Press, 1995), 164.

[15] Mavrodes, "Conventions and the Morality of War," 82.

principle or something similar is accepted, a state is not allowed to break the convention merely because the enemy state has done so. Instead, it has to take into account the wider implications of still further violations of the principle. For instance, retaliation in kind might in the long run make the situation of human beings worse. However, it has to be noted that this will not always be so. There can be specific situations where adopting a rule that identifies precisely these situations as exceptions to the convention of civilian immunity might in the long run produce more good than bad. Sometimes situations are so specific or so extreme that the expected benefit of violating the convention in these situations in pursuit of certain valuable goals is not outweighed by the expected disadvantages of violating the convention. To give a hypothetical example: if by intentionally killing one innocent person one averts the destruction of the whole of humanity, one should kill the innocent person. Less extreme examples are readily available. Thus, the convention theory cannot uphold an absolute immunity of civilians either.

I have so far discussed four approaches to distinguishing the "innocent" from the "noninnocent," that is, distinguishing those who have a right not to be killed or maimed or otherwise subjected to severe violence from those who do not have this right. *Each* of these approaches is centered on its own morally valid principle, namely, the principle of moral guilt, the principle of self-defense, the principle of justifying emergency, and the rule-utilitarian principle. The theories differ from the principles they are based on in that each theory raises its respective principle to an absolute status and uses it as the one and only measure for distinguishing between legitimate and illegitimate targets and acts. Using more than one principle would lead to new and different approaches. In fact, all four principles need to be applied and weighed against each other.

However, neither alone nor in concert can the four theories or principles explain or justify an absolute immunity of civilians. Of course, if one takes into account the epistemic restrictions, that is, the uncertainty and lack of knowledge under which combatants often must act in war, then in many situations the guilt theory, the self-defense theory, and the justifying emergency theory go a long way toward establishing at least a *presumption* of innocence (whether "innocence" is understood in the sense of the first of these theories or of the two latter ones), but this presumption is defeasible. Sometimes combatants *know* or are at least reasonably certain that certain civilians are noninnocent with regard to the unjust war effort and that the combatants are also quite capable of targeting those civilians. This still leaves the rule-utilitarian principle as a last moral defense of even noninnocent civilians. However, under certain circumstances it will not only be outweighed by other principles but also will justify or even require the attack on civilians. Thus, from a moral point of view, pace Sparrow, it is not possible to clearly demarcate "the group of combatants" from civilians in such a way that the former can be permissibly killed while the latter are immune.

A second assumption of Sparrow's that is widely rejected is that there is a symmetry *based on self-defense* between both sides in a conflict. After all, the right to self-defense sides with the defender and thus is far from grounding a *mutual* right of defenders and aggressors to kill each other.[16]

A third assumption Sparrow makes, however, is, as it would seem, shared by many present-day just war theorists, namely, the assumption that self-defense plays the central role in justifying killing in war. However, more important than the self-defense justification is actually the justifying emergency justification. This justification, as we saw, (morally) allows the killing of an aggressor in a much wider range of cases than the self-defense justification and thus circumvents the limitations Sparrow is concerned about anyway.

Fourth, it is not clear *why* Sparrow is concerned about these limitations. After all, he elucidates the distinction between war and policing as follows:

> In war it is legitimate to target and kill enemy combatants—those who are actively involved in the business of warfare...In policing, on the other hand, it is permissible to kill only those who are responsible for serious violations of human rights and even then only in the course of preventing serious rights violations and/or trying to bring the perpetrators of such violations to justice.[17]

Thus, his claim here, again, is that war makes more people legitimate targets, since not all combatants are actually responsible for serious violations of human rights, and in war killing those nonresponsible combatants is,

---

[16] Ibid., 92–95. It is an established principle in criminal law that "there can be no self-defense against self-defense." See, for example, Brien Hallet, "Just War Criteria," in Lester R. Kurtz and Jennifer E. Turpin (eds.), *Encyclopedia of Violence, Peace, and Conflict, Vol. 2,* (Oxford: Elsevier Science & Technology, 1999), 283–294, at 291. The reason for this is precisely that there is a "moral asymmetry" between aggressor and defender, so that the former forfeits his right to life if killing him is necessary and proportionate under the circumstances. This view has a long tradition in natural law thinking and the just war tradition. For a clear and early statement, see Samuel Pufendorf, *De Jure Naturae et Gentium Libri Octo,* Vol. 2, trans. C. H. Oldfather and W. A. Oldfather (Oxford: Clarendon Press, 1934), 323 (219) [III.I.7]. A far-reaching mutual liberty of soldiers on both sides to kill each other would therefore have to be grounded in a different way. See, for such an attempt, Uwe Steinhoff, "Rights, Liability, and the Moral Equality of Combatants," *Journal of Ethics* (2012, Online First).

[17] Sparrow, "Robotic Weapons and the Future of War," 127. Incidentally, Sparrow's account of policing is incorrect: police in most, if not all, jurisdictions are also allowed to kill so-called innocent (nonresponsible) aggressors if this should prove necessary to safe innocent bystanders.

allegedly, legitimate even if it does not happen in the course of preventing serious rights violations. And thus he concludes:

> It is possible, then, that future advances in the development of UMS [unmanned systems] may have the perverse consequence of under-mining the justification of their use in war (or at least, war against certain sorts of enemies). Instead, robotic weapons would need to be used (much) more selectively, to prevent injustice and punish crime in the context of international operations.[18]

In other words, Sparrow claims here that unmanned military systems (UMS) would make it morally imperative to be more discriminate in war fighting. Why that should be deemed "perverse," however, is unclear to me. Rather, it seems that this would, from a *moral* point of view, speak *for* UMS, not against them.

3. Asymmetric War: On Creating the Circumstances for Justified Terrorism

In a very perceptive article, Suzy Killmister argues the following:

> Remote weaponry restricts the moral options for retaliation available to the state under attack. A state under attack from remote weaponry is unable to respond in the traditional, just war sanctioned, manner of targeting combatants on the battlefield—there simply are none. There are thus three options available to such a state: it can surrender; it can target enemy civilians; or it can target what I have termed civilian combatants within the aggressor state.
>
> ...If the operational difficulties of attacking civilian combatants become insurmountable, remote weaponry can create situations in which the targeted state has all moral options for retaliation closed off, forcing it to either surrender or transgress civilian immunity. This places great strain on just war theory. We are left having to claim either that superior military technology engenders a superior moral claim, such that anyone targeted by remote weaponry is morally obliged to submit and/or surrender. Or we must claim that in situations of remote warfare, the principle of civilian immunity cannot hold. In such situations remote weaponry has the consequence of rendering just war theory either an ally of the powerful, or obsolete.[19]

---

[18] Ibid., 130.

[19] Suzy Killmister, "Remote Weaponry: The Ethical Implications," *Journal of Applied Philosophy* 25:2 (2008): 121–133, at 122.

Killmister perceives a disconcerting feature of asymmetric warfare, but her way of expressing her perception is slightly odd, for what should worry us is not so much the consequences of asymmetric warfare for just war *theory* but the consequences for the actual morality of warfare.

Nevertheless, let me point out anyway that she is quite wrong about the alternatives she sees just war theory confronted with. After all, she stresses "that the scenario under discussion is not a war of humanitarian intervention. For there to be a question of just responses to the attack, State Y must have a right of self-defence."[20] Thus, her scenario concerns a state (or community) that does (in principle) have a right to self-defense but cannot legitimately exercise it in the face of the enemy's use of remote weaponry. However, this scenario is then in turn also one where the aggressor state (the one using remote weaponry) has, of course, no right to attack the weaker state in the first place. Thus, while just war theory (on Killmister's interpretation, that is, interpreted as a theory that absolutely prohibits the targeting of innocent people) would in this scenario leave the weak state without legitimate means to defend itself, it also leaves the strong state without any justification to attack the weak one in the first place. While this might be a poor consolation to the weak state and not much help, it is not quite the same as making just war theory an *ally* of the powerful. To simply insist, by the way, that just war theory does become an ally of the powerful if, even though it condemns the aggressor, it also simultaneously prevents the attacked from responding, seems to be nothing more than a one-sided stipulation. After all, one could as well turn the argument around: by preventing (as just war theory does) the aggressor from continuing its fight, just war theory becomes an ally of the defender even though it prohibits the attacked from fighting back under the circumstances. In other words, while Killmister is right in claiming that in this scenario "anyone targeted by remote weaponry is morally obliged to submit and/or surrender" as far as just war theory (on Killmister's interpretation) is concerned, she is *wrong* in asserting that in this scenario just war theory implies "that superior military technology engenders a superior moral claim."

Regarding the claim of "obsoleteness," it has to be said that there are different versions of just war theory. Not all of them endorse an absolute prohibition on targeting the innocent. Michael Walzer's and Igor Primoratz's accounts, both of which Killmister actually discusses herself to this effect, do not. There are a number of further present-day just war theorists who also allow the targeting of the innocent in certain circumstances (Jeff McMahan and Frances Kamm being notable examples). But there are older just war theorists, too, who do not endorse this prohibition. Particularly outspoken (but not alone) in this regard was the sixteenth-century just war theorist Francisco de Vitoria, who

[20] Ibid., 124.

plainly stated that "*the entire community can be punished for the sins of its king*. If a king starts an unjust war with another power, the other power to whom injustice has been done can...kill the subjects of the king, even if they are entirely innocent."[21]

Thus, just war theory can be adapted to the circumstances of extreme asymmetric warfare, and in fact I have tried to do precisely that elsewhere in the context of providing a possible justification for terrorism.[22] As already explained, the four serious approaches one might use in distinguishing illegitimate human targets from legitimate ones do *not* provide distinctions that coincide with the distinction between combatants and civilians in the usual, colloquial sense, or in the sense of the laws of armed conflict, for that matter. None of them can explain why civilians, and only civilians, should be immune from attack.

The convention theory, whose underlying rationale is in some sense "rule-utilitarian" or at least consequentialist, comes closest to upholding the distinction. However, there can be exceptional circumstances where the consequences of upholding or abiding by the convention are actually *bad*. Under such circumstances, then, it would be permissible to widen the scope of one's targets: the obvious first choice being *noninnocent* civilians (Killmister discusses this option too, albeit with a different terminology).Yet, if that proves insufficient, one may be permitted to widen the target range still further. As already discussed, sometimes it can be justified, namely, on grounds of a necessity justification, to violate someone's rights: for example the right of innocent people not to be killed. I said that this justification can be used to justify "collateral damage." But it can also be used to justify, in extreme circumstances, the *targeted* killing of innocents.

To be sure, some people try to use the so-called doctrine of double effect to construe a relevant moral difference between the targeted and the "collateral" killing of innocents. Basically, the doctrine distinguishes between what is intended and what is merely foreseen, or between means, ends, and side effects. It claims that *intentionally* killing an innocent person, so that killing that person is an end in itself or a *means* to further some other end, is absolutely prohibited, while killing an innocent person in such a way that her death is a mere *side effect* of a well-intentioned and not intrinsically evil act (like the attack on an unjust aggressor) is permissible if the (predicted) negative consequences (the death of the innocent person) are not disproportionate in the light of the (predicted) positive effects (the incapacitation of the unjust aggressor and hence the defense of his potential victims). The problem with this theory,

---

[21] Franciscus de Victoria (Francisco de Vitoria), *De Indis Recenter Inventis Et De Jure Belli Hispanorum In Barbaros*, ed. Walter Schätzel (Tübingen: Mohr/Siebeck, 1952). The text is in Latin and German; the translation of the quote from German is mine.

[22] Steinhoff, *On the Ethics of War and Terrorism*, chs. 4 and esp. 5.

however, is that it leads to highly counterintuitive implications. Consider, to give just one example, the following case: Adolf Hitler gives a speech in a stadium in front of 5,000 innocent school children. A bomber of the Royal Air Force is nearby and could drop a bomb on the stadium with the intention to kill Hitler and the foreseen side-effect of killing all the school children. Let us suppose this were proportionate, perhaps because it could end the war and save hundreds of thousands of school children and millions of other innocent people. However, there is also the British spy 003 in the stadium. With his sniper rifle he has no clear shot at Hitler but could shoot the innocent, very corpulent construction worker standing above Hitler on scaffolding. 003 knows that if he shot the worker, the worker would fall down and squash and kill Hitler. The doctrine of double effect would consider killing the construction worker as a *means* to kill Hitler impermissible although this course of action spares the life of 5,000 school children but killing the construction worker along with the 5,000 schoolchildren as a *side effect* of killing Hitler permissible. But then abiding by the doctrine of double effect under such circumstances seems to amount to little more than a rule-fetishism that comes with quite a blatant disregard for human life. The doctrine of double effect cannot be correct.[23]

In contrast to the doctrine of double effect, the convention theory and its consequentialist rationale actually do provide a plausible explanation of why, *under normal circumstances*, the targeted killing of civilians and innocents is worse than their collateral killing, but at the moment we are *ex hypothesi* talking about *exceptional* circumstances.

Under such exceptional circumstances (which have been aptly described by Killmister), then, the consequentialist rationale of the convention theory works against upholding and toward breaking the prohibition. As I explained elsewhere, if strong states are safe from severe reprisals following their attacks on civilians, then, as long as attacks on civilians serve their purposes, they have no reason to refrain from them. From this it follows that such a continuous abstention of weak communities from reacting against the attacks on their civilians with the only strategy still available to them gives the aggressors a free hand. Accordingly, the weak communities' abstaining from the counterattack on civilians is likely to increase, in the future, the overall number of innocents killed or the scale of the deprivation of liberty. This does not lead to the rule, "If a community can protect a large number of their innocents from an aggressor only by attacking a smaller number of the innocents of the aggressor,

---

[23] For a detailed interpretation and critique of this doctrine, see ibid., 33–52. Other critics of the doctrine include Nancy Davis, "The Doctrine of Double Effect: Problems of Interpretation," *Pacific Philosophical Quarterly* 65 (1984): 107–123; Frances M. Kamm, "Failures of Just War Theory: Terror, Harm, and Justice," *Ethics* 114 (2004): 650–692; Alison McIntyre, "Doing Away with Double Effect," *Ethics* 111 (2001): 219–255; Judith Jarvis Thomson (1991), "Self-Defense," *Philosophy & Public Affairs* 20 (1991): 283–310, esp. 290–296.

then this is permissible," but rather to the rule, "If a community can protect a large number of their innocents from an aggressor only by attacking a smaller number of the innocents of the aggressor, then this is permissible *provided that it is not to be expected that a group of aggressors sufficiently large for the purposes of deterrence will be punished for their attacks*." That a rejection of *this* principle cannot be justified in rule-utilitarian terms, while its acceptance can, can already easily be seen in the italicized subordinate clause alone.[24]

Note that this argument does not imply that the weaker side may attack innocent people on the (unjust, as we assume) stronger side whenever the strong side fights in a way that makes it impossible for the weak side to fight or retaliate against combatants. Just war principles like prospects of success (which, however, is not under all circumstances a principle that must be satisfied before a war is just) and proportionality (which *is* a principle that must be satisfied) remain relevant. Thus, if the strong side wages an unjust war to annex some objectively speaking not particularly attractive small patch of land and does not thereby endanger the people on the weak side, the weak side does not yet have a justification to respond with attacks on innocents on the enemy side. However, if the strong state violates sufficiently important rights of the people on the other side, the situation can change.

This, then, is a justification of terrorism. That aggressive asymmetric warfare can beget such a justification of terrorism, however, says something especially damning about aggressive asymmetric warfare too. To wit, if people think that terrorism is something bad (as I do, though I also think that concomitant slaughter, that is, "collateral damage," is something bad), then an extremely asymmetrical aggressive war by the superior side is even worse than a normal unjust aggressive war, all else being equal. After all, under the circumstances described it provides the weaker side with a valid justification to engage in terrorism.

4. Strawser

Bradley Jay Strawser claims that there is a duty to employ uninhabited aerial vehicles (UAVs) in a justified war. He explains:

> The basis for this claim rests upon what I call the principle of unnecessary risk (PUR). PUR proceeds as follows: If X gives Y an order to accomplish good goal G, then X has an obligation, other things being equal, to chose a means to accomplish G that does not violate the

---

[24] Since I do not know how to say it better now than I did then, I basically quote myself in this paragraph after the colon (the reader may forgive me). See ibid., 134–135.

demands of justice, make the world worse, or expose Y to potentially lethal risk unless incurring such risk aids in the accomplishment of G in some way that cannot be gained via less risky means. That is, it is wrong to command someone to take on *unnecessary* potentially lethal risks in an effort to carry out a just action for some good; any potentially lethal risk incurred must be justified by some strong countervailing reason. In the absence of such a reason, ordering someone to incur potentially lethal risk is morally impermissible.[25]

Strawser says that he takes "PUR to be uncontroversial."[26] If it is uncontroversial, then that is because so many provisos are already built in. But this means that an argument for an obligation to employ uninhabited aerial vehicles based on PUR would also have to establish some further premises: (a) that other things are equal (whatever that means in this context, and that would of course have to be explained); (b) that choosing UAVs to obtain a military goal does not violate the demands of justice; (c) that it does not make the world worse off; and (d) that it does not expose Y to potentially lethal risk.

Be that as it may, Strawser seems to think that the following claim OP can somehow be derived from PUR:

(OP) For any just action taken by a given military, if it is possible for the military to use UAV platforms in place of inhabited aerial vehicles without a significant loss of capability, then that military has an ethical obligation to do so.[27]

I have doubts. First of all, all the qualifications and provisos of PUR have suddenly and mysteriously disappeared in OP. However, if this is really how OP is meant, then OP is simply so obviously wrong—for of course there can always be countervailing reasons—that any further discussion of it is not really worthwhile. Thus, for the sake of argument, let us charitably interpret OP as still containing the provisos of PUR.

Note then, second, that PUR starts with: "If X gives Y an order..." Now let us assume that X gives the pilot of a fighter-bomber the order to attack some ammunition factory. But in circumstances where the fighter-bomber cannot operate UAV platforms it then seems to follow from PUR that after giving an order *to the pilot* to achieve goal G, X now is under an obligation to have *someone else*, namely, the operator of the drone, achieve that goal. Thus, a suspicious

---

[25] Bradley Jay Strawser, "Moral Predators: The Duty to Employ Uninhabited Aerial Vehicles," *Journal of Military Ethics* 9:4 (2010): 342–368, at 344.

[26] Ibid.

[27] Ibid., 346.

schizophrenia seems to lurk within PUR. Probably Strawser thinks that the drone operator should get the order in the first place, but it has to be stressed (at the risk of appearing pedantic) that this does simply not follow from PUR.[28]

It is also safe to assume that Strawser thinks that the responsibility to use safe means is owed to the person given the order. After all, Strawser seems to base the elaborate PUR on the more general "premise that if an agent is pursuing a morally justified yet inherently risky action, then there is a moral imperative to protect this agent if it is possible to do so, unless there exists a countervailing good that outweighs the protection of the agent."[29] However, having the pilot replaced by the operator might cost the pilot his job in the long run. It might actually not protect him and his interests: he might prefer a risk of being killed to the certainty of losing his job.

On this note, if persons consent to take certain risks (barring here situations of coercion or exploitation), there is no obvious obligation to neutralize those risks if one can. This argument has actually been pressed against Strawser by Stephen Kershnar.[30] However, Strawser's reply (only in a footnote) is unconvincing (incidentally, Strawser talks about entering into a "foolish" contract; however, the acceptance of certain risks, even ones that could be avoided, is not necessarily foolish—whether it is or not depends on the available alternatives, for example, in terms of available jobs):

> If one wish[es] to grant this is [a] possibility, then PUR can be amended to reflect those relationships where Y enters under the authority of X on the assumption that X will not order him to take on risk for no good reason; that is, Y assumes X will follow PUR. At any rate, I think most military members in Western militaries implicitly expect their commanders not to risk their lives unnecessarily.[31]

There are several problems here. First, why should only what Y assumes count? What if X enters the contract with Y under the assumption that Y will do as he tells him? Second, the "amendment" Strawser suggests has the perhaps

---

[28] Strawser (personal communication) finds my complaint here somewhat unclear and states: "The PUR is a simple conditional claim. *If* one is to give an order to someone, then they have an obligation—as part of giving *that* order—to not put the recipient of that order at unnecessary risk." My question is this: unnecessary risk, period, or unnecessary risk *in following that order*? If it is the latter, then, in the case of my example, nothing about UAVs follows, since the order was to achieve the goal *with* the fighter-bomber. If it is the former, and if unnecessary risk can only be avoided by using the UAVs, the consequence is precisely the one I state in the main text, and, yes, I do indeed think that that would point toward a certain schizophrenia in PUR.

[29] Strawser, "Moral Predators," 343.

[30] Kershnar's point also undermines Strawser's two examples of "Captain Zelda" and "Recklessville."

[31] Strawser, "Moral Predators," 363, n. 6. I have swapped the places of "X" and "Y" in this quote to keep them in line with the formulation of PUR, where X is the authority.

somewhat embarrassing effect that the independent validity of PUR plays no role anymore. Rather, what is actually important is the assumptions the contract partners have when they enter the contract. If they assume PUR, then PUR must govern their interactions—but if not, then not. In other words, this cannot be the basis for a general argument for a duty not to burden soldiers with "unnecessary" risks and hence an implied duty to use drones.

This is also confirmed by Strawser's thought that "most military members in Western militaries implicitly expect their commanders not to risk their lives unnecessarily." After all, given this mere "most" there is no path anymore to the "any" of OP. Again, OP would apply to some commander–subordinate relationships but not to others.

Perhaps an even bigger problem is that this idea of Strawser's, even if it did capture some truth, does not quite represent the whole story. What I mean is that one would have to know what this implicit expectation Strawser mentions in fact amounts to. This, then, is the catch: it is not only quite possible but in all likelihood also a fact that these military members *also* assume that what is and what is not "necessary" is decided by their commanders or political leaders. In other words, they will "implicitly expect" that their commanders will not impose risks upon them that *they, the commanders (or political leaders),* deem unnecessary. There might, however, be quite diverse reasons why political leaders or commanders deem certain weapons or equipment off limits. Thus, Strawser cannot overcome the objection from consent. PUR is *not* a valid principle.

In this context, let me note that the formulation of PUR is not entirely clear on the following point: as we saw, PUR contains the claim that "it is wrong to command someone to take on *unnecessary* potentially lethal risks in an effort to carry out a just action for some good." But this can be interpreted in (at least) two ways: (1) in case the risks R are *in fact* unnecessary, it is wrong to command someone to take on the risks R in an effort to carry out a just action for some good; (2) in case the commander *deems* the risks R to be unnecessary, it is wrong to command someone to take on the risks R in an effort to carry out a just action for some good.

If what is meant is (1), then PUR, in both the original version and in the version in the footnote, is quite implausible from the start. It is counterintuitive to claim that a commander does something wrong, morally speaking, only because the risks R he (and perhaps even every competent observer) reasonably believes to be absolutely necessary for the just mission are not *in fact* necessary. If, however, (2) is what is meant, the original PUR is still wrong in light of Kershnar's objection, and the modified PUR is far too weak to generate the conclusions Strawser is trying to get. For example, Strawser's Captain Zelda, who opts for a suicidal tactic although a nonsuicidal one is readily available, might deem the suicidal one *necessary* (e.g., necessary to please the gods).

By the way, it seems that given PUR Strawser would not only have to endorse OP but ALSO the following principle PGP (for poison gas principle):

> For any just action taken by a given military, if it is possible for the military to deploy poison gas in such a way that it enhances the safety of the members of one's military, the military has an ethical obligation to do so, unless countervailing reasons override this obligation.

It is unclear how Strawser could possibly defend OP on the grounds of PUR but reject PGP. (Of course, poison gas is illegal, whereas UAVs are not. But nothing in OP as formulated refers to legality, and therefore PGP is *not* disanalogous to OP as formulated. I will come back to the significance of legality in a moment.) That in itself, I submit, should give us pause. For one thing, it seems to be intuitively quite implausible to assume that there is any prima facie duty to deploy poison gas if this enhances the safety of the members of one's own military, that is, a duty one needs only then not to comply with if there are countervailing reasons. On the contrary, it appears there is simply *no* such duty *at all*, countervailing reasons or not. If this is true here, however, it would also be true for OP and PUR generally, for it is unclear what is supposed to be the difference that makes OP or PUR so much better.

Strawser, however, claims that "there are some weapons that are simply wrong to use *in principle*, regardless of how they protect or do not protect just agents using them. ... I think poison gas is wrong to use in principle because of the way it kills its victims (cruel and painful and drawn out, etc.), the non-discriminate way it functions, the long-lasting after effect, and so forth."[32] The reply, obviously, is that poison gas is not necessarily more indiscriminate than bombs, and that, second, being mutilated by bombs and shellfire also often leads to painful and drawn-out deaths. But third, and most importantly, whether poison gas has all these negative effects Strawser mentions depends on the nature, that is, the chemistry of the *specific* poison gas in question. *Specific* UAVs (e.g., those equipped with particularly nasty poison gas) might also have these negative effects. However, it still seems counterintuitive to claim that we have at least a prima facie duty to deploy poison gas that is not worse than permissible bombs if this enhances the safety of the members of one's own military.

But let us assume that Strawser would claim that there is a prima facie obligation to deploy poison gas under the pertinent circumstances and holds that there *are* countervailing duties while there are *no* such countervailing duties in the case of UAVs. (Of course, Strawser might think that there are no countervailing reasons in both cases and poison gas should in fact be used. If so, he should say that instead of only discussing UAVs.) In that case, however, one

---

[32] Personal communication.

would like to know what exactly the difference is: what are the countervailing reasons that exist in the former case but not in the latter?

It may appear to many, including the military person Y from Strawser's principle PUR, that a sufficient reason (in the absence of countervailing reasons that override *this* reason) not to use poison gas is that it is *illegal* under international law (and I indeed think that this is *one* of the reasons why we think that even poison gas that is not worse than permissible bombs should not be used). This could, in principle (and, in particular, in the mind of Y), be a good reason even when the law is actually *bad*.[33] If so, then OP would have to be circumscribed still further: it would not be applicable to situations where drones are outlawed by international law (and perhaps Strawser could agree to this). But then it seems it would also not be applicable in situations where they are outlawed by domestic law. Or does Strawser want to claim that the commanding officer X or other high echelons in the military are obliged to break the law? If so, he would have to provide an argument to the effect that PUR overrides reasons to obey the law. So far he has not done that. In fact, he does not address the issue.

So far I have shown that PUR is not plausible and that therefore OP remains unsupported. In fact, we have already seen positive reasons to reject OP. I now want to discuss two further reasons to reject OP. Both of them have already been discussed by Strawser himself (one head-on, one more tangentially). Strawser formulates the first objection I have in mind as follows:

> ...The asymmetry in combat abilities created by the advanced technology of UAVs, and in particular by the massive reduction of risk to the UAV pilot, makes it too easy for the nation employing UAVs to go to war. That is, the asymmetry created by UAVs lowers the *jus ad bellum* threshold such that more unjust wars might be conducted because the risks of war to a nation-state could become so minimal.[34]

Strawser offers some counterarguments to this objection, all of which I find wanting. First, he claims that this argument "strikes at *any* asymmetry in military technological development whatsoever."[35] I think that the "whatsoever" is a severe exaggeration. Even if it is not, however, it would hardly show that the original objection against UAVs is wrong. Be that as it may, more interesting is Strawser's further claim that "following this logic could even lead to the conclusion that a state should have their militaries throw away their weaponry and

---

[33] This claim, incidentally, is compatible with the claim that *the mere fact* that something is the law is no reason at all to abide by it. Not violating certain laws, including some bad ones, might have certain good consequences under particular circumstances, and, if so, it is these consequences that provide the justification for abiding by bad laws, not the bad laws or "the" law itself.

[34] Strawser, "Moral Predators," 358.

[35] Ibid., 359.

all defensive technology, for certainly a neutered military would be less likely to engage in unjust wars in the future."[36] Actually, Strawser is not following the logic of the argument at all here. If asymmetry, or at least extreme asymmetry, is the problem, then obviously one does not solve that problem by throwing one's weapons away. After all, unless potential enemies do the same, such a move will only *create* asymmetry.

Strawser also thinks that the objection "rests on epistemically dubious calculations that are predictive about *themselves* [the citizens of a nation-state of a hypothetical example of his] doing something wrong in the future ('we might be more likely to do wrong action X down the road') over epistemically solid calculations to protect their own just warfighters presently ('our soldiers will be safer *today* if they wear the vests')"[37] However, first, it might well be that a politician calculates what the military will do if the use of drones is allowed or what future politicians will do. This is not that dubious. Moreover, the original objection must of course be amended: it is not only that it is more likely that "our" soldiers will do more wrong action down the road if they use vests but also that it is *virtually certain* that if they do more (or even the usual amount of) wrong action down the road they will do this wrong action, thanks to the vests, much more safely, to the detriment of their victims, who will be much less safe than they otherwise would have been.

Moreover, Strawser actually explicitly admits that if the stakes are high enough, "then perhaps it is justifiable to do a lesser wrong now in order to increase even the slightest chance of avoiding a much greater wrong in the future." However, he states that "the trouble with applying this to our present case is," again, "the high degree of epistemic uncertainty we have in predicting future states of affairs."[38] According to him, "the normative force of PUR upon present actions is too strong to overcome such weak predictive calculations of future possibilities."[39] However, we have seen already that Strawser does not provide any support for PUR in the first place. He just accepts it as "uncontroversial." Yet it is not; in fact, it is wrong, as we also saw. Therefore, it need not be "overcome," and hence Strawser's attempt to undermine this objection to the use of drones fails.

Finally, let me also point out that there is a difference—and one not really discussed by Strawser—between using certain weapons in a concrete situation and producing and distributing them. Consider a case where X, a father, gives Y, his teenage son, the order to go to school and learn. There have been shootings last year at the school, so by sending his son to school

---

[36] Ibid.

[37] Ibid. In his example Strawser refers for reason of illustration to bulletproof vests instead of UAVs.

[38] Ibid., 360.

[39] Ibid., 359.

the father is exposing him "to potentially lethal risk," to use the formulation of PUR. The father owns a pistol and has trained the son how to use it. Now, if the son were to be caught in a firefight in the school and in *that situation* the father could make the son safer by throwing him the gun through the window, this would be morally permissible. But this certainly does not mean that it was and is also permissible for the father to let the son take the gun to school every morning. In fact, if all parents refrain from giving their children guns to take with them to school, all the children will be safer. Thus, there are strong rule-utilitarian and consequentialist considerations that prohibit furnishing the son with a gun for his risky time in school. If the father breaks them, this would also be unfair toward the parents who actually abide by the rule.

This argument, of course, is also applicable to the case of guns for wars, and in particular to guns that give one side a very tempting superiority. Thus, even if it were true that there are situations were drones should be employed when they are already available to soldiers (and I agree with Strawser—without, incidentally, having to rely on PUR—that in principle there are such situations), it might be that such weapons should not be produced and be made available to soldiers in the first place (or should be taken away from them if they already have them).

Strawser says he agrees with me on that and states that his aim was to establish that there are, indeed, situations where there is a moral obligation, not merely permission, to employ drones when they are available.[40] However, in case that was all he wanted to show, that could also be shown in less than 100 words. Here we go: The Evils credibly threaten to blow up Sao Paulo with their nuclear bomb unless the Brazilian military employs one of their drones to destroy, without any collateral damage, an unmanned small swimming vehicle (USSV, for short) of the military's choice. There is no other way to save Sao Paulo than by giving in to the Evils' demand, and giving in to their demand would indeed save Sao Paulo. The Brazilian president orders the military to attack the boat. It is, I submit, entirely obvious that this is a situation where the deployment of a drone would be obligatory.

However, my impression was that Strawser tried to establish the correctness of the thesis that the deployment of UAVs is obligatory *in a wide range* of cases *that are quite common in war*, and thus I argued that Strawser severely underestimates reasons that speak against that claim and does not even mention others. Even if my argument should miss Strawser's claim, it does not miss this thesis.

---

[40] Personal communication.

Let me now turn to the second objection. Strawser quotes me saying:

> To be sure, I do not deny that there is something fishy about attacking the defenseless. What is fishy about it might be captured very well in this passage: "The pilot of a fighter-bomber or the crew of a man-of-war from which the Tomahawk rockets are launched are beyond the reach of the enemy's weapons. War has lost all features of the classical duel situation here and has approached, to put it cynically, certain forms of pest control."[41]

I make this remark in the context of a discussion of torture, and Strawser rightly points out that I say that the prohibition of assaults upon the defenseless is not a principle of just war theory and can be just. He agrees and goes on to say:

> I would add that a crucial element in how one "feels" about imagining such warfare depends on whether or not the precision missile strike in the picture envisioned is justified or not. Is it a military strike as part of a fully justified defense against an aggressing, unjustified, destructive enemy force? Is the strike hitting a legitimate and morally culpable target? If it is, such factors temper our view of the strike considerably and move us away from the "pest control" picture. In such a case, we should desire that the just warrior be well protected from any possible threat that this enemy might proffer—protection that the UAV affords.[42]

Here I am inclined to agree with Strawser. Yet an important piece of the puzzle is missing here—namely, *reality*.[43] Strawser provides it himself at the very end of his paper, but he overlooks what conclusions might be drawn from it:

> Finally, I note that this paper is in the odd position of arguing for the ethical obligation to use UAVs for a putatively just military action in

---

[41] I say this in "Torture: The Case for Dirty Harry and against Alan Dershowitz," *Journal of Applied Philosophy* 23 (2006): 337–353, at 338. I quote here Herfried Münkler, *Die neuen Kriege* (Reinbek bei Hamburg: Rowohlt, 2003), 234, my translation. Strawser quotes me in "Moral Predators," 357.

[42] Ibid., 358.

[43] Strawser (personal communication) complains that it is actually me who is not dealing with reality since drones *are* available and that hence we need to deal with the fact of their availability. True. Handguns are also available, and one of my ways of dealing with their availability lies in insisting that parents should normally not hand them out to their children. And of course recommending that politicians be careful before handing out drones to the military or should consider taking them away if the military already has them is also a way of dealing with reality.

the current context wherein much, if not all, *actual* UAV employment is part of military actions that are morally questionable or outright impermissible. The particular contemporary circumstances and misuses of UAVs, however, do not trump the moral principles underlying the ethical obligation to employ UAVs for *just* actions. Indeed, this highlights the central point well: the first question for the morally permissible use of any weapon technology is, of course, whether the military action itself is morally justified. If it is not a justified undertaking in the first place, then it does not matter if it is carried out via a crossbow, a sniper rifle, or a UAV; it is morally impermissible regardless. If the act is morally justified, however, we are obliged via the demands of PUR to protect the agent ordered to carry out that action as best we can; be it a police officer apprehending a dangerous criminal, an EOD technician disarming a bomb, or a just warrior fighting an unjust enemy. Hence, the ethical obligation to employ UAVs.[44]

First of all, it is certainly not true that it does not matter by which means impermissible actions, including impermissible military actions, are carried out. For example, certain kinds of ammunition are prohibited as particularly cruel; poison gas is prohibited, too. Moreover, some ways of doing an impermissible (kind of) act might show greater depravity and disrespect toward one's victims than others.

Second, and regarding the police officer, the work of police officers can be quite dangerous. Some of them get shot not in the intentional attempt to arrest a criminal but in simple traffic stops. However, when police officers are ordered to make traffic stops and in that context ask for driver's licenses, for instance, we do *not* arm them to the teeth and do *not* put them into heavy body armor. The reason for this is quite simply that the citizens do not want that: they want to be confronted with a recognizable human being, not with a Star Wars storm trooper. If this is already sufficient as regards "countervailing reasons" against the strongest protection, then certainly there will be a lot of countervailing reasons in the case of drones.

In this context, then, it should be remembered that the use of UAVs is the latest incarnation of aerial warfare, a type of warfare whose history consists, for the most part, in white people more or less symmetrically bombing each other but *also*, and this is important, in white people (or people collaborating with and being supported by white people) asymmetrically and criminally (I take natural law as my standard here) bombing black or yellow or brown ones for colonialist, racist, and imperialist reasons and, incidentally, without much regard for civilians. Those black, yellow, or brown people might therefore

---

[44] Strawser, "Moral Predators," 362.

have a somewhat different perspective on the alleged advantages of warfare by drones. They might think that it is bad enough to be treated like the barbarian enemies but, still worse, to be treated like cockroaches on the receiving side of pest control. If the sensitivities of Western citizens are sufficient to forego more efficient protections of their police officers, why shouldn't the sensitivities of Eastern or Southern citizens not be sufficient reason to forego certain extreme types of military superiority?

5. Conclusions

I have not argued here that UAVs are intrinsically bad or that their use is somehow intrinsically wrong. On the contrary, I have argued that even automated ("intelligent") weapon systems are not intrinsically bad and that it is not intrinsically wrong to use them. In a world where we had one just world state and where drones would be used, after scrupulous deliberation, to fight dangerous, unjust and unjustified criminals, their use would not only be justified but, I believe, also morally quite unproblematic. (However, even in such a world there would not necessarily be a *duty* to use UAVs. Whether or not there would be such a duty depends on further characteristics of such a world.) In our world, however, military superiority is used to intimidate and coerce others, and it is employed in wars that are morally problematic at the very least and often undergirded by colonialist, imperialist, or downright racist motivations that remind those on the receiving side of such technology all too much of times allegedly past, where the self-proclaimed *Herrenmenschen* and the harbingers of civilization discipline the brutes, mostly by killing them. This context should perhaps be kept in mind before celebrating the advances of military technology. This is *not* a knockdown argument against UAVs or other extremely superior military technology. It is, however, a strong reminder that things are perhaps a little more complicated than people killing other people by pushing buttons thousands of miles away might want to believe.[45]

[45] I thank Suzy Killmister and Bradley Jay Strawser for very helpful comments on a first draft of this chapter. I also thank two anonymous referees for further useful comments.

PART THREE

AUTONOMOUS DRONES AND THE FUTURE OF UNMANNED WEAPONRY

10

Engineering, Ethics, and Industry: The Moral Challenges of Lethal Autonomy

GEORGE R. LUCAS JR.

1. Introduction

The essays in this volume deal primarily with moral, legal, and policy issues arising from the use of remotely piloted drones (RPVs). In this chapter, by contrast, I will raise and discuss questions concerning the additional, distinctive challenges or liabilities we will confront, primarily in engineering and industry, from what I have elsewhere termed "the relentless drive toward autonomy."[1]

2. Current Ethical Challenges in Unmanned Systems Design and Deployment

A view prevalent among defense industry engineers and US Department of Defense (DoD) policymakers is that, in their present nonautonomous status, unmanned systems raise no genuinely new legal or moral questions. They merely place the operator at a safe distance from the mission, which is otherwise unchanged. Hence, concerns over the development and deployment of these new systems are misplaced. As with most exotic new technologies, the novelty blinds us to the fact that the moral issues involved are entirely familiar and conventional and not appreciably different from those associated with the development of previous and current weapons technology.

---

[1] I use this term in several places to describe the determined, headlong, and stubbornly unreflective insistence on choosing greater degrees of autonomy over alternative solutions to the force multiplication and economy problem. See, most recently, "Industrial Challenges of Military Robotics," *Journal of Military Ethics* 10:4 (December 2011): 274–295. For an illustration of this attitude, see Siva Banda, "The Challenges of Achieving UAV Autonomy," Graduate School of Engineering and Applied Sciences Distinguished Lecture Series, Naval Postgraduate School (December 2, 2010). Excerpted in "Update: Naval Postgraduate School Newsletter" (January 2011), 5: http://www.nps.edu/About/News/World-Renowned-UAV-Control-Expert-Presents-GS EAS-Distinguished-Guest-Lecture.html.

There is some measure of truth in this claim, at least as applied to "remotely piloted" systems. The moral issues *are* nevertheless "technology driven," at least in the sense that RPVs make feasible missions whose objectives would otherwise prove exceptionally risky, dangerous, and difficult (if not impossible) to undertake from a logistical standpoint. Hence, the criticisms of drone warfare in the literature (as well as in this volume) mirror the concerns raised by this dramatic expansion of mission feasibility, to include an increase in the capacity to undertake or inflict:

(1) Assassination or "targeted killing," especially across or within the sovereign borders of nations with whom we are not formally at war.
(2) Collateral damage to innocents and their property; and thereby
(3) Magnifying the probability for errors in targeting judgment (i.e., mistakes) that would not otherwise be made (since many of the missions in question could not otherwise be undertaken); and
(4) Perhaps most troublingly, increasing the opportunities and incidents of use of deadly force in a military context by nonmilitary personnel (such as civilian intelligence operatives, or private security contractors).

The last emerging aspect of drone warfare is disconcerting on many levels, but especially when it involves the summary execution, without any form of "due process," of US citizens allegedly engaged in criminal enterprises abroad.

While it is quite true that such anomalous and morally murky activities often occurred during the conduct of espionage and covert actions, it is equally true that drone technology substantially magnifies the prospects for engaging in such missions. This is one striking feature of unconventional or "irregular" warfare.[2] First, adversaries and insurgent interest groups deal with the radical asymmetries in our favor in conventional settings, by disrupting social systems and attacking the weak links in logistical supply chains through the use (for example) of suicide bombers and improvised explosive devices (IEDs) that throw conventional military forces seriously off balance. Subsequently, a new technology owned initially by the besieged conventional forces becomes the optimal response. "Our" drone attacks are systemic in precisely the same sense as "their" IEDs and suicide bombers, disrupting the adversary's command structure, relentlessly hunting him out where he lives and hides and thus demoralizing him in return and hopefully breaking his ability and will to fight. The host of legal and ethical questions and conundrums described and evaluated in the other essays in this volume arise from this relentless tactical arms

---

[2] See George R. Lucas Jr., "'This Is Not Your Father's War': Confronting the Moral Challenges of 'Unconventional' War," *Journal of National Security Law and Policy* 3:2 (2009): 331–342; Lucas, "Postmodern War," *Journal of Military Ethics* 9:4 (December 2010): 289–298.

race—this perennial "give and take" between political adversaries, or between security forces representing the rule of law, and international criminals intent on circumventing that rule.

3. Introducing Greater Autonomy in Unmanned Systems

In what way, if at all, does rendering the robotic or unmanned systems technology autonomous, self-governed, and self-directed (requiring little or no human oversight, once enabled and launched) significantly alter or transform this debate?

Paradoxically, if we are concerned (as in (4) on the list) about nonmilitary personnel operating military assets and undertaking inherently military operations, then the advent of machine autonomy would indeed transform that debate, since it would no longer be the case that nonuniformed personnel were engaging in military operations. Rather, these missions would henceforth be undertaken solely by machines (presumably with military authorization and oversight). This, in effect, turns "topsy-turvy" the "accountability dilemma" first raised by Robert Sparrow and Noel Sharkey, in that defenders of these practices could now plausibly claim (albeit again rather disingenuously) that no "nonmilitary personnel" are engaged in questionable actions like extrajudicial killing of adversaries or rogue US citizens.[3] Only machines (and not persons) are undertaking the activities in question. In short, we can make many of the moral and legal anxieties raised by the policies and practices considered in the other essays in this volume simply disappear, merely by redefining the activities in question as involving "machine behavior exclusively" and hence immune from the charges leveled against the remotely piloted missions.

This rather odd line of argument merely rings a change on a more familiar denial of responsibility by engineers involved in the research, development, manufacture, and ultimately deployment of any new weapons technology during wartime. That argument consists in the observation that a nation's defense industries, scientists, and privately contracted personnel are, to a large extent,

---

[3] Robert Sparrow, "Killer Robots," *Journal of Applied Philosophy* 24:1 (2007): 62–77; Sparrow, "Predators or Plowshares? Arms Control of Robotic Weapons," *IEEE Technology and Society Magazine* 28:1 (2009): 25–29; Sparrow, "Robotic Weapons and the Future of War," in Paolo Tripodi and Jessica Wolfendale (eds.), *New Wars and New Soldiers: Military Ethics in the Contemporary World* (London: Ashgate Publishing Ltd., 2011), 117–133. See also Noel Sharkey, "Robot Wars Are a Reality," *Guardian* (August 18, 2007): 29; Sharkey, "Automated Killers and the Computing Profession," *Computer* 40 (2007): 122–124; Sharkey, "Cassandra or False Prophet of Doom: AI Robots and War," *IEEE Intelligent Systems* (July–August 2008): 14–17; Sharkey, "Grounds for Discrimination: Autonomous Robot Weapons," *RUSI Defence Systems* 11:2 (2008): 86–89; Sharkey, "Saying 'No!' to Lethal Autonomous Targeting," *Journal of Military Ethics* 9:4 (December 2010): 299–313.

servants or handmaidens of the policy decisions of the ruling government. It is the government and its political leadership, and not its defense industries, scientists, or contractors that determine whether and how to prosecute its military conflicts, and accordingly, whether to use military or nonmilitary means and personnel to do so. Indeed, the senior-level managers and directors of private military contractor and defense contracting firms are often eager to emphasize the point that their efforts support the defense of the State and that their industries and organizations exist solely to support the requirements of the State in carrying out this inherently governmental responsibility.

Such a neat division of labor, also conveniently absolving contractors of their individual or organizational responsibilities, is hardly as definitive as it might appear, of course, inasmuch as leading military and political decision makers (or trusted colleagues and associates) often leave government service to work in defense industries or for private military contractors and vice versa. The boundaries between what or whom is military or nonmilitary, public or private, are extremely porous. Even beyond these potential conflicts of interest, however, the public–private division of authority does not specifically excuse defense industries or their employees, in particular, for performing merely as mindless (let alone narrowly self-interested) technocrats. Chief executive officers as well as essential scientists, engineers, and employees of such industries are also citizens of the State, who should be concerned to avoid increasing either the risk or the incidence of war through their efforts (even if they labor otherwise to lessen war's most destructive effects through their inventions). Their dual responsibilities as citizens, as well as subject-matter experts in military technology, might be said to run parallel to those of military personnel themselves to offer faithful advice, grounded in their professional experience, on the prospects and problems inherent in political policies regarding preparation for or engagement in military conflict.[4] Thus, as P. W. Singer, in particular, has forcibly maintained, scientists, engineers, and captains of industry engaged in the development and manufacture of military robots and unmanned systems generally must take upon themselves much more explicitly the responsibility for ensuring their wise and lawful use.[5] I will return to this important observation on professional ethics in the context of defense engineering in conclusion.

---

[4] On the responsibilities for offering sound military advice, see Martin L. Cook, *The Moral Warrior*, (Albany: State University of New York Press, 2004). See also George R. Lucas Jr., "Advice and Dissent: the 'Uniform' Perspective," *Journal of Military Ethics* 8:2 (2009): 141–161. The tensions inherent in the dual roles of scientist (or engineer) and citizen during military conflicts is addressed in detail in Lucas, *Anthropologists in Arms: the Ethics of Military Anthropology* (Lanham, MD: AltaMira Press, 2009).

[5] Peter W. Singer, *Wired for War* (New York: Penguin Press, 2009); Singer, "The Ethics of 'Killer Apps,'" *Journal of Military Ethics* 9:4 (December 2010): 314–327.

4. Ethics, Engineering Design, and "Force Multiplication"

From yet another vantage point: it is a well-recognized problem in robotics and unmanned systems research that the most substantial dividends from automating certain features of the battlefield would come from what is termed "force multiplication." On one hand, at present, it is already the case that a single Predator or Reaper, remotely piloted by anywhere from one to five human operators, considerably magnifies the ability of military forces engaged in justified missions to accomplish those missions with greater success, precision, and reduction of risk of harm to innocents than their "manned" counterparts. This is an important dimension of what Bradley J. Strawser defines as "the principle of unnecessary risk" (PUR) in undertaking otherwise-justified security operations.[6] The ability to operate several of these platforms simultaneously, under the supervision of a single operator, however, would considerably magnify mission capability without a corresponding increase in scarce and expensive (and nonexpendable) human personnel. Thus, the pursuit of "force multiplication" through some kind of systems engineering modification or technological enhancement of existing military weapons systems is simply an additional logical implication of PUR.

In principle, this objective of "force multiplication" with respect to military robotics in particular can be achieved, in turn, in either of two ways:

1. By improving the human–automation interface (e.g., cleaning up the current messy and cluttered Predator–Reaper control stations, and replacing them with vastly simplified and more effective governance hardware)
2. By endowing each unmanned platform with enhanced autonomy and independence of operation

The first of these alternative strategies is relatively straightforward and achievable through the application of thoroughly conventional engineering ingenuity.[7] Imagine, for example, replacing the four to five computer terminals (and their corresponding keyboards and "mice")—all of which are

---

[6] Bradley J. Strawser, "Moral Predators: the Duty to Employ Uninhabited Vehicles," *Journal of Military Ethics* 9:4 (December 2010): 357–383. This principle essentially holds that, when they are engaged in otherwise morally justifiable military or security missions, military and security personnel are owed as much safety and minimized risk of harm as military technology can afford them.

[7] Mary L. Cummings, et al., "The Role of Human-Automation Consensus in Multiple Unmanned Vehicle Scheduling," *Human Factors: The Journal of the Human Factors and Ergonomics* 52:1 (2010); Cummings, "Assessing Operator Workload and Performance in Expeditionary Multiple Unmanned Vehicle Control," in *Proceedings of the 48th AIAA Aerospace Sciences Meeting* (Orlando, FL: Curran Associates, Inc., January 2010).

presently required to operate a Predator drone—with a single joystick or smartphone "controller." Importantly, *this path of engineering modification in the pursuit of force multiplication would not invoke any new ethical or legal challenges* beyond those already considered by the other contributors to this volume (as well as by many others currently involved in the ongoing debate about the morality and legality of remotely piloted intelligence, surveillance, and reconnaissance (ISR) and lethal missions that are wholly under human supervision and control). That is, *if* it is otherwise deemed ethical as well as legally permissible within the framework of international humanitarian law for a team of operators to conduct a remote strike against a Taliban or al-Qaeda stronghold, then it remains so even if we replace the four or five remotely located operators with a single operator employing more efficient command and control technology. Again, this conclusion is consistent with Strawser's PUR.

Far more esoteric and appealing to engineers and many policy analysts, however, is the "force multiplier" dividend attained by dispensing altogether with the human operator, whether "in," or merely "on" the loop (exercising merely supervisory or "executive" oversight). The appeal is multifaceted, from the straightforward projected cost savings anticipated by acquisitions and supply officers, to the improvements in "latency" (i.e., signal and reaction time), targeting, and overall mission effectiveness imagined by unmanned systems operators and commanders in the field. Computer scientists and artificial intelligence researchers are eager to take on such an interesting and engaging challenge.

But to concerned critics, such as Sparrow, Sharkey, Singer, or the "father" of American robotics, George Bekey, this *relentless drive toward machine autonomy* is the source of the most problematic moral and legal conundrums.[8] The seemingly unreflective eagerness of scientists, engineers, and military and political leaders to move ahead with the development of autonomous weapons systems, notwithstanding these objections and concerns of critics, constitutes an attitude toward public welfare and the substantial risk of unintended consequences that is characterized by these critics as ranging from *reckless endangerment* to outright *criminal negligence*.[9]

---

[8] See the works previously cited for the first three authors. See also George Bekey, *Autonomous Robots: From Biological Inspiration to Implementation and Control* (Cambridge, MA: MIT Press, 2005); George Bekey, Patrick Lin, and Keith Abney, *Autonomous Military Robotics: Risk, Ethics, and Design* (Washington, DC: U.S. Department of the Navy, Office of Naval Research, December 20, 2008).

[9] These are terms and concepts more familiar in domestic tort and criminal law. I have followed Michael Walzer's lead in extending them by straightforward analogy to the realm of war and international conflict, based on what Walzer terms "the doctrine of double intention." See his *Just and Unjust Wars* (New York: Basic Books, 1977).

To make matters even worse, much of this dispute between proponents and critics of enhanced machine autonomy is mired in a nearly hopeless kind of conceptual confusion and linguistic equivocation. Proponents of increased machine autonomy, for their part, sometime complicate the issues unnecessarily by invoking what turn out to be spurious concepts, like machine "morality," or by describing their proposals for an "ethical governor" for lethally armed autonomous robots.[10] They misleadingly describe autonomous combat weapon systems that would be empowered to make "moral decisions and judgments," and that would also (in principle at least) experience the machine equivalent of "guilt" from sorties gone wrong, and "learn" from those experiences. Consequentially, these proponents argue, lethally armed, autonomous military robots will be "more ethical" and even "more humane" than their human counterparts.[11]

Critics for their part worry needlessly about "killer robots" run amok,[12] as well as the presumptive moral inappropriateness of machines "making decisions to kill humans,"[13] or the lack of meaningful accountability for resulting "war crimes" that might consequently be committed.[14] The critics appear to envision cyborgs (like "the Terminator") or the infamous intelligent computer "HAL" (from Arthur C. Clarke's science fiction novel *2001: A Space Odyssey*) in command on the bridge of a nuclear submarine, or "R2D2" and "C3PO," fully weaponized and roaming the mountains of southern Afghanistan but unable to distinguish (without human supervision) between an enemy insurgent and a local shepherd.

Both extremes are, frankly, preposterous. Enhanced machine autonomy, even when married with lethal force, represents something far different from

---

[10] See, for example, Ronald Craig Arkin, Patricik Ulam, and Alana R. Wagner, "Moral Decision Making in Autonomous Systems: Enforcement, Moral Emotions, Dignity, Trust, and Deception." *Proceedings of the IEEE* 100:3 (March 2012): 571–589.

[11] Here I concur with Noel Sharkey, that this use of terminology is highly misleading, and I add, wholly unnecessary. What is being proposed is legal compliance, attained through machine and software program design, and not something akin to human moral judgment.

[12] See, for example, Armin Krishnan, *Killer Robots: Legality and Ethicality of Autonomous Weapons.* (London: Ashgate Press, 2009); Peter Asaro, "How Just Could a Robot War Be?" in P. Brey, A. Briggle, and K. Waelbers (eds.), *Current Issues in Computing and Philosophy* (Amsterdam, The Netherlands: IOS Press, 2008): 50–64.

[13] See Matthew S. Larkin, "Brave New Warfare: Autonomy in Lethal UAVs," Master's thesis, Monterey,CA:NavalPostgraduateSchool.https://wiki.nps.edu/download/attachments/15073701/ Brave+New+Warfare+(Larkin,+Matthew+Thesis).pdf?version=1&modificationDate=1301324 368000; Thomas J. Billitteri, "Drone Warfare: Are Strikes by Unmanned Aircraft Ethical?" *CQ Researcher* 20:28 (August 6, 2010): 653–676.

[14] This presumed lack of accountability for the commission of "war crimes" by robots was first raised by Robert Sparrow, "Killer Robots"; Peter Asaro, "How Just Could a Robot War Be?" and is a principal motivation behind their founding, with Noel Sharkey, the International Committee for Robot Arms Control (ICRAC). I have attempted to address these concerns in George Lucas, "Industrial Challenges of Military Robotics," *Journal of Military Ethics* 10.4 (2011): 274–295.

what either critics or proponents describe or imagine, and presents its own, unique ethical and legal challenges for engineering and industry, often quite different from those currently under discussion. For one thing, nothing so fanciful or technologically infeasible as the previously outlined outlandish scenarios is required, envisioned, or desired. Machines need not be "ethical," and it is highly misleading to speak in this fashion. Likewise, machines cannot commit "war crimes," inasmuch as they lack intentionality or self-motivation, and are utterly devoid of the interests (or emotions) required as ingredients for criminal culpability. Ethics, and accountability under international law, remain firmly and solely in the domain of human experience.

The "autonomy" requisite for moral decision making is something quite distinct from "machine autonomy." The latter merely involves unmanned systems performing in complex environments without the need for continuous human oversight. In the latter, purely mechanical sense of "autonomy," a Patriot cruise missile and my iRobot "Roomba" vacuum cleaner are both "autonomous," in that they perform their assigned missions, including encountering and responding to obstacles, problems, and unforeseen circumstances with minimal human oversight. But the missile does not unilaterally change its mission en route, or re-program its targeting objectives—let alone does it raise "moral objections" about the appropriateness of the targets selected for it. Likewise, I would not wish to have my Roomba "decide" whether or not it is necessary or appropriate to shoot an intruder in my home.[15] In general, we neither need nor desire our autonomous machines to make those kinds of moral judgments.

Here I have come to believe that the rhetoric of ethics and law have not proven very useful analytical tools, largely because they are both so widely misunderstood, misused, and misinterpreted by the participants in this debate. Critics of autonomous lethal platforms worry that these might be indiscriminate and uncontrollable and in any case, unaccountable for their inevitable "war crimes" and thus illegal from the outset. But this concern, likewise, rests upon a conceptual equivocation: "R2D2" and "C3PO" in the aforementioned imaginary Afghan scenario could not ever commit "war crimes." Unlike my alternative namesake's Hollywood portrayals, real autonomous systems have no intentionality or self-awareness. They do not care about their own survival. They have no "interests." Importantly, they cannot "get scared" or "get angry," nor could they possibly try to "get even" by seeking retaliation against enemies for harm done to themselves or their companions (all of these invoking human emotions and intentions, which are most often the source of war crimes). Rather, unmanned autonomous platforms would do precisely and only

---

[15] An exception to this general rule is what are termed "single-state, mission-oriented" robot sentries in what I term a "highly scripted" environment: for example, sentry robots in a border or demilitarized zone, or when protecting what is termed a "no-go" zone around a Naval flotilla, in which ample warning is given and all attempts are made to dissuade violation of the boundaries or prohibited zone.

what they were programmed or commanded to do, *unless they happen to malfunction.* The anthropomorphic, romantic nonsense attached to robotics in the popular minds by "Star Wars," "Blade Runner," and other movie and science fiction fantasies seriously compromises the ethical analysis of the use of genuine, real-world military robots within the confines of international law.

Robots that, by definition, cannot commit *war crimes* per se, but only malfunction or make mistakes, require a radically different metric for assessment than the moral one we tend to apply. Moral evaluation of behavior pertains solely to human agents. For robots, as our tools, by contrast, we must talk instead about *safety, reliability,* and *risk.*

It would be madness, for example, to deploy a weapons system that was unsafe or unreliable, that killed the wrong people, or that killed innocent people, instead of destroying the legitimate enemy targets they were designed to attack. Accordingly, in international law as in domestic law, the expectation that would be laid down regarding accountability for wrongful death and destruction would be "due care" and the absence of reckless endangerment or criminal negligence.[16] Deploying a patently unreliable system is surely reckless (and therefore morally culpable) and in extreme circumstances might be found explicitly to be "criminally negligent."[17] By contrast, deploying an autonomous platform that has proven to be safe and reliable under rigorous testing in stringent conditions would on the whole constitute an acceptable, even a morally responsible, action. If such a system malfunctioned (even as humans and their manned systems sometimes make mistakes, hit the wrong targets, or inadvertently kill the wrong people), then the procedure in the machine case would parallel that of the human case in similar circumstances. An inquiry is held and investigation into circumstances conducted, and if no intentional wrongdoing or culpable error by operators is discerned then well-intentioned governments and their militaries issue an apology and do their best to make restitution for the harm inflicted.[18]

---

[16] I discuss these metrics in detail in "Industrial Challenges of Military Robotics."

[17] The attitude that Singer, Sharkey, and others discern among engineers and defense industries all too ready to pursue autonomy without adequate investigation of these problems would constitute one glaring example of "criminal negligence," which is why I argue that attention must be paid to the "safety, reliability, risk" design specification for any armed unmanned systems endowed with any degree of autonomy.

[18] See "Industrial Challenges of Military Robotics." I there argue that the dilemma of military robotics in this regard differs little from that of human combatants, who must be similarly "trained" (rather than "educated") to follow the applicable rules of engagement for a given conflict, that in turn represent the translations by military lawyers of international humanitarian law and law of armed conflict into actionable mission parameters in given conflicts. Failure to comply due to misjudgments, accidents, and mistakes (that are not attributed to criminal negligence or recklessness, in the human case) are then acknowledged by the respective militaries and their governments: apologies are issued, and compensation for damages (ineffectual though that may be) is offered, in analogy with similar kinds of product liability situations in domestic law.

This process is grounded, however, in the prior expectation of what Michael Walzer first termed "double intention" (in lieu of the more lenient criterion of double effect): in this instance, holding manufacturers and designers strictly accountable for exercising *due care* (as well as simply for not deliberately *intending* to do harm) in testing and assuring the reliability and safety of their commercial and industrial products (for robots and drones, when all is said and done, are nothing more than that).[19] We would certainly define the engineering design specifications as requiring that our autonomous machines perform as well or better than human combats under similar circumstances in complying with the constraints of the law of armed conflict and applicable rules of engagement for a given conflict.[20] If they can, and if they do achieve this benchmark engineering specification, then their use is morally justifiable. If they can't, *or if our designers and manufacturers have not taken due care to ensure that they can,* they we have no business building or deploying them. It is really just as simple as that. And like Aegis and Patriot missiles and other semiautonomous systems, this *due care* requires a system of reliable target recognition and threat-level escalation, leading to a proportionate, discriminate, and therefore appropriate response in the use of deadly force.

That is quite enough of a technological challenge, without muddying the waters with science fiction, or with specious metaphysical worries about "machines targeting and killing humans." We are not yet even remotely close to being able to have our machines engage in such activities, in any case, in terms of character recognition software and hardware, for example. And the systems we do propose to build and deploy at present have "autonomy" only in a very limited and highly scripted sense. Platforms such as "Sea Scouts," Israeli-designed "Harpies," and Korean "border sentry" robots are all designed to reliably target adversarial threats in extremely limited and very well-defined scenarios. In addition, these weapons systems usually focus on disarming a perceived threat or (as in the case of "Harpies") dismantling the target's weapons, radar, and command–control technology.[21] Such systems are designed to

---

[19] See Michael Walzer, *Just and Unjust Wars* (New York: Basic Books, 1977; 4th ed., 2010).

[20] This criterion—that robots comply as or more effectively with applicable constraints of law of armed conflict on their use of force and doing of harm than human combatants under similar circumstances—constitutes what I have termed the "Arkin Test" for robot "morality" (although that is likewise somewhat misleading, as the criterion pertains straightforwardly to compliance with international law, not with the exhibiting of moral judgment). In this sense, the test for "morality" (i.e., for the limited ability to comply with legal restrictions on the use of force) is similar to the "Turing Test" for machine intelligence: we have satisfied the demand when machine behavior is indistinguishable from (let alone better than) human behavior in any given context.

[21] Naval engineer John Canning has long argued that this targeting of an adversary's weapon systems (rather than the adversaries themselves) is the proper objective of lethally armed, fully autonomous unmanned systems. Otherwise, such systems should at most be armed with nonlethal weapons or programmed to undertake evasive action rather than use force in self-defense. See John Canning, G. W. Riggs, O. Thomas Holland, Carolyn Blakelock, "A Concept for the Operation

employ force only in very limited situations that leave little room for ambiguity or error. The mistakes that might nonetheless be made are regrettable, but usually not criminally negligent or culpable (as when a child strays into the demilitarized zone or a boater foolishly transgresses the well-defined and well-publicized "no-go" zone around a Navy aircraft carrier).

Policy guidance on future unmanned systems, recently released by the the Office of the US Secretary of Defense, now distinguishes more carefully between "fully autonomous" unmanned systems and systems that exhibit various degrees of "semiautonomy."[22] DoD policy will likely specify that lethal kinetic force may be integrated only, at most, with semiautonomous platforms, involving set mission scripts with ongoing executive oversight by human operators. Fully autonomous systems, by contrast, will be armed at most with nonlethal weapons and more likely will employ evasive action as their principal form of protection. Fully autonomous systems will not be designed or approved to undertake independent target identification and mission execution. In that event, the forthcoming OSD policy statement would be fully in concurrence with recommendations on the future of lethal autonomous systems originally offered in the "Executive Summary and Command Brief" issuing from the symposium of military and civilian robotics authorities participating in the 2010 McCain Conference at the United States Naval Academy.[23]

5. Folk Psychology, "Folk Morality," and Computational Models for Machine Morality

To this point, I have raised questions concerning the diminishing value of "ethics language" and the language of morality as useful approaches to formulating meaningful engineering design specifications for unmanned systems.

---

of Armed Autonomous Systems on the Battlefield," *Proceedings of Association for Unmanned Vehicle Systems International's (AUVSI) Unmanned Systems North America* (Anaheim, CA: August 3–5, 2004); John Canning, "Weaponized Unmanned Systems: A Transformational Warfighting Opportunity, Government Roles in Making it Happen," in *Proceedings of Engineering the Total Ship (ETS)* (Falls Church, VA: September 23–25, 2008).

[22] See "Autonomy in Weapons Systems," Department of Defense Directive (DoDD) 3000.09 (21 November 2012), 3. Accessed on January 9, 2013. http://www.dtic.mil/whs/directives/corres/pdf/300009p.pdf.

[23] See "Executive Summary and Command Brief: 10th Annual McCain Conference," in G. R. Lucas Jr. (ed.), "New Warriors and New Weapons: Ethics & Emerging Military Technologies," *Journal of Military Ethics* 9:4 (December 2010): 416–423. Note that John Canning, "A Concept for the Operation of Armed Autonomous Systems," played an important role in helping to draft these recommendations, as did Ronald C. Arkin, Singer, and a number of other figures cited in this essay. The recommendations thus represent the "best advice" of the most significant engineers, scientists, military officials, and critics of unmanned systems weapons research.

The earliest discussions of "machine morality" nevertheless focused largely on conventional moral theory, often from a purely philosophical perspective, and proceeded to question whether machines could be designed to develop their own "moral intuitions" of right and wrong in situ.[24] The resulting design approaches to "robot morality" appeared technologically challenging, if not wholly infeasible.

Scientists and engineers, however, are loath to be told by nonexperts that their goals and aspirations are "technologically infeasible." One might rather phrase the quest for something analogous to authentic human moral judgment and practical reasoning as "technologically challenging" or "formidable" and wonder about the design specifications that would, at minimum, be required to attain that goal. And here we might well observe that the conventional frameworks for thinking about ethical decision making largely presupposed in these earliest discussions (a set of assumptions concerning intentionality and agency that are sometimes collectively termed "folk morality") as the sort of "morality" to be programmed or simulated in machines are not always themselves well informed by the most recent biological, cognitive, or neurobiological discoveries pertaining to the origins and functioning of moral cognition in overall human behavior.

Rationality-based conceptions of moral deliberation within the framework of "folk morality" often tend, for example, to ignore or downplay the origins and functions of emotions as essential components of moral cognition and utterly ignore the biological and evolutionary basis of human moral behavior. Partly as a result of this rationalistic, ahistorical, and antipsychological bias in conventional morality, very little basic research has been conducted that might contribute to the feasibility of autonomous systems one day possessing the requisite capacities for full character recognition and "situational awareness"—including sensitivity to "moral dilemmas" and the ability to "deliberate" meaningfully about such dilemmas—that would be required, in turn, to achieve some sort of reliable analogue to ethical judgment and practical reasoning in the human case.

If we fail to recognize the significance of this novel research in the psychological and neurobiological foundations of human moral behavior, that is, then it is highly unlikely that we would be led, in turn, to incorporate such discoveries in the design of governance architecture for machine behavior. The future ability of unmanned systems to possess these capacities, however, might prove absolutely essential both to their safe operation as well as to their

---

[24] For example, Robert Sparrow, "Building a Better WarBot: Ethical Issues in the Design of Unmanned Systems for Military Applications," *Science and Engineering Ethics* 15:2 (2008): 169–187. Wendell Wallach, *Moral Machines: Teaching Robots Right from Wrong* (New York: Oxford University Press, 2009).

full acceptance on the part of their human end users. Greater acceptance of robot "combatants" by their human users in what the military, for example, terms its "force mix," depends both upon the reliability of robotic intelligence as a guide to the overall functioning of these machines, and also upon the human users' *ability to trust* in the reliability of that functioning. Fostering the required degree of trust on the part of human users would be essential, in turn, to the effective functioning of these otherwise-autonomous systems within the larger human social matrix (including the resulting military "force-mix" of human and robotic combatants).

Hence, any meaningful research effort aimed toward producing "intelligent, moral machines," would, at minimum, have to incorporate these most recent advances in scientific understanding of human moral behavior itself as a guide toward addressing these parallel engineering concerns in the case of machines. Ethics, after all, may itself be portrayed as largely a matter of good strategic planning regarding the most appropriate ends or goals to pursue, followed by the tactical pursuit of the most appropriate lawful and socially-acceptable means of attaining those goals. Why couldn't this observation be translated into programmable behavioral guidance or "governance architecture" for otherwise-autonomous unmanned systems? An alternative, and as-yet untried approach to robot morality, accordingly, might be to analyze more carefully and precisely the larger social context or matrix within which strategic ends are envisioned, and the appropriate tactical means to achieving them formulated and operationalized.

In pursuing this line of investigation, we might observe, first, that *the evaluative responses of other persons* to an individual agent's decisions and actions (responses such as bestowing praise, ascribing blame, or prescribing punishment, for example) comprise a significant element in the process of individual human moral deliberation, judgment, and action. Absent the corresponding features of "folk psychology" (e.g., the beliefs, intentions, and even basic self-regard described earlier in this essay)—autonomous unmanned systems seem inherently to lack the feedback capacities for governing behavior that emerge or result from them. For what forms or patterns of machine behavior, for example (as Robert Sparrow wonders in this volume), would human operators be willing to confer a Medal of Honor or other recognition for "courage and valor" on an unmanned system? And for what morally-proscribed actions (as Sparrow asked in earlier publications) would we be willing to condemn or "punish" the machine itself? As noted above, these are the features of conventional "folk morality" that Sparrow, and also Noel Sharkey and Peter Singer, find utterly ludicrous when extrapolated to machine behavior.

I propose that we take such critiques instead as posing admittedly-formidable (rather than "impossible") design specifications that robot engineers and computer programmers should be required to address. In fact, some engineers and computer scientists are attempting to do just that. Arkin, for example, has more recently proposed what I would call an "operational" or "functional" morality for unmanned systems. Arkin's approach accepts the accounts of conventional "folk morality" as fully legitimate, and then attempts to *model elements of the underlying folk psychology* (e.g., intentions, and emotions, such as "guilt") that might well prove essential in devising computational analogues of human moral behavior.[25]

An alternative approach, as yet untried and untested, would constitute a kind of physicalist, or "eliminative materialist" approach to the "deep-structure" of moral behavior—the sort of view that philosopher Daniel Dennett has championed for decades—based upon an enhanced understanding of the biological and evolutionary basis of human moral behavior.[26] Promising new lines of biological, psychological, and neurological research *[Gazzaniga, Gratch, Baillargeon], for example,[27] appear to provide insights leading to a more thorough and unified "deep-structure" causal understanding of the place and role of moral cognition and intentional deliberation in the human case. If their work is found plausible in the human context, it might readily be extrapolated to the design of analogous computational, programmable machine governance. Such research would also need to explore the realistic prospects for computational

[25] See, for example, Paul Hyman, "Ethical Robots: Let Their Artificial Consciences be their Guides," *Communications of the Association for Computing Machinery* (September 18, 2012): http://cacm.acm.org/news/155361; Don Troop, "Robots at War," *Chronicle of Higher Education* (September 10, 2012), p. A1. http://chronicle.com/article/Moral-Robots-the-Future-of/134240/.

[26] While he has more recently moved away from a strict reductionist approach to cognition and elements of human behavior to neurological brain states, Dennett's earlier work steadfastly maintains the prospect of one day determining the correlation between brain-states and epiphenomena such as "consciousness" and "intentionality," that form the cornerstone of practical human behavior (including, but not limited to moral behavior). See, for example, *Elbow Room: the Varieties of Free Will worth Wanting* (Cambridge, MA: MIT Press, 1984), *The Intentional Stance* (Cambridge, MA: MIT Bradford Press, 1989), *Brain-children: Essays on Designing Minds* (Cambridge, MA: MIT Bradford Press, 1998), *Consciousness Explained* (Boston, MA: Back Bay Books, 1991), and *Darwin's Dangerous Idea: Evolution and Ethics* (New York: Simon & Schuster, 1995).

[27] A representative sample of this work would include Michael S. Gazzaniga, *The Ethical Brain* (New York: Harper Perennial, 2005); Gazzaniga and Funk, "The functional brain architecture of human morality," *Current Opinion in Neurobiology* 19, no.6 (2009):, 678–681; J. E. Laird, *The Soar Cognitive Architecture* (Cambridge, MA: MIT Press, 2012); Dimitrios Antos, Barbara Grosz, Jonathan Gratch and Celso de Melo, "The influence of emotion expression on perceptions of trustworthiness in negotiation," *25th AAAI Conference on Artificial intelligence* (San Francisco, CA, 2011); Wenji Mao and Jonathan Gratch. "Modeling Social Causality and Responsibility Judgment in Multi-Agent Interactions," *Journal of Artificial Intelligence Research* 44 (2012): 223–273; Lewis, G.J., Kanai, R., Bates, T.C., & Rees, G., "Moral values are associated with individual differences in regional brain volume" *Journal of Cognitive Neuroscience*, 24 (2012): 1657–1663; Baillargeon, R., He, Z., Setoh, P., Scott, R., Sloane, S., & Yang, Y., "False-belief understanding and why it matters: The social-acting hypothesis," M. R. Banaji & S. Gelman (Eds.), *Navigating the social world: What infants, children, and other species can teach us.* (New York: Oxford University Press, forthcoming).

models of the underlying neurological states and processes discerned, within evolutionary biology and current moral psychology, as key drivers of moral behavior. Finally, such research agendas would bear importantly on the safe and reliable operation of autonomous systems, and would powerfully assist in meeting objections or concerns regarding the compliance of unmanned systems with relevant Rules of Engagement and applicable international humanitarian law.

6. Due Care, "Ethical Illiteracy," and Criminal Liability in Unmanned Systems Design

In sum, and regardless of what specific avenues of research are finally pursued, machines equipped with lethal force need to be designed to operate according to precise engineering specifications, including the specifications that their actions comply accurately and unerringly with relevant international law pertaining to distinction, proportionality, and the avoidance of needless suffering (the so-called "cardinal principles" of international humanitarian law), as well as to the operant constraints of "Standing" and specific rules of engagement (ROE). Such constraints are identical to those currently imposed upon human combatants in the field (often with less than perfect success).

Arkin, in particular (whose efforts in this field I greatly admire in other respects), has sometimes seemed needlessly provocative in citing the potential capacity for robots to behave "more ethically," or for autonomous, lethally armed platforms to be "more humane" than human combatants. Autonomous military robots operating on land, in or beneath the sea, or in the air, seem to constitute an entirely different class of entity. Like our rifles, missiles, undersea torpedoes, and jet aircraft, we demand that our military robots be reliable and safe to operate (meaning that they won't malfunction and inadvertently destroy the operator or creator, or wantonly destroy property or innocent human life).

Ever greater degrees of machine autonomy are desirable in order to increase the efficiency and "force multiplier" effects of using unmanned systems in our overall force mix. But they cannot, nor, in the final analysis, do we need to have them, "behave ethically." That is certainly asking for much more than we can currently deliver, and probably much more than we really require of them. We wish, instead, for military robots to be *safe and reliable* in their functioning, and to perform their assigned missions effectively, including following instructions that comply with the laws of armed conflict (just as human combatants do). Invoking "ethics," in lieu of strict compliance with the law (a far simpler domain of behavior to design), may simply serve to confuse or frustrate the proper objectives of robotics research.

If the proper engineering parameters and specifications for lethally-armed autonomous systems are "safety and reliability" within defined limits of tolerable risk (as pertains to matters such as target recognition and threat-level escalation), then what is demanded of engineers, industrial designers and producers, and military end users of such potentially lethal and destructive weapons, in turn, is *due care*, and an absence of reckless, negligent, or criminally-liable disregard for the possible risks of malfunctions, mistakes, or misuse. Those are entirely different matters than the spurious "ethical concerns" raised for or against lethally armed autonomous systems.

Such concerns are of paramount importance to efforts to increase the degree of autonomy, without loss of safety and reliability, in our unmanned military platforms. In ISR* missions, unmanned systems should track and survey appropriate targets, while avoiding doing any harm inadvertently to civilian bystanders or objects within the operational environment. We also want these systems to avoid surveillance (and violation of privacy) of inappropriate or impermissible targets. This is the very meaning of safety and reliability of operation, and ensures that our increasing reliance on such systems conforms to the demands of ethics and the law. Success in this "moral dimension" of robotics research is especially of importance to future DoD* initiatives to combine the force-multiplying effects of greater machine autonomy with lethal force. If responsibly and thoroughly undertaken, such research may lead to marked improvements in both the proportional and highly discriminate ability of the U.S. military to project requisite force in conflict while greatly reducing collateral damage, thereby lessening the generalized destruction and loss of life that otherwise routinely accompany the pursuit of armed conflict.

Although these alternative challenges are themselves extremely grave and very serious, they are nonetheless entirely encompassed within the existing governance framework for manned weapons and systems.[28] Autonomous systems must likewise be designed within carefully defined limits of mechanical tolerance and risk, and operated or deployed only for very specific, scripted missions (what computer scientists and systems engineers describe as "finite state" machines). In that capacity, lethal autonomous platforms are not required to "decide," or to "judge" anything: they merely execute assigned missions, recognize varying contexts, and respond as programmed for each contingency. In case of error or malfunction, the designer or end user is responsible, either criminally (for careless or willful misuse), or civilly (for restitution of harm inflicted or for damage done). Morality and legality (just as with manned

---

[28] For the current status of international law respecting the development and use of unmanned systems, as well as constructive proposals for strengthening this legal regime, see the exhaustive review by Gary Marchant, et al., "International Governance of Autonomous Military Robotics," *Columbia Science and Technology Law Review* 12.272 (2011). http://www.stlr.org/cite.cgi?volume=12&article=7.

weapons systems currently employed in combat) are ultimately a property, and the responsibility, of the system as a whole, not solely its machine components. This presents a radically different and reassuringly more attainable operational goal than critics or proponents of machine autonomy currently envision.

Finally, I return to the point initially raised regarding ethics and the engineering profession itself. Peter Singer is highly critical of what might be characterized as "ethical illiteracy" among engineers, whom he describes as uncomfortable with these questions and all too willing to proceed with their scientific and technological work while leaving the moral concerns to others outside their field.[29] This criticism is not entirely fair: in this article, we have considered the extensive contributions to moral debate and the framing of moral issues in military robotics made by a number of scientists and engineers in the field (e.g., Arkin, Canning, Sharkey). Their work is every bit as significant, and perhaps more credible, in their fields as that undertaken by moral philosophers or experts in international relations. Moreover, much of the engineering contributions to the ethics of unmanned and future autonomous systems is appropriately published in scientific and professional journals, such as the well-regarded *Proceedings of the IEEE*.

Singer is correct to complain, however, that despite these features of the moral debate, far too many practitioners in the field are simply unaware of, or unconcerned with, such matters. Far too many members of the engineering profession simply have not stayed current with the ongoing and published research undertaken by their colleagues. Arkin, for example, has developed methods and a plan for operationalizing what he labels the "ethical governance" (i.e., legal compliance) for autonomous machine behavior. Other research teams (e.g., Brutzman et al.) are pursuing alternative, and occasionally less complex, methods of achieving this goal and hence for satisfying the "Arkin Test."[30] Satisfying this test in *some* fashion, however, is not "optional," but constitutes instead a *strict operational and design specification* for future unmanned systems armed with lethal force. Together, these efforts define a program of research involving alternative testable and falsifiable operational parameters, designed to address this essential design specification for future autonomous systems. It therefore constitutes a serious lapse of professional ethics and must henceforth be recognized as professionally inexcusable for practitioners in the field of military robotics engineering to remain unaware, unconcerned, and uninvolved in this scientific research. Deliberate and willful neglect of this essential dimension of the overall robotics engineering project constitutes

[29] Singer, *Wired for War;* Singer, "Ethics of 'Killer Apps.'"

[30] See Don Brutzman, Bob McGhee, and Duane Davis, "An Implemented Universal Mission Controller with Run-Time Ethics Checking for Autonomous Unmanned Vehicles—A UUV Example," *Proceedings of the IEEE-OES Autonomous Underwater Vehicles* (Southampton, UK: National Oceanography Center (NOC), September 2012).

what is known in law and morality as "culpable ignorance." Practitioners guilty of it could henceforth find themselves morally culpable, and very possibly criminally liable as well, simply for pursuing their current lines of research while ignoring this key engineering design specification.[31]

[31] In my earlier article "Industrial Challenges of Military Robotics" I proposed that the time had come to move beyond speculation about the relative efficacy of LOAC compliance of autonomous unmanned systems to the development and testing of such systems, designed to operate effectively within the constraints of specific rules of engagement (ROE). ROE are specific findings and interpretations specifying lawful conduct in a specific theater of combat operations. I obtained a grant from the Office of the Secretary of Defense via our robotics consortium at the Naval Postgraduate School, on the topic of operationalizing the laws of war for unmanned systems, in which I sought to enlist engineering, computer science, and robotics graduate students and faculty to develop testable guidance software for specific systems we are developing, such as for autonomous underwater warfare, to determine whether such systems could be made "safe and reliable" with respect to compliance with international law. I was not, however, able to encourage any of my colleagues in engineering to sponsor or supervise master's- or doctoral-level research in this topic, as they found it "insufficiently empirical and not really focused on engineering." I believe this attitude reflects not just a bias against the unfamiliar but also an abject failure to remain current in scholarship and research in the field. Leading roboticists, engineers, and scientists engaged in robotics (like Ronald Arkin) have persuaded the field that this is among the most important scientific challenges faced and have published their work to this effect in leading peer-reviewed technical journals. It strikes me as inexcusable academically, as well as professionally dangerous, to continue to fail to acknowledge the significance of designing and testing alternative models for achieving an acceptable level of legal and moral guidance and compliance in future unmanned systems.

11

Autonomous Weapons Pose No Moral Problem

STEPHEN KERSHNAR

1. Introduction

In this chapter, I argue that autonomous weapons pose no moral special problem. By posing no special problem, I mean that the producing and using of autonomous weapons is wrong under the same conditions as the use of nonautonomous weapons. That is, whether the weapon is morally autonomous does raise a distinct moral issue.

2. Argument

Here is my argument:

(P1) Necessarily, if an act is wrong, then it wrongs someone.
(P2) Necessarily, if an act wrongs someone, then it infringes on his right.
(C1) Hence, necessarily, if an act is wrong, then it infringes on his right. [(P1), (P2)]
(P3) Producing or using autonomous weapons does not necessarily infringe on someone's moral right.
(C2) Hence, producing or using autonomous weapons is not necessarily wrong. [(C1), (P3)]

My argument begins with two assumptions. First, autonomy is a matter of degree. Weapons can differ in their autonomy from no autonomy (e.g., a club) to maximum autonomy (e.g., a robot with god-like capacities). In the context of war, a weapon is autonomous, roughly, when it decides whom to attack. A weapon is autonomous to the degree that it decides whom to attack. Very sophisticated autonomous machines might also decide whether to go to war and, if at war, how to conduct it. The latter involves specific targeting decisions.

An individual is morally autonomous, roughly, when it has the internal features that make it morally responsible. These features involve the capacity to guide one's life according to self-chosen principles and, perhaps, doing so. On my account, moral responsibility is a basic notion. That is, it is not analyzable into other notions. On other accounts, an individual is morally responsible just in case he is apt for praise and blame. At some point of moral autonomy, individuals become morally responsible agents (persons) and are not morally different from human persons.[1]

Second, people have natural, negative, and strong moral rights (or claims) to their bodies and properties and these claims are accompanied by powers. By "natural," I mean they are had in virtue of the holders being persons. By "negative," I mean that they are rights to an omission. By "strong," I mean that very weighty moral considerations are needed to override the rights. A power is the standing to leave, modify, or eliminate another moral relation, usually a claim. All other moral rights are derived from these natural rights via commitment (that is, promise or consent) or injustice (i.e., compensatory or punitive justice). I'll later weaken this assumption and note that doing so does not sink the previous argument.

Let us visit these premises.

2.1 Premise (P1) (If an Act Is Wrong, Then It Wrongs Someone)

A wrong act is one that an agent has a duty not to do. Premise (P1) asserts that an act is wrong only if it wrongs someone. This denies free-floating wrongs. A free-floating wrong is a type of wrong act that does not wrong anyone.[2] Candidate free-floating wrongs involve degradation, attitudinal wrongs, and exploitation. The idea here is that some feature of an individual acted on is what explains a duty to act (e.g., moral autonomy or sentience).

2.2 Premise (P2) (If an Act Wrongs Someone, Then It Infringes on His Right)

Premise (P2) asserts that an act wrongs someone only if it infringes on his moral right. This notion fails if there are ways to wrong someone without

[1] For the notion that robots can be moral agents, see John Sullins, "When Is a Robot a Moral Agent?" *International Review of Information Ethics* 6 (2006): 23–30. For the notion that even if robots are persons, they might still be designed so as to serve human interests, see Stephen Peterson, "The Ethics of Robot Servitude," *Journal of Experimental & Theoretical Artificial Intelligence* 19 (2007): 43–54. One concern is that robots do not have emotions and other capacities outside of rationality that are necessary for morality, see Wendell Wallach and Colin Allen, *Moral Machines: Teaching Robots Right from Wrong* (New York: Oxford University Press, 2009), esp. ch. 10.

[2] See Joel Feinberg, *Harmless Wrongdoing* (New York: Oxford University Press, 1988), 19.

infringing on her rights. If we view a right as a claim and a claim as a duty one individual owes a second, then this notion intuitively seems obvious. After all, if one person satisfies all of his duties toward a second, then it is intuitively hard to see how he could wrong the second.

One might argue that one person can wrong a second if the first has a moral reason not to do certain things to a second, even if the reason does not ground a duty.[3] For example, a utilitarian might assert that where one person, Al, has a reason not to steal Bob's car, the reason occurs not because Al owes Bob a duty but because there is a utility-based fact that weighs against his doing so. I have my doubts whether such an act wrongs Bob because the wrongness of the action is explained in terms of the utility of the state of affairs and Al's well-being is only part of that state of affairs. In any case, the utilitarian reason is not always present when autonomous weapons are produced or used. For short, I'll refer to both actions simply as "autonomous weapons."

2.3 Premise (P3) (Producing or Using Autonomous Weapons Does Not Necessarily Infringe on Someone's Moral Right)

The argument for premise (P3) has several parts. Just defense does not infringe anyone's moral rights. I provide a separate analysis of attackers', defenders', or third-parties' rights.

2.3.1 Autonomous Weapon Use Does Not Necessarily Infringe Attackers' Rights

2.3.1.1 Unjust Attackers Forfeit Their Rights

Premise (P3) rests on the notion that the use of autonomous weapons does not pose a distinct moral problem because the use does not necessarily infringe on someone's moral right. Specifically, it need not infringe on the rights of the persons who are targeted by them, those who create or target the weapons, or third parties. Consider the notion that the production and use of autonomous weapons does not infringe on those targeted by them. The argument is that there is a contingent relation between a weapon's autonomy and whether its use unjustly wrongs a victim.

The underlying picture here is that, if autonomy grounds rights, then autonomy does not prevent right alienation because autonomy is reflexive and protects an individual's opportunity to shape his own life. A person is autonomous if he uses self-chosen principles to guide his own life (exercise version) or he

---

[3] For the notion that utilitarians have reasons to act rather than duties, see Alastair Norcross, "Reasons without Demands: Rethinking Rightness," in Jaimie Dreier (ed.), *Blackwell Contemporary Debates in Moral Theory* (New York: Blackwell, 2006), 38–53.

has the ability to do so (capacity version).[4] It thus involves narrative control, that is, the shaping or ability to shape one's life according to one's own narration. Because this narrative might involve less total autonomy, it is not a maximizing notion. This narrative control might involve the shortening of the narrative (consider, e.g., the choice to commit suicide or to do life-shortening acts like smoking) or the ceding of narrative control to another (e.g., imagine someone who lets her husband, Rabbi, or God make her major decisions in life). This shows that autonomy is reflexive, that is, that it includes within itself the control over whether to continue to be autonomous and, if so, how this is to be done. If autonomy is reflexive, then the rights that are grounded by it are alienable because only alienable rights allow one to eliminate or lessen autonomy. Note the shortening or ceding of narrative control need not involve the loss of rights as in the above cases (e.g., suicide, husband, Rabbi).

If the rights protecting autonomy are alienable, then they can be waived. They can also be forfeited. It intuitively seems that a person can forfeit some of his rights.[5] Consider the following case:

Rapist

Outside a bar, a fully responsible attacker, Don, tries to rape and kill a woman, Erin, and she defends herself by hitting him with a tire iron, thereby badly bruising his leg and discouraging him from continuing the attack.

---

[4] For the exercise concept of autonomy and the related notion of freedom of the will, see John Martin Fischer, "Responsiveness and Moral Responsibility," in Derek Pereboom (ed.), *Free Will* (Indianapolis: Hackett Publishing Company, 1997), 214–241; John Christman, "Autonomy and Personal History," *Canadian Journal of Philosophy* 21 (1991): 1–24. For the capacity notion, see Gerald Dworkin, *The Theory and Practice of Autonomy* (New York: Cambridge University Press, 1988), ch. 1; Harry Frankfurt, "Freedom of the Will and the Concept of a Person," *Journal of Philosophy* 68 (1971): 5–29; Gary Watson, "Free Agency," *Journal of Philosophy* 72 (1975): 205–220. On some accounts, the capacity notion includes external conditions that allow an individual the opportunity to shape his own life. See Joseph Raz, *The Morality of Freedom* (Oxford: Clarendon Books, 1986), 150–157.

[5] Other people who assert that a criminal forfeits some of his moral rights include A. John Simmons, "Locke and the Right to Punish," in A. John Simmons et al. (eds.), *Punishment* (Princeton, NJ: Princeton University Press, 1995), 238–252; Judith Jarvis Thomson, *The Realm of Rights* (Cambridge, MA: Harvard University Press, 1990), 365–366; Vinit Haksar, "Excuses and Voluntary Conduct," *Ethics* 96 (1986): 317–329; Murray Rothbard, *The Ethics of Liberty* (Atlantic Highlands, NJ: Humanities Press, 1982); Alan Goldman, "The Paradox of Punishment," *Philosophy and Public Affairs* 9 (1979): 30–46; Roger Pilon, "Criminal Remedies: Restitution, Punishment, or Both?" *Ethics* 88 (1978): 348–357. I make this case in Stephen Kershnar, "The Structure of Rights Forfeiture in the Context of Culpable Wrongdoing," *Philosophia* 29 (2002): 57–88. These theories differ with regard to whether right forfeiture is a fundamental feature of rights or explained by a more fundamental principle.

Consider what happened to the attacker's right to his body. If the right is neither overridden nor alienated, then Erin's hitting Don was wrong, although perhaps excused.[6] This intuitively seems incorrect. If the defensive action is permissible, then the right is either overridden or not infringed. If it is merely overridden by Erin's right to control her body, then there is a residue duty that Erin owes Don. She thus owes him an apology, if not compensation. This is implausible.

If Don's right has a complex content: do-not-hit-unless-necessary-for-defense-or-punishment-or-..., then the right presupposes the conditions under which defensive violence, punishment, and so forth can be done.[7] If so, then the right does not explain when and why such actions may be taken; it merely reflects the conclusion with regard to these things. However, rights theorists often think that rights are part of the moral world precisely because they do such explanatory work. This explains why theorists reason from rights to conclusions about abortion, free speech, and the right to privacy rather than vice versa.[8] Also, the various exceptions (defense, punishment, and consent) are likely ad hoc and not justified by whatever justifies the right. In addition, the logic of such content involves reasoning from *duty-to-X-unless-Y* and *Y* and the rules for such reasoning are unclear.

The best explanation of Don's right is that it is lost. Because Don does not intend this to happen, it is forfeited rather than waived. Right forfeiture is consistent with the alienability of rights and inconsistent with inalienability of them. Just as rights can be waived as part of a self-shaping life, rights can also be forfeited as a way of restricting some individuals from interfering with others having self-shaping lives.[9] The underlying picture of both is that rights protect a self-shaping life, although waiver is more directly connected to the exercise of the shaping process than is forfeiture.

In addition, the right forfeited is either the right in question or an equivalent right. This is in part because otherwise defense would be impossible in some cases. For example, a blind man who attempts to blind another cannot be blinded if that is one way the intended victim could defend herself. Nor could

---

[6] The notion that it is a permissible right infringement can be seen in Phillip Montague, *Punishment as Societal Defense* (Boston: Rowman & Littlefield Publishers, Inc., 1995), ch. 5.

[7] The notion that self-defense involves a narrowly bounded right (e.g., a right to life-except-where-necessary-to-save-someone's-life) is discussed in Judith Jarvis Thomson, "Self-Defense and Rights," in William Parent (ed.), *Rights, Restitution, and Risk* (Cambridge, MA: Harvard University Press, 1990), 37–42.

[8] See Judith Jarvis Thomson, "A Defense of Abortion," *Philosophy and Public Affairs* 1 (1971): 47–66; Judith Jarvis Thomson, "The Right to Privacy," *Philosophy and Public Affairs* 4 (1975): 295–314.

[9] For the notion that forfeiture applies to unjust aggressors, but not just ones, see Jeff McMahan, "On the Moral Equality of Combatants," *Journal of Political Philosophy* 14 (2006): 377–393, esp. 379; and Jeff McMahan, *Killing in War* (New York: Oxford University Press, 2009).

anyone defend against a man who does not own a car and attempts to steal one from another by stealing the would-be thief's car. Note whether the right that is lost has a limited scope in time or whether the right is only temporarily lost is a distinction without a difference, because both descriptions are equivalent and there is no reason to prefer one over the other. On this account, the forfeited right acts as the ceiling on the amount of just defense.

The right to defend is a claim to noninterference against the wrongdoer. The right to defend is accompanied by a liberty against the victimizer to impose defense violence. This liberty is an absence of a duty owed to him not to impose violence. This right is usually, if not always, accompanied by a power over the claim. A claim is a duty owed by one individual to another. A power is the moral standing to eliminate, modify, or leave in place this duty.

On a different account, defensive violence is permissible because it involves the fair distribution of the risk of harm from an attack.[10] The problem with this account is that it does not address how fairness affects the rights of the two parties. In addition, if fairness is a value that depends on other values (e.g., desert, rights, or equality), then fairness-based arguments likely need to be recast in terms of the more fundamental values before we can assess them.

2.3.1.2 If Unjust Attackers Forfeit Their Rights, Then Autonomous Weapons Do Not Necessarily Infringe on the Attackers' Rights

If wrongdoers forfeit their right against (proportional and defensive) violence against defenders, then defenders may use a reasonable means of violence. In general, if one person has a right to something, X, against a second person, Y is a reasonable means to X and does not infringe on an additional right of the second, then the first has a right against the second to do Y. For example, if Erin has a right to prevent Don's attack and her stabbing him with a knife is a reasonable means of her doing so, then she has a right to stab Don. What means are reasonable depends in part on the content of the right that is forfeited. On different accounts of just defense, the violence must be likely to succeed, proportionate, necessary, respond to an immediate threat, or have an appropriate intention or motivation. None of these conditions are plausible.

Defensive efforts are sometimes just even if they are unlikely to succeed, will likely produce greater injury, and are not necessary to stop the violence.[11]

[10] For such an account in the context of torture, see Michael Moore, "Torture and the Balance of Evils," in his *Placing Blame* (Oxford: Clarendon Press, 1997), 726–736.

[11] This is relevant to objections to the interrogational torture used for defensive purposes that rest on its being an ineffective way to gain information. See Bob Brecher, *Torture and the Ticking Time Bomb* (Malden, MA: Blackwell, 2007), 25.

Prison Attack

In prison, the Aryan Brotherhood decides to send a message to the Jewish inmates by giving one Jewish inmate a severe beating, thereby showing the rest that they are all vulnerable and should transfer out of C-Block. They attack Morty. He knows that any defensive violence is unlikely to stop the attack and in fact is likely to make it even more savage.

Cavalry Defense

Polish horse cavalry face overwhelming force by a Nazi blitzkrieg. Cavalry members know that launching horse based attacks will likely result in their death, their horses' death, and the fruitless killing of a few Nazi soldiers.

In these cases, the defensive efforts are permissible because the attackers have forfeited their rights. This is true despite the fact that defensive violence produces, or is likely to produce, unproductive harm to both victim and attacker.

Rape Defense

A small inmate faces a rape attack from a powerfully built member of an Aryan gang. The only way he can defend himself is to stab the gang member in the neck with a shank (prison knife), which will kill him.[12] The small prisoner knows this.

The small prisoner may stab the Aryan gang member despite the fact that killing someone to prevent rape is disproportionate violence. This is because the harm he would inflict (death) is larger than the harm he seeks to avoid (rape). Thus, the assertion that defensive violence must, for example, work, be known to work, or be proportionate is not true. Nor need defensive violence be in response to an immediate threat. The temporal distance between when

---

[12] In women, the notion that defending oneself against rape increases the victim's chance of injury is probably false. Defensive actions appear to have better mental health outcomes than those that did not resist. See S. E. Ullman, "Rape Avoidance: Self-Protection Strategies for Women," in S. Schewe (ed.), *Preventing Violence in Relationships: Interventions across the Life Span* (Washington, DC: American Psychological Association, 2002), 137–162.

the threat is organized and when it is likely to be effectuated is as irrelevant as the spatial distance between where the threat is organized and where it will be effectuated. The other intention and motivation conditions are also morally irrelevant if we are to distinguish someone's blameworthiness for an attack and whether the attack was wrong.

Even if these conditions are morally relevant, in some cases the use of an autonomous weapon might be likely to succeed, proportionate, necessary, in response to an immediate threat, and done with an appropriate intention or motivation.

Consider first an objection that the use of such weapons infringes on the right of targeted persons. There are three reasons someone might think this. On one version, the weapons are not moral agents and persons have a right not to be attacked by nonmoral agents.[13] On another version, use of the weapons do not always allow someone to be held accountable for their decision and it is wrong to cause persons to be attacked when no one can be held accountable.[14] On a third version, use of the weapons assaults defenseless unjust attackers and so infringes on their rights.[15] I argue that all three versions fail because there is no right against these things, and, even if there *were* such a right, then it could be forfeited.

The problem with all three versions is that people have rights to their body and property. This is the simplest and best explanation of why the same rights protect against unwanted control of one's body or property, regardless of how and why foreign control is tried. For example, it is independent of whether the control is intentional, voluntary, or blameworthy. The problem with the first and second versions is that people's rights are justified by autonomy and people's autonomy is not affected by whether the (lethal) attacking object is a moral agent or accountable (that is, can be punished or provide compensation).

Consider the first version that weapons are not moral agents and persons have a right not to be attacked by nonmoral agents. If this were true, then unjust attackers would have a right not to be disabled or killed by land mines,

---

[13] For the notion that human beings and not machines should decide whom to kill, see Noel Sharkey, "Saying 'No!' to Lethal Autonomous Targeting," *Journal of Military Ethics* 9 (2010): 369–383, esp. 380, citing Colonel Lee Fetterman.

[14] See Robert Sparrow, "Killer Robots," *Journal of Applied Philosophy* 24 (2007): 62–77.

[15] See Henry Shue, "Torture," *Philosophy and Public Affairs* 7 (Spring 1978): 124–143. For the notion that the rules of warfare allow assaults on soldiers who are in effect defenseless, see Bradley Jay Strawser, "Moral Predators: The Duty to Employ Uninhabited Aerial Vehicles," *Journal of Military Ethics* 9 (2010): 342–368, esp. 355–358; Uwe Steinhoff, "Torture—The Case for Dirty Harry and against Alan Dershowitz," *Journal of Applied Philosophy* 23 (2006): 337–353. That the actual unmanned aerial vehicles have been used as part of an assassination program, see Jane Mayer, "The Predator War: What Are the Risks of the C.I.A.'s Covert Drone Program?" *New Yorker* (October 26, 2009).

heat-seeking missiles, and smart bombs. The self-guiding nature of a weapon is irrelevant to the forfeited right.

On another version, use of the weapons does not always allow someone to be held accountable for his decision, and it is wrong to cause persons to be attacked when no one can be held accountable. Having someone to hold accountable does not affect the permissibility of defensive violence. To see this, consider the following case. A person who is about to die from cancer may still use lethal violence to defend his family or friends from attack even though his imminent death prevents those whom he attacks from being able to hold someone accountable. The accountability proponent might still assert that there is someone who can be held accountable, namely the decedent, even if that person no longer exists or exists but can't be harmed or punished. However, if this move is allowed, then the same can be said for the person who deployed an autonomous weapon. Even if the targeting of the autonomous weapon is in principle unpredictable, blame would still attach to the person who deployed it without being able to accurately predict whom it will target.

2.3.2 *Autonomous Weapons Do Not Infringe Defenders' Rights*

On a different theory, the autonomous weapon user infringes his own right (i.e., a reflexive right). That is, he infringes on a right concerning how he may treat himself. The notion that a defender who uses autonomous weapons infringes on a reflexive right is a little hard to see if natural rights are exclusively focused on bodies and property. This is because an autonomous weapon user does not infringe on his own right to body or property. This picture of rights rests on a controversial theory of rights. If a more expansive view is correct, then this response is unconvincing.

On a variant of this theory, autonomous weapons might become so sophisticated that they make our moral decisions for us. This might be done by making our normative ethical decisions (our commitments to specific theories of the right and the good) or our applied-ethical decisions (given our notions of the right and the good, decisions as to when to go to war and when at war whom we target).[16] The idea is that, in turning these decisions over to machines, human persons fail to satisfy reflexive duties to respect their own rationality, autonomy, or dignity, fail to take responsibility for their actions, or in effect give up their autonomy by failing to have

---

[16] On one account of what should govern lethal behavior in autonomous robots, Ronald Arkin includes conditions that adopt normative ethical principles (e.g., not targeting noncombatants). See Ronald Arkin, *Governing Lethal Behavior in Autonomous Robots* (New York: Chapman & Hall, 2009), ch. 9. One can imagine an autonomous robot that can revise its design commitment to these principles. For a discussion of the possibility of programming robots so that they may not harm human beings, see P. W. Singer, *Wired for War: The Robotics Revolution and Conflict in the 21st Century* (New York: Penguin Press, 2009), ch. 21.

attitudes required for autonomy.[17] Reliance on autonomous machines with regard to these decisions is analogous to a person who willingly turns over his life-shaping decisions, or perhaps merely his moral decisions, to another person. Such an abdication might be seen as inconsistent with someone being autonomous or properly valuing autonomy. A political analogy to this situation might be if a society were to turn over legislative, executive, or judicial functions to autonomous robots.[18]

On the narrative-control theory of autonomy, it is consistent with autonomy for people to give up narrative control. This is because autonomy is reflexive in the sense that one guides his life according to self-chosen principles even when he adopts a principle of handing over such guidance to another or ends his life so that there is nothing more to guide. An example of an autonomous decision to temporarily suspend autonomy occurs when Odysseus has the sailors bind him to the mast. Even if one restricts the reflexivity of autonomy to when one guides his life according to principles that are rational, reflect the deep self, connect to the good and the true, and connect to one's values, this still allows persons to turn over some principle selection or application to others.[19] This might occur when the others make better decisions than we would. This is true whether the others are persons, machines, or both.

A person can decide autonomously even when he sacrifices future autonomy for a prioritized and rational goal. Consider, for example, when a person donates his vital organs to his spouse and children so that they might survive an accidental poisoning. This might also occur in ordinary areas of life when a person recognizes that others make better decisions than he does. For example, a person who turns over life-and-death decisions about surgery to a trusted

---

[17] For the notion that autonomy presupposes the agent adopt certain attitudes, see Marilyn Friedman, *Autonomy, Gender, Politics* (Oxford: Oxford University Press, 2003), 19; Paul Benson, "Feminist Intuitions and the Normative Substance of Autonomy," in James Stacey Taylor (ed.), *Personal Autonomy* (Cambridge: Cambridge University Press, 2005), 124–142, esp. 125; Catriona Mackenzie and Natalie Stoljar, "Introduction: Autonomy Refigured," in Catriona Mackenzie and Natalie Stoljar (eds.), *Relational Autonomy* (Oxford: Oxford University Press, 2000), 3–31, esp. 19. This might involve a commitment to a particular value (e.g., autonomy itself), a reflexive normative attitude (e.g., sense of self-trust), or a normative competency (the ability to recognize and be motivated by what is actually valuable). See Mark Piper, "The Impossibility of Purely Content-Neutral Accounts of Autonomy," unpublished manuscript (2012).

[18] For the notion that persons cannot abdicate their moral decision making, see Robert Paul Wolff, *In Defense of Anarchism* (Berkeley: University of California Press, 1980). There is an issue as to whether turning decisions over to robots involves using them to gain more knowledge of how to govern ourselves or allowing others to give us commands. Wolff argues that the latter is morally problematic.

[19] For the notion that moral responsibility requires that one's choices and acts be guided by one's deep self, see Frankfurt, "Freedom of the Will." For the notion that moral responsibility requires the person's psychology be connected to the true and the good, see Susan Wolf, *Freedom within Reason* (New York: Oxford University Press, 1990). For the notion that moral responsibility requires one's choices and acts be connected to his values, see Gary Watson, "Free Agency," *Journal of Philosophy* 72 (1975): 205–220.

and wise physician, on the basis that the latter makes better decisions, makes an autonomous choice. The same is true with regard to targeting issues during wartime. This is true whether the thing making the surgical or targeting decision is a person, machine, or both. If the decision maker is worse than the person who turns over the decisions, then the turning over is, perhaps, irrational, bad, or wrong. This is not a problem unique to autonomous machines. It also occurs when a person chooses a poor physician to make his medical decisions or when a commander allows a poor subordinate to make targeting decisions.

If in some cases it is rational to hand decision making to another party because of the other party's expertise regarding medical care or targeting, then it is hard to see why this would not be true with regard to moral values (specifically, what theories of the good and right to accept). The same is true with regard to applying one's values (e.g., targeting issues in relation to the theories of the good and right). Again, problems of unreliable decision making are not unique to autonomous weapons systems even when the systems make fundamental decisions.

On another variant of this theory, the right infringed is the inalienable right the autonomous weapon user holds against himself. In the context of torture, Jeremy Wisnewski and R. D. Emerick argue that a torturer loses himself and an opportunity for the expression of dignity, at least temporarily, because he overly embraces a role.[20] An analogous claim might be made with regard to an autonomous weapon user. However, it is not clear in what sense a person loses himself. In addition, the notion that user fails to express his own dignity likely depends on the claim that he does not respect the victim's dignity, and this returns us to the focus on the victim. In addition, if the reflexive right protects narrative control, then for the reason mentioned above it is alienable.

2.3.3 *Autonomous Weapons Do Not Infringe on Third-Parties' Rights*

An opponent of autonomous weapons might argue that the autonomous weapon user infringes on a right of the victim's family, community, ethnic group, or other relevant third party. In the realm of torture, Richard Matthews asserts that some torture assaults an entire culture.[21] An analogous claim might be made with regard to autonomous weapons. This might occur if the death of one person leads to the rest of the community being terrified, enraged, disbanded, or succumbing to various mental disorders, such as posttraumatic stress.

[20] See Jeremy Wisnewski and R. D. Emerick, *The Ethics of Torture* (New York: Continuum, 2009), 98.

[21] See Richard Matthews, *The Absolute Violation: Why Torture Must Be Prohibited* (Montreal: McGill-Queen's University Press, 2008), 51–59, esp. 56.

One concern is that this allows one person to have rights over the body of another. On this account, if Al's autonomous weapon attacks Bob, this can infringe on Charlene's right. Here Charlene might be Bob's spouse, child, or fellow community member. If an adult is the sole owner of his body, at least in the absence of a contract or other commitment transferring his right, it is unclear how attack via autonomous weapon can wrong a third party. In a few cases, US law does allow one person to recover for injury done to another. For example, in a wrongful death suit, the family of a decedent may recover for lost economic support and companionship.[22] These cases are narrow and arguably based on efficiency.

The more pressing concern is that the third party's right is infringed only if the victim's right is infringed. In the absence of a contract or other commitment, even if a third person can have rights over the body of a victim, the third party's right is likely infringed only if the victim's right is infringed. After all, it is hard to see how a third party can be wronged because of what is done to someone who is not himself wronged. If this is correct, then the claim of the third party depends on a showing that the victim's right is infringed and this again returns the focus to the victim.

2.4   Objection #1: Autonomous Weapon Use Is Necessarily Wrong Even If It Does Not Necessarily Wrong Anyone or Infringe on Anyone's Moral Rights

An objector might claim that there are reasons to think that autonomous weapon use is wrong even if it does not necessarily wrong anyone or infringe on anyone's moral rights. The objector might claim that either (P1) or (P2) is mistaken, so the overall argument fails.

2.4.1   Objection #1a: Autonomous Weapon Use Is Necessarily Wrong but Does Not Necessarily Wrong Anyone

On some accounts, there are free-floating duties. Free-floating duties are duties to do certain acts that are not owed to anyone. For example, utilitarianism posits a duty to reproduce if one's children will have ecstatic lives, even though the duty is not owed to anyone in particular. Some utilitarians have argued that there is no such duty; rather, there is merely a reason to do so.[23] Immanuel Kant asserted there was an imperfect duty to act charitably, even though there is no

---

[22] See *Blacks's Law Dictionary*, 5th ed., s.v. "Wrongful Death Statutes."

[23] See Alastair Norcross, "Reasons without Demands," in James Drier (ed.), *Blackwell Contemporary Debates in Moral Theory* (Oxford: Blackwell, 2006), 38–54.

one to whom the duty was owed.[24] It is not clear that a nonconsequentialist should think that there are free-floating duties. Even if there are such duties, it intuitively seems they are forward-looking or imperfect. In the absence of a perfect duty against autonomous weapon use owed to everyone, there is no free-floating duty against autonomous weapon use. Such use might still wrong someone but not by infringing his moral right. Let us consider this possibility.

2.4.2 Objection #1b: Autonomous Weapon Use Necessarily Wrongs Someone but Does Not Infringe on His Moral Right

It might be thought that the side constraint against autonomous weapon use is subject centered. A side constraint (feature that makes certain acts wrong) is subject centered if it depends primarily on a property of the agent. The property of the agent might be the value of his acting in accord with rationality or virtue or his having a correct attitude (e.g., a correct intention or motive). The idea behind the rationality requirement is that morality is a part of rationality and it is the incorrectness of irrationality that explains the wrongness of immoral action. The idea behind virtue is that it is the concern for an individual's own virtue that explains why nonconsequentialism is true. Consider the following case:

Trade-off

Bad guy never lies. He tells good guy that he (bad guy) will kill five innocent people if good guy doesn't kill one innocent.

The reason that it would be wrong for the good guy to kill the one innocent is that in so doing he would make himself vicious in some way, the particular way depending on the nonconsequentialist theory. This concern for virtue also explains why an agent should not have certain attitudes toward others.[25]

None of these theories are particularly plausible if the explanation is filled out in terms of the badness of irrationality or vice because there can be cases where killing, torturing, or battering innocents will prevent even more irrationality or vice from occurring in others. Think of a case analogous to *Trade-off*. If the explanation for the side constraint is not filled out in terms of the badness of irrationality or vice, then it is hard to see what the explanation for

---

[24] See Immanuel Kant, *Groundwork of the Metaphysics of Morals*, trans. H. J. Paton (New York: Harper Torchbooks, 1964), 89.

[25] For the role of virtue in nonconsequentialism, see Samuel Scheffler, "Introduction," in Samuel Scheffler (ed.), *Consequentialism and Its Critics* (Oxford: Oxford University Press, 1988), 1–13.

the side-constraint is. We can leave this concern aside because none of these subject-centered side constraints rule out all cases of autonomous weapon usage.

It is not irrational to engage in autonomous weapons use if rationality is filled out in terms of individual or aggregate self-interest and if in some cases such use maximizes interest satisfaction. If rationality is filled out in moral terms, then the proponent of the autonomous weapon side constraint has the burden of filling out what is the feature of rationality that explains such a constraint. It can't be a purely formal feature like universalization because it is likely that such a feature can be met. For example, it is possible to universalize the following maxim: if one person is in a situation where a second has launched an attack on innocents can be stopped only via autonomous weapon use and doing so stops the attack, then he uses the weapon.

Nor is it necessarily vicious to use such weapons. Consider the following theory of a vicious attitude: an attitude is vicious if and only if it involves the love of (intrinsic) evil or the hatred of (intrinsic) good.[26] An agent who uses such weapons need not love any aspect of it, but instead see it as a means to avoid greater evil. Similarly, the user might not hate, or be indifferent to, the victim's pleasure. He might instead love it but still view it as an obstacle to overcome in protecting others. If this is correct, then autonomous weapon use has at most a contingent connection to vicious attitudes. Whether such vicious attitudes tend to accompany such use is an empirical question. It is hard to imagine, though, that the wrongness of such use rests on how much pleasure the user takes from his job.

On a different theory of a vicious or indifferent attitude, an attitude is vicious if it is one that would not be held by a virtuous person.[27] A virtuous person is one who has the disposition to act in certain ways in certain types of situations (and perhaps for a certain range of reasons). If this is conjoined with the notion that the disposition results largely from a golden mean in emotion and action, then it appears possible that a person satisfying the golden mean uses autonomous weapons to prevent an attack. In any case, an argument to the contrary would have to be made and it is hard to see what it would look like.

Christopher Tindale puts forth a version of the subject-centered constraint.[28] On his account, if an act is wrong then the agent has control over the wrong-making feature. Tindale does not provide the basis for this assumption,

---

[26] For this account, see Thomas Hurka, *Virtue, Vice, and Value* (New York: Oxford University Press, 2001), chs. 1–2; Thomas Hurka, "The Common Structure of Virtue and Desert," *Ethics* 112 (2001): 6–31.

[27] See Aristotle, *The Nichomachean Ethics*, trans. J. E. C. Welldon (Buffalo, NY: Prometheus Books, 1987).

[28] See Christopher Tindale, "Tragic Choices: Reaffirming Absolutes in the Torture Debate," *International Journal of Applied Philosophy* 19 (2005): 209–222.

but it is probably the claim that if an act is wrong, then what makes it wrong is something for which the agent is morally responsible and the claim that a person is morally responsible for something only if he can control it. On Tindale's account, if the agent has control over the wrong-making feature, then what makes an act wrong is an incorrect intention. Because autonomous weapon use is always done with an incorrect intention, it is absolutely wrong.

One objection to this argument is that control might be necessary for blame, but it is not so necessary for an act to be wrong. The possibility of an excuse for certain acts, acts that are wrong but for which the agent lacked a culpable mental state, suggests that control is not so closely tied to an act's deontic status. A second objection is that it is not clear, of course, that autonomous weapon use always involves an incorrect intention. Tindale does not make it clear on what this claim rests. It might involve a vicious attitude or viewing another merely as a means. The former has the aforementioned problems, and the latter likely cannot be distinguished from permissible defense whereby a person is harmed in ways he does not consent to as a way of stopping or preventing an attack.

Another version of the subject-centered constraint looks at the kingdom-of-ends version of the Categorical Imperative. On this version, each person's contingent goals, the goals that are closely tied to their happiness, should be given equal consideration. This is not done when one person's goals or interests are subordinated to another's.[29] This is unfitting for rational equals. This constraint either cuts too wide or is satisfied by some autonomous weapon use. If this constraint prevents individuals from blocking others' projects, then it rules out all defensive force and punishment and perhaps even some business transactions to which third parties object. If it prevents individuals from blocking others' rational or moral projects, then it does not prevent autonomous weapon use when used to block unjust aggressive attacks. This is because the attackers' projects are neither rational nor moral and because their avoidance of intense pain is at least in part a means by which to further these attacks.

The subject-centered side constraint is a two-person side constraint because it involves a relational property. Specifically, the agent must act in accord with rationality or virtue toward another or have a correct attitude toward her. The requirement thus relates two individuals. Were this not correct, the subject-centered constraint would be a case where the victim is wronged.

Subject-centered accounts of side constraints are likely false because they do not explain why there are side constraints in morality. Even if they are plausible,

---

[29] For this version of the Categorical Imperative, see Kant, *Groundwork of the Metaphysics of Morals*, 100–102. For a similar interpretation of it, see Michael Cholbi, "On Hazing," *Public Affairs Quarterly* 23 (2009): 143–160, esp. 149–154.

the two most plausible versions, rationality- and virtue-based constraints fail because neither disallows autonomous weapons use. The former does not do so because it is sometimes rational to use such weapons. The latter does not do so because it is not obviously vicious to use such weapons on someone who is part of an attack on innocents.

2.5 Objection #2: Autonomous Weapon Use Is Contingently Wrong

A third objection is that autonomous weapon use is contingently wrong. On this objection, the use is wrong for the same sorts of reasons that nonautonomous weapon use is wrong, namely, when it is not used for just defense or when it is used for just defense but violates one of the standard conditions for just defense, such as discrimination between combatants and noncombatants, proportionality, and necessity. If this is correct, then there is no moral problem that is unique to autonomous weapons. Instead, the standard moral restrictions on just defense of self and others apply and a defensive attack must satisfy them. This is true whether the defense occurs via punches, revolver, or fully autonomous robot.

The same is true for a consequentialist analysis of autonomous weapon use. It might be argued that autonomous weapons open up the door to catastrophes, whether expected or possible. Whether the use of such weapons maximizes the good depends on how and when they are used. There is no one answer to this any more than there is to whether it is wrong to throw a punch, make or use a revolver, or make and deploy nuclear weapons.[30]

3. Conclusion

In this chapter, I argue that autonomous weapons pose no moral special problem. By posing no special problem, I mean that producing and using autonomous weapons is wrong under the same conditions that the use of nonautonomous weapons or no weapons is wrong. That is, the use does not raise a distinct moral issue. I argued that if an act is wrong, then it wrongs someone, and if an act wrongs someone, then it infringes on his right. Producing or using autonomous weapons does not necessarily infringe on someone's moral right. Hence, producing or using autonomous weapons is not necessarily wrong.

The central argument here is that autonomous weapon use does not necessarily infringe attackers' rights. This is because unjust attackers forfeit their

---

[30] For the notion that the autonomous weapon use could lead to greater targeting of noncombatants and violate the Law of Armed Conflict, see Robert Sparrow, "Predators or Plowshares? Arms Control of Robotic Weapons," *IEEE Technology and Society and Magazine* (Spring 2009): 25–29, esp. 27.

rights. If unjust attackers forfeit their rights, then autonomous weapons do not necessarily infringe on the attackers' rights. The secondary argument is that the use of such weapons does not infringe on defenders' or third-parties' rights.

The chapter then discusses objections based on the notion that autonomous weapon use is necessarily wrong even if it does not necessarily wrong anyone or infringe on anyone's moral rights. Another objection holds that autonomous weapon use is contingently wrong. The objections all failed.[31]

[31] I am thankful to Neil Feit and Bradley Jay Strawser for their helpful comments and criticisms of this chapter.

BIBLIOGRAPHY

Ackerman, Spencer. "New Study Suggests Drone Strikes Don't Kill as Many Pakistani Civilians as Claimed." *Washington Independent*, May 28, 2010. Accessed February 25, 2012. http://washingtonindependent.com/85945/new-study-suggests-drone-strikes-dont-kill-as-many-pakistani-civilians-as-claimed.

Adams, T.K. "Future Warfare and the Decline of Human Decisionmaking." *Parameters: US Army War College Quarterly* (Winter 2001): 57–71.

Alexander, Lawrence A. "Self-Defense and the Killing of Noncombatants: A Reply to Fullinwider." In *International Ethics: A Philosophy & Public Affairs Reader*, edited by Charles Beitz et al., 98–105. Princeton: Princeton University Press, 1990.

Alexandra, Andrew, Deane-Peter Baker, and Marina Caparini, eds. *Private Military and Security Companies: Ethics, Policies and Civil-Military Relations.* London: Routledge, 2008.

Alston, Philip. *Report of the Special Rapporteur on extrajudicial, summary or arbitrary executions: Addendum, Study on Targeted Killings.* New York: United Nations Human Rights Council, May 28, 2010.

Antos, Dimitrios, Barbara Grosz, Jonathan Gratch and Celso de Melo. "The influence of emotion expression on perceptions of trustworthiness in negotiation." Paper presented at 25th AAAI Conference on Artificial Intelligence, San Francisco, CA, 2011.

Aristotle. *The Nichomachean Ethics.* Translated by J. E. C. Welldon. Buffalo: Prometheus Books, 1987.

Arkin, Ronald. *Governing Lethal Behavior in Autonomous Robots.* New York: Chapman & Hall, 2009.

Arkin, Ronald. "The Case for Ethical Autonomy in Unmanned Systems." *Journal of Military Ethics* 9 (2010): 332–341.

Arkin, Ronald, Craig Patrick Ulam, and Alana R. Wagner. "Moral Decision Making in Autonomous Systems: Enforcement, Moral Emotions, Dignity, Trust, and Deception." *Proceedings of the IEEE* 100/3 (March 2012): 571–589.

Arneson, Richard. "Just Warfare Theory and Noncombatant Immunity." *Cornell International Law Journal* 39 (2006): 101–126.

Aronovitch, Hilliard. "Good Soldiers, A Traditional Approach." *Journal of Applied Philosophy* 18:1 (2001): 13–23.

Asaro, Peter. "What Should We Want From a Robot Ethic?" *International Review of Information Ethics* 6 (2006): 9–16.

Asaro, Peter. "Robots and Responsibility from a Legal Perspective." Paper presented at IEEE International Conference on Robotics and Automation, Rome, 2007.

Asaro, Peter. "How Just Could a Robot War Be?" In *Current Issues in Computing And Philosophy*, edited by Philip Brey, Adam Briggle and Katinka Waelbers, 50–64. Amsterdam, The Netherlands: IOS Press, 2008.

"Attorney General Eric Holder Speaks at Northwestern University School of Law." Chicago, March 5, 2012. Accessed May 29, 2012. http://www.justice.gov/iso/opa/ag/speeches/2012/ag-speech-1203051.html

Axe, David. "Decoy Swarm Could Overwhelm Enemy Defenses." *Wired* (June 1, 2011). http://www.wired.com/dangerroom/2011/06/decoy-swarm-could-overload-enemy-defenses/.

Baillargeon, R., He, Z., Setoh, P., Scott, R., Sloane, S., and Yang, Y. "False-belief understanding and why it matters: The social-acting hypothesis." In *Navigating the social world: What infants, children, and other species can teach us*, edited by M. R. Banaji and S. Gelman. New York: Oxford University Press, forthcoming.

Banda, Siva. "The Challenges of Achieving UAV Autonomy." *Graduate School of Engineering and Applied Sciences Distinguished Lecture Series*. Naval Postgraduate School (December 2, 2010). Excerpted in "Update: Naval Postgraduate School Newsletter." (January 2011): 5. http://www.nps.edu/About/News/World-Renowned-UAV-Control-Expert-Presents-GSEAS-Distinguished-Guest-Lecture.html.

Barnes, Julian and Charles Levinson. "US Drones Hit Targets in Libya." *Wall Street Journal*, April 25, 2011. Accessed May 19, 2012. http://online.wsj.com/article/SB10001424052748704489604576282703009692640.html.

Bekey, George. *Autonomous Robots: From Biological Inspiration to Implementation and Control.* Cambridge, MA: MIT Press, 2005.

Bekey, George, Patrick Lin, and Keith Abney. *Autonomous Military Robotics: Risk, Ethics, and Design*. Washington, D.C.: U.S. Department of the Navy, Office of Naval Research, December 20, 2008.

Belasco, Amy. *Troop Levels in the Afghan and Iraq Wars, FY2001-FY2012: Cost and Other Potential Issues*. Washington, D.C.: Congressional Research Service, 2009.

Bellamy, Alex. *Just Wars: From Cicero to Iraq*. Malden, MA: Polity Press, 2006.

Benbaji, Yitzhak. "A Defense of the Traditional War Convention." *Ethics* 118 (2008): 464–495.

Bender, Bryan. "Attacking Iraq, from a Nev. Computer." *Boston Globe,* April 3, 2005.

Benson, Paul. "Feminist Intuitions and the Normative Substance of Autonomy." In *Personal Autonomy*, edited by James Stacey Taylor. Cambridge: Cambridge University Press, 2005.

Bergen, Peter and Katherine Tiedemann. "The Year of the Drone: an Analysis of U.S. Drone Strikes in Pakistan 2004–2010." *Foreign Policy*, April 26, 2010. Accessed October 28, 2011. http://www.foreignpolicy.com/articles/2010/04/26/the_year_of_the_drone.

Bergen, Peter and Katherine Tiedemann. "Washington's Phantom War: The Effects of the U.S. Drone Program in Pakistan." *Foreign Affairs*, July–August 2011.

Billitteri, Thomas J. "Drone Warfare: Are strikes by unmanned aircraft ethical?" *CQ Researcher* 20:28 (August 6, 2010): 653–676.

Blacks's Law Dictionary, 5th ed., s.v. "Wrongful death statutes."

Blumenfeld, Laura. "In Israel, a Divisive Struggle Over Targeted Killing." *The Washington Post* August 27, 2006. Accessed May 29, 2012. http://www.washingtonpost.com/wp-dyn/content/article/2006/08/26/AR2006082600917.html?sid=ST2007112401542.

Bonadonna, Reed R. "Above and Beyond: Marines and Virtue Ethics." *Marine Corps Gazette* 78:1 (1994): 18–20.

Bone, Elizabeth and Christopher Bolkcom. "Unmanned Aerial Vehicles: Background and Issues for Congress." Report for Congress, April 25, 2003. http://www.fas.org/irp/crs/RL31872.pdf.

Brecher, Bob. *Torture and the Ticking Time Bomb*. Malden, MA: Blackwell, 2007.

Brennan, John. "The Efficacy and Ethics of U.S. Counterterrorism Strategy." Woodrow Wilson Center, April 30, 2012. Accessed May 1, 2012. http://www.wilsoncenter.org/event/the-efficacy-and-ethics-us-counterterrorism-strategy.

Brock, Peter. *The Quaker Peace Testimony: 1660 to 1914*. Syracuse: Syracuse University Press, 1990.

Canning, John, Riggs, G.W. Holland, O. Thomas, and Carolyn Blakelock. "A Concept for the Operation of Armed Autonomous Systems on the Battlefield." *Proceedings of Association for Unmanned Vehicle Systems International's (AUVSI) Unmanned Systems North America*. Anaheim, CA: August 3–5, 2004.

Canning, John. "Weaponized Unmanned Systems: A Transformational Warfighting Opportunity, Government Roles in Making it Happen." *Proceedings of Engineering the Total Ship (ETS).* Falls Church, VA: September 23–25. 2008.

Cappacio, Tony and Jeff Bliss. "U.S. Said to Reduce Civilian Deaths after Increasing CIA Pakistan Strikes." *Bloomberg,* January 31, 2011. Accessed March 22, 2011. http://www.bloomberg.com/news/2011-01-31/u-s-said-to-reduce-civilian-deaths-after-increasing-cia-pakistan-strikes.html.

Card, Joseph. "Killer Machines." *Foreign Policy,* 2007.

Caryl, Christian. "Predators and Robots at War." *New York Review of Books,* September 29, 2011. Accessed December 20, 2011. http://www.nybooks.com/articles/archives/2011/sep/29/predators-and-robots-war/?pagination=false.

Cholbi, Michael. "On Hazing." *Public Affairs Quarterly* 23 (2009): 143–160.

Christman, John. "Autonomy and Personal History." *Canadian Journal of Philosophy* 21 (1991): 1–24.

Clare, Andrew S., Christin S. Hart, and Mary L. Cummings. "Assessing Operator Workload and Performance in Expeditionary Multiple Unmanned Vehicle Control." Paper presented at 48th AIAA Aerospace Sciences Meeting, Orlando, FL, January 2010.

Cochran, David Carroll. "War-Pacifism." *Social Theory and Practice* 22 (1996): 161–180.

Codevilla, Angelo. "Get Rid of Saddam Hussein Now: The Moral Justification." *Wall Street Journal,* February 25, 1991.

Cook, Martin L. *The Moral Warrior.* Albany, NY: State University of New York Press, 2004.

Corn, Geoffrey and Chris Jenks. "Two Sides of the Combatant COIN: Untangling Direct Participation in Hostilities from Belligerent Status in Non-International Armed Conflicts." *University of Pennsylvania Journal of International Law* 33 (2011).

Crawford, Neta C. "The Cost of War Since 2001: Afghanistan, Iraq, and Pakistan, Executive Summary." *The Costs of War Project.* Providence, RI: Watson Institute for International Studies, 2011.

Cummings, Mary L., et al., "The Role of Human-Automation Consensus in Multiple Unmanned Vehicle Scheduling." *Human Factors: The Journal of the Human Factors and Ergonomics* 52:1 (2010).

Davis, Nancy. "The Doctrine of Double Effect: Problems of Interpretation." *Pacific Philosophical Quarterly* 65 (1984): 107–123.

Dennett, Daniel C. *The Intentional Stance.* Cambridge, MA: MIT Bradford Press, 1989.

Dennett, Daniel C. *Consciousness Explained.* Boston, MA: Back Bay Books, 1991.

Dennett, Daniel C. *Darwin's Dangerous Idea: Evolution and Ethics.* New York: Simon & Schuster, 1995.

Dennett, Daniel C. *Brain-children: Essays on Designing Minds.* Cambridge, MA: MIT Bradford Press, 1998.

Department of the Army. *FM 3-24: Counterinsurgency.* Washington, DC: Department of the Army, 2006.

Dilanian, Ken. "CIA Drones May be Avoiding Pakistani Civilians." *Los Angeles Times,* February 22, 2011. Accessed March 18, 2011. http://articles.latimes.com/2011/feb/22/world/la-fg-drone-strikes-20110222.

Dipert, Randall. "The Ethics of Cyberwarfare." *Journal of Military Ethics* 9:4 (2010): 384–410.

Dipert, Randall. "The Ethics of Cyberwarfare." Paper presented at International Society of Military Ethics Annual Conference, San Diego, January, 2010.

DoD Dictionary of Military and Associated Terms. Joint Publication 1–02, 2008.

DoD Directive 2311.01E, May 9, 2006.

"DoD News Briefing with Geoff Morrell at the Pentagon Briefing Room, Arlington, VA." September 9, 2009. http://www.defenselink.mil/transcripts/transcript.aspx?transcriptid=4475.

Drones Team. "Covert US Strikes in Pakistan, Somalia and Yemen—Our Methodology." *The Bureau of Investigative Journalism.* August 10, 2011. Accessed February 28, 2012. http://www.thebureauinvestigates.com/2011/08/10/pakistan-drone-strikes-the-methodology2/.

Dworkin, Gerald. *The Theory and Practice of Autonomy*. New York: Cambridge University Press, 1988.

Eck, Kristine and Lisa Hultman. "One-Sided Violence Against Civilians in War: Insights from new Fatality Data." *Journal of Peace Research* 44:2 (2007).

Elbow Room: the Varieties of Free Will worth Wanting (Cambridge, MA: MIT Press, 1984),

Elshtain, Jean Bethke. "The Third Annual Grotius Lecture: Just War and Humanitarian Intervention." *American University International Law Review* 17:1 (2001): 17–18.

Elshtain, Jean Bethke. *Just War Against Terror*. New York: Basic Books, 2004.

Emerton, P. and T. Handfield. "Order and Affray: Defensive Privileges in Warfare." *Philosophy and Public Affairs* 37 (2009): 382–414.

"Ending Drone Attacks." *The Nation*, March 26, 2011. Accessed March 30, 2011. http://www. nation.com.pk/pakistan-news-newspaper-daily-english-online/ editorials/26-Mar-2011/Ending-drone-attacks.

Engeland, Anisseh van. *Civilian or Combatant? A Challenge for the 21st Century*. New York: Oxford University Press, 2010.

Entous, Adam Siobhan Gorman, and Julian Barnes. "U.S. Tightens Drone Rules." *Wall Street Journal*, November 4, 2011. Accessed May 19, 2012. http://online.wsj.com/article/SB100 01424052970204621904577013982672973836.html.

Entous, Adam. "Special Report—How the White House learned to love the drone." *Reuters. com*. Accessed February 29, 2012. www.uk.reuters.com/article/2010/05/19/uk- pakistan -drones-idUKTRE64H5U720100519?pageNumber=3.

Entous, Adam, Siobhan Gorman, and Julian Barnes. "U.S. Relaxes Drone Rules; Obama Gives CIA, Military Greater Leeway in Use Against Militants in Yemen." *Wall Street Journal*, April 26, 2012.

"Executive Summary and Command Brief: 10th Annual McCain Conference." In "New Warriors and New Weapons: Ethics & Emerging Military Technologies." Edited by G.R. Lucas, Jr. *Journal of Military Ethics* 9:4 (December 2010): 416–423.

Exum, Andrew, Nathaniel Fick, Ahmed Humayun, and David Kilcullen. "Triage: the Next Twelve Months in Afghanistan and Pakistan." Center for a New American Security, June 2009, 18, Accessed February 25, 2012. http://www.cnas.org/files/documents/ publications/ExumFickHumayun_TriageAfPak_June09.pdf (accessed February 25, 2012).

Fabre, Cécile. "Mandatory Rescue Killings." *The Journal of Political Philosophy* 15:4 (2007).

Fair, C. Christine. "Drone Wars." *Foreign Policy*, May 28, 2010. Accessed February 25, 2012. http://www.foreignpolicy.com/articles/2010/05/28/drone_wars?page=0,0

Fehrenbach, T.R. *This Kind of War*. New York: Macmillan, 1963.

Feinberg, Joel. *Harmless Wrongdoing*. New York: Oxford University Press, 1988.

Finkelstein, Claire, Jens David Ohlin, and Andrew Altman, editors. *Targeted Killings: Law and Morality in an Asymmetrical World*. Oxford: Oxford University Press, 2012.

Finn, Peter. "In Russia, A Secretive Force Widens." *The Washington Post*, December 12, 2006. Accessed March 5, 2012. http://www.washingtonpost.com/wp-dyn/content/ article/2006/12/11/AR2006121101434_2.html. Accessed March 5, 2012.

Finnemore, Martha. *The Purpose of Humanitarian Intervention: Changing Beliefs about the Use of Force*. Ithaca and London: Cornell University Press, 2003.

Fischer, John Martin. "Responsiveness and Moral Responsibility." In *Free Will*, edited by Derek Pereboom, 214–241. Indianapolis: Hackett Publishing Company, 1997.

Fitzsimonds, J.R. and T.G. Mahnken. "Military Officer Attitudes Toward UAV Adoption: Exploring Institutional Impediments to Innovation." *Joint Forces Quarterly* 46 (2007): 96–103.

"Fox and Hague slapped down by the generals after suggesting that Gaddafi could be personally targeted." In "Is Gaddafi a legitimate target." *New Statesman*, March 21, 2011. Accessed February 29, 2012. www.newstatesman.com/blogs/the-staggers/2011/03/ gaddafi- generals-hague-fox. Accessed February 29, 2012.

Frankfurt, Harry. "Freedom of the Will and the Concept of a Person." *Journal of Philosophy* 68 (1971): 5–29

French, Shannon E. *The Code of the Warrior: Exploring Warrior Values, Past and Present*. Lanham, Md.: Rowman & Littlefield, 2003.

Friedman, Marilyn. *Autonomy, Gender, Politics*. Oxford: Oxford University Press, 2003.

Galliot, Jai C. "Uninhabited Aerial Vehicles and the Asymmetry Objection: A Reply to Strawser." *Journal of Military Ethics* 11:1 (2012): 58–66.

Galliott, Jai C. "The Rise of Uninhabited Military Systems" In "Saving Soldiers and the Ethics of Uninhabited Military Systems." Doctoral Dissertation, Macquarie University, Forthcoming.

Galula, David. *Counterinsurgency Warfare: Theory and Practice*. New York: Frederick A. Praeger, 1964.

Garamone, Jim. "Allen: Troops Will Accomplish Afghan Mission." *American Forces Press Service*, March 20, 2012. http://www.defense.gov/news/newsarticle.aspx?id=67611.

Gazzaniga, Michael S. *The Ethical Brain*. New York: Harper Perennial, 2005.

Gazzaniga and Funk. "The functional brain architecture of human morality." *Current Opinion in Neurobiology* 19:6 (2009): 678–681.

Gentile, Gian P. "A Strategy of Tactics: Population-centric COIN and the Army." *Parameters: US Army War College Quarterly* (Autumn 2009): 5–17.

Gentry, John A. "Doomed to Fail: America's Blind Faith in Military Technology." *Parameters: US Army War College Quarterly* (Winter 2002): 88–103.

Glover, Jonathan. *Causing Death and Saving Lives*. New York: Penguin Books, 1990.

Goldman, Alan. "The Paradox of Punishment." *Philosophy and Public Affairs* 9 (1979): 30–46.

Gorman, Ryan R. "War and the Virtues in Aquinas's Ethical Thought." *Journal of Military Ethics* 9.3 (2010): 257–258.

Grayling, AC. *Among the Dead Cities: Was the Allied Bombing of Civilians in WWII A Necessity or a Crime?* London: Bloomsbury, 2006.

Green, Michael. "War, Innocence, and Theories of Sovereignty." *Social Theory and Practice* 18 (1992): 39–62.

Gross, Michael. "Assassination and Targeted Killing: Law Enforcement, Execution, or Self-Defence?" *Journal of Applied Philosophy* 23:3 (2006): 323–335.

Gross, Michael L. *Moral Dilemmas of Modern War: Torture, Assassination and Blackmail in an Age of Asymmetric Conflict*. Cambridge: Cambridge University Press, 2009.

Guiora, Amos. "Targeted Killing as Active Self-Defense." *Case Western Reserve Journal of International Law* 36 (2004): 319–329.

Haksar, Vinit. "Excuses and Voluntary Conduct." *Ethics* 96 (1986): 317–329.

Hallet, Brien. "Just War Criteria." In *Encyclopedia of Violence, Peace, and Conflict, Vol. 2*, edited by Lester R. Kurtz and Jennifer E. Turpin, 283–294. Atlanta, GA: Academic Press, 1999.

Harding, Luke. "Alexander Litvinenko poisoning: move to extradite second murder suspect." *The Guardian*, February 29, 2012. Accessed March 1, 2012. http://www.guardian.co.uk/world/2012/feb/29/alexander-litvinenko-polonium-suspect-charged.

Harley, Jeffrey A. "Information, Technology, and Center of Gravity." *Naval War College Review* 50.1(1997): 66–87.

Hehdal, Markus. "Blood and Blackwaters: A call to arms for the profession of arms." *Journal of Military Ethics* 8:1 (2009): 19–33.

Hencaerts, Jean-Marie and Louise Doswald-Beck. *Customary International Humanitarian Law*. Cambridge: Cambridge University Press, 2006.

Himma, Ken. "Artificial Agency, Consciousness, and the Criteria for Moral Agency: What Properties Must an Artificial Agent Have to be a Moral Agent?" Paper presented at 7th International Computer Ethics Conference, San Diego, July, 2007.

Hosmer, Steven T. *The Conflict over Kosovo: Why Milosevic Decided to Settle When He Did*. Santa Monica, Arlington, and Pittsburgh: RAND Corporation, 2001.

Human Rights Institute, Columbia Law School. "Targeting Operations with Drone Technology: Humanitarian Law Implications." Background Note for the American Society of International Law Annual Meeting, March 25, 2011, 25–36.

Hurka, Thomas. "The Common Structure of Virtue and Desert." *Ethics* 112 (2001): 6–31.

Hurka, Thomas. *Virtue, Vice, and Value*. New York: Oxford University Press, 2001.

Hursthouse, Rosalind. *On Virtue Ethics*. Oxford: Oxford University Press, 2001.

International Commission on Intervention and State Sovereignty (ICISS). *The Responsibility to Protect*. Ottawa: International Development Research Centre, 2001.

International Committee of the Red Cross. "Convention (III) Relative to the Treatment of Prisoners of War." *International Humanitarian Law—Treaties and Documents*. Geneva: Red Cross, 1949.

International Committee of the Red Cross. *Interpretive Guidance on the Notion of Direct Participation in Hostilities under International Humanitarian Law*. Geneva: Red Cross, 2009.

International Criminal Tribunal for the former Yugoslavia. *Kupreskic Case (Judgment of 14 January 2000)*, paragraph 524.

"Interpretive Guidance on the Notion of Direct Participation in Hostilities under IHL." *International Review of the Red Cross* 90 (2008): 991–1047.

"ISAF Troops Kill Seven Innocent Civilians in NWA: ISPR." *Associated Press of Pakistan*, September 3, 2008. Accessed January 11, 2011. http://www.app.com.pk/en_/index.php?option=com_content&task=view&id=51444&Itemid=2 (accessed January 11, 2011).

"John Brennan talks War on Terror." Fox News Sunday, April 29, 2012. Accessed April 29, 2012. http://www.foxnews.com/on-air/fox-news-sunday/2012/04/29/john-brennan-talks-war- terror-joel-and-victoria-osteens-message-hope?page=2.

Johnson, Rebecca. "Doing More with More: The Ethics of Counterinsurgency." Paper presented at International Symposium of Military Ethics, San Diego, January 2010.

Johnson, Rebecca. "Fight Right to Fight Well: General McChrystal's Approach to Preserving Noncombatant Immunity." *Small Wars Journal* 6 (April 2010): 12–18.

Johnston, Patrick B. and Anoop Sarbahi. "The Impact of U.S. Drone Strikes on Terrorism in Pakistan." Belfer Center for Science and International Affairs, John F. Kennedy School of Government, February 25, 2012. Accessed March 1, 2012. http://patrickjohnston.info/materials/drones.pdf (accessed March 1, 2012).

Kahl, Colin. "In the Crossfire or the Crosshairs: Norms, Civilian Casualties, and U.S. Conduct in Iraq." *International Security* 32:1 (Summer 2007): 7–46.

Kahn, Paul W. "The Paradox of Riskless Warfare." *Philosophy and Public Policy Quarterly* 22 (2002): 2–8.

Kaldor, Mary. *New and Old Wars*. Palo Alto, CA: Stanford University Press, 1999.

Kamm, Frances M. "Failures of Just War Theory: Terror, Harm, and Justice." *Ethics* 114 (2004): 650–692.

Kant, Immanuel. *Groundwork of the Metaphysics of Morals*. Translated by H. J. Paton. New York: Harper Torchbooks, 1964.

Kant, Immanuel. "Perpetual Peace." In *The Ethics of War: Classic and Contemporary Readings*, edited by Gregory Reichberg, Henrik Syse, and Endre Begby. Oxford: Blackwell, 2006.

Kant, Immanuel. *Critique of Pure Reason*. New York: Penguin Classics, 2008.

Kasher. Asa & Amos Yadlin. "Military Ethics of Fighting Terror: An Israeli Perspective." *Journal of Military Ethics* 4:1 (2005): 60–70.

Kasher, Asa. "The Principle of Distinction." *Journal of Military Ethics* 6:2 (2007): 152–167.

Kaufman, Frederick. "Just War Theory and Killing the Innocent." In *Rethinking the Just War Tradition*, edited by Michael Brough, John Lango, and Harry van der Linden, 99–114. New York: SUNY Press, 2007.

Kaufman, W.R.P. "Rethinking the Ban on Assassination." In *Rethinking the Just War Tradition*, edited by Michael Brough, John Lango, and Harry van der Linden. New York: SUNY Press, 2007.

Kaurin, Pauline. "When Less Is *Not* More: Expanding the Combatant/Noncombatant Distinction." In *Rethinking the Just War Tradition*, edited by Michael Brough, John Lango, and Harry van der Linden, 115–130. New York: SUNY Press, 2007.

Kennan, George. "Morality and Foreign Policy." *Foreign Affairs* 64 (Winter 1985/1986).

Kershnar, Stephen. "The Structure of Rights Forfeiture in the Context of Culpable Wrongdoing." *Philosophia* 29 (2002): 57–88.

Kershnar, Stephen. "The Moral Argument for a Policy of Assassination." *Reason Papers* 27 (2004): 45–67.

Kershnar, Stephen. "Assassination and the Immunity Theory." *Philosophia* 33:4 (2005): 129–147.

Kilcullen, David. *The Accidental Guerilla*. New York: Oxford University Press, 2009.

Kilcullen, David and Andrew Exum. "Death from Above, Outrage from Below." *New York Times*, May 16, 2009. Accessed September 15, 2011. http://www.nytimes.com/2009/05/17/opinion/17exum.html?pagewanted=all&_r=0.

Killmister, Suzy. "Remote Weaponry: The Ethical Implications." *Journal of Applied Philosophy* 25:2 (2008): 121–133.

Knickmeyer, Ellen and Jonathan Finer. "Insurgent Leader Al-Zarqawi Killed in Iraq." *Washington Post* June 8, 2006. Accessed March 1, 2012. http://www.washingtonpost.com/wp-dyn/content/article/2006/06/08/AR2006060800114.html.

Koh, Harold. "The Obama Administration and International Law." American Society for International Law. Accessed February 25, 2012. http://www.state.gov/s/l/releases/remarks/139119.htm.

Kolff, D. W. "'Missile Strike Carried Out with Yemeni Cooperation'—Using UCAVs to Kill Alleged Terrorists: A Professional Approach to the Normative Basis of Military Ethics." *Journal of Military Ethics*, 2:3 (2003): 240–244.

Kreps, Sarah. "The Second Lebanon War: Lessons Learned." *Parameters* 37 (2007): 72–84.

Kreps, Sarah and John Kaag. "The Use of Unmanned Aerial Vehicles in Contemporary Conflict: A Legal and Ethical Analysis." *Polity* 44 (2012).

Krishnan, Armin. *Killer Robots: Legality and Ethicality of Autonomous Weapons*. London: Ashgate Press, 2009.

Lacina, Bethany and Nils Gleditsch. "Monitoring Trends in Global Combat: A New Dataset of Battle Deaths." *European Journal of Population* 21:2–3 (2005): 145–165.

Laird, J.E. *The Soar Cognitive Architecture*. Cambridge, MA: MIT Press, 2012.

Landay, Jonathan. "'We're Pinned Down: 4 U.S. Marines Die in Afghan Ambush." McClatchy News Service, September 9, 2009. Accessed September 20, 2012. http://www.mcclatchydc.com/227/story/75036.html.

Lang, Gerald, Michael Otsuka, and Bradley Jay Strawser. "Symposium on Jeff McMahan, Killing in War." *Analysis* 71 (2011): 511–559.

Larkin, Matthew S. *Brave New Warfare: Autonomy in Lethal UAVs*. Master's Thesis. Monterey, CA: Naval Postgraduate School. Accessed September 15, 2012. https://wiki.nps.edu/download/attachments/15073701/Brave+New+Warfare+(Larkin,+Matthew+Thesis).pdf?version=1&modificationDate=1301324368000

Lazar, Seth. "Responsibility, Risk, and Killing in Self-Defense." *Ethics* 199 (2009): 699–728.

Lazar, Seth. "The Responsibility Dilemma for Killing in War: A Review Essay." *Philosophy and Public Affairs* 38:2 (2010): 180–213.

Lazar, Seth. "Necessity in Self-Defence and War." *Philosophy and Public Affairs* (forthcoming Winter 2012).

Levy, Jack S. and William R. Thompson. *Causes of War*. West Sussex: Wiley-Blackwell, 2010.

Lewis, G.J., Kanai, R., Bates, T.C., & Rees, G. "Moral values are associated with individual differences in regional brain volume." *Journal of Cognitive Neuroscience* 24 (2012): 1657–1663.

Long, Austin. *On "Other War": Lessons from Five Decades of RAND Counterinsurgency Research*. Santa Monica, CA: RAND, 2006.

Lucas, Jr., George R. "Advice and Dissent: the 'Uniform' Perspective." *Journal of Military Ethics* 8:2 (2009): 141–161.

Lucas, Jr. George R. *Anthropologists in Arms: the Ethics of Military Anthropology*. Lanham, MD: AltaMira Press, 2009.

Lucas, Jr., George R. "'This is Not Your Father's War': Confronting the Moral Challenges of 'Unconventional' War." *Journal of National Security Law and Policy* 3:2 (2009): 331–342.

Lucas, Jr., George R. "Postmodern War." In *New Warriors and New Weapons: Ethics & Emerging Military Technologies, Journal of Military Ethics* 9:4 (December 2010): 289–298.

Lucas, Jr., George R. "Industrial Challenges of Military Robotics." *Journal of Military Ethics* 10:4 (December 2011): 274–295.

Mackenzie, Catriona and Natalie Stoljar. "Introduction: Autonomy Refigured." In *Relational Autonomy*, edited by Catriona Mackenzie and Natalie Stoljar, 3–31. Oxford: Oxford University Press, 2000.

Mander, Jerry. *Four Arguments for the Elimination of Television*. New York: Morrow Quill Paperbacks, 1978.

Mao, Wenji and Jonathan Gratch. "Modeling Social Causality and Responsibility Judgment in Multi-Agent Interactions." *Journal of Artificial Intelligence Research* 44 (2012): 223–273.

Maqbool, Aleem. "Mapping US Drone and Islamic Militant Attacks in Pakistan." *BBC News South Asia*, July 22, 2010. Accessed September 26, 2010. http://www.bbc.co.uk/news/world-south-asia-10728844.

Marchant, Gary, et al. "International Governance of Autonomous Military Robotics." *Columbia Science and Technology Law Review* 12:272 (2011).

Marston, Daniel and Carter Malkasian, eds. *Counterinsurgency in Modern Warfare*. New York: Osprey Publishing 2008.

Matthews, Richard. *The Absolute Violation: Why Torture Must Be Prohibited*. Montreal: McGill-Queen's University Press, 2008.

Mavrodes, George I. "Conventions and the Morality of War." *Philosophy and Public Affairs* 4:2 (1975): 117–131.

Maxwell, Dave. "Is COIN the Graduate Level of War?" *Small Wars Journal Blog* 20 (July 2008).

Mayer, Chris. "Nonlethal Weapons and Noncombatant Immunity: Is it Permissible to Target Noncombatants?" *Journal of Military Ethics* 6:3 (September 2007): 221–231.

Mayer, Jane. "The Predator War: What are the Risks of the C.I.A.'s Covert Drone Program?" *The New Yorker*, October 26, 2009.

Mazetti, Mark. "C.I.A. Drone Is Said to Kill Al Qaeda's No. 2." *New York Times*, August 27, 2011.

McIntyre, Alison. "Doing Away with Double Effect." *Ethics* 111 (2001): 219–255.

McKeogh, Colm. "Civilian Immunity in War: From Augustine to Vattel." In *Civilian Immunity in War*, edited by Igor Primoratz, 61–83. Oxford: Oxford University Press, 2007.

McMahan, Jeff. "The Ethics of Killing in War." *Ethics* 114:4 (2004): 708–718.

McMahan, Jeff. "Just Cause for War." *Ethics and International Affairs* 19 (2005): 1–21.

McMahan, Jeff. "On the Moral Equality of Combatants." *Journal of Political Philosophy* 14 (2006): 377–393.

McMahan, Jeff. "Debate: Justification and Liability in War." *Journal of Political Philosophy* 16:2 (2008): 227–244.

McMahan, Jeff. *Killing in War*. New York: Oxford University Press, 2009.

McMahan, Jeff. "Targeted Killing: Murder, Combat, or Law Enforcement?" In *Targeted Killings: Law and Morality in an Asymmetrical World*, edited by Andrew Altman, Claire Finkelstein, and Jens David Ohlin, 135–155. New York: Oxford University Press, 2012.

Meilinger, Phillip. "Precision Aerospace Power, Discrimination, and the Future of Warfare." *Aerospace Power Journal* 15 (2001).

Melzer, Nils. "Interpretive Guidance on the Notion of Direct Participation on Hostilities under International Humanitarian Law." *International Committee of the Red Cross*. Geneva: Red Cross, 2008.

Merchant, Gary E., Braden Allenby, Ronald Arkin, Edward T. Barrett, Jason Borenstein, Lyn M. Gaudet, Orde Kittrie, Patrick Lin, George R. Lucas, Richard O'Meara and Jared Silberman. "International Governance of Autonomous Military Robots." *The Columbia Science and Technology Law Review* 12 (2011): 272–315.

Metz, Steven and Raymond Millen. *Insurgency and Counterinsurgency in the 21st Century: Reconceptualizing Threat and Response*. Carlisle Barracks, PA: Strategic Studies Institute, U.S. Army War College, 2004.

Mir, Amir. "60 Drone Hits Kill 14 Al-Qaeda Men, 687 Civilians." *The News*, April 10, 2009.

Mir, Amir. "US Drones Killed 123 Civilians, 3 al-Qaeda Men in January." *The News*, February 1, 2010.

Moelker, Renee and Peter Olsthoorn. "Virtue Ethics and Military Ethics." *Journal of Military Ethics* 6:4 (2007): 257–258.

Monbiot, George. "With its Deadly Drones the U.S. is fighting a Coward's War." *The Guardian* January 30, 2012.

Montague, Phillip. *Punishment as Societal Defense*. Boston: Rowman & Littlefield Publishers, Inc., 1995.

Moore, Michael. "Torture and the Balance of Evils." *Placing Blame*. Oxford: Clarendon Press, 1997.

Münkler, Herfried. *Die neuen Kriege*. Reinbek bei Hamburg: Rowohlt, 2003.

Mustin, J. Future Employment of Unmanned Aerial Vehicles. *Air and Space Power Journal* 16:2 (2002): 86–97.

Nagel, Thomas. "War and Massacre." *Philosophy and Public Affairs* 1 (1972): 123–144.

Nagl, John. *Learning to Eat Soup with the Knife: Counterinsurgency Lessons from Malaya and Vietnam*. Chicago, University of Chicago Press, 2005.

National Priorities Project. *Cost of War*. Accessed September 1, 2010. http://www.national-priorities.org/costofwar_home.

Norcross, Alastair. "Reasons without Demands: Rethinking Rightness." In *Blackwell Contemporary Debates in Moral Theory*, edited by Jaimie Dreier, 38–53. New York: Blackwell, 2006.

Norman, Richard. *Ethics, Killing and War*. Cambridge: Cambridge University Press, 1995.

"Obama Administration Counter-Terrorism Strategy." C-Span. June 29, 2011. Accessed October 14, 2011. http://www.c-spanvideo.org/program/AdministrationCo.

"Obama Defends US Drone Strikes in Pakistan." *BBC News*, January 31, 2012. Accessed February 25, 2012. http://www.bbc.co.uk/news/mobile/world-us-canada-16804247.

O'Connell, Mary Ellen. "Lawful Use of Combat Drones." Testimony before the House of Representatives Subcommittee on National Security and Foreign Affairs, April 28, 2010. Accessed February 25, 2012. http://www.fas.org/irp/congress/2010_hr/042810oconnell.pdf.

O'Connell, Mary Ellen. "Unlawful Killing with Combat Drones: A Case Study of Pakistan, 2004–2009." Notre Dame Law School Legal Studies Research Paper No. 09-43, 20. Accessed February 25, 2012. https://webspace.utexas.edu/rmc2289/LT/Mary%20Ellen%20OConnell%20on%20Drones.pdf.

O'Donovan, Oliver. *The Just War Revisited*. New York: Cambridge University Press, 2003.

Office of the Under Secretary of Defense. *Unmanned Aircraft Systems Roadmap: 2005–2030*. Washington DC: Office of the Under Secretary of Defense, 2006.

Olsthoorn, Peter. "Honor as a Motive for Making Sacrifices." *Journal of Military Ethics* 4.3 (2005):183–197.

Olsthoorn, Peter. "Courage in the Military: Physical and Moral." *Journal of Military Ethics* 6:4(2007): 270–279.

Olsthoorn, Peter. *Military Ethics and Virtues: An Interdisciplinary Approach for the 21st Century*. London and New York: Routledge, 2011.

Orend, Brian. *The Morality of War*. Toronto: Broadview Press, 2006.

Osiel, Mark. *The End of Reciprocity*. Cambridge: Cambridge University Press, 2009.

"Over 700 Killed in 44 Drone Strikes in 2009." *Dawn*, January 2, 2010. Accessed March 20, 2010. http://archives.dawn.com/archives/144960.

"Pakistan Troops 'Repel' US Raid." BBC News, September 22, 2008. Accessed July 10, 2010. http://news.bbc.co.uk/2/hi/south_asia/7628890.stm.

Pape, Robert. *Bombing To Win: Air Power and Coercion in War*. Ithaca and London: Cornell University Press, 1996.

Perlez, Jane. "Pakistan's Military Chief Criticizes U.S. Over Raid." *New York Times*, September 10, 2008. Accessed July 10, 2010. http://www.nytimes.com/2008/09/11/world/asia/11pstan.html?scp=2&sq=kayani%20at%20all%20costs&st=cse.

Perry, David L. *Partly Cloudy: Ethics in War, Espionage, Covert Action, and Interrogation*. Lanham, MD: Scarecrow Press, 2009.

Peterson, Stephen. "The Ethics of Robot Servitude." *Journal of Experimental & Theoretical Artificial Intelligence* 19 (2007): 43–54.

Pfaff, Tony. "Ethics in Complex Contingencies: New Demands on the Warrior Ethics." Paper presented at the Joint Services Conference on Professional Ethics (JSCOPE), 2004.

Phythian, Mark. "Ethics and Intelligence: The Implications of the Rise of the Armed Drone." Paper presented at 7th Global Conference on War and Peace, Prague, April 30, 2010.

Pilon, Roger. "Criminal Remedies: Restitution, Punishment, or Both?" *Ethics* 88 (1978): 348–357.

Piper, Mark. "The Impossibility of Purely Content-Neutral Accounts of Autonomy." Unpublished manuscript, 2012.

Plaw, Avery. "Sudden Justice." Paper presented at 7th Annual Global Conference on War and Peace, Prague, May 1, 2010.

Plaw, Avery, Matt Fricker, and Brian Glynn Williams, "Practice Makes Perfect? The Changing Civilian Toll of CIA Drone Strikes in Pakistan." *Perspectives on Terrorism* 5:5–6 (2011): 57–58.

Pogge, Thomas. "Preempting Humanitarian Intervention." In *Humanitarian Intervention: Moral and Philosophical Issues*, edited by Aleksander Jokic. Peterborough: Broadview Press, 2003.

Power, Samantha. *A Problem from Hell: America and the Age of Genocide.* New York: Harper Perennial, 2003.

Pufendorf, Samuel. *De Jure Naturae Et Gentium Libri Octo.* Translated by C. H. Oldfather and W. A. Oldfather. Oxford: Clarendon Press, and London: Humphrey Milford, 1934.

Rabasa, Angel, Lesley Anne Warner, et al. *Money in the Bank: Lessons Learned from Past Counterinsurgency (COIN) Operations.* Santa Monica, CA: RAND, 2007.

Ramsey, Paul. *The Just War: Force and Political Responsibility.* Lanham, MD: Rowman & Littlefield, 2002.

Rawls, John. *Law of Peoples.* Cambridge: Harvard University Press, 2001.

Raz, Joseph. *The Morality of Freedom.* Oxford: Clarendon Books, 1986.

Ricks, Tom. "A rare disagreement with Ignatius, on the deployment of armed Predators to Libya." *The Best Defense,* April 22, 2011.

Robinson, Paul. "Magnanimity and Integrity as Military Virtues." *Journal of Military Ethics* 6:4 (2007): 259–269.

Rodley, Nigel. *The Treatment of Prisoners under International Law.* Oxford: Clarendon Press, 1999.

Rohde, David. "The Obama Doctrine." *Foreign Policy,* March/April 2012.

Ross, Alice. "Untangling the Data." *The Bureau of Investigative Journalism,* August 10, 2011. Accessed February 20, 2012. http://www.thebureauinvestigates.com/2011/08/10/ drones- untangling-the-data/.

Rothbard, Murray. *The Ethics of Liberty.* Atlantic Highlands, NJ: Humanities Press, 1982.

Russett, Bruce. *Grasping the Democratic Peace.* Princeton: Princeton University Press, 1993.

Saeed, Traiq. "Drone Strikes Kill 6 in NWA." *Pakistan Observer,* March 12, 2011. Accessed April 4, 2011. http://pakobserver.net/detailnews.asp?id=80509.

Sassoli, Marco and Laura M. Olson. "The Relationship between International Humanitarian Law and Human Rights Law Where it Matters: Admissible Killing and Internment of Fighters in Non-International Armed Conflicts." *International Review of the Red Cross* 90, 2008.

Scheffler, Samuel. "Introduction." In *Consequentialism and Its Critics,* edited by Samuel Scheffler, 1–13. Oxford: Oxford University Press, 1988.

Schelling, Thomas. *The Diplomacy of Violence.* New Haven: Yale University Press, 1964.

Schmitt, Eric. "Precision Attack and International Humanitarian Law." *International Review of the Red Cross* 87, 2005.

Schmitt, Eric. "Intelligence Report Lists Iran and Cyberattacks as Leading Concerns." *New York Times,* 31 January 2012. Accessed February 25, 2012. http://www.nytimes. com/2012/02/01/world/intelligence-chief-sees-al-qaeda-likely-to-continue-fragmentin g.html?_r=1&scp=2&sq=al%20qaeda%20fragment&st=cse.

Schultz, William F. "Security is a Human Right Too." *New York Times,* April 18, 2004. Accessed March 3, 2012. http://www.ngo-monitor.org/article/_security_is_a_human_right_too_.

Shactman, Noah. "Drone School, a ground's-eye view." *Wired Magazine,* May 27, 2005. Accessed August 1, 2012. http://www.wired.com/science/discoveries/ news/2005/05/67655.

Shachtman, Noah. "First Armed Robots on Patrol in Iraq (Updated)." *Wired Online*, August 2, 2007.

Shah, Pir Zubair. "My Drone Wars." *Foreign Policy*, March/April 2012.

Shane, Scott. "CIA to Expand use of Drones in Pakistan." *New York Times*, December 3, 2009. Accessed October 28, 2011. http://www.nytimes.com/2009/12/04/world/asia/04drones.html?pagewanted=all.

Sharkey, Noel. "Automated Killers and the Computing Profession." *Computer* 40 (2007): 122–124.

Sharkey, Noel. "Robot Wars are a Reality." *The Guardian*, August 18, 2007.

Sharkey, Noel. "Cassandra or False Prophet of Doom: AI Robots and War." *IEEE Intelligent Systems* 23:4 (2008):14–17.

Sharkey, Noel. "Grounds for Discrimination: Autonomous Robot Weapons." *RUSI Defence Systems* 11:2 (2008): 86–89.

Sharkey, Noel. "Saying 'No!' to Lethal Autonomous Targeting." In "New Warriors and New Weapons: Ethics & Emerging Military Technologies," edited by G.R. Lucas, Jr. *Journal of Military Ethics* 9:4 (December 2010): 299–313.

Shaw, Saeed and Peter Beaumont. "US Drone Attacks in Pakistan Claiming Many Civilian Lives, Says Campaigner." *The Guardian*, July 17, 2011.

Shue, Henry and David Rodin. *Preemption: Military Action and Moral Justification*. Oxford: Oxford University Press, 2010.

Silver, Steven M. "Ethics and Combat: Thoughts for Small Unit Leaders." *Marine Corps Gazette* 90.11 (2006): 76–78.

Simmons, John A. "Locke and the Right to Punish." In *Punishment*, edited by A. John Simmons et al. Princeton: Princeton University Press, 1995.

Singer, Peter W. *Wired For War: The Robotics Revolution in the 21st Century*. New York: Penguin Press, 2009.

Singer, Peter W. "The Ethics of 'Killer Apps.'" In "New Warriors and New Weapons: Ethics & Emerging Military Technologies," edited by G.R. Lucas, Jr. *Journal of Military Ethics* 9:4 (December 2010): 314–327.

Sluka, Jeffrey. "Death From Above: UAVs and Losing Hearts and Minds." *Military Review* (May–June 2011).

Solis, Gary. *The Law of Armed Conflict: International Humanitarian Law in War*. Cambridge: Cambridge University Press, 2010.

Sparrow, Jeff. *Killing: Misadventures in Violence*. Carlton, Vic.: Melbourne University Publishing, 2009.

Sparrow, Robert. "Killer Robots." *Journal of Applied Philosophy* 24:1 (2007): 62–77.

Sparrow, Robert. "Building a Better Warbot: Ethical Issues in the Design of Unmanned Systems for Military Applications." *Science and Engineering Ethics* 15 (2009): 169–187.

Sparrow, Robert. "Predators or Plowshares? Arms Control of Robotic Weapons." *IEEE Technology and Society* 28:1 (2009): 25–29.

Sparrow, Robert. "Robotic Weapons and the Future of War." In *New Wars and New Soldiers: Military Ethics in the Contemporary World*, edited by Jessica Wolfendale and Paolo Tripodi, 117–133. Surrey, UK & Burlington, VA: Ashgate, 2011.

Stanton, Doug. *Horse Soldiers: The Extraordinary Story of a Band of US Soldiers Who Rode to Victory in Afghanistan*. New York: Scribner, 2009.

Steinhoff, Uwe. "Torture: The Case for Dirty Harry and against Alan Dershowitz." *Journal of Applied Philosophy* 23 (2006): 337–353.

Steinhoff, Uwe. *On the Ethics of War and Terrorism*. Oxford: Oxford University Press, 2007.

Steinhoff, Uwe. "Jeff McMahan on the Moral Inequality of Combatants." *Journal of Political Philosophy*, 16:2 (2008): 220–226.

Steinhoff, Uwe. "Killing Civilians." In *The Changing Character of War*, edited by Hew Strachan and Sibylle Scheipers, 381–394. Oxford: Oxford University Press, 2011.

Steinhoff, Uwe. "Rights, Liability, and the Moral Equality of Combatants." *The Journal of Ethics* (2012, Online First).

Strawser, Bradley "Moral Predators: The Duty to Employ Uninhabited Aerial Vehicles." *Journal of Military Ethics* 9:4 (December 2010): 342–368.

Sullins, John. "When is a Robot a Moral Agent?" *International Review of Information Ethics* 6 (2006): 23–30.

Taj, Farhat. "Drone Attacks." *Daily Times*, January 2, 2010. Accessed November 22, 2010. http://www.dailytimes.com.pk/default.asp?page=2010%5C01%5C02%5Cstory_2-1-2010_pg3_5

Teson, Fernando. "Eight Principles for Humanitarian Intervention." *Journal of Military Ethics* 5 (June 2006): 99–101.

"The secret plan to kill Hitler," *BBC News*, July 23, 1998.

"The West are terrorists." *MSN News*, March 20, 2011. Accessed March 4, 2012. http://news.uk.msn.com/articles.aspx?cp-documentid=156584494. Accessed March 4, 2012.

Thompson, Judith Jarvis. "A Defense of Abortion." *Philosophy and Public Affairs* 1 (1971): 47–66

Thomson, Judith Jarvis. "The Right to Privacy." *Philosophy and Public Affairs* 4 (1975): 295–314.

Thomson, Judith Jarvis. "Self-Defense and Rights." In *Rights, Restitution, and Risk*, edited by William Parent, 37–42. Cambridge: Harvard University Press, 1990.

Thomson, Judith Jarvis. *The Realm of Rights*. Cambridge: Harvard University Press, 1990.

Thomson, Judith Jarvis. "Self-Defense" *Philosophy & Public Affairs* 20 (1991): 283–310.

Tindale, Christopher. "Tragic Choices: Reaffirming Absolutes in the Torture Debate." *International Journal of Applied Philosophy* 19 (2005): 209–222.

Troop, Don. "Robots at War." *Chronicle of Higher Education*, September 10, 2012.

UK Ministry of Defence. *The Manual of the Law of Armed Conflict*. Oxford: Oxford University Press, 2004.

Ullman, S. E. "Rape avoidance: Self-protection strategies for women." In *Preventing Violence in Relationships: Interventions Across the Life Span*, edited by S. Schewe, 137–162. Washington, DC: American Psychological Association, 2002.

United Nations Mission in Afghanistan. *Afghanistan Annual Report 2011: Protection of Civilians in Armed Conflict*. Kabul: United Nations, 2012.

United States Army. *Field Manual (FM) 3-24: Counterinsurgency*. Washington, D.C.: U.S. Government Printing Office, 2006.

U.S. Army. *FM 3-24: Counterinsurgency*. Ft. Leavenworth: Army Field Manual, 2006.

US Navy. "United States Navy Fact File: Tomahawk Cruise Missile." US Navy, April 23, 2010.

Vidal, John. "Nigeria's agony dwarfs the Gulf oil spill. The US and Europe ignore it." *The Guardian*, May 30, 2010. Accessed March 5, 2012. http://www.guardian.co.uk/world/2010/may/30/oil-spills-nigeria-niger-delta-shell.

"Vietnam: Policy and Prospects." *Hearings Before the Committee on Foreign Relations, United States Senate*. Washington: US Government Printing Office, 1970.

Vitoria, Franciscus de. *De Indis Recenter Inventis Et De Jure Belli Hispanorum In Barbaros*. Edited by Walter Schätzel. Tübingen: Mohr/Siebeck, 1952.

Waldron, Jeremy. "Can Targeted Killing Work as a Neutral Principle." NYU Public Law and Legal Theory Working Papers, March 1, 2011.

Wallach, Wendell. *Moral Machines: Teaching Robots Right from Wrong*. New York: Oxford University Press, 2009.

Walzer, Michael. *Just and Unjust Wars: A Moral Argument with Historical Illustrations*. New York: Basic Books, 1977.

Walzer, Michael. "Five Questions About Terrorism." *Dissent*, Winter 2002.

Walzer, Michael. *Arguing About War*. New Haven: Yale University Press, 2004.

Walzer, Michael. "Response." *Journal of Military Ethics* 6:2 (2007): 168–171.

Warrick, Joby & Peter Finn. "Amid Outrage over Civilian Deaths in Pakistan, CIA Turns to Smaller Missiles." *Washington Post*, April 26, 2010.

Watson, Bradley C.S. "The Western Ethical Tradition and the Morality of the Warrior." *Armed Forces and Society* 26:1 (1999): 55–72.

Watson, Gary. "Free Agency." *Journal of Philosophy* 72 (1975): 205–220.

Waycoff, Chris and Matthew Russell. "The Nine Post-Reform Scenarios." In *Project on National Security Reform Vision Working Group Report and Scenarios*, edited by Sheila R. Ronis, 54–57. Carlisle: Strategic Studies Institute, 2010.

Weiss, Thomas G. "Overcoming the Somalia Syndrome—Operation Rekindle Hope?" *Global Governance* 1 (1995).

Whetham, David. *Just Wars and Moral Victories: surprise, deception and the normative framework of European War in the later Middle Ages*. Leiden: Brill, 2009.

Whetham, David. "Remote Killing and Drive-By Wars." In *Protecting Civilians During Armed Conflict: Theoretical and Practical Issues During Violent Conflict*, edited by David Lovell and Igor Primoratz. Ashgate, May 2012.

Williams, Brian. "Pakistani Responses to the CIA's Predator Drone Campaign and Al Qaeda and the Taliban." *Terrorism Monitor* 8:7 (2009).

Wisnewski, Jeremy and R. D. Emerick. *The Ethics of Torture*. New York: Continuum, 2009.

Wolf, Susan. *Freedom within Reason*. New York: Oxford University Press, 1990.

Wolff, Robert Paul. *In Defense of Anarchism*. Berkeley: University of California Press, 1980.

Woods, Chris. "US claims of 'no civilian deaths' are untrue." *The Bureau of Investigative Journalism*, July 18, 2011. Accessed August 25, 2011. http://www.thebureauinvestigates. com/2011/07/18/washingtons-untrue-claims-no-civilian-deaths-in-pakistan-drone-st rikes/

Woods, Chris. "Witnesses Speak Out." *Bureau of Investigative Journalism*, February 4, 2012, Accessed February 25, 2012. http://www.thebureauinvestigates.com/2012/02/04/ witnesses-speak-out/.

World Press Freedom Review. International Press Institute, 2002.

Yi, Jamison. "MCMAP and the Marine Warrior Ethos." *Military Review* 846 (2004): 17–24.

Zaloga, Steven. *Unmanned Aerial Vehicles: Robotic Air Warfare 1917–2007*. New York: Osprey Press, 2008.

Zino, Aviram. "High Court: Targeted killing permissible." *Ynetnews*, December 14, 2006. Accessed May 29, 2012. http://www.ynetnews.com/articles/0,7340,L-3339905,00.html.

INDEX

References "132–135" indicate (not necessarily continuous) discussion of a topic across a range of pages. Because the entire work is about the "ethics of drones" in some fashion or other, the use of this and related terms (UAVs, etc.) as an entry point has been intentionally minimized. Information will be found under the corresponding detailed topics.